National Security, Leaks and Freedom of the Press

National Security, Leaks and Freedom of the Press

The Pentagon Papers Fifty Years On

EDITED BY

LEE C. BOLLINGER

and

GEOFFREY R. STONE

OXFORD
UNIVERSITY PRESS

OXFORD
UNIVERSITY PRESS

Oxford University Press is a department of the University of Oxford. It furthers
the University's objective of excellence in research, scholarship, and education
by publishing worldwide. Oxford is a registered trade mark of Oxford University
Press in the UK and certain other countries.

Published in the United States of America by Oxford University Press
198 Madison Avenue, New York, NY 10016, United States of America.

Library of Congress Cataloging-in-Publication Data
Names: Bollinger, Lee C., 1946– author. | Stone, Geoffrey R., author.
Title: National security, leaks, and freedom of the press : the Pentagon papers
fifty years on / edited by Lee C. Bollinger and Geoffrey R. Stone.
Description: New York, NY : Oxford University Press, [2021] | Includes index.
Identifiers: LCCN 2020041790 (print) | LCCN 2020041791 (ebook) |
ISBN 9780197519387 (hardback) | ISBN 9780197519394 (paperback) |
ISBN 9780197519417 (epub) | ISBN 9780197519424
Subjects: LCSH: Government information—Law and legislation—United States. |
Public records—Access control—United States. | National security—Law
and legislation—United States. | Security classification (Government documents)—United States. |
Leaks (Disclosure of information)—United States—History. | Freedom of the press—United States. |
Government and the press—United States. | Pentagon Papers. | Snowden, Edward J., 1983–
Classification: LCC KF5753 .B675 2021 (print) | LCC KF5753 (ebook) |
DDC 342.7308/53—dc23
LC record available at https://lccn.loc.gov/2020041790
LC ebook record available at https://lccn.loc.gov/2020041791

DOI: 10.1093/oso/9780197519387.001.0001

1 3 5 7 9 8 6 4 2

Paperback printed by LSC Communications, United States of America
Hardback printed by Bridgeport National Bindery, Inc., United States of America

To Jean and Jane
And to the next generation:
Emma, Colin, Katelyn, Sawyer, and Cooper
Julie, Mollie, Maddie, Jackson, Bee, and Leni

CONTENTS

ACKNOWLEDGMENTS

We begin our thanks to our authors and to members of the commission, an extraordinary group of individuals from diverse backgrounds and perspectives of national security, journalism, and academia. Included here, too, must be Paul Wolfson and Seth Waxman and their colleagues at WilmerHale, who provided the comprehensive background document and other assistance along the way. Altogether, it is difficult to imagine a more distinguished or more thoughtful group of colleagues to undertake this effort to understand and resolve these persistent, complex, and highly important issues. And every one of them was an absolute pleasure to work with.

It is easy to underestimate the enormous labor involved in bringing a scholarly book to publication, and there are always numerous people who play central roles. Jane Booth, general counsel of Columbia University, helped to orchestrate the process of working with WilmerHale and brought to bear her own wisdom. The staff in the president's office of Columbia was indispensable, with special thanks to Christina Shelby, senior executive director.

We are also grateful to Dave McBride and to the entire staff at Oxford University Press who worked with us so diligently to bring this volume into being. Needless to say, this would not have been possible without their assistance and guidance.

No one can feel more fortunate for the close counsel and inexpressible collaboration in life than we do to Jean Magnano Bollinger (Lee's spouse) and Jane Dailey (Geof's spouse).

And finally, what we said in the acknowledgments to *The Free Speech Century* is equally true here: we owe more than we can say to Carey Bollinger Danielson, who oversaw every detail of the editing, cite checking, organizing, copyediting, and coordinating of this work (with the help of research assistants Bret Matera and Ellie Dupler). She has been tireless in her efforts, generous with her time, and an absolutely perfect colleague. Given our other commitments, we can honestly say that without Carey, this project would never have seen the light of day. Thank you!

CONTRIBUTORS

Stephen J. Adler, Editor-in-Chief of Reuters.

Keith B. Alexander, former Director of the National Security Agency, currently Chairman and Co-CEO of IronNet Cybersecurity.

Lee C. Bollinger, President and Seth Low Professor of the University at Columbia University.

John O. Brennan, former Director of the Central Intelligence Agency.

Bruce D. Brown, Executive Director of the Reporters Committee for Freedom of the Press.

Kathleen Carroll, former Executive Editor and Senior Vice President of the Associated Press.

Richard A. Clarke, former National Coordinator for Security, Infrastructure Protection, and Counter-Terrorism for the United States.

Stephen W. Coll, Dean of Columbia Journalism School, Henry R. Luce Professor of Journalism at Columbia University.

Jack Goldsmith, Learned Hand Professor of Law at Harvard University.

Avril Haines, former White House Deputy National Security Advisor.

Eric Holder, former Attorney General of the United States.

Jameel Jaffer, Executive Director of the Knight First Amendment Institute at Columbia University.

Jamil N. Jaffer, Founder and Executive Director of the National Security Institute and Professor at the Antonin Scalia Law School at George Mason University.

Ann Marie Lipinski, Curator of the Nieman Foundation for Journalism at Harvard University, former Editor-in-Chief and Senior Vice President of the *Chicago Tribune*.

Judith Miller, Investigative Journalist formerly with the *New York Times*, Adjunct Fellow at the Manhattan Institute, Contributing Editor at *City Journal*.

Lisa O. Monaco, former Homeland Security and Counter-terrorism Advisor and Deputy National Security Advisor, currently Distinguished Senior Fellow at the Reiss Center on Law and Security at New York University..

Michael Morell, former Acting and Deputy Director of the Central Intelligence Agency.

Ellen Nakashima, National Security Reporter at the *Washington Post*.

Mary-Rose Papandrea, Samuel Ashe Distinguished Professor of Constitutional Law at the University of North Carolina School of Law.

David E. Sanger, National Security Correspondent and Senior Writer at the *New York Times*.

Louis Michael Seidman, Carmack Waterhouse Professor of Constitutional Law at the Georgetown University Law Center.

Allison Stanger, Russell Leng '60 Professor of International Politics and Economics at Middlebury College.

Geoffrey R. Stone, Edward H. Levi Distinguished Service Professor of Law at the University of Chicago.

David A. Strauss, Gerald Ratner Distinguished Service Professor of Law at the University of Chicago.

Cass R. Sunstein, Robert Walmsley University Professor at Harvard Law School.

WilmerHale attorneys: Allison Aviki, Jonathan G. Cedarbaum, Rebecca Lee, Jessica Lutkenhaus, Seth P. Waxman, and Paul R. Q. Wolfson.

OPENING STATEMENT

LEE C. BOLLINGER AND GEOFFREY R. STONE

Among the greatest human achievements of the last century, one that stands out is the Supreme Court's evolution of an extensive jurisprudence defining the meaning of the First Amendment rights of freedom of speech and press. The constitutional language—"Congress shall make no law . . . abridging the freedom of speech, or of the press"—was an essential part of the Bill of Rights, which was adopted in 1789, but it was not until 1919 that the Supreme Court decided a case that gave it the opportunity to explore what those words actually mean.[1] Since then, the Court has issued hundreds of opinions that collectively address the many profound questions about the proper functioning of a democratic society, and of the United States, in particular. The resulting jurisprudence affords the rights of freedom of speech and freedom of the press a degree of protection that is unique in world history and has had enormous influence around the globe. In *The Free Speech Century*, published in 2018 to mark the centennial anniversary of the Supreme Court's first decisions on the meaning of the First Amendment, we invited a group of distinguished scholars to join us in celebrating and marking that achievement.[2]

One of the most vexing and perennial questions facing any democracy is how to balance the government's legitimate need to conduct its operations— especially those related to protecting national security—with the public's right and responsibility to know what its government is doing. There is no easy answer to this issue, and different nations embrace different solutions. In the United States, at the constitutional level, the answer begins exactly half a century ago with the Supreme Court's landmark 1971 decision in *New York Times Co. v. United States*, or, as it is familiarly known, the Pentagon Papers case.[3] As with so many facets of First Amendment jurisprudence, this decision was a uniquely American response to a classic dilemma. A government employee (Daniel Ellsberg) working in the Defense Department made Xerox copies of a classified, multivolume, seven-thousand-page document, which had been commissioned by Secretary of Defense Robert McNamara in 1967 to recount in great detail the history of America's involvement in the Vietnam War.[4] After carefully reviewing the document and eliminating those portions of the publication that Ellsberg thought might harm the national interests of the United States, he gave the "Pentagon Papers" first to journalists working for the *New York Times* and then, later, to journalists working for the *Washington Post*.[5] After reviewing the materials, the newspapers began publishing excerpts.[6] Upon realizing what was happening, officials of the Nixon administration went immediately to federal district courts in New York and Washington, DC, seeking injunctions against publication of the classified information.[7] On a highly expedited basis, the combined cases reached the Supreme Court, which issued a stunning decision rejecting the government's position and protecting the right of the press to proceed with publication.[8]

Although the Justices issued multiple opinions, there was a clear majority for the proposition that so-called prior restraints, which include judicial injunctions against publication, are presumptively unconstitutional under the First Amendment absent proof of grave and irreparable damage to the nation, which, the Court concluded, the government had not established in this case.[9] The *New York Times* and the *Washington Post* were, therefore, free to publish these classified secrets, even though they had been illegally stolen from the government and knowingly received by the journalists.[10]

Sometimes cases stand for more in the public mind, and even in the law itself, than their specific holding on the facts presented would suggest. That could certainly be said of the Pentagon Papers decision. One reading of the holding is that the extraordinary protection the Court afforded the press to publish national secrets extends only to prior restraints and not to criminal prosecutions initiated after publication. Obviously, if that were true, any publisher of classified information would find the value of a shield against injunctions rather hollow. Although we do not think this is a sensible understanding of the decision, the matter remains unclear and has left a degree of uncertainty hanging over the law for half a century.

At the time it was handed down, the Pentagon Papers decision was hailed as an enormous victory for the press and for the public's reliance on the press for information, particularly in the face of a government that was widely perceived as excessively secretive.[11] Over the years, the decision has become the foundation for our nation's answer to the classic and perennial question noted earlier: how should a democracy balance the needs of the government to conduct at least some of its affairs in secret with the needs of citizens to have the necessary information about their government's actions to be able intelligently and thoughtfully to exercise their sovereign authority?

In fact, though, as already noted, the Pentagon Papers decision left many important questions unresolved. For example, should the press have a right not only to publish such information if it comes into its hands but also to demand that the government disclose information that on balance would be better in the public domain? This idea of a First Amendment "right of access" was largely rejected by the Court in a series of cases around the same time as the Pentagon Papers decision.[12] Another issue is whether government employees who leak classified information to the press (or to others) should have a right to do so if the value of the information disclosed to the public outweighs the harm to the state. Over the years, this approach, too, has been rejected by courts.[13]

The current state of the law, stated simply, is as follows: Because the government often needs to be able to operate in secret in order to protect the national interest, it is under no obligation to publicly disclose classified information, even though public officials may have a strong bias toward being excessively secretive for a host of reasons. Under current law, there is no constitutionally based remedy for that problem. Leakers who hand over classified documents to the press can be prosecuted and punished by the government for doing so, and they will be afforded no constitutional defense.[14] On the other hand, the press that receives the unlawfully leaked documents and information, even though properly classified as national secrets, may publish the information without suffering any legal consequences for doing so.[15]

This has been the system in the United States since the Pentagon Papers era. It is unique in the world. To some, it represents a structure for utter chaos, with the government too vulnerable to the unauthorized and illegal actions of government employees who choose to take the fate of the nation into their own hands and with an unelected press possessing the unrestrained authority to make profoundly important national security decisions that they are neither authorized nor equipped to make. On the other hand, others view the Pentagon Papers regime as consistent with the genius of the American system of checks and balances and of dispersing power in circumstances in which the dangers of lodging full authority in any single entity are simply too great to risk. Uncertainty is sometimes said to be the best strategy, and nowhere is that view better represented than in the strange balance created by the Pentagon Papers case.

Nonetheless, it seems to have worked reasonably well—or at least that is the debatable premise on which we put together this volume. But even if the seemingly odd approach embraced by the Pentagon Papers case has arguably worked reasonably well for most of the last fifty years, it is undebatable that the circumstances that undergirded the Pentagon Papers system have changed fundamentally in the last decade or so. This does not *necessarily* mean that a new way of balancing the interests is called for, but it does mean that reconsideration in light of new circumstances is both appropriate and necessary.

One primary change over the years concerns the introduction of the internet and the digitization of information. The nature of government is to keep secrets, and the exponential growth in both the felt need for secrecy (especially after 9/11) and the capacity to satisfy that need through digitization has been highly significant. Another primary change is that the risk of leaks has seemingly increased. The number of government employees and contractors with access to classified information has skyrocketed, and the ability of leakers to disclose unprecedented amounts of potentially damaging information has escalated beyond anything Ellsberg could have contemplated half a century ago.[16] And beyond that, the internet has significantly undermined the business model of traditional press like the *New York Times* and the *Washington Post* and opened the floodgates to would-be "publishers" of all kinds. While some of these publishers adhere to longstanding standards of journalistic practice, others do not. In short, the risks of both too much secrecy and too much disclosure are arguably very different from what they were in 1971 and the ensuing decades.

This new reality led us to this book. Difficult problems call for a range of different perspectives. We therefore decided to bring together an amazing array of individuals with deep and broad expertise in the national security world, journalism, and academia. We asked each of them to delve into important dimensions of the current system, to explain how we should think about them, and to offer as many solutions as possible. We also invited five experts from the national security and journalism worlds to join us as a "Commission" in discussing these issues, especially against the background of the essays, to see whether we could come to a consensus about how best to refine the system inherited from the Pentagon Papers era. The "report" of this Commission follows the essays in this volume. The book opens with a comprehensive background memorandum prepared by Paul Wolfson and his colleagues at the law firm WilmerHale.

We are proud of the rigorous and serious thinking that has gone into this volume. Most of all, we believe it is reflective of the incredibly complex and important issues that our nation must continue to address and strive to resolve as we move into the future.

National Security, Leaks and Freedom of the Press

The Pentagon Papers Framework, Fifty Years Later

ALLISON AVIKI, JONATHAN CEDARBAUM, REBECCA LEE,
JESSICA LUTKENHAUS, SETH P. WAXMAN, AND PAUL R. Q. WOLFSON

In *New York Times Co. v. United States*,[1] the Supreme Court confronted a problem that is inherent in a democratic society that values freedom of expression and, in particular, the role of the press in challenging the truthfulness of claims by the government, especially in the realm of national security. On the one hand, as Justice Potter Stewart wrote in his concurring opinion, "it is elementary" that "the maintenance of an effective national defense require[s] both confidentiality and secrecy."[2] On the other hand, as described by Justice Hugo Black, the First Amendment protects the press so that it may "bare the secrets of government and inform the people."[3] Our democracy, like all democracies, has confronted how to balance these competing interests, particularly when leaked information can be "*both* potentially harmful to the national security *and* quite valuable to public debate."[4]

Four days after hearing an extraordinary oral argument in late June 1971, the Court issued a three-paragraph per curiam decision holding only that the government had not met the burden necessary to establish the need for a prior restraint.[5] Every Justice on the Court issued a separate opinion—six in concurrence, three in dissent. Whether the separate opinions of five of the Justices might be combined to discern a precise majority rationale is uncertain. Nonetheless, there appears to be consensus that the Court's decision set forth the following basic framework within which legal disputes over disclosure of national security information have been assessed in the United States:

1. The government can block the publication of sensitive national security information only in extraordinary circumstances.

2. Even when publication may not be restrained, press outlets are not insulated from criminal prosecution for publication.

3. Because the newspapers had not solicited the leaked materials or participated in Daniel Ellsberg's acquisition or copying of the materials, the Court did not decide whether the press possesses a right to elicit classified information or to assist potential leakers in obtaining it and transferring it to the press.

4. Leakers possess no First Amendment right to make unauthorized disclosures. Ellsberg, the leaker, subsequently faced criminal prosecution.

5. Although the Court did not adopt the government's position that the very fact that documents were classified demonstrated that their disclosure would seriously threaten national security, neither did the Court challenge the government's ability to deem material classified in the first instance.

6. The Court did not recognize any constitutional right of the public to have access to information in the hands of the government.

This introductory essay principally reviews the development of the law in the United States since the Pentagon Papers decision. It then more briefly addresses three related subjects: the difficulties in assessing the effectiveness of the Pentagon Papers regime in permitting disclosures that benefit public debate more than they harm national security while discouraging leaks that cause more harm than good, how the US legal framework for handling national security information compares to the United Kingdom's, and how technological and institutional changes over the five decades since the Pentagon Papers decision have called into question some of that decision's premises.

Developments in US Law

Since the Pentagon Papers case, the government only rarely has sought to enjoin publication of material—and only once succeeded in winning an injunction on the ground that publication threatened national security. When courts have examined questions of prior restraints, they have consistently looked to the Pentagon Papers decision's reaffirmance of the presumptive unconstitutionality of prior restraints.

Since 1971, the government has never sought criminal penalties against the press for merely receiving or publishing classified information. It has, however, brought criminal prosecutions against government employees who leaked classified information to the press without authorization, and it has also sought to prosecute non-media third parties for their role in disseminating information leaked to them by government insiders.[6] The influence of *New York Times Co.* has been much more limited in these prosecutions. Indeed, in criminal prosecutions brought against leakers, the Pentagon Papers case has often been sidelined as a "prior restraint case" or not mentioned at all. Recently, the government has broken new ground by bringing criminal charges against an organization that some consider to be part of the press—WikiLeaks—alleging that it actively participated in and abetted a leak of classified information. The relevance of *New York Times Co.* to that situation is uncertain.

The law on a constitutional right of access to government-held information has also developed since the Pentagon Papers decision. The Supreme Court has consistently rejected a broad First Amendment right of access to information in the hands of the executive branch, although it has recognized limited rights of access to certain criminal proceedings. Those cases, too, have been decided almost entirely without reference to the Pentagon Papers case.

Prior Restraints on the Press

Only once since the Pentagon Papers case has any federal court concluded that a prior restraint against publication, based on a claim that disclosure would threaten national security, was constitutionally permissible.[7] In 1979, a district court enjoined the *Progressive* magazine from publishing an article about how to make a hydrogen bomb.[8] The court distinguished the Pentagon Papers case on several grounds. First, the court found that the Pentagon Papers study involved only historical information and the government had advanced "no cogent reasons ... as to why [its publication] affected national security."[9] By contrast, the *Progressive* sought to publish information about the "most destructive weapon in the history of mankind."[10] Second, information about the hydrogen bomb fell within the Atomic Energy Act's prohibition on communicating "restricted data" about the construction of nuclear weapons.[11] No similar statutory grounds for relief were at issue in the Pentagon Papers case. The court balanced those factors against the public's "need[] to know" and identified "no plausible reason why the public needs to know the technical details about hydrogen bomb construction to carry on an informed debate on this issue."[12] The court accordingly concluded that the government had overcome the "heavy presumption against [the prior restraint's] constitutional validity."[13]

In so holding, the court specifically found that the "[s]ecret" of the hydrogen bomb, if published, posed "grave, direct, immediate and irreparable harm to the United States," and so publication of those secrets could be restrained under the rationale adopted by Justices Stewart and White in the Pentagon Papers case.[14] The court also found that the government had met the standard for prior restraint set forth in *Near v. Minnesota*[15] because publishing technical material about the hydrogen bomb was analogous "to publication of troop movements or locations in time of war."[16]

The court's reasoning was never reviewed by an appellate court. The Seventh Circuit dismissed the *Progressive*'s appeal[17] after other newspapers published the key concepts and the government abandoned its efforts to restrain publication.[18] The *Progressive* ultimately published its article about the hydrogen bomb in November 1979.[19]

The validity of a prior restraint against the press has reached the Supreme Court rarely since the Pentagon Papers, and never in a case relating to national security. In *Nebraska Press Association v. Stuart,* the Supreme Court overturned an injunction against the press in the context of a defendant's right to a fair and impartial trial under the Sixth Amendment. The defendant had been charged with murdering six people in a small town.[20] The case "attracted widespread news coverage."[21] Because the pretrial publicity could have undermined the defendant's right to a fair trial, the state trial court restrained the press from publishing any articles about the defendant's confessions or other facts "strongly implicative" of the defendant.[22]

The Supreme Court unanimously concluded that the restraining order violated the First Amendment. Although the Supreme Court recognized the danger that pretrial publicity posed to the defendant's right to a fair trial, it faulted the state court for failing to explore whether other measures would mitigate that danger.[23] The Supreme Court also questioned the efficacy of the prior restraint given the "practical problems" in enforcing the restraint against publishers in multiple jurisdictions.[24] Taking those factors into account, the Court ruled that the proffered justifications for the restraint were not sufficient to overcome the presumption against constitutionality recognized in *New York Times Co.* and *Near.*[25]

Pre-Publication Restraints on Government Employees

In contrast to the strong protections courts have established for the press, courts have repeatedly permitted prior restraints on publications by government employees who sought to disclose national-security-related information that they obtained in the course of their employment. In several key cases— *United States v. Marchetti, Alfred A. Knopf Inc. v. Colby, Snepp v. United States,* and *Agee v. Central Intelligence Agency*—the Central Intelligence Agency (CIA) successfully enforced a system of pre-publication restrictions against its former employees. The courts did not apply the Pentagon Papers standard for prior restraints. Rather, in each case, the courts concluded that traditional First

Amendment principles were inapplicable due to the former employees' relationship with the CIA.[26]

Victor Marchetti was a former CIA employee who agreed in writing that he would not publish information about the CIA unless authorized to do so in advance.[27] Marchetti later sought to publish a book and article based on his experiences as an agent.[28] Because Marchetti had not submitted the material to the CIA for review, the government sued to enforce the agreement. The district court enjoined publication, and the Fourth Circuit affirmed. The court found that secrecy agreements are an "entirely appropriate" means to effectuate the CIA director's statutory responsibility to protect intelligence sources and methods.[29] It then found that the agreement did not violate Marchetti's constitutional rights. The court agreed with Marchetti that the First Amendment "limits the extent to which the United States, contractually or otherwise, may impose secrecy requirements upon its employees and enforce them with a system of prior censorship."[30] Accordingly, the court said that the First Amendment would protect Marchetti's publication of unclassified information.[31] As to classified information obtained during Marchetti's employment, however, "the risk of harm from disclosure [was] so great and maintenance of the confidentiality of the information so necessary" that prior restraint was appropriate so the CIA could ensure no classified information appeared in the book.[32] To ensure the "reasonableness" of the restraint, the Fourth Circuit ordered the CIA to promptly approve or disapprove any material submitted by Marchetti for publication.[33]

Following pre-publication review, Marchetti and his publisher challenged more than one hundred redactions the CIA had demanded.[34] In *Alfred A. Knopf Inc. v. Colby*, the Fourth Circuit took a stronger view of Marchetti's secrecy agreement. By signing the agreement, the court held, Marchetti "effectively relinquished his First Amendment rights."[35] The court also construed its earlier decision as announcing a general rule: prior restraints against the disclosure of classified information do not violate the First Amendment when "(1) the classified information was acquired during the course of his employment, by an employee of a United States agency or department in which such information is handled and (2) its disclosure would violate a solemn agreement made by the employee at the commencement of his employment."[36] In addition, the Fourth Circuit rejected what it characterized as the district court's imposition of a "far too stringent" burden of proof on the government to justify the classification decisions, and instead emphasized the "presumption of regularity in the performance by a public official of his public duty"—in effect, closing the door to substantive judicial review of the CIA's classification decisions.[37] As the Fourth Circuit stated, "the government was required to show no more than that each deletion item disclosed information which was required to be classified in any degree and which was contained in a document bearing a classification stamp."[38] Other courts of appeals have insisted on a more searching review of government classification decisions in this context.[39]

The Supreme Court endorsed a similar view of national security employees' secrecy obligations in *Snepp v. United States*.[40] Frank Snepp, a former CIA analyst, had signed a secrecy agreement similar to Marchetti's.[41] In violation of that agreement, Snepp published a book about the CIA without submitting it for pre-publication review.[42] The book criticized the CIA's actions during the Vietnam War.[43] The government sued, demanding Snepp submit future publications for review and that he lose all profits from the book. The Supreme Court resolved the case in a per curiam opinion without receiving merits briefs or holding oral argument.[44] It rejected Snepp's claim that the pre-publication review requirement violated his First Amendment rights. The agreement, the Court held, was a "reasonable means" for protecting the government's "compelling interest in protecting both the secrecy of information important to our national security and the appearance of confidentiality so essential to the effective operation of our foreign intelligence service."[45] It made no difference that Snepp's book concededly contained no classified information.[46] Nor did the Court place any weight on Snepp's undisputed constitutional right to publish unclassified information.[47] Because the agreement required Snepp to submit for review any information relating to the CIA—not only classified information—his failure to do so constituted a breach of trust that "irreparably harmed" the United States.[48] The Supreme Court enjoined Snepp from future violations and ordered him to place his book profits into a constructive trust.[49]

Like Marchetti and Snepp, Philip Agee signed a secrecy agreement as a condition of his employment with the CIA.[50] He wrote several books after leaving the Agency "containing intelligence information relating to CIA activities without prior submission to the agency and in violation of the Secrecy Agreement."[51] In reliance on *Snepp*, a district court ordered Agee to submit his future writings to the CIA for review.[52] Then, in *Haig v. Agee* the following year, the Supreme Court upheld the State Department's revocation of Agee's passport.[53] The Court rejected Agee's argument that the revocation violated his First Amendment right to criticize the government: "Agee's disclosures, among other things, have the declared purpose of obstructing intelligence operations and the recruiting of intelligence personnel. They are clearly not protected by the Constitution."[54] Citing *Near v. Minnesota*, the Court noted that the government can prevent such harmful disclosures.[55]

The Pentagon Papers decision exerted little apparent influence in the decisions just described. In *Marchetti*, the Fourth Circuit did not analyze *New York Times Co.*, even though the court recognized that "Marchetti claims that the present injunction is barred by the Supreme Court decision in the Pentagon Papers case because the Government has failed to meet the very heavy burden against any system of prior restraints on expression."[56] The Supreme Court's decision in *Snepp* similarly "circumvent[ed] the doctrine against prior restraint."[57]

The government's system of pre-publication review for former government employees has come under renewed scrutiny in recent years,[58] and it has catapulted into the popular press as a result of several controversies over publication of memoirs by senior Trump administration officials.

The most widely covered dispute has arisen over *The Room Where It Happened*, a memoir by John Bolton, President Trump's former national security advisor.[59] Upon joining the White House staff, Bolton signed standard confidentiality agreements concerning classified information. After leaving his position, he quickly wrote a book and submitted it for pre-publication review. After four months of review, the senior National Security Council staffer responsible for review informed Bolton that she believed the manuscript was free of classified information, but the government refrained from providing a formal approval for publication. Bolton authorized his publisher to proceed with producing and distributing the book. In the meantime, other officials determined that the book still contained classified information. Less than a week before the book's release date in June 2020 and with many embargoed copies already distributed, the government sued Bolton for breaching his confidentiality agreements and sought an injunction preventing Bolton from "publi[shing] and disseminati[ng]" the book until conclusion of the pre-publication review.[60] The government argued that the memoir "contain[ed] classified information" and that "[d]isclosure of the manuscript [would] damage the national security of the United States."[61] Judge Royce Lamberth on the US District Court for the District of Columbia declined to issue the requested injunction.[62] Although Judge Lamberth concluded that the government was likely to succeed on the merits, he held that the government had failed to show that an injunction would prevent irreparable injury: "With hundreds of thousands of copies around the globe—many in newsrooms—the damage is done. There is no restoring the status quo."[63]

Another former government employee, Guy Snodgrass, who served as chief speechwriter to former secretary of defense James Mattis, brought a lawsuit challenging the Department of Defense's (DOD's) failure to clear the manuscript of his memoir, alleging that the DOD was violating the First Amendment and exceeding its authority to classify records.[64] Facing a motion for a preliminary injunction, the DOD largely cleared the manuscript within a month after the lawsuit was filed.[65] Finally, a group of five former government employees who wish to publish written work have brought a lawsuit challenging the system of pre-publication review as violative of the First and Fifth Amendments.[66] Those plaintiffs make allegations of extensive delays and arbitrary and capricious decisions in the pre-publication review process. The district court granted the government's motion to dismiss, holding that the plaintiffs' prior restraint claim was "simply untenable in light of *Snepp*"[67] and that the policies at issue were not impermissibly vague.[68]

Relying on the principles of *Snepp*, the United States has recently brought a suit against Edward Snowden and his publishers, asserting that publication of his book *Permanent Record* (and certain speeches and public statements Snowden made) violate nondisclosure agreements he had entered into with the government and fiduciary duties he owed the government. In December 2019, the district court granted partial summary judgment in the government's favor, concluding that the nondisclosure agreements were unambiguous in "requir[ing] prepublication review of a signatory's disclosures which refer to, mention, or are based upon, classified information or intelligence activities or materials."[69] The court refused to consider Snowden's affirmative defenses based on alleged bias and prejudgment in the prepublication review process because Snowden had failed to submit his manuscript for review.[70]

Criminal Exposure for the Media

One year after the Pentagon Papers case, in *Branzburg v. Hayes*, the Supreme Court rejected the idea of a reporter's privilege under the First Amendment that would immunize members of the press from being required to appear and testify before state or federal grand juries about information they obtained from their confidential sources.[71] The Court declined to "interpret[] the First Amendment to grant newsmen a testimonial privilege that other citizens do not enjoy" and remarked that "the press is not free to publish with impunity everything and anything it desires to publish."[72]

Two other Supreme Court decisions—*Landmark Communications, Inc. v. Virginia*, 435 U.S. 829 (1978), and *Bartnicki v. Vopper*, 532 U.S. 514, 528 (2001)—have set much of the framework for assessing criminal exposure for the press.

In 1975, the *Virginian-Pilot*, a newspaper owned by Landmark Communications, published an article describing the investigation of a state court judge by the Virginia Judicial Inquiry and Review Commission. A grand jury subsequently indicted the paper's owner for violating a Virginia statute rendering it unlawful to divulge information about proceedings before the Commission.[73] After a bench trial, the newspaper was found guilty and fined $500, and the Supreme Court of Virginia affirmed the conviction.[74]

The US Supreme Court reversed in a unanimous opinion.[75] It concluded that the newspaper's publication lay "near the core of the First Amendment" and that Virginia's "interests advanced by imposition of criminal sanctions were insufficient to justify the actual and potential encroachments on freedom of speech and of the press which follow therefrom."[76] Justice Stewart, concurring in the judgment, cited *New York Times Co. v. United States* and wrote that "[t]hough government may deny access to information and punish its theft, government may not prohibit or punish the publication of that information once it falls into the hands of the press, unless the need for secrecy is manifestly overwhelming."[77]

In a series of decisions, the Supreme Court has extended the holding of *Landmark Communications* and prohibited the imposition of criminal—and civil—sanctions on a newspaper for publishing truthful information, absent evidence that the newspaper had acted illegally in acquiring the information. In *Smith v. Daily Mail Publishing Co.*, the Court considered a West Virginia statute making it a crime for newspapers to publish the name of any youth charged as a juvenile offender.[78] Because a "free press cannot be made to rely solely upon the sufferance of government to supply it with information," the Court held, "the state may not punish [the] publication [of lawfully obtained information] except when necessary to further an interest more substantial" than was present in *Daily Mail*.[79] Similarly, in *Florida Star v. B.J.F.*, the Supreme Court took up a Florida statute making it unlawful to print the names of victims of sexual assault.[80] Applying the "*Daily Mail* principle," the Court held that imposing damages on a newspaper for publishing a victim's name violated the First Amendment.[81] In a footnote, the Court stressed that its holding concerned only cases in which neither the source nor the newspaper participated in illegal conduct in acquiring the information: "The *Daily Mail* principle does not settle the issue whether, *in cases where information has been acquired unlawfully by a newspaper or by a source*, government may ever punish not only the unlawful acquisition, but the ensuing publication as well."[82] "This issue," the Court explained, "was raised but not definitively resolved in *New York Times Co. v. United States*."[83]

In *Bartnicki v. Vopper*, the Supreme Court analyzed "a narrower version" of the still-open issue it identified in *Florida Star* and *Daily Mail*, which *New York Times Co. v. United States* had "raised" but not resolved.[84] The Court characterized the question presented this way: "Where the punished publisher of information has obtained the information in question in a manner lawful in itself but from a source who has obtained it unlawfully, may the government punish the ensuing publication of that information based on the defect in a chain?"[85] A radio station (among others) had received—and proceeded to play on the air—a recording of a phone conversation among union leaders who were discussing contentious bargaining negotiations with a school board.[86] Relying on a private right of action in a federal statute prohibiting wiretapping, some of the participants in the recorded conversation sued those who played it on the air. Because of the posture of the case, the Supreme Court accepted the plaintiffs' submission that the radio host (and others) who had played the recording on air "had reason to know" that the recording had been obtained unlawfully.[87] The Court also proceeded on the assumption that the defendants (1) had played no part in the illegal interception and (2) had obtained the tapes lawfully.[88]

Pointing to *New York Times Co. v. United States*, the Court stated that it had "upheld the right of the press to publish information of great public concern obtained from documents stolen by a third party."[89] The majority concluded that "it would be quite remarkable to hold that speech by a law-abiding possessor of information can be suppressed in order to deter conduct by a non-law-abiding third party."[90] On a practical point, the Court added, "there is no basis for assuming that imposing sanctions upon the press recipients will deter" the party that had acted unlawfully from continuing to engage in such behavior.[91]

Criminal Exposure for Leakers

The Supreme Court has not decided any case directly involving criminal prosecution for leaks of classified material to the press. Several Justices in the Pentagon Papers case suggested that the government could have prosecuted the *New York Times* and the *Washington Post* but did not directly address whether the government could also have prosecuted the leaker.[92] Since that decision— and as discussed in a number of the later essays in this book—leakers have been prosecuted for disclosing information to the press. Here we provide a brief overview of the legal framework.

The primary statute used to prosecute leakers is the Espionage Act of 1917, which has several provisions prohibiting a range of activity associated with receiving, possessing, and communicating information relating to the national defense.[93] Among the most important of those is 18 U.S.C. § 793(d), which subjects to criminal punishment

> Whoever, lawfully having possession of, access to, control over, or being entrusted with any document, . . . relating to the national defense, or information relating to the national defense which information the possessor has reason to believe could be used to the injury of the United States or to the advantage of any foreign nation, willfully communicates, delivers, transmits or causes to be communicated, delivered, or transmitted . . . to any person not entitled to receive it, or willfully retains the same and fails to deliver it on demand to the officer or employee of the United States entitled to receive it.[94]

Section 793(e) creates a parallel prohibition reaching those with unauthorized *access* to information relating to the national defense and subjects to punishment anyone with unauthorized access who transmits the information further or who even "willfully retains the same and fails to deliver it to the officer or employee of the United States entitled to receive it."[95]

A leading decision interpreting these provisions is *United States v. Morison*,[96] the first case in which the government obtained a conviction of a government employee for leaking classified information to the media.[97] Samuel Loring Morison, a Navy analyst with a Top Secret security clearance, transmitted classified photographs of a Soviet naval shipyard to the British publication *Jane's Defence Weekly*, which published them several days later.[98] Morison was convicted following a jury trial of violating §§ 793(d) and (e) (in addition to other crimes).[99]

On appeal, the Fourth Circuit rejected Morison's contention that the Espionage Act applies only in cases of "classic spying and espionage."[100] The court also rejected Morison's First Amendment argument that leaks to the press were exempt from the Espionage Act.[101] The court distinguished the Pentagon Papers decision as one about prior restraint against the press—not prosecution of a leaker.[102] Relying instead on *Snepp* and *Marchetti*, as well as *Branzburg v. Hayes*[103] (which had rejected a constitutionally based reporter's privilege), the court concluded that the First Amendment does not provide special protections for disclosures by government employees to the press.[104] The court thus observed that an "intelligence department employee who had abstracted from the government files secret intelligence information . . . is not entitled to invoke the First Amendment as a shield to immunize his act of thievery."[105]

The Fourth Circuit also rejected vagueness and overbreadth challenges to §§ 793(d) and (e). The court affirmed the trial court's jury instructions defining the scope of information covered by the phrase "relating to the national defense" as requiring the government to show (1) the photographs were "closely held," and (2) their disclosure would be "potentially damaging to the United States or might be useful to an enemy of the United States."[106] In approving the instructions, the Fourth Circuit pointed to Justice White's concurrence in *New York Times Co.*, which noted that Congress had enacted the Espionage Act to punish disclosures of "potentially damaging" information.[107]

Two judges concurring in *Morison* emphasized the importance of the First Amendment rights implicated by Morison's conviction. Judge J. Harvie Wilkinson observed that "[c]riminal restraints on the disclosure of information threaten the ability of the press to scrutinize and report on government activity."[108] Nonetheless, he indicated the courts must accord substantial deference to the government's "compelling interest in protecting . . . the secrecy of information important to our national security."[109] Judge Wilkinson distinguished Morison from a leaker who "truly expose[s] governmental waste and misconduct."[110] In a separate concurrence, Judge Phillips echoed that "the first amendment issues raised by Morison are real and substantial."[111] Although the Espionage Act was, "as facially stated," both overbroad and vague, Judge Phillips agreed that the instructions provided by the trial court, which required the government to prove that the leaked information "was either 'potentially damaging to the United States or might be useful to an enemy' " sufficiently limited the Act's scope.[112]

Subsequent decisions about leak prosecutions under §§ 793(d) and (e) have generally followed *Morison*'s key holdings. First, most courts have adopted *Morison*'s requirement that to fall within the statutory prohibition, information "relating to the national defense" must be (1) "closely held" information, (2) the disclosure of which "could harm" the United States.[113] Second, courts consistently have looked to the executive branch's classification regulations to define who is and is not "entitled to receive" national defense information.[114] Third, courts have continued to reject any special protections for leaks to the press.[115]

Later decisions have clarified the scienter requirement for oral disclosures, an issue left open in *Morison*. In *United States v. Rosen*, the government charged two lobbyists for the American Israel Public Affairs Committee, who had received classified information from government sources without authorization, for orally sharing the information with colleagues, journalists, and Israeli officials not entitled to receive it.[116] The court concluded that the Espionage Act imposes an additional scienter requirement with respect to such intangible communications. The district court held that the requirement in §§ 793(d) and (e) that the leaker "has reason to believe" the information "could be used to the injury of the United States or to the advantage of any foreign nation" requires the government to prove that intangible information was communicated with "bad faith purpose to either harm the United States or aid a foreign government."[117] No such requirement, the court concluded, applies to disclosure of tangible documents or records.[118]

The Espionage Act is not the only federal criminal statute available to prosecute leakers. Others include:[119]

- 18 U.S.C. § 641: prohibits the theft or conversion of government documents and "things of value of the United States";
- 18 U.S.C. § 794: prohibits communicating or attempting to communicate "information relating to the national defense" to "any foreign government" or its representative;
- 18 U.S.C. §§ 795, 797: prohibits unauthorized creation, publication, or sale of photographs or sketches of "vital military and naval installations or equipment";
- 18 U.S.C. § 796: prohibits using aircraft for the purpose of making photographs or sketches of "vital military or naval installations or equipment";

- 18 U.S.C. § 798: prohibits disseminating "classified information . . . concerning the communication intelligence activities of the United States";
- 18 U.S.C. § 952: prohibits disclosure of diplomatic code or coded correspondence by government employees;
- 18 U.S.C. § 1030(a): prohibits communicating classified information retrieved by accessing a computer without or in excess of authorization;
- 18 U.S.C. § 1924: prohibits the unauthorized removal, retention, or storage of classified information by a government employee, contractor, or consultant;
- 42 U.S.C. § 2274: prohibits the communication of "Restricted Data" related to the design, manufacture, or use of atomic weapons and atomic material;
- 50 U.S.C. § 783: prohibits government employees from communicating classified information to "an agent or representative of any foreign government"; and
- 50 U.S.C. § 3121: prohibits disclosing the identity of a "covert agent" to unauthorized persons.

Many of these criminal prohibitions are limited to particular types of information or particular kinds of disclosures. Some apply only to government employees. The most notable exception is the government property theft statute, 18 U.S.C. § 641, which imposes liability on anyone who "embezzles, steals, purloins or knowingly converts to his use or the use of another, or without authority, sells, conveys or disposes of any record . . . or thing of value of the United States." It "does not require any showing of harm to the United States or any consideration of the public interest."[120] Moreover, several federal courts of appeals have ruled that § 641 applies to disclosures of intangible information as well as documents and other tangible items.[121] Several courts have recognized that applying § 641 to government information raises First Amendment concerns, although they have not reversed convictions on that ground.[122]

No Broad Public Right of Access

The leading Supreme Court decision about a constitutional right of access to government information is *Houchins v. KQED*.[123] KQED, a news broadcaster, sued the sheriff of Alameda County in California after the sheriff denied KQED permission to inspect and take photographs of the part of the county jail where an inmate had reportedly committed suicide.[124] A district court issued an injunction ordering that KQED and the news media be afforded (1) access to all parts of the jail at reasonable times, (2) use of recording equipment, and (3) the opportunity to interview inmates.[125] A divided seven-Justice Supreme Court reversed.[126] Both the three-Justice plurality, per Chief Justice Warren E. Burger, and Justice Stewart, concurring in the judgment, concluded that the First Amendment does not provide a right of access to government-held or government-controlled information, nor does it guarantee the press a greater right of access than the public.[127] Justice Stewart clarified in his concurrence, however, that the Constitution "assure[s] the public and the press equal access once government has opened its doors."[128] That guarantee required the sheriff to provide KQED "*effective* access to the same areas" of the jail open to the public.[129] Thus, Justice Stewart indicated that the First Amendment would support requiring the press to receive access to the jail on a more frequent basis than the public and to bring sound and photography equipment—both elements that allow journalists "to gather information to be passed on to others" consistent with "the critical role played by the press in American society."[130] The three Justices in dissent, however, suggested some support for constitutional "protection for the acquisition of information about the operation of public institutions."[131]

The Supreme Court later recognized a limited constitutional right of access to criminal trials. In *Richmond Newspapers, Inc. v. Virginia*, the Court reversed an order excluding both the press and the public from observing a murder trial.[132] Although there was no majority opinion, seven of the eight Justices participating held that the First Amendment guaranteed a right of access to criminal trials.[133] The plurality opinion, per Chief Justice Burger, relied on the historic openness of criminal trials as well as the public value of open trials.[134] Three concurring Justices—Brennan, Marshall, and Stevens—suggested that the public right of access went beyond criminal trials.

Later court decisions have not extended *Richmond Newspapers* to national security information held by the executive branch. In 2013, the DC Circuit held that the government did not need to release information about individuals detained after the September 11, 2001, terrorist attacks.[135] It concluded: "The narrow First Amendment right of access to information recognized in *Richmond Newspapers* does not extend to non-judicial documents that are not part of a criminal trial."[136] The Constitution, the court observed, is not a "Freedom of Information Act," and "disclosure of government information generally is left to the 'political forces.' "[137]

Challenges in Evaluating the Impact of the Pentagon Papers Regime

Has the Pentagon Papers regime—which Alexander Bickel deemed a "disorderly situation"—led to the release of highly damaging information or, conversely, prevented the release of important information that the public should know? As other essays in this book reflect, some insist that the nation would be

better off with more disclosures,[138] while others believe that leaks have been destructive and have undermined US military operations, endangering the lives of
informants and hindering diplomatic efforts.[139]

It is difficult to evaluate the consequences of the Pentagon Papers framework
with precision. The first, most obvious impediment is that typically only government insiders with access to classified information are in a position to evaluate the
impact of a disclosure on national security.[140] Those insiders are often unwilling
or unable to share their evaluations with the public, or they choose to release only
heavily redacted assessments.[141] For example, when *Vice News* sued the Defense
Intelligence Agency (DIA) to release its internal evaluation of the leaks by National
Security Agency (NSA) contractor Snowden, the DIA redacted every page of
its internal assessment, excluding only some subheadings.[142] The lack of meaningful disclosure made it difficult to evaluate whether officials who had read an
unredacted version of the assessment were accurately representing its findings.[143]

Second, even government insiders may struggle to identify and articulate the
impact of a leak ex post. A leak's effects may take time to become apparent. For
example, intelligence officials complain that nearly five years after the original
Snowden release, revelations in the media have continued, making any evaluation of harm premature.[144] In addition, harms flowing from a leak may be indirect
or unquantifiable—such as the possibility that a leak reduces the level of confidence that informants or diplomatic contacts have in the United States' ability
to keep information secure, thus reducing the likelihood of cooperation from
those sources.[145] Relatedly, because classified information is often combined
with nonclassified information, it can be difficult even for insiders to distinguish
leaks from effective open-source reporting.[146]

Third, it is difficult to evaluate the harms arising from failures to disclose.
How can one determine what secrets the public should have been told without
knowing first what the secrets are? Although organizations such as Transparency
International have proposed types of information that national security agencies
should disclose—thus creating a benchmark by which to compare the transparency of various countries—their metrics focus more on budgets and auditing
than on secret programs and operations.[147]

Observers from many points along the political spectrum have argued that
more information is classified than needs to be and that much information that
is secret could be disclosed without threatening national security.[148] In a 2016
hearing before the House Committee on Oversight and Government Reform,
Chairman Jason Chaffetz noted that an estimated 50 to 90 percent of classified material is not correctly labeled.[149] A witness at the same hearing, the director of the National Security Archive at George Washington University, noted
that "when a security official—officials—tell you something is classified, don't

believe them. Most of the time they are wrong."[150] Nearly a decade earlier, former US diplomat George Kennan similarly said that "upwards of 95% of what we need to know about foreign countries could be very well obtained [from other] perfectly legitimate sources of information open and available to us."[151]

Overclassification has many causes. First, government insiders may mistakenly believe intelligence is more important than it is. Because there is no clear guidance for what constitutes "damage to national security," insiders have discretion, and perhaps an inclination, to overclassify.[152] Although those with authority to classify materials must supposedly be "able" to articulate the anticipated damage resulting from each disclosure, they do not need to spell out their reasoning when making the classification decision.[153] Recent legislative reforms to limit overclassification, such as the Reducing Over-Classification Act,[154] have failed to define what overclassification entails.[155] Second, government officials may intentionally overclassify information to avoid public controversy or to serve the bureaucratic interests of their agency.

Some studies suggest that, far from protecting national security, overclassification can threaten national security in several ways.[156] First, it can undermine information sharing—making agencies less capable of anticipating threats and carrying out their missions effectively.[157] Second, excessive classification can lead US officials to overvalue their own intelligence and ignore important sources of open-source intelligence. For example, former US senator Daniel Patrick Moynihan found that excessive secrecy caused intelligence officers to ignore contradictory sources of open-source intelligence in the run-up to the Bay of Pigs invasion. As a result, US officials ignored important sources of open-source intelligence that showed Cubans were highly supportive of Fidel Castro and therefore unlikely to support the US-orchestrated uprising.[158] Third, overclassification is expensive, diverting national security dollars that might otherwise have gone to strategic initiatives. The Information Security Oversight Office estimates that in 2017, the government spent $18.39 billion on security classification,[159] nearly half the amount the United Kingdom spent on its entire defense budget that year.[160] Lastly, overclassification may encourage harmful leaks. When overclassification is pervasive, the credibility of the entire classification system is compromised, leading insiders to make their own decisions about what should be declassified.[161] As Justice Stewart predicted in 1971:

> [W]hen everything is classified, then nothing is classified, and the system becomes one to be disregarded by the cynical or the careless, and to be manipulated by those intent on self-protection or self-promotion.... [S]ecrecy can best be preserved only when credibility is truly maintained.[162]

Comparing the United States and the United Kingdom

Different countries, including advanced democracies, have drawn different lines to prevent the dissemination of national security information.[163] One way to evaluate the Pentagon Papers framework is to compare the balance it struck between secrecy and disclosure with that struck by other nations. A common comparator is the United Kingdom. Although some emphasize formal differences between US and UK anti-leaking laws, evidence suggests that the laws are enforced similarly in practice. Nonetheless, leaking patterns still differ across the two countries, suggesting that perhaps anti-leaking laws and leak prosecutions alone do not explain the varied results in each country.

Both the United States and the United Kingdom have statutes criminalizing unauthorized disclosures of national security information. In the United States, the cornerstone law is the 1917 Espionage Act. In the United Kingdom, it is the Official Secrets Act of 1989. There are two striking differences between the two laws. First, the Official Secrets Act criminalizes all unauthorized disclosures by members of the security and intelligence services, even if the information disclosed is not necessarily "damaging."[164] Under the Espionage Act, by contrast, many courts have held that disclosures must be potentially damaging to the United States or useful to an enemy of the United States to constitute an offense.[165] Second, the Espionage Act does not explicitly state that publishers can be prosecuted for printing leaked information, whereas § 5 of the Official Secrets Act specifically allows for publishers—or any other member of the public—to be prosecuted when they publish information that they have reasonable cause to believe has been unlawfully disclosed to them.[166]

Although the Official Secrets Act is broader on paper than the Espionage Act, enforcement patterns do not appear to be strikingly different. The British government has not published updated information about prosecutions under the Official Secrets Act, but most sources suggest that prosecutions are rare.[167] In the few cases when an individual has been prosecuted for transferring top-secret documents to a publication, there is no evidence to suggest the media outlet disseminating the leak was also prosecuted. For example, former MI5 officer David Shayler was sentenced to six months in jail in 2002 after he sold top-secret documents to the *Mail on Sunday*, but the *Mail* was not prosecuted.[168]

The British government attempts to prevent leaks not only through criminal prosecution but also through the work of the Defence and Security Media Advisory (DSMA) Committee, which has no analogue in the United States. This independent advisory group consists of five members of the British government from four agencies, along with seventeen members of the media.[169] The DSMA

Committee issues guidance aimed at avoiding disclosures that harm national security, known as "DSMA notices" or, previously, "DA notices," and more specific "letters of advice" about particular leaks.[170] Standing DSMA notices recommend that the media refrain from disclosing certain categories of sensitive national security information, including military operations, plans, and capabilities.[171] These notices and letters are not legally binding.[172] Even so, the press reportedly regularly complies with the DSMA Committee's requests for self-censorship.[173] The DSMA notice system may be one reason the British government does not appear to experience as many leaks as the US government does.[174]

How Circumstances Today Differ

The same year that the Supreme Court handed down *New York Times Co. v. United States*, Intel released the first general-purpose microprocessor.[175] Advertised as "A New Era in Integrated Electronics," Intel's chip was "the size of a little fingernail" but "delivered the same computing power as the first electronic computer," which had taken up an entire room in 1946.[176] Early personal computers found their way into American homes roughly a decade later,[177] and the launch of the World Wide Web occurred in 1990.[178] Dramatic technological changes in the way we produce, duplicate, transmit, and consume information present significant challenges to the stability of the Pentagon Papers framework, as do related changes in the structure of the press.

The Digital National Security State

Since the 1990s, the government, like other large organizations, has increasingly kept its records in electronic rather than paper form. This shift to digital records, combined with the rise of the internet, has had many implications for the secrecy and disclosure of confidential government information.

First, it has facilitated a dramatic expansion in access to classified and other government documents, particularly in the aftermath of the September 11 attacks and the 9/11 Commission's conclusion that "too little access to information and sharing [between agencies] was the problem, not too much."[179] That includes people who may hold relatively low-level positions and may have little familiarity with the information's significance.[180] Whereas Ellsberg was a "member of the elite with an academic pedigree from some of the world's finest universities and some of the highest security clearance," Chelsea Manning was "a low-level security analyst, a node in a vast industry of networked individuals."[181] Snowden, to take another example, "had access to all that information not because he was an expert but because he was an IT guy."[182] Examples of low-level government employees and contractors disclosing large caches of information have led some to accuse the government of failing to take proper security measures[183] and to propose that the government focus on developing better technological defenses to protect sensitive information in the first place.[184] The expansion of the population with access to classified information has also been driven by the dramatic growth in the contractor workforce assisting US defense and intelligence agencies.[185]

Increased digitization has also both expanded the volume of classified information and made it easier for would-be leakers to disclose information.[186] Consider the physical work of copying and disclosing documents. Whereas Ellsberg had to spend many hours over many nights physically transporting and photocopying classified documents, Snowden was able to download 1.7 million files, in large part using "inexpensive and widely available software" that scraped NSA networks as he went about his normal job.[187] Several scholars have written about "deluge leaks," characterized by the unauthorized release of previously unimaginable amounts of data.[188] The peril of such leaks, as Margaret Kwoka has observed, is that "whenever hundreds of thousands of records (exponentially larger than even the 7,000 pages of Pentagon Papers) are released, the risk is magnified that some information turns out to have a direct, harmful effect."[189] And whereas leakers and the press may once have been capable (assuming they were willing) of reviewing documents before their release, the scale of modern disclosures may render such pre-publication review a logistical impossibility.[190]

In 1993, the *New Yorker* published a now-famous cartoon with the caption "On the Internet, nobody knows you're a dog." Today, "leaking without consequences" may be possible,[191] as the strong anonymity protections that online platforms can afford leakers hampers the government's ability to identify and prosecute leakers,[192] as well as the basic ability to authenticate leaked information.[193] Greater anonymity itself may encourage leaking.[194]

Today's leakers may also have different interests from their predecessors; they may, some have observed, believe in a broader notion of transparency and may reject the guardianship role of the institutional press.[195]

The Digital Media

The shift to ubiquitous reliance on computers and digital information and the rise of the internet have also reshaped the nature of the press and the universe of possible recipients of leaked information. The press has become more difficult to define in the online era.[196] Many have applauded the internet for democratizing access to information.[197] As law professor Mary-Rose Papandrea has observed, "In the digital age, . . . [t]hose who want to reveal information to the public have a wide variety of foreign and domestic intermediaries to reach their desired audience."[198] At the same time, unlike during the Pentagon Papers era, would-be leakers no longer have to wait for traditional newspapers such as the *New York Times* or the *Washington Post* to publish their leaks.[199] "[T]hey can forgo intermediation entirely and distribute their information directly to the public."[200]

The number of these nontraditional publishers is effectively limitless—"and they appear to be constrained only by the number of people willing to create them."[201] This capability, along with the fact that many traditional news companies are struggling to remain solvent,[202] may mean that the traditional press is no longer integral to mediating between the interests of the government and those of leakers.

Many new nontraditional publishers may not adhere to the norms concerning consultation with the government and patriotic regard for guarding US national security followed by many traditional news organizations.[203] WikiLeaks, in particular, has shown "no sense of an institutional obligation systematically to consult with officials about the release of government secrets."[204] Many other online platforms may not "self-censor to avoid disclosing harmful national security information" in the way that an institution like the *New York Times* sometimes has.[205] Of course, "concerns about publications with bad motives existed long before WikiLeaks came on the scene." But they have been greatly magnified as traditional editorial practices of reviewing documents before publishing and seeking government input on whether certain information should be redacted are embraced by fewer potential recipients of leaks.[206]

Challenges to Enforcement

The international presence of platforms such as WikiLeaks poses new law enforcement challenges. Foreign-based online organizations may be shielded from legal liability because of limits on US jurisdiction.[207] WikiLeaks, for example, "has relied mainly on infrastructure outside of the United States to host its site" and has no physical presence in the United States.[208] Without the threat of US jurisdiction hanging over their actions, publishers like WikiLeaks may feel little pressure from domestic laws meant to deter leaks.[209]

Nor are such concerns limited to new, nontraditional platforms. In 2013, for example, British newspaper the *Guardian* strategically shared documents leaked to it by Snowden with the *New York Times*, in order to take advantage of the comparatively robust First Amendment protection against prior restraint available to publishers in the United States.[210] The *Guardian*'s decision to partner with a US newspaper was driven by pressure from the UK government to turn over the leaked documents.[211] A similar "partnership" had been "forged in 2010 between the *Guardian*, the *New York Times* and *Der Spiegel* in relation to WikiLeaks's release of US military and diplomatic documents."[212]

PART ONE

THE NATIONAL SECURITY
PERSPECTIVE

Fighting for Balance

AVRIL HAINES

I have yet to encounter anyone who thinks that we are striking the right balance between the public's right to know and the government's legitimate interests in secrecy in the United States, though there is little agreement about the direction in which we are leaning too far and even less agreement about what should be done to address the situation. Dissatisfaction with the status quo tends to be framed by seemingly opposing views. Some critics focus on what they perceive to be an "avalanche" of national security leaks and argue that the existing legal and policy frameworks should provide the government with greater tools to prevent the publication of classified information and support a more aggressive pursuit and punishment of "leakers"—whether employees of the government, reporters, or media institutions—to deter the disclosure of such information and prevent the damage that such leaks can do.[1] On the other side, critics focus on the overclassification of national security information, which they believe is stifling public debate and thereby corroding effective self-governance. These critics advocate for reforming the classification and declassification process to better promote transparency, enhancing protections for whistleblowers, and providing greater protection for journalists and the press, including immunity from prosecution when publishing classified information.[2] Both sides have reason to be concerned. It is true that there is an increase in the quantity of unauthorized disclosures of classified information and that some of these disclosures have had a serious and damaging impact on our national security, but it is also true that too much information that should not be classified is classified and that we desperately need to improve government transparency in support of an informed citizenry that is critical to the functioning of our democracy.

Of course, these perspectives are not mutually exclusive, though they do tend to be motivated, in large part, by different underlying interests that need to be balanced. Framing the problem in this way, however, obscures the fundamental challenge at the heart of the debate and allows one to take the moderate but overly simplistic and entirely unrealistic position in response to both critiques that we need to restructure the system to address overclassification, and having achieved this ideal state—one in which the government only classifies information that truly warrants classification—we should indeed pursue leakers aggressively in order to protect our national security. This apparent solution fails to take into account the fact that many would disagree over what warrants classification, and although the existing classification system can be improved, there is little hope of producing a system within the executive branch that does not overclassify information to some degree. Most important, however, such a solution fails to address the more challenging question of how to establish a framework that promotes as a matter of course the disclosure of information that is properly classified but that nevertheless should be declassified because its importance to the underlying purpose of the free speech guarantee outweighs the national security interest in maintaining secrecy. This is the fundamental objective that we should be focused on achieving.

There are at least some who will question whether it is ever necessary or wise to expose information that could reasonably be assessed to do damage to our national security, but such disclosures can be critically important to informing the public debate over government action. For example, when President Obama declassified and publicly disclosed that the United States had during the course of his administration targeted and killed four US citizens in the course of counter-terrorism operations,[3] no one questioned whether the information had been properly classified, and yet most would agree, I suspect, that such information both was newsworthy and contributed to a public debate consistent with the underlying purposes of the free speech guarantee.[4] The disclosure of such information is fundamental to a functioning democracy, for how can the public reward or sanction elected leaders for their actions if they do not know, even in general terms, what activities the government is engaged in at their direction? In such a case, risking some potential harm to national security is warranted in light of the public interest in an informed discussion. Nevertheless, it took an enormous amount of time and effort at the highest levels of government to manage that disclosure and many others like it.[5] In my view, this balancing of interests would require disclosure in only rare scenarios when the government is engaged in major, potentially controversial activities that are already or would almost certainly be the subject of substantive debate if known and when such disclosures can avoid severe and irreparable national security harm. I recognize that such decisions rest on judgment calls that defy easy characterization, but at the very least, a mechanism should be established to promote such disclosures, which should be tailored and timed to minimize the damage to national security.

This question of when and how to promote the disclosure of classified information when the public's need to know outweighs the national security interest was at the heart of the Supreme Court's Pentagon Papers case in 1971.[6] The Court sought a balance of these interests that remains salient today and established a framework for promoting that balance by effectively encouraging different actors—individuals with access to classified information, the press, and the courts—to weigh the public's right to know against the national security interests at stake in the context of each disclosure. Due to changes in the landscape since the 1970s, however, the Pentagon Papers framework has become less workable and effective. While the need for a mechanism that extends beyond the executive branch to promote the disclosure of national security information that is of critical importance to our public debate has only increased, the current framework is not accomplishing this goal.

The Existing Framework

In 1971, the Supreme Court decided that an injunction prohibiting the publication of a classified study titled the *History of U.S. Decision-Making Process on Viet Nam Policy* would constitute an impermissible prior restraint on free speech. Despite the fact that the government claimed that publication of the study would do irreparable harm to national security and no Justice disputed this conclusion, several Justices noted that a heavy presumption against the constitutional validity of injunctions preventing the publication of information was fundamental to the protection of free speech and that the information in the study did not overcome that presumption. The Justices simultaneously acknowledged the power of Congress and the executive branch to sanction, including through the imposition of criminal penalties, individuals for certain unauthorized disclosures of classified information. As a result, the Court's framework for protecting free speech in this area effectively—and bizarrely—relies on government employees, contractors, or others to break the law and, where relevant, the terms they have agreed to in the course of their employment, in order to disclose information that many of the Justices indicated was precisely what the Founders would have wanted to see published under the First Amendment—information exposing controversial governmental action essential for the public to know in order to hold the government accountable, as our political system envisions.

The framework established by the Pentagon Papers case implicitly assumes that the executive branch cannot be trusted on its own to appropriately balance the public's right to know and the government's legitimate interests in secrecy. This is, frankly, not an unreasonable assumption—perhaps most obviously in light of overclassification but more fundamentally because there is no institutional structure, beyond enlightened leadership and pressure from the press when a leak has already occurred,[7] that incentivizes the declassification of information when the potential damage that such a disclosure would cause is outweighed by the importance of making such information public. The holding consequently supports the construction of a safety valve in the system that relies on people who have access to classified information to disclose such information if they believe it is sufficiently important to do so and are willing to accept the risk of perhaps even criminal sanctions for having done so. If the press is willing to publish the information, however, the Court's decision rules out the possibility of preventing the publication of such information in all but exceptional circumstances.

The framework, however, contains certain safeguards presumably intended to help tailor the information disclosed to what would be most important to the public debate and to avoid severe national security damage. First, the framework relies not only on the judgment of the individual willing to leak the classified information but also on the press's judgment that the information is newsworthy and thus worth publishing.[8] Second, the Court built into the system a second safety valve for the government, though it has only once been successfully applied: a majority of Justices made clear that although the First Amendment's protection can extend to classified information, it will not do so if the classified information at issue is of a nature that is virtually certain to do grave harm to our national security. In other words, the right to free speech is not an absolute right, and although it applies to some classified information, the framework supports weighing the extent of the national security interest against the value of disclosure by leaving open the possibility that when particularly damaging information is at stake, the executive branch can go to court, and if, as Justice Stewart articulated, the judiciary agrees that the classified information at stake would "surely result in direct, immediate, and irreparable damage to our Nation or its people," it would be possible to overcome the presumption against prior restraints and prevent publication of the information.[9] Yet, as discussed further below, both safeguards have been rendered effectively irrelevant today as a consequence of technological developments.

Interestingly, although a majority of Justices distinguished, for purposes of whether prior restraints should be made available, the degree of damage that might occur as a consequence of public disclosure of the classified information at issue, they did not explicitly indicate that the relative value of the speech to the public debate should be formally weighed in making such decisions. Nevertheless, it seems reasonable to assume that this would be the case, and there are signs that the nature of the information was considered by at least some of the Justices.[10] Moreover, there is precedent in First Amendment jurisprudence for distinguishing among different categories of speech in accordance with the importance of such speech to the underlying purposes of the free speech guarantee, which suggests that this factor might be taken into account in future cases, despite the heavy presumption against such restraints on publication.[11]

Certainly, from a policy perspective, I would hope that any framework that is intended to promote the declassification of information along these lines would look at the degree of harm that is likely to occur from a national security perspective and weigh it against the value that such information would have to public debate. In practice, I have found that this can mean that while certain important decisions or activities can and should be disclosed, there may be details that surround such a decision or activity that would not add anything to the debate but would likely result in some damage to national security and thus would be better left out of any proposed disclosure. For example, while it may be important to publicly disclose the fact of US military action against a particular target and the nature of the threat posed by that target in order to promote a debate on the wisdom of such action, it may not be as important to disclose the specific weapons, tactics, techniques, or procedures used by the military in the course of such an operation. Doing so could serve the purpose of informing US adversaries about our military methods, which may be damaging for future operations without providing the public with information that is necessary for a debate about the underlying action. The challenge, of course, is that this is inevitably a judgment call, and one might reasonably question whether the national security community within the executive branch can be relied upon to judge by themselves what information is most important to disclose in order to promote an informed public debate. One can see, therefore, the wisdom of the safety valve established in the Pentagon Papers framework, which relies on a decision by the press to determine if the information is worth publishing. In today's world, however, this is not a workable solution. The ease with which anyone can publish information means that such decisions are often made by individuals who are not professional journalists, or even state actors such as Russia, using social-media cut-outs to publish "news." Consequently, the press is no longer in a position to provide an additional layer of considered judgment, and without that additional layer, there is no second opportunity for a responsible actor to tailor the publication to avoid unnecessary damage to our national security.

Relevant Shifts in the Landscape since the 1970s

There have been a series of shifts in the landscape since the 1970s that are relevant to the Pentagon Papers framework. On the one hand, given the increasing power of the executive branch, a relatively weak Congress, and US engagement in lengthy conflicts involving US military force abroad, the need for a framework that promotes the appropriate disclosure of national-security-related information to the public is arguably more important today than ever before as a way of holding the executive branch accountable. On the other hand, largely as a consequence of technological advancements, the framework is less effective at maintaining the balance it was designed to achieve. The danger of massive and seriously damaging leaks being broadly disseminated through publication on the internet that do not contribute to the public discourse has increased, the use of prior restraints as a tool for preventing the dissemination of information is increasingly impractical even if permitted by law, and the press, however defined, no longer appears to have a role in making the kind of considered judgment that the framework envisioned.

Growing Executive Power

Despite the fact that the Framers of the American Constitution were particularly focused on constraining presidential power, having revolted against monarchical power, the executive branch has increasingly gained more influence and control than the Framers intended.[12] Over the last two hundred years or so, the power of the presidency has generally expanded, frequently to fill the demands placed on the executive branch by economic expansion and industrialization with a growing number of administrative agencies under the president's control but also as a consequence of structural advantages, political developments, and the extraordinary role that the United States has played internationally, where the executive branch is the authoritative actor for the United States as a matter of international law. Still, the expansion of executive power, principally at the cost of congressional power, has not been smooth.[13] In the 1970s, there were a number of efforts to rein in unilateral presidential authority on a variety of fronts, such as the War Powers Resolution of 1973, the Hughes-Ryan Amendment of 1974, the Domestic Intelligence Guidelines of 1976, the National Emergencies Act of 1976, and the Foreign Intelligence Surveillance Act of 1978. Yet these efforts and others were short-lived, and over time, these laws were interpreted and applied in ways that ultimately strengthened the executive branch's power to act without the explicit consent of Congress. The result is that the president is today the dominant force in national security and foreign policy formation, and Congress, rather than being alert to "dangerous encroachments" by the executive branch,[14] has effectively ceded power to the president in a whole series of areas that were traditionally dominated by Congress earlier in our history, such as foreign commerce, war powers, immigration, and international agreements.

For example, two critical structural advantages that have allowed the executive branch to accrue power are its "first mover" advantage and veto leverage, both of which are particularly effective in the context of the use of military force by the United States. In most deployments, presidents act under their own authority, but even when Congress explicitly legislates, the executive branch generally maintains control over the scope and nature of the US government's activities in conflicts today. Congress can pass an authorization to use military force, as it did in the wake of the attacks on September 11, 2001, and the president has the power to act under that president's own expansive interpretation of that law, without seeking any additional approval from Congress. In this context, no case or controversy regarding the deployment of such troops is likely to be reviewed by the judiciary, and even if Congress is capable of passing a joint resolution to attempt to rein in the president's deployments or the president's use of military force under these circumstances, it would presumably be vetoed by the president and thus would require a supermajority to become law over the president's veto. Such a scenario is extremely unlikely to occur in today's highly partisan environment, in which members of Congress from both parties tend to rely heavily on their party and the president, if the president is of their party, for support in any re-election campaign, so that controversial issues tend to be voted on along party lines, rather than on an institutional basis, even when institutional prerogatives are at stake, which of course is inconsistent with the structural opposition that the separation-of-powers framework relies upon.

In general, when it comes to activities that must be conducted secretly, such as certain aspects of military operations and intelligence activities, the appropriate committees in Congress with access to relevant classified information needed to provide oversight are expected to ensure that the executive branch is held accountable and that its programs are legal, ethical, wise, and protective of people's civil liberties.[15] This is particularly important in light of the fact that the public does not have access to this information and consequently must rely on congressional representatives' judgment and engagement to shape the executive branch's activities in this realm. Given, however, the increasing power of the executive branch, not only are members of Congress cut out of the conversation leading up to most major decisions in the context of national security, but they also find it increasingly challenging to shape executive branch action after a decision is taken, especially when the president is determined to follow a particular course of action. While Congress continues to maintain some significant leverage in the context of appropriations and the approval of nominees, these are ultimately levers that can only be used sparingly and with considerable political pushback, particularly if members cannot explain to constituents why they are withholding congressional approval for executive action that sometimes appears unrelated and perfectly sensible because the activities at issue are classified.[16]

With a legislative branch today that is unable or unwilling, as a consequence of structural and political challenges, to rein in the executive branch when it overreaches, even when a majority is inclined to do so, we would normally turn to the judiciary under our separation-of-powers framework, which should be active in correcting this imbalance by enforcing principles allocating power between the president and Congress. In the context of national security, however, the judiciary is rarely effective at guarding against overreaches by the executive branch. This is in part because most critical national security decisions and activities will never be reviewed by a court, which must await a case or controversy presented by a litigant with standing,[17] and in many national security cases, this is not an easy barrier to overcome, but even when such issues are reviewed by the courts, judges tend to be extremely deferential to the executive branch in this arena[18] and on occasion will determine that the issue is a non-justiciable political question.[19]

Furthermore, the problem is exacerbated during times of crisis, when the president's ability to control the levers of power tends to be augmented, especially in the context of conflicts.[20] This is particularly relevant at this moment in our history, as we enter the nineteenth year of the conflict in Afghanistan.[21] The number of national security areas in which executive branch power has been expanded and decisions made in secrecy in the wake of 9/11, generally with congressional support in the context of conflicts that the United States is engaged in, has been widely reported.[22] Moreover, with increasing mobility, globalized trade, and technological developments that further integrate us with, and make us more reliant on, other countries, it is hard to imagine a time when foreign policy, as well as national security, have had more relevance to domestic matters or when the decisions being made in this arena were of greater significance to the public and the fate of the nation.

In sum, with an increasingly powerful executive branch, a weak Congress, and the likely continued use of US military force abroad, it seems clear that the need has never been greater for a framework that promotes the disclosure of classified information when it is important to an informed public debate, as the public may be the only effective restraint on executive policy and power in this realm. This challenge was foreshadowed to some extent by Justice Stewart, who noted in the Pentagon Papers case that the executive branch, in the areas of national defense and international relations, is endowed with enormous power by the Constitution, and with the advent of the nuclear age, that power has been "pressed to the very hilt," so that the "only effective restraint upon executive policy and power in the areas of national defense and international affairs may lie in an enlightened citizenry—in an informed and critical public opinion which alone can here protect the values of democratic government."[23]

Despite all this, I remain convinced that some information must remain classified, that this includes certain activities that are taken in the interest of national security, and that in the majority of cases, congressional oversight, with full access to relevant classified information, can and should be sufficient to ensure that the executive branch is held accountable and that its programs are legal, ethical, wise, and protective of people's civil liberties. Nevertheless, it is hard to ignore the degree to which unauthorized leaks regarding certain executive branch programs have resulted in significant changes over the last several decades, even when these programs were known and understood by at least some members of Congress.[24] While it might be that the members who knew about the programs were supportive of them and simply were not a good proxy for the public's reaction to their existence, in at least some cases it is clear that members either did not think they had been given sufficient information to judge the activities, or they understood them but disagreed with them and were not sufficiently empowered to change the executive branch's trajectory. What is apparent is that the initial checks intended to hold the executive branch accountable when its activities are not disclosed publicly rarely wield sufficient power to shape the executive branch's activities, and consequently it is likely even more important than it was in 1971, when the Pentagon Papers case was decided, to maintain a mechanism for promoting greater transparency of the executive branch's activities in national security.[25]

Technological Developments

A second cluster of trends that are relevant to the Pentagon Papers framework relates to developments in technology. Technology has revolutionized the way information is created, stored, communicated, and accessed, thereby making it far easier to leak massive amounts of classified information and to disseminate such information without the need for traditional media outlets.

In the context of the Pentagon Papers, Daniel Ellsberg, even with help from his kids, spent days copying the Pentagon Papers and then had to carry the roughly seven-thousand-page report to the media by hand—something that would take less than a minute to accomplish today.[26] Digitization makes accessing, copying, and disseminating information exponentially easier, as was demonstrated by the leaks effected by both Chelsea Manning and Edward Snowden, each of which involved hundreds of thousands of unauthorized disclosures. In fact, the role of information and communication technology in both classified leaks and espionage is growing,[27] and the damage to our national security is not trivial.[28] Furthermore, when information is disclosed at such volume, the resulting disclosures do not tend to be tailored to reveal only what would contribute meaningfully to an informed public debate but instead result in significant collateral harm by disclosing additional classified information of little or no benefit to such debate, along with information that might reasonably be judged to be important to disclose for First Amendment purposes. For example, while Snowden's leaks clearly prompted a useful debate regarding government surveillance programs, his leaks also exposed how the United States tracked members of al-Qaeda via emails, social media, and cell phones, giving them the ability to change their practices and thereby avoid US surveillance. Such tactical information could have been protected without reducing the overall value of the disclosures regarding the fact that we are involved in such surveillance and the scope of such surveillance. Similarly, as a consequence of Manning's leak of State Department cables, civil society activists in certain countries who were talking to US officials on a confidential basis were put at risk. Such information was unnecessary to promote public debate and harmful to our ability to obtain such information.[29] To some extent, this is not a new problem. I suspect the same criticism was made of the information disclosed in the Pentagon Papers, but because technology has increased the ease and scale with which such information can be accessed and disseminated through online publication without a media intermediary making a judgment about what is most newsworthy, the challenge is clearly exacerbated today.

Additionally, the easy dissemination of information online reduces the opportunity to exercise prior restraints on publication, even for the kind of information that a majority of Justices in the Pentagon Papers case indicated could be subject to prior constraints—information that would result in direct, immediate, and irreparable damage to the United States if disclosed. Consequently, the second safety valve in the Pentagon Papers framework has been rendered effectively irrelevant as a consequence of how our information technology has evolved.

In sum, developments in technology have not only significantly exacerbated the problem of leaks, making them easier to occur at scale, but have also effectively eliminated the remaining checks in the system that were envisioned in the Pentagon Papers for the purpose of protecting national security. In other words, given that it is no longer necessary to rely on traditional media outlets to broadly disseminate such information, we cannot rely on the press to be a separate actor in the framework capable of making a considered judgment about what is newsworthy, and furthermore, the second safety valve built into the framework that is intended to help protect against the disclosure of especially damaging information is no longer a realistic constraint.

Overclassification of Information

Finally, it is worth taking a moment to consider the challenges associated with overclassification and how that interacts with the existing Pentagon Papers framework. As many have noted, the amount of information that is classified, whether properly or not, has generally increased significantly over the last fifty years, and many, myself included, believe that the current system results in overclassification that undermines critical democratic objectives such as increasing transparency to promote an informed citizenry, negatively impacts national security and other objectives because it actually encourages leaking,[30] and increases the challenges associated with sharing information that should not be classified, or at least not classified at the level at which it is classified, and undermines the basic trust that the public has in government.[31] This is not a new challenge for government, but it is one that has been exacerbated by the expansion of classified materials across a range of agencies at a time when national security issues have been particularly prominent. The fact that the government overclassifies information is yet another reason to promote a mechanism for the media or some other entity outside of the executive branch to have access to information that is likely to be important to the public discourse while still finding a way to protect our most important secrets. Of course, coming up with a mechanism that is plausibly capable of accomplishing this is not easy, and it seems obvious that even if such a mechanism were designed, we would still want to find ways to reduce the degree of overclassification that occurs throughout the US government.

Numerous investigations and reviews have been done in an attempt to identify ways to address the challenge of overclassification.[32] During his time in office, President Obama issued presidential memoranda on this subject, established a board on declassification, and attempted to change the standards and the culture surrounding declassification in a revised executive order on classification. Despite these efforts and others throughout the US government, only modest improvements were achieved in reforming the system. The fact remains that the challenges are incredibly hard to overcome. There are virtually no incentives in the bureaucracy to declassify or to refrain from classifying a document, yet there are plenty of incentives to classify. Even the logistics of minimizing classification are surprisingly challenging for national security professionals. Reducing the amount of classified material takes additional time, which is at a premium in most of these jobs. Just to give an example, of which there are many, it takes extra time when writing emails or memos to mark the classification of each paragraph, in order to ensure that any unclassified information is marked as such, and thus, most people simply classify the entire email or memo at a level of classification that is based on the existence of one or two details that require that level of classification. Furthermore, national security professionals are trained to mitigate risks to national security, which makes it likely that they will be naturally biased toward classifying information that they believe could cause any damage to US national security interests, even if it is not likely.[33] In fact, if national security professionals make the mistake of classifying a document at a lower level than it should be classified at, they risk losing their clearance. Additionally, the process for declassifying information before it would automatically be declassified is more complicated and generally requires a higher-level authorization than classifying a document, and numerous reports on classification have demonstrated that many employees remain uneducated about the requirements and standards to be applied when properly classifying documents, which can also lead to overclassification.[34] There are also those who argue that government employees will classify information to avoid revealing embarrassing information, which, of course, is not a legitimate basis for classification.[35] In my experience, this was not a significant issue, and in fact, the reasons I have listed above were a far greater problem than what some call the "pretext effect," but regardless, the problem of overclassification remains an issue that leaders must continue to combat, despite the fact that a perfect system is almost certainly unachievable.

The fact that overclassification is a systemic problem creates a number of challenges, not the least of which is that it highlights the problem associated with relying on the existing system within the executive branch to promote the disclosure of information important to public debate when doing so might create even a minor risk of national security harm.

Elements of a New Framework?

The objectives and interests identified and weighed in the context of the Pentagon Papers case remain, in my view, the right ones, though perhaps with an even greater emphasis on the imperative of disclosing as much information as possible to further public debate in light of the growth of executive power. The framework must be reformed, however, to better promote this balance and to minimize the risk of national security damage done by massive leaks.[36] In sum, we should be looking for mechanisms, supported by law, regulation, institutional structures, culture, and resources, that will promote the disclosure of classified information when the public's need to know outweighs the national security interest. Furthermore, although I have no perfect answers or comprehensive recommendations for establishing such mechanisms, I am convinced that (1) we cannot, in today's world, rely on prior restraints as an effective method for addressing leaks that will cause grave damage to our national security when that damage is not outweighed by the value of the information to the underlying purposes of the First Amendment; (2) we should not rely on a system that leaves it up to every individual who obtains access to classified information and is willing to risk sanctions that he or she may in any case avoid by going to jurisdictions in which he or she can escape accountability, to decide what can and should be disclosed and disseminated publicly; and (3) we should not rely solely on national security professionals to weigh the national security implications of disclosing classified information against the public's need to know.

With these objectives and principles in mind, it is worth considering some of the tools we might deploy to achieve the superior balance we are seeking in this realm. For example, it would make sense to continue to improve the classification system, so as to minimize overclassification; improve the security surrounding classified information that will result in direct, immediate, and irreparable harm to national security objectives; and pursue sanctions against those who "leak" and widely disseminate classified information without a legitimate basis for doing so, as long as there is a protected way for individuals to raise this issue outside of the executive branch. Additionally, it may make sense to establish a commission with rotating participation that includes members of the national security community and the press, to be selected in accordance with a process outlined by Congress in law. This commission could consider petitions from inside and outside of government, including the executive and legislative branches, to disclose certain classified information because its value to the public debate outweighs the national security damage likely to result from its disclosure and make recommendations to Congress and the executive branch regarding the disposition of such information.

Relatedly, a "whistleblower" pathway could be established across the federal government for petitioning this new commission with respect to classified information, providing petitioners with the ability to remain anonymous and protected from retaliation for submitting such petitions. Whistleblowing is typically defined as the "act of reporting waste, fraud, abuse, and corruption in a lawful manner to those who can correct the wrongdoing," but in this case, such petitions should not have to assert wrongdoing, as the information to be disclosed may be properly classified.[37] Congress might additionally provide certain privileges and immunities to media institutions and journalists that meet specific apolitical journalistic standards established in law and regulation to access executive branch information in a timely fashion through mechanisms such as the Freedom of Information Act (FOIA).[38] Positions might be established in the Office of the Director of National Intelligence as well as at the Department of Justice that work with the new commission and are focused on ensuring that a process exists for reviewing and declassifying information across the federal government that the commission recommends be disclosed.

In sum, while the Pentagon Papers framework was a creative way to promote a better balance between the public's right to know and important national security interests in 1971, and has served our democracy well over the intervening years, we need to make adjustments to promote a better balance through a more effective framework that is capable of promoting as a matter of course the disclosure of information that is properly classified but that nevertheless should be declassified because its importance to the underlying purpose of the free speech guarantee outweighs the national security interest in maintaining secrecy. The current system simply does not reliably provide a safe outlet for doing this, and it should, for without it, we cannot hope to achieve the balance of interests sought in the Pentagon Papers case.

Crafting a New Compact in the Public Interest

Protecting the National Security in an Era of Leaks

KEITH B. ALEXANDER AND JAMIL N. JAFFER

Introduction

When it comes to unauthorized media disclosures of highly classified government information, two seminal moments occurred in the last couple of gen-
erations. In June 1971, the *New York Times* published the first tranche of the
Pentagon Papers, the results of a classified historical study of the Vietnam War
leaked to the *Times* by RAND researcher Daniel Ellsberg.[1] Almost forty-two
years later, a British newspaper, the *Guardian*, published the first tranche of US
government material stolen by Edward Snowden, a former NSA and CIA IT
contractor, who revealed an ongoing and, at the time, highly classified government counter-terrorism program to collect massive amounts of telecommunica-
tions metadata inside the United States.[2]

The events that followed these two seminal publications, in many ways, significantly muddled our collective thinking on dealing with the modern problem
of unauthorized disclosures of classified information. This essay suggests that
the general approach to such disclosures in the aftermath of the Pentagon Papers
case—with the government prosecuting those who leak such information while
largely holding the media unaccountable and the media generally engaging in
a broad defense of its ability to (aggressively) seek, obtain, and publish an extremely wide range of classified information—may no longer make sense in the
context of the modern media environment. However, rather than argue that the
government should engage in a new, sustained effort to pursue media companies
for publication of classified information or that the media should halt its efforts

to obtain and publish classified information, the essay argues that a more modest approach—essentially, the creation of a new national security and public interest bargain between the government, the public, and the (responsible) media—is key to addressing this problem going forward.

Specifically, this essay argues that there should be a significant measure of internal recalibration within the government and the media to develop a new compact to serve the public interest that (1) accounts for modern changes in the way information is communicated and utilized, (2) reassesses the values behind the government's classification and declassification of information, (3) re-evaluates the media's role in the solicitation and disclosure of classified information, (4) engages both sides in a more serious effort to measure the relative benefits of a given disclosure to the public interest versus the impact of the disclosure on the government's ability to protect the national security, and (5) seeks to ensure that government descriptions of national security programs *and* media reporting on such programs fairly and accurately characterize such programs. The essay also argues that this internal recalibration should be accompanied by (and perhaps prompted by) specific, targeted changes in the law and practice to provide (1) additional transparency from the government, (2) more rapid and robust consideration of classification and declassification decisions, (3) broader and more robust oversight of classified programs by Congress, (4) options for incentivizing responsible behavior by publishers, accompanied by measures that would hold irresponsible publishers—particularly those who directly aid and abet violations of the law—directly liable, and (5) access to a more diverse set of remedies, including civil fines, that might be employed to disincentivize illegal disclosures and the inappropriate publication of classified information. In our view, such a new compact between the government and the media, as well as the public they both serve, would be best able to protect the legitimate interest in the public having as much information as possible about government programs while preserving the ability of the government to defend our nation and preserve the very rights and liberties at the heart of our system of government.

The Pentagon Papers, the Legal Aftermath, and the Snowden Disclosures

As briefly noted above, the modern story of classified leaks has been shaped by the events that took place in the days and weeks after Ellsberg handed over the Pentagon Papers to the *New York Times*. Within days of the *New York Times'* initial publication of parts of the report (and with the *Washington Post* joining the fray), the federal government went to court in New York and DC, intent on stopping the further publication of the papers (and seeking their immediate return).[3] The court proceedings moved quickly, and by the end of June 1971, the Supreme Court issued a short, unsigned opinion holding that the government had not met its burden to restrain further publication of the papers.[4] While the Court's short opinion was accompanied by nine separate signed opinions—one for each Justice, with six in the majority and three in dissent (and various Justices joining others) —there rapidly hardened in place a general understanding of the Supreme Court's core decision. Namely, there would be very rare circumstances, if any, in which the government could prevent the publication of classified information, particularly if there was no evidence that the newspapers had solicited or materially participated in the effort to purloin classified materials or if the government could not demonstrate that the release of materials would have an immediate impact on its ability to protect the nation.[5] At the same time, there was also a general understanding that, while the media wouldn't be restrained from publication of such material, the government could put some limits on disclosures by former government employees[6] and could punish the leakers themselves.[7]

Moreover, while at least one Supreme Court case suggests that the government might theoretically be able to bring criminal charges against the media engaging in illegal activities related to a publication,[8] a number of more recent cases also hold that the media may not be criminally punished *solely* for publishing information that is illegally obtained through a third party's independent conduct.[9] While there remains some debate whether certain prosecutions of leakers may raise First Amendment concerns,[10] this understanding of the Pentagon Papers decision has largely held until the modern day. Given this background, since the 1970s, the executive branch has only rarely sought to enjoin publication of classified material and has succeeded only once (and then only temporarily).[11] Given these constraints, the government has generally only sought to prosecute those who leak classified information—with such prosecutions rising significantly during the last two administrations—while largely avoiding any effort to hold the media accountable for its role in such disclosures (save for trying to identify the sources of classified information provided to reporters in certain cases).[12]

On a parallel path, the media has aggressively sought to protect its own right to publish a broad range of information, whether classified or not and no matter how obtained. Reporters regularly (and often aggressively) seek to encourage sources to disclose properly classified information in order to inform the public about the government's activities. These efforts—while obviously beginning long before the Pentagon Papers case—have accelerated significantly in scope and scale since the 1970s. In particular, the digitization of data and miniaturization of computing devices in recent years have supercharged this trend, making it significantly easier to access, obtain, and convey large amounts of classified information. This change in the availability of data has also taken place in the context of a dramatic expansion in the number of methods for sharing information among a wide range of individuals on a massive scale. The nature of the popular media itself has also changed with the growth of organizations like the Intercept, whose very purpose is to publicly disclose information about how governments conduct their most secret activities.

This expansion likewise takes place in the context of a growing sense among many reporters and media executives alike—even in "mainstream" institutions (and perhaps even with some portion of the public writ large)—that the government is not always an honest actor and that key components of the government—and particularly intelligence agencies—may be acting in service of agendas not necessarily in the national interest. At the same time, there has been a similar trend taking hold on both sides of the political spectrum. Specifically, bipartisan concerns among elected leaders about the government using its law enforcement and intelligence capabilities to unfairly target unpopular populations or perspectives have become a staple of public debate and discussion. This new (and often vitriolic) debate is part and parcel of a broader decay in the historic, bipartisan national security consensus that has been a feature of American politics since at least the early 1980s.

It is this evolving environment into which the Snowden disclosures dropped in June 2013. Those disclosures, as noted above, initially focused on a major classified government program whose sheer scale and scope gave rise to significant privacy and civil liberties concerns. The revelation of the government's metadata program led to a substantive public debate about the value and nature of the program, with the executive branch mounting only a limited defense, failing to make compelling public arguments for the value of the program in its then-current state. Nonetheless, in 2015, more than a year and a half after the initial disclosure, the executive branch was able to convince members of Congress that the program presented sufficient counterterrorism value to be permitted to continue, albeit in a significantly modified form, under the USA Freedom Act. This aspect of the Snowden disclosures has led to significant praise for Snowden in major parts of the academic, civil liberties, and privacy communities, notwithstanding the admittedly illegal nature of his actions.

What has been significantly undercounted in the aftermath of Snowden's initial disclosures, however, are the nature, scope, and breadth of his actual theft of highly classified US government information and the more voluminous disclosures that followed. In particular, since late 2013 the relative impact of Snowden's disclosures on US national security has been nearly completely ignored, particularly as weighed against the potential privacy and civil liberties benefits of those revelations. Following the initial Snowden disclosure of the government metadata program was more than two years of near-constant disclosures (and more since then) about the alleged details of how the United States (and other allied governments) conduct specific surveillance operations, the vast majority of which had little to no impact whatsoever on the privacy and civil liberties of Americans. Many of these disclosures related to specific technical capabilities, access to certain systems or providers, relationships between the governments and private entities, and ongoing military operations.

To be sure, many of these disclosures, if accurate, demonstrated the ability of the US government (and others) to access overseas communications, including those that might incidentally contain communications of Americans. However, in surveying the vast amount of disclosures that took place in the months and years following the initial Snowden disclosures, it becomes clear that none of these other programs could credibly be seen as having anywhere near as significant an impact on the privacy and civil liberties of Americans. Even where there was an ostensible impact, as in the case of the metadata program, independent government reviews later found that these programs were neither pervasive nor indiscriminate, as breathless media reports initially indicated, nor were there any systemic, intentional privacy or civil liberties abuses by the government, as claimed by a range of advocacy groups.[13]

When viewed in this context, one might argue that these massive leaks of highly classified information—if accurate—almost certainly resulted in tremendous damage to the US government, while yielding precious little in substantive public value with respect to core privacy and civil liberties interests. In many ways, one might argue that the vast majority of the Snowden disclosures did little more than satisfy the prurient interests of intelligence voyeurs, while simultaneously aiding our enemies and doing significant damage to government national security programs.

Both American and allied officials have described the catastrophic impact of these disclosures on our national security. For example, in 2014, James Clapper, the former director of national intelligence, referred to Snowden's actions as "potentially the most massive and damaging theft of intelligence information in our history."[14] In his public testimony before the House Intelligence Committee, Clapper said that Snowden's disclosures "went way, way beyond [Snowden's] professed concerns with so-called domestic surveillance programs" and caused "profound damage," making the United States "less safe and its people less secure."[15] Specifically, Clapper argued that the United States had "lost critical foreign intelligence collection[] sources, including some shared with us by valued partners," that "the lives of members or assets of the intelligence community . . . as well as our armed forces, diplomats, and our citizens" were put "at risk" by Snowden's disclosures.[16] He likewise argued that Snowden's disclosures allowed "[t]errorists and other adversaries of this country [to] go[] to school on US intelligence sources, methods and tradecraft," leading to "changes in the communications behavior of adversaries, particularly terrorists."[17]

Other officials such as Matt Olsen, the former director of the National Counter-terrorism Center, have been a bit more granular, with Olsen indicating that the Snowden revelations specifically led to the loss of "collection against some individuals, people that we were concerned about," and that terrorists had "changed how they encrypt their communications[, had] adopted more stringent encryption techniques[,]" and "[had] changed service providers and email addresses and . . . in some cases, just dropped off all together."[18] This view was reiterated more recently in 2018 by the National Counterintelligence and Security Center, which publicly stated that Snowden's disclosures "put U.S. personnel or facilities at risk around the world, damaged intelligence collection efforts, exposed tools used to amass intelligence, destabilized U.S. partnerships abroad and exposed U.S. intelligence operations, capabilities and priorities."[19] And Sir David Omand, the former head of the United Kingdom's Government Communications Headquarters (GCHQ), likewise referred to the Snowden theft of classified information as "the most catastrophic loss to British intelligence ever."[20]

Moreover, these concerns don't even address the corrosive effect that the disclosures had on the relationship between the US government and American companies, particularly in the technology sector, or the potential economic losses caused by the disclosures, which some estimate could go as high as $180 billion.[21]

The challenge, of course, in evaluating these claims of harm, particularly those relating to national security, is that the US government has presented little, if any, factual evidence to support these statements. This failure is not especially surprising, given the government's strong interest in protecting its sources and methods, particularly in the aftermath of a massive disclosure. The most detailed, unclassified public analysis available is nonetheless still deeply troubling. The House Intelligence Committee's 2016 report, which examined a number of the underlying government damage assessments conducted to date, including a comprehensive review by the Defense Department and a more targeted review by the IC, revealed that Snowden had stolen more than 1.5 million documents, which if printed out and stacked up would reach three miles high.[22] More important, however, according to the Committee—and consistent with the public disclosures we've seen thus far—the "vast majority of the documents Snowden removed were unrelated to electronic surveillance or any issue associated with privacy and civil liberties."[23] In fact, the Committee found that the information taken by Snowden, if made available to nations like China and Russia, could put US troops at greater risk in a future conflict.[24] Overall, the Committee's review determined that the documents released publicly by August 2016—which themselves made up only one-tenth of one percent of the total documents stolen by Snowden—had "caused massive damage to national security."[25] Indeed, the Committee cited thirteen high-risk categories of data taken by Snowden and specifically provided—albeit in completely redacted form—nearly four pages of specific examples of damage caused by the Snowden disclosures.[26]

A Method for Evaluating Public Disclosures of Classified Information

In our view, the aftermath of the Snowden disclosures reveals that while there are critically important values to be served by a free and open press, these values— and, alongside them, the ability to maintain a strong free and open press—can be undermined by leaks that damage national security with no countervailing benefit, as well as by broad, unequivocal defenses of leaking in general. A critical part of the analysis of leaks and the law and policy surrounding them in a healthy, democratic society is the need to fully account for the relative costs and benefits to society of unauthorized disclosures. Our sense is that, at least historically, the vast majority of major media outlets actually engaged in this type of robust analysis before publication. There are numerous historical examples of the media voluntarily holding off—sometimes temporarily—on publication of details of highly classified programs at the government's request and sometimes even of its own accord. And while some might quibble with particular publication decisions by the media in the past, there is a general sense that, at least until recently, the post–Pentagon Papers détente worked well for the American people, both from the national security perspective and from a public disclosure perspective. Unfortunately, key aspects of the modern media environment— including technological evolution and economic realities, as well as changes in social norms and politics—have begun to eat away at the ability of responsible media outlets to make reasonable, independent publication decisions.

In order to help return us to that relative détente, it may be useful to categorize potential media disclosures based in part on their potential benefit to the public discourse. In our view, the vast majority of unauthorized revelations of highly classified information by the media can be said to fall into five broad categories: (1) allegations regarding potentially serious waste, fraud, and intentional abuse by the government, including claims of intentional violations of the law that have a direct and material impact on the privacy or civil liberties of Americans; (2) descriptions of government activities that, because of unintentional actions by the government or others (e.g., human mistakes, technical errors, or otherwise), involve some impact on the privacy or civil liberties of Americans; (3) allegations of government activities that, while lawful, may nonetheless have a privacy or civil liberties impact that ought to be (re)considered by policymakers; (4) details of American foreign relations or operational activities that have little impact on the privacy or civil liberties of Americans but may have an impact on policymaking decisions related to our national security, foreign policy, warfighting, or our conduct of overseas intelligence activities; (5) details of American foreign relations, intelligence, or military operational activities that have no impact on the privacy and civil liberties of Americans and no significant impact on policymaking decisions but nonetheless reveal information about our national security, foreign policy, warfighting, or the conduct of intelligence activities that could be highly useful to our enemies.

One key concern in the new media environment we find ourselves in as a nation—highlighted perhaps most clearly by the Snowden disclosures—is that while there may be some salutary benefits to certain media-led disclosures of classified information in all of the first four categories listed above, the relative benefits, at least outside of category one, can vary widely. This concern is particularly heightened when the benefits of disclosures in categories 2 through 4 are measured against the potential national security impact of the given disclosure. The initial Snowden disclosure about the US government's metadata program is a good example. Under the rubric set out above, the metadata program revealed by Snowden falls not into category 1, as one might assume based on the initial press reports, but rather in a combination of categories 2 and 3. Namely, the metadata program, while fully authorized by law in the aftermath of the 9/11 attacks and carefully overseen by federal judges, the executive branch, and Congress, nonetheless had both structural components and unintentional challenges that created privacy and civil liberties impacts. It was these impacts, or at least the perception of these impacts in popular culture, that led Congress to make specific modifications to the program after its details came to light. One might argue, of course, whether such disclosures needed to be made in the public arena directly or whether the same issues might usefully have been addressed and resolved in a different manner, such as the IC whistleblower process. In such cases, a robust discussion between the government and media outlets might be quite valuable. In these scenarios, in particular, the lack of a solid détente today is particularly concerning.

The other key concern raised by the new media environment is that while media-led disclosures can make hugely important contributions to the public debate, particularly where the underlying claims fit into category 1, the reality is that very few modern examples actually meet that test. That is, where intentional violations of the law that have a direct and material impact on the privacy and civil liberties of Americans are alleged to have taken place, there may be a reasonably strong debate about the need for disclosure outside the normal whistleblower processes. Rather than falling into this category, however, a significant number of modern disclosures, including the majority of the now-public Snowden disclosures (and likely all of the as-yet-undisclosed Snowden materials), fall squarely into the fifth category, well outside any reasonable justi-fication for media-led publication.

In fact, our review of the media landscape of major recent classified disclosures indicates that the strong trend of such disclosures in recent years is in the direc-tion of the latter categories, principally the fourth and fifth categories, with very few media disclosures of classified information going to the first category. Of all the recent public disclosures we are aware of relating to highly classified infor-mation, the principal ones that identify intentional violations of the law gen-erally revolve around individual bad actors (e.g., the individual Federal Bureau of Investigation [FBI] lawyer's actions on the Carter Page Foreign Intelligence Surveillance Act [FISA] application or the rare instance of NSA or FBI employees using government databases to collect "LOVEINT"). Even when it comes to some of the most prominent disclosures in recent years that fall into the other three categories, it is worth noting that these disclosures did not dem-onstrate massive illegality conducted by the government but rather simply raised concerns that otherwise authorized programs might go too far or implicate pri-vacy concerns that some believe ought to be re-evaluated by policymakers.

In our view, an examination of the massive disclosure of classified infor-mation over the last half dozen years reveals (1) a good deal of unintentional errors, all of which were self-reported or identified by the government; (2) the occasional individual bad actor; and (3) a handful of potentially serious policy disagreements about the scope of government activities. It is important, how-ever, that such an examination does not reveal any evidence whatsoever of mas-sive, intentional illegality in government programs. Yet the story conveyed to the public—or at least the manner in which it is conveyed—often suggests a very different scenario. More often than not, when classified information about national security programs is revealed in the media, the underlying claim is that the programs involve actual violations of the law, including the legally protected privacy and civil liberties of Americans. But when one gets down to brass tacks, the reality is often quite different.

Even more concerning, in our view, are stories purporting to raise serious violations of privacy rights but which don't effectively articulate the often ex-tensive efforts the government undertakes to protect the privacy of Americans. Indeed, in our experience, there is distinctly little media coverage describing the government's efforts to safeguard the data it collects under lawful authority, even where the government undertakes protective efforts that have the result of lim-iting, segregating, or halting otherwise potentially valuable collection. Instead, media coverage of government national security efforts where privacy concerns of Americans are implicated often suggests a government run amok, engaging in massive violations of privacy and civil liberties, rather than a committed work-force of dedicated public servants undertaking a legally authorized and carefully calibrated balance of intelligence efforts designed to protect the security and safety of American citizens.[27]

Take, for example, the Terrorist Surveillance Program (TSP), first revealed by the *New York Times* in 2005 and declassified by the president shortly there-after, as well as its follow-on program, the § 702 surveillance program conducted under the FISA Amendments Act of 2008. This program, which was initiated in the aftermath of the 9/11 attacks, was designed, along with the metadata program, to serve as an early warning system to identify potential overseas ter-rorist threats against the homeland. Indeed, the TSP itself—unlike the meta-data program—was focused on collecting only international communications, where one participant was a known or suspected terrorist or related party. From the date of the first disclosure of these programs up to the present day, however, much of the media coverage around these programs describes it as "warrantless" surveillance, notwithstanding the fact that the program is focused on targeting foreigners located overseas (i.e., in circumstances where a warrant is simply not applicable or even appropriate). While it is true that the communications of non-targeted Americans might be incidentally acquired, this is no less true than where any innocent party is incidentally acquired on a court-authorized foreign intelligence intercept. In that case, just as with the 702 Program, court-authorized minimization procedures are applied to protect the privacy and civil liberties interests of the non-targeted American.

Thus, the use of the term *warrantless* in this context is not only inaccurate, but it also undermines and nearly completely discounts the very real efforts undertaken by the government to protect the privacy and civil liberties of Americans. As in the famous paraphrase of Justice Robert Jackson,[28] the Constitution is not a suicide pact, and where the government takes legitimate action to protect national security, if that action has some impact on the pri-vacy and civil liberties of Americans, it is critical that the right balance be struck. For the public and the government to be able to focus on getting the balance right, the media coverage of such issues must be accurate and even-handed. If the media is to truly fulfill its own self-conception as a resource that creates an informed electorate able to make good choices for its own future, being accurate and even-handed in the context of such important and hard-fought debates is crucial.

This, then, is yet another context where if classified information is to be disclosed, there is significant reason for the government and the media to work together to more accurately and effectively inform the public. In particular, this example demonstrates an opportunity for both sides to work together to buttress traditional journalistic norms, presenting reasonable perspectives on both sides of the debate on classified activities, and undergirding the core First Amendment values inherent in unbiased reporting.

There are similar values to be supported on the government side as well. For example, the government is more likely to be able to engage in robust, legal programs to protect the national security if it appropriately classifies material consistent with legal requirements and traditional norms. The government's ability to maintain robust national security authorities can be (and will continue to be) significantly undermined if the government broadly engages in overclassification, illegitimate classification of information in order to protect against embarrassing or unhelpful disclosures, or continued classification of information that no longer meets the relevant requirements. Likewise, the government must be prepared to forthrightly defend its own programs on the basis of their value and capability, including publicly wherever possible. If the government is unable to demonstrate to the satisfaction of the public (or at least to its elected representatives in Congress) that it has conducted itself appropriately, it will not be surprising if the government is unable to maintain such programs.

Striking a New Balance: Internal Recalibration and Potential Changes to Law and Practice

Taking a Principled Approach

It goes without saying that the government has an inherent responsibility to protect the nation. Likewise, in our political system, the media plays a central role in informing the public and policymakers on issues of public concern. And yet in recent years, both have come to be viewed as not accurately characterizing the facts and circumstances on particular issues, including those in the national security arena. This creates a very muddled situation, where it is hard to sort out how these key bastions of our democratic system—the government and the media—can be encouraged to work better together. This problem, of course, is an age-old one, but it is increasingly complicated by the expanding scope of information available to the public, the diverse nature of the modern information and media environment, and the collapse, in recent years, of the nearly four-decade-long bipartisan consensus on national security matters. As a result, getting out of this muddle, in our view, will require both a clear-eyed analysis of the very real challenges that face our national security community and a serious accounting of the need to protect and defend the privacy and civil liberties of our citizens.

The key to solving this problem is to create a system that takes a principled approach to these issues and that effectively balances these critically important interests. Moreover, we cannot simply exchange platitudes about balancing these interests. Rather, we must, as a society, accept that there are times at which we will choose to balance our privacy and civil liberties in a way that prioritizes national security and that there are also times at which we must reveal information that otherwise ought to be classified in order to have a robust discussion about the relevant equities.

We also believe that the solution to this cannot originate from legislation or executive action standing alone but must emerge, at its core, from the building of a new national security and public interest ethical bargain between the government and the (responsible) media. This new bargain must include the creation of new mores about the classification and declassification of government information, the transparency that should attach to government intelligence activities, and the re-establishment of a responsible approach to the disclosure of otherwise properly classified government information by the media.

What is needed today, in our view, is a fundamentally new compact between the government and the media. For its part, the government needs to be significantly more transparent about the efforts it undertakes on behalf of the nation and must be significantly more self-critical in evaluating what data must be classified, at what level, for how long, and when it might be revealed publicly. At the same time, major press institutions must be willing to give the government fair treatment—not simply accepting the most tawdry explanation for government activities but instead calling them what they are and recognizing the differences between, on the one hand, active, intentional violations of the privacy and civil liberties of Americans and, on the other, efforts where the government is seeking to carefully balance the public interest in security with the need to preserve the rights and liberties that we cherish as Americans.

It is likewise incumbent upon the government—not just the executive branch but also the legislature—to undertake serious efforts to explain, up front, the national security activities that it is undertaking, as well as to defend classified programs when they come to light, regardless of how that happens. More often than not, the government is terrible at playing effective defense and explaining itself when it comes to classified programs. It simply is not good at defending the legitimacy of such programs or convincingly laying out the justification behind them, even where there is a strong basis for both. This may be in part because of discomfort with the programs themselves, but it is typically because the government so jealously guards the classification of information once attached that it is unwilling to declassify the information necessary to defend itself effectively. And occasionally, the government can be bad at disclosing programs publicly because political leaders are unwilling to take responsibility for their decisions or those of their predecessors.

In defending and justifying its intelligence collection and national security programs, the government must therefore be willing to go into some significant amount of detail, all while still carefully protecting sources and methods. Specifically, the government needs to be able to talk about what its programs do and don't do, particularly when it comes to their impact on Americans, what steps it takes to protect Americans and their information, and what oversight is conducted—both within and outside of the executive branch—to ensure that the rights and liberties of Americans are strongly preserved. Likewise, when errors or mistakes happen, the government must be willing to come clean about them and to talk about what it is doing to correct those errors. It must be willing to do so, where appropriate, in public, rather than, as historically has been done, in private, behind closed doors, in a classified setting.

Members of Congress must likewise take responsibility for the information they are given, for reviewing it, and for making decisions based on it. To be sure, internal processes within Congress about what information is shared, with whom, and when ought to be revised, including broadening the scope of members both on and off the intelligence committees who are made aware of major intelligence programs. However, it is also critically important that we dispel the notion that members of Congress are free to feign ignorance about—or, worse, to criticize or misrepresent—government programs that they are informed about (or given the opportunity to learn about). Such behavior from elected officials is totally unacceptable. The American people—and the media working on their behalf— must be willing to call out members of Congress who, ostensibly in the name of defending privacy and civil liberties, refuse to take responsibility for information they were given or who misrepresent the facts in an effort to score political points or vindicate a particular policy perspective. Regardless of whether their goals may be laudable, such behavior is not something the American people ought to accept if we are truly trying to build a more robust and honest debate in this arena. To that end, holding elected leadership accountable on national security issues—in both the executive branch and Congress—is one way the media can help the American people gain more knowledge and insight on these issues and therefore make better, more educated decisions about the trade-offs inherent in such important policy choices.

Another key to addressing the challenges we face in this area is re-establishing a bipartisan approach to these matters. As mentioned briefly above, the long-standing bipartisan collaboration on national security—modeled by congressional leaders such as former House Intelligence Committee chairman Mike Rogers (R-MI) and ranking member Dutch Ruppersberger (D-MD), as well as current Senate Intelligence Committee chairman Richard Burr (R-NC) and vice chairman Mark Warner (D-VA), Senate Armed Services chairman Jim Inhofe (R-OK) and ranking member Jack Reed (D-RI), House Armed Services chairman Adam Smith (D-WA) and ranking member Mac Thornberry (R-TX), and other members such as congresspersons Will Hurd (R-TX), and Elissa Slotkin (D-MI) and former senators John McCain (R-AZ), Daniel Inouye (D-HI), Bob Corker (R-TN), Sam Nunn (D-GA), Ted Stevens (R-AK), and Mark Kirk (R-IL)—has largely decayed. Instead, we see more partisan infighting on a range of issues—including matters that go to the heart of our ability to address the very real (and current) threats to our national security.

The most obvious example in the current era of such unhelpful infighting is the threat that Russia and other nations pose to the functioning of our government through their ongoing—and highly successful—campaign to undermine the faith of Americans in our key governmental institutions. These nations have actively, and successfully, sought to corrode the trust and confidence of the American populace in key rule of law and national security organizations, including key parts of the Intelligence Community (IC), the Justice Department, and the FBI, as well as in our elected officials writ large. Both the office of the President and Congress have seen the confidence of the American people drop off drastically in recent years, and while some of that may be attributable to domestic politics, much of it is the result of discord actively stoked by foreign actors. These efforts have been assisted, unfortunately, by the behavior of partisan political leaders on both ends of Pennsylvania Avenue. The partisanship we've seen in recent years hasn't been limited to Russia or foreign influence matters but has extended to other core issues of national security such as those surrounding North Korea, Iran, and government counter-terrorism efforts. In these areas also, such partisanship and public carping are hugely unhelpful.

Rather than focus on the very real threats posed by external actors, we have turned inward and have attacked one another, effectively carrying out the very wishes of those that oppose us. Resolving this issue is highly relevant to our proposed effort to rebuild the relationship between the media and the government. This is so because, if the government itself cannot internally find common cause on national security matters, particularly those related to active efforts by our enemies to undermine confidence in our system of government, it is hard to imagine how the government, writ large, can establish a robust new compact with the media, much less the public, to addresses these tough issues.

Specific Recommendations to Help Establish a New Compact

To achieve these goals and return us closer to the détente that generally governed media and national security relationships in the past, we propose a series of five concrete efforts that should be undertaken to establish a new national security and public interest bargain between the government, the public, and the (responsible) media.

Recognizing that not all media outlets will be willing to come to the table (including, in some cases, independent publishers, individuals, and agenda-driven organizations), these recommendations focus on major media outlets that subscribe to core journalistic ethical values. In our view, while focusing on these institutions may not completely prevent the inappropriate disclosure of classified information in all cases, agreeing to a set of basic values and approaches and voluntarily limiting the further dissemination of highly classified information by organizations that are trusted by a significant majority of the public (and that have massive scale) can nonetheless serve to best protect properly classified information in the current environment.

1. *Increasing Government Transparency on Classified Programs.* The government's decision, post-Snowden, to broadly undertake a review of certain existing surveillance programs and declassify appropriate details as well as relevant legal analysis, internal policies, legal filings, and judicial decisions has publicly provided a wide range of information about government intelligence efforts while having a fairly limited impact on the sources and methods of intelligence collection. This effort should therefore be standardized and significantly expanded in order to identify other programs and efforts where similar declassification takes place, providing more information to the public while still preserving our ability to collect intelligence and protect the nation. The more the government is able to tell the public about what it is doing, why, and (to an appropriate extent) how it is doing so, the more likely it is that it will be able to effectively conduct other highly classified programs and to sustain both in the long run.

2. *Modifying the Rules and Procedures around Classification and Declassification of Government Information.* It is estimated that a huge portion of classified information—between 50 and 90 percent—is mislabeled and that much information could be declassified with fairly limited, if any, harm to national security.[29] Given the corrosive effect that overclassification has on internal government information sharing as well as on public confidence in the overall system, the executive branch and Congress ought to work closely on efforts to fundamentally restructure government classification procedures. Specifically, these reforms should significantly limit the scope and nature of classification at the highest levels and modify the relevant incentives in order to (1) disincentivize overclassification, (2) create and strengthen internal and external penalties for inappropriate classification (i.e., classification imposed for improper purposes, such as avoiding embarrassment or the hiding of inappropriate or illegal activity), (3) significantly shorten general declassification

timelines to the minimal amount of time necessary to strictly protect sources and methods (particularly in light of the rapidly evolving technological environment), and (4) eliminate most mandatory declassification exceptions and limit the use of existing declassification exceptions to the minimum amount possible.

3. *Limiting the Disclosure of Certain Classified Information That Has No Public Policy Value.* The government and major media organizations should work together to identify and evaluate whether properly classified information provided in an unauthorized manner to the media falls into the last category we set out above—namely, where there is little to no public policy value to the disclosure of the information but the information would nonetheless be valuable to our enemies. In such cases, the media should voluntarily take steps to limit the disclosure and dissemination of such information. One method for conducting this dialogue could be through a voluntary joint body, such as the British DSMA Committee, that evaluates such issues and issues non-legally-binding recommendations on what information the (responsible) media should avoid publishing.[30] While this organization would likely primarily be staffed with representatives of the executive branch and the media, key members of Congress ought to play a role also to ensure that the political branches are aligned on the right approach to classified information. Regardless of whether such a committee is set up, as a general matter, responsible media outlets should voluntarily decline to publish information that adds limited to no public policy value, as it generally does today in the case of sensitive subject matters, such as the names of covert operatives, whistleblowers, or victims of particularly heinous crimes. In addition, responsible media outlets should likewise decline to further disseminate such information even where it is made public by other nontraditional or less responsible outlets. Should such voluntary efforts fail, the government might consider whether specific prohibitions on the disclosure of specific categories of information—enforced perhaps not by criminal penalties but by civil fines—may be another effective remedy to such disclosures.

4. *Holding Irresponsible Publishers Accountable and Incentivizing Responsible Outlets.* The government should strongly enforce existing laws and work to establish new specific procedures and laws (where necessary) to address and prosecute illegal activity by both traditional and nontraditional media outlets. Specifically, where a media entity either has engaged in illegal activity itself to obtain properly classified information or has actively engaged in aiding and abetting the violation of law by individuals with authorized access to classified information, the fact that they are a media entity should not present a legal or policy barrier to taking action to address such illegality. To the contrary, our

existing applicable laws ought to be clarified to apply extraterritorially against media outlets and leakers who intentionally locate (or flee) abroad to avoid the consequences of such illegal behaviors. In addition, in order to provide more flexibility in enforcing these laws, the government should use both civil and criminal penalties to address such violations of the law. In order to engender more positive, forward-leaning decisions by the (responsible) media, the government should consider incentivizing participation in a US DSMA-type process (like that described in recommendation 3 above) by presumptively exempting those that participate in such a process from the application of such criminal or civil penalties.

5. *Improving and Broadening Legislative Oversight of Classified Programs.* One of the key challenges facing the government when it comes to defending highly classified programs is a lack of public access to information. While granting broad access to the general public while protecting sources and methods may be quite difficult, given that members of Congress (like federal judges) are generally given access to highly classified information by virtue of their office, the executive branch should work with Congress to broaden the scope of members who have access to such information on a regular basis. The executive branch also, with some exceptions (focused on specific sources and methods of collection), should broadly brief *all* members of Congress on key capabilities and programs—and specifically on the benefits and successes achieved through such programs, as well as any challenges they face or errors or mistakes made and corrective actions taken. While specific oversight would continue to be conducted by the intelligence committees, these committees' virtual monopoly on compartmented data— as well as that of the Armed Services and Appropriations Committees— should be limited to only the truly most sensitive of information (e.g., the names of particular assets and the like). In addition, members and staff with appropriate clearances should have regular and simplified access to executive branch classified computer systems containing such information, including Joint Worldwide Intelligence Communications System (JWICS), and should not be limited to relying only on the highly limited access currently provided to Congress.

We recognize that the specific efforts described above may be seen as only an initial step in the effort to build a fundamentally new national security and public interest compact between the government, the public, and the (responsible) media. Nonetheless, we believe that such an effort is critical and that we must begin now. Technology—and the access to data that it affords—is changing rapidly as we write, and as a nation, we need to be sure we appropriately protect properly classified information in this new, evolving construct. In our view, these efforts, which put significant responsibility on both sides to do their respective parts, can eventually lead to the creation of a baseline of trust and cooperation that will best serve the needs of the American public in the modern era and most effectively preserve the rights and liberties that we so rightly cherish as Americans.

‖ 3 ‖

Leaks of Classified Information

Lessons Learned from a Lifetime on the Inside

MICHAEL MORELL

Introduction

This might sound strange coming from a career intelligence officer (and alleged member of the "deep state"), but the US government has a history of abusing its power. From the 1798 Sedition Act and the widespread suspension of habeas corpus during the Civil War to the harassment of people suspected of being "disloyal" during the McCarthy era and the unlawful surveillance of domestic critics of the Vietnam War, the government has shown itself fully capable of violating the constitutional rights of the American people.

This history has helped to reinforce a natural distrust in government on the part of the citizenry that has been present in our political culture since our founding. Wanting to avoid the abuses of power inflicted on the colonies by the British government, the Founders wrote at length in the *Federalist Papers* about their concern that our new nation's leaders might be tempted, for any number of reasons, to abuse their power. They therefore built into our governing structure a system of checks and balances along with a Bill of Rights to mitigate that risk.

This natural distrust on the part of citizens is healthy, in that it has led to congressional and judicial structures to oversee executive branch activities, statutes to create channels and protections for whistleblowers, and even protections for journalists to publish classified information provided to them by government employees with security clearances, which we all call leaks. These protections are important with regard to limiting government abuse with regard to all government activities, but they are particularly important to limiting abuses by intelligence agencies because they are secret organizations operating in a democracy with little public transparency.

Having said all that, there are many interesting and important questions when it comes to leaks. What share of the total leaks of classified information reflects true whistleblowers motivated by a view that the public needs to be told of government wrongdoing? What are the damages to national security that occur as we protect the media's constitutional right to share classified information with the public? What are the media's responsibilities that should accompany these rights? And how can the government play a role in helping the media find the right balance? This essay attempts to answer these questions, all within the context of the government's requirement captured in the Preamble to the Constitution to provide for both our liberty and our security.

The Taxonomy of Leaks

During the seven years that I served on the senior leadership team at the CIA, I would start each day by spending an hour with my "PDB briefer."[1] This person would come to work in the middle of the night and put together a thick binder that contained that day's President's Daily Brief (a compilation of the most important intelligence analysis produced by the Intelligence Community [IC], largely from the CIA), other intelligence analysis produced by the CIA and other IC agencies, and raw intelligence reports—accounts from spies, intercepts of communications, and other things—from across the IC. The briefer would then walk me through each of the pieces in the book to make sure I understood the key points. It was the best part of my day—taking a deep dive into the newest information and freshest analysis on all the national security issues facing the United States.

At my request, the first document in the briefing book, sitting atop the intelligence information, was that day's "CIA Media Highlights," a compilation of all the media stories from the previous twenty-four hours that had some relevance to the CIA. These stories could range from reports on recent developments on key national security issues to exposés on the CIA's in-house Starbucks to allegations of CIA human rights abuses overseas. The Media Highlights was the first thing I read every day, even before the President's Daily Brief, because a media story with the CIA as the subject—whether the contents of the story was right or wrong—was the thing that could most easily hijack my day.

While reading the Media Highlights, I would see the publication of classified intelligence information, some fully accurate, some only partially so. This was not a rare occurrence; it took place with a frequency that I don't want to specify here but that I and other intelligence officers found frustrating. If the classified information belonged to the CIA—either intelligence reports disseminated by the CIA or analysis produced by the CIA—we would create a "crimes report" and deliver it to the Department of Justice (DOJ), reporting that we believed that a crime had been committed in that someone with access to classified information had provided it to someone they should not have. The DOJ would then decide whether to investigate the possible violation of law or not. The filing of a crimes report is a requirement anytime a federal department or agency believes the law has been broken. During my tenure in the leadership, the CIA filed crimes reports for all sorts of reasons, but among the top were leaks of classified information.

An Important Bottom Line

In seeing a multitude of leaks over the years, I came to be able to categorize them—in short, to analyze them—from the perspective of where they might have come from organizationally, what might have motivated the leaker, how much damage to national security might result, and whether, in my personal view, the public had a need to know in order to check government wrongdoing.

Here is the most important conclusion from my informal analysis: *The contents of the vast majority of leaks have nothing to do with government wrongdoing, and the vast majority of leakers are not motivated by a belief that the public needs to know about government overreach. Those instances are extremely rare. They are few and far between.*

Definitions and Authorities

Before delving into what I think about the different types of leaks, I think it's important to first broadly define a leak of intelligence information. A leak is the intentional sharing of classified US government intelligence information—such as details about covert action programs, intelligence sources and methods, raw intelligence reporting, or analytic assessments—without the approval of a properly designated official with the authority to declassify information. In my experience, there are only a handful of officials inside a government department or agency with such authority, granted to them by the director of that organization, and then only with authority over information that was originally classified by that organization.

The president and the director of national intelligence (DNI) are the only two officials with the authority to broadly declassify intelligence information.[2] The DNI can do so for any information originally classified by a component of the IC, and the president can do so for any information originally classified by an executive department or agency. And both can delegate that authority to others (the DNI can do so only to his or her principal deputy), as President Donald

Trump did in 2019 by granting Attorney General William Barr the authority to declassify any IC information he sees fit to declassify with regard to the DOJ's investigation into the origins of the FBI's probe into a possible relationship between the Trump campaign and the Russians during the 2016 election.[3]

Categories of Leakers

With that in mind, and in my experience, here are the key categories of leakers:

- *Currently serving policy officials*, including those at the White House, are the most frequent source of leaks. Currently serving congressional officials, particularly staff, do the same but to a lesser degree than officials in the executive branch. It is a common misconception that Congress leaks more than the executive branch.
- *Former government policy officials*, in contact with currently serving officials, are another common source of leaks. Currently serving officials feel free to share classified information with former officials with whom they once worked, and then those former officials talk to the media. Reporters frequently cite "former government officials" when sourcing the facts of their stories.
- *Currently serving intelligence officials*, contrary to popular thought, are only rarely the *direct* source of leaks, because such officials are subject to regular security reinvestigations, including polygraphs, in a way that policy officials are not. These, not surprisingly, create a strong disincentive to leak.

Leaks that do originate with currently serving intelligence officials fall into two categories:

- The majority of leaks that originate within the IC go from current officials to former intelligence officials to the media. There is a strong sense of family in the IC, and former employees tend to stay in that family even after they leave government. Reporters target former IC officials for just this reason.
- Though less common, there are leaks that come from "troubled" employees—IC officers who are struggling in some way with their careers, with getting along with their colleagues, or with psychological issues. These leaks often capture the most attention because of their magnitude and because of the resulting damage.

Motivations of Leakers

There are a handful of core reasons for *why* leakers leak. These, of course, are not mutually exclusive. I believe that the most frequently occurring motivations are the following:

- Most leakers divulge classified information to reporters in an attempt to influence policy in a particular direction. One example of this, *if true*, would be the executive branch policy official or congressional official who leaked the CIA's alleged assessment that Saudi Crown Prince Mohammad bin Salman was culpable for the 2018 death of Saudi dissident Jamal Khashoggi. The leaker, in this case, was most likely trying to influence US policy toward Saudi Arabia. (I should add that I am not aware if this was or was not the CIA's conclusion on the matter.)
- Many leakers also divulge classified information in an attempt to gain an upper hand against domestic political rivals. Many of the leaks that followed the attacks in Benghazi that killed four Americans—most spun well beyond the truth—were done in an attempt to undermine President Obama's 2012 re-election bid as well as Secretary of State Hillary Clinton's then-likely candidacy for president in 2016.
- Some leakers divulge classified information simply to feel like players. This is particularly true of former officials who still wish they were in the game. They are motivated largely by ego, as they want to see themselves as influencing policy. Some former officials, including former intelligence officials, want the historical record to display them and/or their work as important.
- There are also some leakers who leak because they actually want to damage the US government. That is their goal. I believe Edward Snowden falls into this category. (I discuss this further below.)
- And finally, there are leakers who disclose classified information because they truly believe the American public has a right to know about government wrongdoings. Daniel Ellsberg, the leaker of the Pentagon Papers, is clearly in this category. Chelsea Manning's leak of US military abuses in Iraq may also be in this category (though her case is muddled by leaking classified materials well beyond the Iraq issue).

Others may disagree, but I find only the last category to be in any way admirable and honorable (and *only* if preceded by a good-faith effort at using an internal whistleblower process before turning to the media and *only* if the leaker takes full responsibility for the leak). The first four categories do not come even close to that for me. I find those motivations shameful and dishonorable. *Another key lesson that I learned about leakers during my time in the IC is the sheer number who leak for one of the top four reasons only to claim that they were motivated by the fifth.* Many leakers who either go public after a leak or who get caught claim they are whistleblowers; they claim that they were motivated by a belief that the government was involved in wrongdoing and that the public needed to know. In my experience, most of those who make this claim are not being truthful, certainly not with the public and probably not with themselves.

The Snowden Example

In my view, Snowden is the best example of someone who leaked classified information for one reason but claimed another. Here is what I wrote about the Snowden leak in my 2015 memoir, *The Great War of Our Time*:[4]

> What were Snowden's motives? One thing I am sure of is that he was not acting out of a simple desire to protect the privacy and civil liberties of Americans or even citizens overseas. And this takes any idea that he was a whistleblower off the table. The vast amount of information he stole and disclosed to journalists had nothing to do with privacy. . . .
>
> So, if his primary motivation was not the protection of privacy and civil liberties, what was it? I don't know for sure, but I strongly suspect that his actions were all about his favorite subject: Edward J. Snowden. It is clear that Snowden has an enormous ego—one that had to be quite large for him to convince himself that he knew better than two presidents (of different parties), the intelligence committees of multiple congresses, the Justice Departments of two administrations, and tens of FISA court judges appointed by the chief justice of the Supreme Court. That is arrogance.
>
> A full answer to the question of why he did what he did would require that he sit down for months with . . . top-notch psychologists. But my hunch is that Snowden is someone who felt underappreciated and insufficiently recognized for his self-perceived brilliance while working for the CIA and the NSA, a feeling that left a huge chip on his shoulder. This is a classic attitude that intelligence officers try to exploit among the enemy. You find someone working for the other side and tell him that he is not receiving the recognition, pay, and honors due him, and you provide those in return for the individual's betrayal of his country. This was the psychology that led Aldrich Ames and Robert Hanssen to commit espionage.[5] Let me stress that I am not suggesting here that Snowden was encouraged by a foreign intelligence service to act as he did—only that the same psychological dynamic can motivate someone to act alone and still do as much damage. In short, I think he wanted to show the world how smart he was by crippling the agencies that did not recognize his brilliance.

The most important point above for Snowden not being a true whistleblower is the vast amount of information he stole and provided to the media. The leaks amounted to millions and millions of documents and went well beyond the two terrorist-related surveillance programs that he says he found so troubling.

Snowden could not have possibly known anywhere near the totality of what he leaked. A true whistleblower would have been much more selective in what he or she leaked.

It is worth noting two other arguments for why Snowden is not who he says he is. First, he made no effort to raise alarm bells within the system. He made no effort to use the dissent or whistleblower channels that were open to him. If he had, he would have had it explained to him that the programs he was worried about did not in fact do what he says he believed they did—that is, that the government was, without a warrant, listening to the phone calls and reading the emails of American citizens.

Second, and perhaps most important, is how Snowden handled himself after he walked out of the NSA with the treasure trove of documents he stole. Snowden did not take credit for his leaks until he was overseas, and he has refused to return to the United States to be judged by a jury made up of the very US citizens whom he claimed to be supporting by leaking.

Contrast Snowden with Ellsberg. On June 28, 1971, after he had given the Pentagon Papers to the *New York Times*, Ellsberg turned himself in to a US Attorney's Office. In doing so, Ellsberg said the following:

> I felt that as an American citizen, as a responsible citizen, I could no longer cooperate in concealing this information from the American public. I did this clearly at my own jeopardy and I am prepared to answer to all the consequences of this decision.[6]

Ellsberg stood up and took responsibility for his leak. Snowden did not do so until he felt secure outside the United States in Hong Kong and Moscow, two places from which he could be confident he would not be extradited.

Even if we take Snowden at his word that he was motivated by uncovering wrongdoing, there is a logical inconsistency in his actions. Snowden claims that he wanted the public to know what the government was doing and to decide for itself whether the surveillance programs should continue or not. But in refusing to stand trial in the United States, he does not want that very same public to have a say in whether what he did was right or wrong.

Snowden recognizes this inconsistency, and he has tried to square it by arguing that he would not get a fair trial in the United States. In response to President Obama's 2014 request for him to return to the United States to stand trial, Snowden said the following:

> [T]he crimes that he [Obama] has charged me with are crimes that don't allow me to make my case. They don't allow me to defend myself

in an open court to the public and convince a jury that what I did was to their benefit.[7]

While there is some truth in what Snowden says, the totality of his argument does not hold. I am not a lawyer, but I have consulted a number of them on this issue. Snowden would be charged under the Espionage Act of 1917, and the key question would center around his ability to make a "public defense" argument or a "necessity" defense—that is, that when he leaked classified information, he had no choice but to do so because his conscience was bearing so heavily on him due to the magnitude of the government's wrongdoing.

One former senior DOJ official I spoke with put it this way: (1) Could Snowden get a jury instruction at trial directing the jury to acquit him if his otherwise certain criminal actions were "necessary"? (2) Could Snowden formally or informally introduce at least some evidence at trial that bears on the claim of "necessity"? And (3) if convicted, could Snowden introduce information or evidence at sentencing bearing on "necessity" in an effort to reduce his punishment? The former DOJ official said he thought the answers to those questions would be (1) "probably no" (for many reasons, but certainly because Snowden did not first try the formal dissent or whistleblower channels), (2) "probably yes," and (3) "almost certainly yes."

In short, Snowden could make the arguments he says he would want to make to a jury. My hunch, however, is that Snowden has a different motive for not wanting to face trial. My bet is that he and his attorneys are well aware that any reasonable jury would look at his leaks, their scope, and the context surrounding them and determine several things:

1. That Snowden, prior to leaking classified information, had a history of making false accusations against the US government—particularly about the IC.
2. That Snowden had felt wronged by the US IC for not, in his mind, placing enough value on his perceived genius.
3. That Snowden made little to no effort to take his concerns through the proper channels prior to leaking the information.
4. That Snowden significantly overstated the risk to the privacy and civil liberties of Americans from the two programs he was concerned about.
5. That Snowden's release of dozens of US IC programs well beyond the scope of the privacy concerns is indicative that Snowden wasn't just motivated by a desire to tell the public about the US government's two primary terrorist surveillance programs.
6. And finally, that the unauthorized disclosure of classified information did significant damage to the national security of the United States (see below).

In other words, I think Snowden knows that his paper-thin veil of purported public altruism would quickly fall apart under scrutiny and that he would face significant punishment.

The Damage from Leaks

During my time at the Agency, I was involved in—and read the results of—dozens of damage assessments. In one case, I was asked by the DOJ to testify during the sentencing phase of a leaker, although that testimony was ultimately overtaken by events. In short, I know a lot of about the damage done by leaks.

Indeed, my time at the CIA taught me that the leaking of classified information can be tremendously damaging to US national security. I have seen firsthand the effect that leaks have on the IC's ability to collect information, on the capabilities of our adversaries to advance their interests against us, on America's intelligence-sharing relationships with some of our closest allies, and on American diplomacy. Although not a reason to classify US government information, I have also seen the deleterious impact of leaks on US businesses and on the American economy. Two examples will illustrate these points.

Manning in 2010 provided WikiLeaks with a trove of classified information. Manning alleges that she was motivated to do so by videos of the US military abusing prisoners in Iraq, and perhaps she was. I agree with Manning that the videos released demonstrate abhorrent and illegal behavior on the part of the soldiers involved—with which the government needed to deal. However, Manning, who, like Snowden, didn't work her issue through the whistleblower process, also released hundreds of thousands of Department of State cables that had nothing to do with alleged abuses by the US military.

These cables detailed the conversations that US diplomats had with their foreign counterparts and outlined the private thoughts of ambassadors, deputy chiefs of mission, and senior diplomats on leaders and developments within the countries in which they served. After these cables were released, key US allies felt less comfortable participating in candid conversations with US diplomats, undermining our understanding of important issues and therefore affecting US national security. They also damaged some important bilateral relationships where diplomats' private reports to Washington were critical of the country in which they served, undermining US policy equities.

There has always been a debate about how much damage Manning did directly to national security and to national defense, but there is no doubt she did real damage to the diplomacy of the United States—cutting off a key source of information that US policymakers need to make sound foreign policy and national security decisions.

I mentioned earlier that the damage done by the Snowden leaks has been immense. One of the many things Snowden leaked was the IC's collection of email information from foreign-based terrorists. Just weeks after the Snowden leaks, terrorist organizations around the world—including ISIS, which was ascendant at the time—were already starting to modify their actions to protect against this collection method. Traditional communication sources dried up, and terrorists moved to encrypted communication methods. Some stopped using electronic communication altogether. It's disheartening to think what the IC could have done to curtail the rise of ISIS had those communication channels not ceased. With the leak of just this one program, Snowden made the United States and our allies considerably less safe.

The damage caused by Snowden was almost certainly not limited to terrorists' adjusting of their tactics. Foreign intelligence services undoubtedly studied the tremendous amount of intelligence data made available to them in the media and derived workarounds to thwart US collection efforts. You can bet that outfits like the Iranian MOIS, Iran's CIA, assigned cells of smart young people to study the news articles and to work on countermeasures. What is more, we can assume that foreign intelligence services have exported their lessons learned. Countries such as Russia and China probably learned from our tactics and then shared that information with other, less sophisticated intelligence services and offered tips about how to frustrate US collection efforts. In return, the Russians and Chinese would have been given access and influence that would have weakened the US security.

You don't have to take my word for the damage done by the Manning and Snowden leaks, just two examples of the damage from leakers that I've chosen to highlight here. Here are some quotes from others on the damage done to US national security by Manning and Snowden:

- In 2013, a senior State Department official testifying under oath at Manning's trial said that Manning's leaks had a "chilling effect" on US foreign relations. The official noted that the leaks made foreign contacts of our embassies "reticent to provide their full and frank opinions and share them with us." He said that "every single embassy was affected" and that "the chilling effect would go on for some time."[8]
- In 2016, the House Intelligence Committee, on a bipartisan basis, said publicly that the Snowden leaks "caused tremendous damage" to US national security. The committee added that a review of the materials he compromised "makes clear that he handed over secrets that protect American troops overseas and secrets that provide vital defenses against terrorists and nation-states."[9]

I should also add that the damage from the Snowden leaks wasn't limited to national security. It impacted American business as well. Foreign customers' trust in American products was significantly damaged as a result of Snowden's leaks. Consumers overseas incorrectly assumed that the US IC was using American information technology to broadly spy on them. As a result of that lack of trust, US information technology companies lost hundreds of millions of dollars in sales overseas. Sue Gordon, the just-retired number two in the IC, recently said publicly that she thought that the economic damage done by Snowden was even more severe than the damage to national security (which she did not discount, calling the national security damage "massive").[10]

I want to deal with two arguments that I've heard over the years about the damage from leaks. One refrain I have heard many times is that leaks do little to no damage to US national security, because either information is seldom leaked that isn't already in the public domain or the IC activity in question is so obvious that anyone, including our adversaries, would assume that the IC would be doing it. I often heard things like "But surely Iran already knew about that program," or "There's no way al-Qaeda didn't know you guys can do that."

The truth is that our adversaries spend countless hours trying to gain more insight into US intelligence capabilities, and, like our analysts, their analysts put bits of information together to paint a picture—and to have confidence in it—in order to take the actions and spend the resources necessary to defeat it. Information that confirms preconceived notions and/or multiple leaks about the same issues not only give our adversaries pieces of a puzzle, but they also build confidence in the judgments to which they have come.

And one single leak published in a prominent place can itself make a huge difference, even if it is easy to argue that "surely the adversary knows." In August 1998, the *Washington Times* published the fact that the United States could listen to Osama bin Laden's communications. After that leak was published, bin Laden never again made a call for the rest of his life. This undoubtedly lengthened the amount of time it took to find the al-Qaeda leader and therefore the time it took to significantly degrade the group that attacked us on 9/11. One of the arguments made at the time was that surely bin Laden knew that the United States had this capability. (The accuracy of this story has been debated over the years, but it was cited by the 9/11 Commission as one of the reasons the United States had a difficult time tracking bin Laden's whereabouts).[11]

Another argument I've heard claims that the damage done to US national security by leaking is a form of collateral damage, an inevitable side effect whenever a "whistleblower" places information into the public square. You'll see advocates of this view say, "Well, any damage done by Snowden's leaks was overshadowed by the tremendous service he did to the American public," or

"So what if Manning's leaks damaged our relationship with other countries? The truth about the abuse of Iraqi prisoners needed to come out, and it did."

This view is also misguided. To take it to its logical conclusion, a collateral damage argument requires a judgment that the damage is necessary to achieve the benefit, that the benefit is real and significant, and that the damage is worth the benefit. One or more of these pieces of a "collateral defense" is often missing. For example, Manning could have achieved the same effect with regard to the military's abuse of Iraqi detainees by working within the system—without damaging our diplomacy and therefore our national security. And, as argued earlier, Snowden was wrong in claiming that the two terrorist surveillance programs he leaked undermined the privacy and civil liberties of Americans (the presidential commission on which I served to look into the Snowden disclosures did not agree with Snowden, recommending no changes to one of the programs and only moderate changes to the other).[12] People who make the collateral damage argument simply have not thought it through—either in general or in the specific cases they cite.

The Media and the Intelligence Community

There's yet another element that I think needs to be a part of the larger conversation about leaks, and that's the media's responsibilities when it comes to leaks and the importance of the relationship between the IC and the media when it comes to how well the media meets those responsibilities.

The Media's Responsibility

We all know, as stated earlier, that the media has the right to publish classified information that comes into its possession. And this right, a critical part of the First Amendment, is vitally important to the maintenance of our democracy. I would fight for that right. Indeed, I saw my entire career as an intelligence officer as defending that right and the others outlined in our Constitution. Sometimes when some of my officers at the Agency would sarcastically ask, "Who gave the media the right to publish classified information," I would answer, "James Madison."

But just because the media has a *right to* publish classified information, that doesn't mean they necessarily *should* publish it. I believe the media has a responsibility to handle classified information in a responsible manner. With great rights come great responsibilities. This means only publishing classified information that the media actually believes is in the public interest, that serves the greater good—not what is good for the media outlet's financial bottom line or a journalist's career advancement. And it means that the media itself should weigh what it thinks is in the public good versus what it thinks might be the negative consequences to our national security.

There is a spectrum of how well media outlets handle this responsibility. It ranges from the irresponsible on one the end of the spectrum, for example, publishing, without even knowing what you are publishing, large data dumps of classified information, to the fully responsible, such as not publishing the name of the Ukraine whistleblower even as some irresponsible media outlets do so.

I've seen both ends of the spectrum. Based on conversations with reporters, I believe the *Washington Post* in the wake of the Snowden leaks was at one end of the spectrum. Indeed, the *Post* behaved, I think, in a way on which other media outlets should model themselves. The *Post* created an IC-style secure room to hold and protect the vast volume of documents that Snowden leaked. *Post* reporters reviewed the material in this room, only drafting stories and drawing on the classified documents when they thought it in the public interest to do so. The *Post* also shared each of those stories with the IC before publication, giving the IC an opportunity to make a case for a complete withholding of the story or the excising of particularly sensitive materials. The *Post* ultimately made the final call on what to publish and what not to publish, but it could not have acted any more responsibly.

At the other end of the spectrum is WikiLeaks, which publishes online everything it can get its hands on, without any care and without any discussion with the US government. Also, WikiLeaks, unlike traditional outlets, does not validate the documents it publishes, running the risk of a foreign intelligence service using the site to spread misinformation. WikiLeaks is completely irresponsible.

I would go even further. I believe WikiLeaks acts more like a foreign intelligence service than a legitimate media outlet. WikiLeaks actively tries to recruit insiders, as it did with Manning, and then manipulates those insiders to leak as much information as they can. WikiLeaks also provides advice to those insiders to help them break into secure systems, and it encourages like-minded individuals to get jobs at US intelligence agencies for the sole purpose of being a source of leaks. No publisher or editor for a legitimate media outlet would allow its reporters to behave in this way.

Finally, WikiLeaks' objectives are fundamentally different from those of traditional media outlets. Traditional outlets believe that by reporting on government wrongdoing, they are strengthening American democracy and society, and they are in general right in concept, even if we can debate individual instances. WikiLeaks' intent is absolutely clear and just the opposite: it is to weaken America. It is to weaken what WikiLeaks sees as a threat to the world.

The IC's Role in the Media's Search for Responsibility

Due to the First Amendment, the IC is nearly powerless to stop a media outlet from running a story, except in circumstances where it can establish that there is a "clear and present danger" that "grave damage" would result from publication, a nearly impossible bar to meet. As I have already noted, that is a good thing for our democracy. Anything to the contrary would be a chilling violation of our freedom of speech and press.

While the IC cannot and should not be able to tell a media outlet what to do, it can make requests of the media—for example, not to publish an entire story or not to publish specific elements of a story. Making such requests—of media outlets responsible enough to inform IC agencies of what is coming—was a routine affair during my time as a senior leader at the CIA. I know of dozens of cases where media outlets have chosen to shelve a story completely or, more often, for a period of time. Even more have removed from stories specific information at our request.

I was personally involved in a good number of those cases—talking to reporters, editors, and even a publisher or two, making a case for why something should not be published. Occasionally, Agency officers would approach me, saying that they had been told by a media outlet that it planned to run a story that was related to the CIA in some way, shape, or form. These officers would ask if I could make a phone call to that media outlet on behalf of the CIA and ask them not to run the story. I didn't always say yes. There were occasions when I judged that the story being reported wouldn't damage national security equities as much as my team thought or that our argument for why it was critical to hold a piece was just not compelling enough. I always thought it best never to use hyperbole and to save my powder for the stories that really mattered. When I chose to engage, when Agency officers convinced me to intervene with a media outlet and ask it not to publish, I was frequently successful (roughly on the order of an NBA free-throw percentage).

The Importance of the Relationship

Why was I successful? For two reasons, I think. The first was the healthy relationship that the Agency had built with individual journalists and with individual media outlets. The CIA directors with whom I worked closely devoted time to making the relationship between the IC and the media as cordial and productive as possible. The relationship was one I was taught to prioritize, and I did so as well when I was in leadership positions. We invited journalists to the CIA to meet with us for off-the-record dinners, attended discussions with editorial boards, and even invited the journalists covering the intelligence beat to our annual holiday party. The second reason for our success was our level of candor when making a request. As I noted earlier, no hyping of an argument, no spinning of the facts, no hyperbole. The result of both of these factors was a level of trust that made the media open to hearing our arguments and believing what we were saying.

Let me provide two specific examples. Once a veteran journalist was planning to write a story containing intelligence we had collected from a human source. It was our belief that if published, it would be obvious to the country involved that it came from a human source, and it would have pinpointed, at least, the organization where he or she worked, putting that person at significant risk of discovery and, in this case, execution. At the request of my staff, I called the reporter, said to him essentially what I just wrote above, and his or her answer was a quick "I will take it out." This would not have happened if the Agency did not have a relationship with the reporter and if I did not have a reputation with the reporter for calling things straight.

Another case involved the veteran *New York Times* journalist David Sanger (I can discuss this case specifically because the Agency several years ago released, under FOIA, email correspondence between our then-head of public affairs and Sanger regarding the issue). Sanger had notified the White House that he intended to publish a chapter in a book on an Obama administration sensitive program. The White House, in turn, asked me to meet with Sanger, go over a draft of his book, and work with him to mitigate the potential damage from what he wanted to publish. While I made it absolutely clear to Sanger that we didn't want him to publish the chapter at all, there were specific references that Sanger agreed to delete or alter after listening to my arguments about why it was important to do so. Sanger did not agree to every request, but he did agree to the vast majority. Again, this would not have happened if the Agency did not have a good relationship with Sanger and if he had not trusted that I was being truthful with him.

The bottom line here is that while journalists need to be responsible, it is up to the IC to work with them in an honest way in order to help them be responsible, in order to help them see the damage of exercising their First Amendment rights.

Conclusion

Some of the best pieces of CIA analysis finish with a section of "opportunity analysis," providing policymakers with thoughts on the opportunities we see for them to more effectively meet their goals. Since I spent a career as an analyst, I see no reason to do anything different now.

With that in mind, if the US government's goal is to disincentivize leaks, strike a healthy balance between national security and privacy and civil liberties, and maintain a positive relationship between the media and the government, here's my "opportunity analysis," developed over the course of more than thirty years in the IC.

To the DOJ: Prosecute every leak to the fullest extent possible. It doesn't matter who is responsible—it could be a current policymaker, former intelligence officer, Senate staffer, contractor, and so on. Indeed, the DOJ has a responsibility to bring a case against a leaker if it can successfully prosecute the case and if it can do so without further damaging US national security. It's also important to note that the DOJ has an obligation to take on these cases regardless of the leakers' motivation. It doesn't matter whether someone leaked information because they thought they were doing the right thing or because they wanted to one-up their political adversary—any unauthorized disclosure of classified information is a federal crime. Why be aggressive here? Because the only way to deter future leaking is to ensure a consistent punishment of leakers.

What about leakers who really believe they are doing the right thing, who really believe that they are serving the public good? The answer is to allow that defense to play out in the courtroom and let the judge and jury decide. Questions to be answered include: Did the leaker attempt to go through a whistleblower process before leaking? Did they turn themselves in to the authorities? Are they willing to take responsibility for what they have done? Does the jury see the same need for the transparency of the information as the leaker? If the answer to all these questions is yes, I would advocate a degree of leniency in how the leaker is treated.

To reiterate, though, I believe that even leakers who truly believe they are doing the right thing need to face a judicial process. This is to ensure that people don't claim "public good" when that was not their intention. And even more important, we simply can't have a system in which individuals feel free to determine themselves what is government wrongdoing and what is not. The classification system simply could not survive allowing the individual officer to decide. There needs to be a check on that, and a judicial check makes the most sense.

To the media: You play a critical role in our democracy and in defending the Constitution. Your right to publish whatever you deem necessary is a sacred part of our democracy. But understand the responsibilities you have as well. The Constitution includes a call on government to "secure the people," and your defense of the Constitution should take that into account. Be open to frequent discussions with the IC. Listen to what career professionals have to say about the costs of publishing a leak prior to doing so. The power is in your hands. Don't abuse it.

And finally, to would-be leakers: When you receive a security clearance, an enormous amount of trust is placed in you—a trust in your judgment and your ability to do the right thing when no one else is looking. Part of the understanding behind this trust is that it is your responsibility to defend the Constitution and to protect classified information.

Sometimes it might seem like these responsibilities are in tension, but they are typically not. Even Ellsberg could have accomplished his goal by providing the Pentagon Papers to Congress rather than the media. The same is true of Manning.

If you see what you believe to be wrongdoing, you have a responsibility to speak up. But you also have a responsibility to use the whistleblowing process and/or other dissent channels that are available to you. My recommendation to you is to trust this process. This process works, as was made so crystal clear by the Ukraine whistleblower. He or she should be a role model for all.

4

Reform and Renewal

Lessons from Snowden and the 215 Program

LISA O. MONACO

Introduction

In 2013, Edward Snowden unleashed a torrent of unauthorized disclosures of classified information, marking a transition from the analog era of leaks to the digital era. It was not the first time that technology and media combined to facilitate a large-scale leak of classified information by one who occupied a position of trust. But the Snowden leaks—especially about the 215 Program—prompted an important debate and marked a sea change in our evaluation of the importance of transparency to the legitimacy of government actions—particularly with regard to national security and intelligence gathering. Whatever one's views of Snowden, hero or villain, even ardent skeptics of the man and his leaks acknowledge that his actions prompted an important and democracy-enhancing debate. A debate that was overdue. How might we have had that debate sooner? And how might we have done so without the damage to national security, the undermining of diplomatic relationships, and the gut punch to trust between government and the technology industry that Snowden's leaks engendered? How might we derive the benefits of increased transparency and the legitimacy and increased confidence it confers on our national security efforts without damaging leaks?

For almost fifty years, the law has treated differently government leakers of classified information and the press that publishes that information—imposing a restraint on the speech of government employees who swear an oath and occupy a position of trust with respect to classified information and our national security. This is true even when the information disclosed may expose waste, fraud, abuse, and even potential government wrongdoing. Such disparate treatment— while the subject of legitimate debate—is appropriate and consistent with the rule of law. But such an extraordinary bifurcation of constitutional protection should be accompanied by mechanisms that maximize the opportunity for democratic debate about the exercise of government power using the system of checks and balances inherent in our separation-of-powers framework. The exposure of the 215 Program and the ensuing debate and reforms provide a useful case study in how vigorous debate, rigorous oversight, independent perspective, and increased transparency can enhance democratic decision-making about national security programs.

On June 5, 2013, the first of many stories appeared in the media based on unauthorized disclosures by Snowden.[1] Over the course of the next year, these disclosures continued in online and print outlets spanning the globe and prompted a national debate about the nature of government surveillance programs, changing attitudes toward privacy, and the potential damage to national security of exposing such programs. The first disclosure, and the one that captured public attention in the United States, exposed the so-called 215 Program, named for the relevant section of the USA Patriot Act.[2] Designed to identify terrorism suspects, the 215 Program authorized the NSA to collect millions of telephone records or metadata—but not the content—of the daily calls made by Americans pursuant to classified approvals issued by the Foreign Intelligence Surveillance Court (FISC).[3]

Snowden revealed himself to the world in an interview with Glenn Greenwald and Laura Poitras from a hotel suite in Hong Kong on June 11, 2013.[4] He had flown there from Hawaii, where he had been working as a contractor for the NSA. He had downloaded onto a thumb drive 1.7 million of the country's most highly classified documents[5] regarding the US government's signals intelligence capabilities.[6] This was certainly not the first time a US government employee had violated his oath to protect classified information and done so on a massive scale. Just three years earlier, then–Private First Class Bradley (now Chelsea) Manning had provided a trove of State Department cables to the transparency activist website WikiLeaks using a thumb drive and a CD.[7] But the Snowden leaks marked a new era in which a US government employee lifted the government's surveillance secrets from under its nose to expose what in Snowden's view was an unlawful combination of technology and government authority in the name of national security. Daniel Ellsberg stood at a copy machine for days[8] and carried seven thousand documents in hard copy out into the Virginia night,[9] and the *New York Times* published the Pentagon Papers over a period of three weeks; online distribution that would ricochet around the world in moments was decades away.[10] With the Snowden disclosures, beginning with the 215 Program, we crossed the Rubicon from the analog era to the digital era of leaks.

Snowden's leaks reflect the outsized harm and "benefit" from unauthorized disclosures in the digital age—the quintessential double-edged sword. In their aftermath, the government needed to rethink how to weigh the interests of security and privacy in an increasingly complex and rapidly changing technology landscape. The US government had responded to 9/11 by harnessing technology to increase exponentially the information available to intelligence analysts to protect the nation, but prior to Snowden had not fully grappled with technology's corresponding danger: viral exposure of its intelligence capabilities. From this point forward, the government would need to consider the risks that leaks posed not only to its capabilities but also to relationships with its allies and to US companies' competitiveness. In other words, the Snowden leaks precipitated an important conversation about the principles that guide "why, whether, when and how the US conducts signals intelligence."[11]

Policymakers would now wrestle with how technology enabled both voluminous intelligence collection and Snowden's extraordinary theft and the dissemination of purloined government secrets. The Snowden disclosures prompted an extraordinary cycle of viral exposure and public and diplomatic blowback, ruptured relations and trust with allies and the technology industry, and engendered a new level of public distrust of government. A series of reforms followed that were intended to inject new input and oversight from policymakers into the intelligence-gathering enterprise; reorient the Intelligence Community (IC) toward transparency; improve the security of intelligence systems and data; and bring new voices into the debate about the (sometimes secret) law undergirding national security programs.[12] But none of this would have happened without the debate that exploded after Snowden's disclosures. What if we had been able to have at least some of that debate in advance?

In the midst of these events, Snowden retreated to Moscow, where he lives to this day,[13] and was indicted by a grand jury in Virginia for, among other things, theft of government property and violation of the Espionage Act.[14] Snowden's indictment is one example of the way the law distinguishes between those who occupy a position of trust, and who have sworn an oath to protect national security secrets, and the press, whose job is to hold to account those who exercise power in the people's name. Indeed, the Snowden fallout is a prominent example of the framework laid out in the Pentagon Papers case, under which the government does not criminally charge traditional press outlets for receiving or publishing classified information but has repeatedly prosecuted leakers who worked for the government and non-media third parties.[15]

In 2013, the challenge was a hard but familiar one: balancing government responsibility for national security with the transparency necessary for those actions to have legitimacy and for the public to hold government accountable. This balance has always included debating and challenging government's actions—in Congress, in the executive branch, in the courts, and in the press. We did so after the leaks, but what if we had done so before?

The Pentagon Papers Framework and the Rule of Law

In 1971, the Supreme Court decided *New York Times Co. v. United States*, popularly known as the Pentagon Papers case, which governs how we balance the public's right to know information about the government's actions in its name against the need for the government to act in secrecy to protect the national security of the United States.[16] The Court held that the government could not restrain the *New York Times* and the *Washington Post* from publishing the Pentagon's classified study of the Vietnam War. To do so would violate the freedom of the press protected by the First Amendment.[17] Because the study detailed the history of the war, not real-time troop movements, the Court was unpersuaded by the government's arguments that publication would hinder national security.[18] At the same time, the Court held that the First Amendment did not authorize the leaker—a government employee—to provide classified information to the press;[19] nor did the Court recognize a constitutional right of public access to government information.[20] Nearly fifty years after this landmark decision, the law still affords different treatment to government employees (rooted in the government's interest in protecting national security) and later speech flowing from those employees' words and conduct.

Under the Pentagon Papers framework and a series of court decisions dating back to 1972, courts have concluded that it is consistent with the First Amendment for government employees to be restrained from disclosing national security information from their government service.[21] Courts have often reached this result not by referring explicitly to the Pentagon Papers case but rather by emphasizing the right of the government to enforce secrecy agreements entered into by employees in order to protect national security information such as sources and methods.[22] Courts have recognized that a contrary rule would put courts in the untenable position of engaging in subjective and inappropriate assessments regarding the value of leaked information.[23] (Note that courts often weigh the validity of national security concerns against the public interest in transparency when adjudicating FOIA disputes, but that is a distinct body of law.) So the question arises, if courts are not always the appropriate place to balance the value of disclosing certain information to the public against the government's national security interest, should those judgments be left to individual government employees? Our rule-of-law system answers this question. That answer is no.[24]

Even those most disturbed by expansive government secrecy acknowledge that intelligence activity requires some degree of secrecy; and most advocates of national security powers acknowledge that such power must operate pursuant to the constraints of a rule-of-law system. As President Obama observed in 2014, "our nation's defense depends in part on the fidelity of those entrusted with our nation's secrets. If any individual who objects to government policy can take it into their own hands to publicly disclose classified information, then we will not be able to keep our people safe or conduct foreign policy."[25]

Nevertheless, some have argued that the current framework imposes a system of unconstitutional prior restraint on the legitimate right of individuals to speak to the press and to expose government action with which they disagree, including government wrongdoing.[26] To do so imposes a restraint that chills government officials in speaking to the press and thereby frustrates the press from performing its constitutionally protected function of exposing government wrongdoing and holding power to account. But a contrary approach would place in the hands of an individual employee the power to decide what laws are worth adhering to based on that person's view of what the public needs to know.

Setting aside one's views of the unauthorized manner in which Snowden disclosed government secrets, the disclosures nonetheless set in motion important reforms around surveillance authorities and transparency. But the debate over the damage to national security and our rule-of-law system caused by unauthorized disclosures rages on. There are at least four reasons explaining why the Pentagon Papers framework that permits prior restraint on government employee speech with respect to classified information remains appropriate.[27]

First, individual employees should not be vested with the power to unilaterally reverse classification decisions based on a subjective view of the value of that information to the public. Courts have determined that they themselves are poorly equipped to make such calls. In *Nebraska Press Association v. Stuart*, Justice Brennan warned of the dangers of forcing the courts to engage in "an ad hoc evaluation of the need for the public to receive particular information."[28] Of course, courts have long adjudicated lawsuits under FOIA and the disclosure of classified information in that context—but in those cases, the courts have the benefit of classified submissions and affidavits from knowledgeable experts to weigh the harm done against the principles enshrined in the FOIA statute.[29] Absent this type of process, the government interest in protecting national security cannot adequately and responsibly be addressed.

Second, even government employees in a position of trust who have been granted a security clearance and take on responsibility to protect classified information from unauthorized disclosure may not be best positioned to determine when something should be exposed. Snowden was a systems administrator, not an intelligence professional with expertise in determining the harm to intelligence collection or diplomatic relations from certain disclosures, let alone a legal expert equipped to assess the legality of the programs he exposed.[30] To vest in a single individual the unilateral power (i.e., unchecked by whistleblower procedures) to judge what the "public needs to know" based on subjective conclusions about what is good or bad policy would, in the words of Judge Donald Stewart Russell in *United States v. Morison,* "convert the First Amendment into a warrant for thievery."[31] Of course, the president of the United States has plenary power to declassify information, but the president is ultimately a politically accountable actor and has historically exercised that power pursuant to norms that include hearing from experts and weighing competing policy interests prior to making declassification decisions.[32]

Third, unauthorized disclosures based on individual agendas can not only damage relationships with allies and partners but also do great harm to government institutions. As Susan Hennessey and Helen Murillo have observed, the unauthorized disclosure of classified transcripts of calls between President Trump and foreign leaders, prompted perhaps by frustration with the president's norm-busting foreign policy practices, itself busted norms in a damaging way, as did other leaks.[33] Such leaks risk eroding the nonpartisan nature of the IC and career national security professionals and precipitating a breakdown of the "grand bargain" set up in the 1970s, under which the bipartisan congressional intelligence committees conduct oversight and approve intelligence activities as long as they are kept "fully and currently informed" of how those authorities are used.[34] In other words, a government employee's belief that the executive branch has busted norms (or laws) does not justify that employee taking it upon himself or herself to decide that certain laws are not worth upholding.

Fourth, information dumps like Snowden's are more fraught in the era of big data. Technological advances have enabled the vast collection, analysis, and dissemination of data and in turn expanded the potential harm from leaks. Our adversaries are able to combine seemingly harmless or isolated buckets of data included in the dumps to amass profiles for counterintelligence purposes, socially engineered hacking efforts, and other harms.[35] Data has become a crucial target for nation-states and criminals alike, with stolen information a weapon of choice for nation-states using that information to conduct cyberattacks and attacks on our democracy.[36]

The internet has expanded the public square. And on the whole, the press endeavors to act responsibly, resisting the temptation for wholesale document dumps and exercising judgment informed by an understanding of the national security—and privacy—consequences of reporting. For example, during the Snowden disclosures, many publications sought input from the government about the potential damage to national security prior to publishing.[37] But technological advances and the ability of foreign adversaries to correlate big data make responsible decision-making about disclosures—be they about intelligence programs, source names, or disinformation—even more difficult and even more important.

The Cycle of Crisis and Response

Policy reform following public outcry resulting from unauthorized disclosures is not a new phenomenon. Until the 1970s, Congress had been essentially silent on intelligence activity.[38] But following Watergate, Congress enacted reforms like the FISA statute and FISC and created the intelligence committee structure, which facilitates oversight of sensitive intelligence activities by a subset of the people's representatives.[39] This oversight and compliance architecture remains in place today.[40]

At its most basic, the reforms adopted in the 1970s constructed a process in which different bodies act as stand-ins for the public in order to promote the democratic accountability for sensitive operations that is so vital to our system of government. For instance, the intelligence committees act as proxies for the people and exercise oversight in their name.[41] FISC, acting in secret and made up of Article III judges, authorizes surveillance on particular individuals based on detailed applications from the government.[42]

But evolving threats and technology have challenged these efforts. The FISC's original mandate—adjudicating individual foreign intelligence warrants—was narrow. After 9/11, the FISC took on an additional role—acting as a "superintendent" of sorts over broader, programmatic surveillance—programs such as Section 215.[43] It took years and the Snowden disclosures for the court's structure and processes to change to reflect its new role and for public debate to bring about the passage of the USA Freedom Act, which opens the FISA process to nongovernment voices as amicus curiae when adjudicating "any application for an order or review that, in the opinion of the court, presents a novel or significant interpretation of the law."[44]

Snowden's Disclosures Revealed Weaknesses in the Post-Watergate System

The debate that followed the Snowden revelations revealed weaknesses in the system created after the 1970s. Perhaps it is not surprising that the system that was created after Watergate would strain under a technology and threat environment that had changed dramatically some forty years later. The Snowden disclosures revealed that all three branches struggled to keep up with the legal, technological, and cultural shifts of multiple decades, all of which was buffeted by the worst terror attack this nation has ever experienced.

This strain became evident in the debate surrounding the Section 215 Program after it was exposed by Snowden in the summer of 2013. The 215

Program was originally part of a series of measures undertaken without FISC approval to address terrorist threats after 9/11.[45] A report by the Privacy and Civil Liberties Oversight Board, an independent agency created after 9/11 to ensure that the nation's counter-terrorism programs are balanced with privacy and civil liberties concerns, detailed that the NSA began collecting telephone metadata in bulk in the aftermath of 9/11 and from 2001 to 2006 relied on presidential authorization—not court orders—to conduct the program. Then, in 2004, without public debate, the executive branch sought and obtained FISC approval for the bulk collection of internet metadata pursuant to FISA. The government later relied on this FISC order when it went to the court in 2006 to seek court approval for the bulk collection of telephone records from US providers utilizing Section 215 of the Patriot Act, the program that remained classified and hidden from public view until Snowden exposed it in 2013.[46]

The IC leaders feared that exposure of the program would impact the ability to identify terrorist threats and would expose sensitive collection techniques.[47] Accordingly, the executive branch used the nonpublic option available to it to ensure that the program was conducted within the rule of law—it sought court approval of the program and orders compelling cooperation from the phone companies. But the FISC's consideration of this technically complex collection program was, necessarily, conducted entirely in secret and was rooted in a novel legal argument advanced by the government without the benefit of other perspectives.[48] While Section 215 (a public law) plainly permits acquisition of non-content, transaction records, that is, metadata, relevant to national investigations, the novelty came in the government's (then-classified) interpretation of "relevance" under that statute, an interpretation that one court and an outside panel would come to see as fundamentally flawed, namely, that records could be collected in bulk because only in doing so could the government later discover whether a particular number was relevant to a national security investigation.[49]

Congress Considers the 215 Program

While the intelligence oversight structure erected after Watergate was used to oversee and approve the 215 Program, the Snowden revelations prompted a debate that revealed the limits of that process. Certain congressional committees and cleared staff at times had access to classified information about the program and the government's interpretation of Section 215 to support bulk collection.[50] The relevant committees received information from the executive branch pursuant to the provision of FISA requiring regular reporting to Congress on "significant legal interpretations" of matters before the FISC.[51]

But the nature and scope of information available to Congress about the government's activities pursuant to Section 215 have been the subject of significant debate.[52] Prior to the 2010 and 2011 reauthorization debates for provisions of the Patriot Act, including Section 215, only certain members and cleared staff could review the government's application to the FISC and related classified FISC materials, such as the initial order granting the application.[53] As for information available to all legislators, the DOJ provided a five-page classified briefing paper to House and Senate intelligence committee chairs and asked that it be made available to all members of Congress in an effort to inform the legislative debate about reauthorization of Section 215. Ultimately, many legislators did not read or fully understand the program.[54] Thus, although the executive branch tried to ensure that Congress was informed about its interpretation of the provision of the Patriot Act that formed the basis of the 215 bulk telephony metadata records collection program, the 1970s framework of intelligence committees serving as proxies for the entire Congress and for the public writ large came up short; many legislators who voted on the statute did not know or understand how it would be interpreted.[55]

The issues around this legislative process—the complexity of the program, the limited number of cleared staff to assist the legislators they worked for, and the executive branch's failure to provide Congress with comprehensive legal analysis that might have assisted members of Congress in evaluating the program—later led many inside and outside the Capitol to heavily criticize Congress's failure to fulfill its oversight function.[56] Ultimately, the information provided and the forum in which it was considered did not precipitate the national debate and transparency that, in the words of one knowledgeable commentator, would have served the "educative and legitimating function" important to representative democracy and to the national security.[57] In the end, a program that all three branches of government took part in approving and overseeing was deemed illegitimate by many.

Similarly, from a legal perspective, despite involvement of all three branches of government in the 215 Program, the Privacy and Civil Liberties Oversight Board ultimately concluded, "While the Board believes that this program has been conducted in good faith to vigorously pursue the government's counter-terrorism mission and appreciates the government's efforts to bring the program under the oversight of the FISA court, the Board concludes that Section 215 does not provide an adequate legal basis to support the program."[58]

Reform and Renewal

In January 2014, President Obama announced the culmination of a review examining how, "in light of new and changing technologies, we can use our intelligence capabilities in a way that optimally protects our national security while supporting our foreign policy, respecting privacy and civil liberties, maintaining the public trust and reducing the risk of unauthorized disclosures."[59] From the Great Hall of the DOJ, the president laid out a series of reforms, including one that got significant attention: that the 215 Program as it was known would cease to exist.[60] But the reforms he announced went well beyond that and addressed how, in the future, programs like 215 would be considered, overseen, and made more transparent to the American people.[61]

Recognizing the need for greater accountability and public confidence in the government's actions, the reforms reflected the impact of rapidly evolving technology on our security, privacy, foreign alliances, and economic competitiveness. The reforms announced included a new presidential directive and new principles regarding signals intelligence collection, accountability from senior policymakers for sensitive collection decisions, incorporating new voices and transparency into FISC opinions, and the transition of the 215 Program to one where the government no longer holds the data. While the 2014 reforms were an important start, in a world where the law lags behind technology and the privacy implications of new technologies and the programs they enable may not be apparent on day one, additional institutional mechanisms are needed to ensure reform and renewal of those efforts.

Incorporating Broader Perspectives

Informing many of the reforms directed by the president and adopted in the aftermath of the Snowden revelations was a chorus of outside perspectives. The president sought formal recommendations from several entities, including two that gathered public comments, as part of a comprehensive review of US signals intelligence:[62] the Privacy and Civil Liberties Oversight Board (PCLOB), whose bipartisan appointees, confirmed by the Senate, have two primary responsibilities, (1) to analyze and review actions by the executive branch with regard to terrorism, balancing the need for those actions with the need to protect privacy and civil liberties, and (2) to ensure that liberty concerns are considered in the development and implementation of terrorism laws and policies; and the President's Review Group on Intelligence and Communications Technologies (the Review Group), a group of five intelligence, counter-terrorism, legal, and privacy experts formed by the director of national intelligence (DNI) in 2013 at the direction of the president specifically in response to concerns at home and abroad generated by the Snowden leaks. The president heeded many of the recommendations from both groups.

For instance, President Obama endorsed the PCLOB's recommendation for nongovernmental views to be considered by the FISC in significant or novel matters.[63] Giving a forum for independent privacy and civil liberties voices in a classified setting would enhance public confidence in the process by ensuring that a court that operates in secret is not hearing only one side. This idea was codified in the USA Freedom Act.[64] The FISC has since relied on amici in some cases.[65] Moving forward, democratic legitimacy for classified programs could be further enhanced with a reporting requirement by DOJ to Congress on programmatic surveillance that has not been the subject of adversary/amici briefing.

This was an important step in opening up an opaque process and assisting the court in its role as "superintendent" of a complex program while protecting the national security equities at stake.[66] One expert commentator has urged additional mechanisms, for instance, importing the intelligence discipline of redteaming into this process by expanding the ranks of the career legal advisors who staff the FISC and assist the judges in considering FISA applications and establishing a mechanism whereby a legal advisor takes on the role of skeptic to test the government's argument.[67] Injecting skepticism into the process in this way may be especially useful as we move further away from some of the processes implemented in the wake of 9/11 and confront new threats that test existing structures.[68]

Adding different voices during FISC consideration of certain programs will challenge the government arguments in novel cases, but how do we ensure that the legal underpinnings—that is to say, the laws—for programs like 215 are strong, are resilient, and have legitimacy in the eyes of the public? The congressional role in the consideration and subsequent renewal of the 215 Program is instructive. As discussed above, when the program was disclosed in the summer of 2013, a debate ensued about who had approved this program and under what rationale.[69] The executive branch rooted arguments for its legitimacy in the fact that the program had been approved by all three branches of government.[70] But the defense of the program as one that reflected interbranch approval was immediately attacked by those in Congress who had long decried the illegitimacy of "secret law" and from others who believed that the executive branch's efforts to educate Congress on its novel interpretation was both too little and too late.[71] Both sides have legitimate grievances with the approach that was followed in the case of the 215 Program. The process employed can be fairly viewed—even in today's cynical climate—as two coequal branches of government operating in good faith within the constraints of their institutions and authorities.

Faced with the belief that disclosing the program and its legal basis would be an unacceptable tip-off to our adversaries, the executive branch sought and obtained democratic buy-in through the mechanisms—albeit classified—available to it. Congress, for its part, used the system of oversight developed after Watergate, acting as proxies for the people through the intelligence committees, to consider and review the program—but in doing so arguably provided too little information to members and staff. In some sense, Congress was asked to vote on what was in effect "secret law," and many of those who attempted to fulfill their duty as legislators were understandably frustrated. Ultimately, the public—through its elected proxies—was not aware of the manner in which the government was exercising the law that had been passed in its name.

With the benefit of hindsight, it is worth asking how this situation could be avoided in the future. A lesson from the review of the 215 Program experience was summed up by the PCLOB, rejecting secret law: "The government should not base an ongoing program affecting the rights of Americans on an interpretation of a statute that is not apparent from a natural reading of the text."[72] The PCLOB went on to observe that the specifics of how a program is conducted may require secrecy so as to frustrate our adversaries and noted that this need would inevitably result in detailed explanations and oversight hearings being held behind closed doors but urged that a general description of how an authority is being used be public.[73] The PCLOB also called for criteria to be developed to guide transparency in congressional consideration of classified programs affecting the rights of Americans. These include requiring at least "the purposes and framework" of domestic intelligence programs to be debated publicly and distinguishing ongoing programs from specific operations.[74] This might better strike the balance between the need for secrecy in intelligence programs and operations and the need for transparency in the authority claimed by the government.[75] With post-Snowden hindsight, this seems quite reasonable, although we should not minimize the challenges facing professionals operating in good faith in the midst of a crisis and unrelenting threat streams that characterized the era that spawned the 215 Program.

The challenge of balancing the need for secrecy about specific operations with transparency about the authority under which the government is operating is all the more reason why establishing criteria and guidance that is public makes sense; codified policy can be available to guide policymakers in future crises. Toward that end, further consideration might also be given to a recommendation made by the Review Group for a heightened standard and reporting by the DNI when and if a program—of the magnitude of the 215 Program—must be kept secret. The Review Group recommended that it be done only after high-level deliberation and a certification that the program serves a compelling government interest and that its efficacy would be substantially impaired if our enemies were to learn of its existence.[76]

Enhancing Executive Branch Oversight

Disclosure of myriad intelligence programs and the backlash from allies and industry alike made apparent the need to adjust the government's approach to signals intelligence. The need to weigh the risk and consequences for security and foreign policy of massive disclosures against the need for collection in the first place was clear in hindsight, but how might we have factored in those risks ahead of time?

One answer to that question comes in the form of Presidential Policy Directive 28 (PPD-28). Issued as part of the 2014 reforms, PPD-28 is an unprecedented set of new guidelines to govern signals intelligence activity at home and abroad. Acting on a set of principles set forth by the Review Group for signals intelligence activities, the directive set forth greater executive branch oversight of signals intelligence activities and a process for weighing the risk of surveillance to national security as well as our alliances, economic relationships and US commercial interests, and our commitment to privacy and basic liberties against the potential for disclosure.[77] For the first time, it extended certain protections for Americans to people overseas and directed the attorney general and the DNI to develop new safeguards limiting the retention and dissemination of this information.[78] The directive also institutionalized greater oversight of future programs, in part by requiring that an annual review of decisions of intelligence priorities and sensitive targets be conducted by the president's national security team.[79]

Regular review by policymakers of the broader implications of intelligence collection requires different members of the president's national security team to come to the table and confront hard choices. Although the Trump administration has not withdrawn PPD-28 and the DNI has continued to publish certain statistics regarding national security authorities and has conducted FISC declassification reviews, it is not clear that the National Security Council deputy- and principal-level process of review of sensitive intelligence decisions called for in PPD-28 has continued; the Obama-era public reports by the DNI on progress in implementing the directive have ceased.[80] One step to enhance executive branch oversight and transparency would be an annual public report to Congress on the progress of implementation of these reforms and certifying that this review is in fact conducted on an annual basis.[81] Another would be to institute a practice of DNI consultation with the PCLOB before the adoption of certain collection programs. The PCLOB served an important function after disclosures precisely because it is charged with considering privacy and civil liberties implications *as well as* the national security implications of counter-terrorism programs.[82] It could be a valuable addition to the consideration and review of some intelligence programs for a standing body with the infrastructure to handle classified information to work with privacy officers in each agency to assess privacy concerns and conduct privacy impact assessments that are reported to the DNI.

Notwithstanding the controversy about its origins in Congress, once implemented, the 215 Program operated with robust oversight by all three branches.[83] Throughout its operation, the program was subject to regular reviews by executive branch lawyers, reporting to the FISC and to Congress regarding errors and compliance-driven changes. This may be one reason the PCLOB concluded that there was no intentional misuse of the authority.[84] It was the *potential* for abuse that ultimately prompted the reforms in 2014.

Whistleblowing

One of the most important checks within the executive branch for identifying and rectifying abuse is the whistleblower process. The whistleblower process can enhance democratic oversight of intelligence programs only if it is used. Regardless of your view on labeling Snowden a whistleblower, there is little dispute that he did not actually avail himself of the formal whistleblower process when he disclosed and sounded the alarm about the US government's surveillance programs.[85] But even if someone blows the whistle the "right way," there can still be problems. The intelligence whistleblower process has been criticized as ineffective; as insufficiently protective of those seeking to expose waste, fraud, and abuse; and as fundamentally flawed because it requires reporting to the same branch that has an interest in protecting information from disclosure.[86] If a would-be whistleblower does not exercise her rights because she believes doing so will have no effect or, worse, will result in retaliation, or if she does exercise her rights but then the process fails, the result is the same. Either way, information that may be important to bring to light, problems that may need fixing, or wrongdoing that should be exposed are left unaddressed. That does not serve national security or our democracy.[87]

The whistleblower process recently has gained widespread attention after President Trump's call with Ukrainian president Volodymyr Zelensky seeking foreign interference in the 2020 election. Most commentary regarding the Ukraine whistleblower episode cites it as an example of the process working, because the whistleblower did not expose classified information directly to the press but rather followed the process established under law.[88] The process, however, revealed a weakness: in a temporary standoff, the acting DNI initially withheld the complaint from Congress, relying on the limiting language in the whistleblower statute that only an "urgent concern"—defined as a "serious or flagrant problem, abuse, violation of law or Executive order, or deficiency relating to the funding, administration, or operation of an intelligence activity within the responsibility and authority of the Director of National Intelligence involving classified information"—must be transmitted to Congress.[89] A thoughtful and experienced commentator on this issue has noted that this limit on the DNI's responsibility is "not a frivolous one."[90] It is not clear what impact this controversy will have on future whistleblowers, although it is reasonable to conclude that some whistleblowers may be dissuaded from coming forward through this process in the future if this avenue is viewed as subject to such limitations—more still if the whistleblower becomes the object of threats, derision, and public scrutiny, as has happened now.[91]

I share the concerns expressed by my former colleagues Michael Morell and David Kris that impasses like the recent one risk discouraging lawful whistleblowing in favor of unauthorized disclosures and risk frustrating legitimate oversight.[92] Faced with these challenges, some have advocated following the example of states like New York where there is an affirmative duty to report wrongdoing.[93] Others have urged direct reporting to Congress and bypassing the DNI and affording protection to such disclosures.[94] The Review Group recommended that the PCLOB (or a "strengthened" version of the agency) be an authorized recipient of whistleblower complaints regarding privacy and civil liberties concerns from IC employees.[95]

At the time of Snowden's disclosures, there was a gap in the reprisal protections afforded to contractors, though this gap has been filled.[96] The more significant gap—and an understandable one given that uncovering waste, fraud, and abuse is the purpose of the whistleblower statute—is the inapplicability of the whistleblower protections to policy issues. "An urgent concern" does not include "differences of opinions concerning public policy matters," so a whistleblower who seeks to expose a policy she disagrees with is unlikely to be satisfied with the whistleblower process.[97]

Enhancing Transparency and Public Confidence

In the months immediately following the first Snowden disclosures, the government declassified more than forty opinions and orders of the FISC.[98] These declassifications were reactive, slow, and often accompanied by substantial redactions. As part of the new reforms, the president directed the DNI and the attorney general to conduct an annual review for declassification of future FISC opinions with privacy implications and to report to Congress on these efforts.[99] The DNI also created a new "hub" for transparency in IC on the Record, an IC website that would include postings of declassified FISC materials and statistics about FISA orders. The IC continues to post an annual transparency report.[100] These steps, while important, do not go far enough.

Another practice cited favorably by the PCLOB that could enhance transparency if adopted more regularly as an institutional norm is the practice of "writing for release"[101] (i.e., writing policies and guidance in order to minimize the amount of classified information and with the purpose of making such documents public). This practice can create a virtuous cycle wherein public interest organizations, the press, and Congress focus on new policies or programs, which in turn results in greater oversight and more ideas for reform. A case in point: the Brennan Center's Liza Goitein recommended publishing a docket cataloguing secret presidential directives.[102] While certain policies and PPDs must remain classified in whole or in part, there may be virtue in lifting the veil in part on the volume of secrecy, while withholding specifics consistent with national security.

Another virtue of publishing such documents when possible is to enable the citizens to hold the executive branch accountable. For instance, in 2015, in the wake of the brutal murder of brave American aid workers and journalists who had been taken hostage by ISIS, the Obama administration issued Executive Order 13698 and a corresponding unclassified PPD reforming the government's approach to hostage recovery activities.[103] To ensure accountability for the reforms, the executive order publicly directed relevant agencies to publish a status report on implementation of the order and required consultation with stakeholders, including hostage families.[104] Making this a public document allowed the families to hold successive administrations accountable for the reforms. Similarly, in response to the urging of numerous human rights organizations concerned with the expansion of the use of military force in the war on terrorism and the lack of transparency about the standards being applied in those operations, in 2016, the administration issued a public report on the legal and policy framework of US military force in national security operations.[105] While these types of reports and requirements are far from a panacea for the concerns about lack of government transparency and are only as effective as the consistency applied to them across administrations, they can establish an expectation among the public, press, and Congress.

Obama's speech in the Great Hall acknowledged that intelligence needs secrecy, but transparency is indispensable for a well-functioning democracy.[106] Transparency for transparency's sake will always be unsatisfactory; government will never be able to provide enough transparency to satisfy everyone without jeopardizing national security.[107] The goal should be to build confidence in and thereby enhance the legitimacy of secret operations conducted in the people's name. Thus, the reforms announced in 2014 aimed to inject transparency into the signals intelligence process, consistent with national security. Similarly, the PCLOB report never strays far from this construct in its recommendations, often qualifying them by what can be done consistent with national security.[108]

If the Snowden disclosures of the 215 Program taught us anything, it is that neither the government's nor the public's appetite for certain programs is static. The government's fear that the program would be useless if exposed as well as the public's tolerance for government action in the name of national security both have demonstrated considerable elasticity over time.[109] Because of this dynamism, as with the sunset clause that has forced regular reauthorization debate about several post-9/11 intelligence authorities (including Section 215), democratic oversight of programs like 215 would be enhanced by regular review to determine if the need for secrecy is still operative.

As we saw in 2013, the consequences of certain leaks can be chaos in foreign relations, strained intelligence relationships, and damage to national security from exposing sources and methods and enabling adversaries to change their tactics, though the extent of damage is often controversial.[110] As a result, debates about the degree of national security damage from leaks and whether such leaks are a necessary price to pay for greater transparency and accountability often end in stalemates. Rather than wait for a leak to expose a controversial program and incur the potential damage to national security and undermine public confidence in government's activities, a more effective and meaningful answer may come from trying to carefully maximize debate and transparency before, during, and after programs like 215 are implemented. The goal should be to provide accountability and hold the government's feet to the fire in order to both protect civil liberties and incentivize national security agencies to expend their resources wisely. In rejecting the notion that national security and privacy must be in conflict, the Review Group captured well the idea that far from being in conflict, safety and civil liberties are inextricably intertwined as two essential elements of security: "Free societies can and must take the necessary steps to protect national security by enabling public officials to counteract and to anticipate genuine threats, while also ensuring that the people are secure 'in their persons, houses, papers, and effects.'"[111]

The author gratefully acknowledges the invaluable research and editorial assistance of Aaron Mattis, JD candidate at New York University School of Law, as well as the support of NYU's Reiss Center on Law and Security.

Government Needs to Get Its Own House in Order

RICHARD A. CLARKE

The most effective solutions to damaging leaks of classified information may in-volve not harassing reporters and media outlets but rather having the govern-ment do a better job of managing such information, those who have access to it, and the ways in which supposedly secret data is made available to the public. This essay addresses two issues: (1) underutilization of available machine learning technology to monitor sensitive data and those with access to it and (2) the climate created when senior government officials leak classified informa-tion. The former concerns unauthorized disclosures, and the latter derives from supposedly "authorized leaks."

Unauthorized Disclosures: Nobody Actually Is Watching Most of the Time

For more than three decades, I had a US government security clearance or, more precisely, many of them.[1] Beyond the canonical Secret and Top Secret categories, there are many exotic variations of Top Secret for special access to highly clan-destine intelligence collection programs, or deniable covert action programs, or developmental "black" weapons systems, or operational capabilities of a spe-cial law enforcement or military unit. There are scores of these compartments, usually created and operated by an agency, or even a branch within an agency, without telling any other agency, because, of course, the others do not have a "need to know."

The proliferation of these special compartments has made them something of a status symbol for new programs. How important can a new effort be if it is just Secret? If security professionals really worry about something being exposed despite routine Secret or Top Secret designation, they will create a "Special Handling" system for it, complete with its own odd code-word name, one known only to a few cognoscenti. On the one hand, the perception among national security professionals that routine designations are no longer providing intended security levels highlights a need for better access management. On the other hand, increased usage of special systems further devalues Secret and Top Secret designations and makes keeping track of who has access to what information an even greater challenge.

At one point, I realized that I was the only person who knew how many of these exotic clearances I had. My parent agency, the White House's National Security Council staff, did not know all of the clearances I had. They did not even know some of the compartments existed. That was the first time that I thought, admittedly very fleetingly, that maybe I knew too much, or at least had too much access for one person who frequently traveled to "interesting" parts of the world with minimal protection.

It was not, however, the first or the last time I thought that someone ought to reform the clearance and access process across the whole of government. The fact that there is such a large patchwork quilt of classified access programs managed by so many agencies is indicative of a broader classification control process run amok. (Although to label it a process implies a greater degree of order than exists.)

The moment when I was most convinced of the need to reform how we grant access to and control highly classified information came in the wake of the disclosure of thousands of highly classified documents by a low-level Booz Allen contractor who had been assigned to do technical support for the NSA, the now-famous (or, more accurately, infamous) Edward Snowden.

President Obama had empaneled a group of five old men (hence the self-attributed name of the group, the Five Guys, after the hamburger chain) to answer for him three very basic questions: (1) What flaws in the system made it possible for all of this information to be disclosed? (2) Did the disclosures highlight any NSA or other government agency activities that we need not or should not have been doing. And (3) what do we need to do to fix the conditions prompting the first two questions? I was one of the Five Guys.

The Five Guys were formally known as the President's Review Group on Intelligence and Communications Technology, and their report to the president is unclassified in its entirety, a condition the panel members insisted on, and is formally titled *Liberty and Security in a Changing World*.[2] The president accepted almost all of its forty-six recommendations in whole or in part, including a series of ideas about using information systems technology to better monitor sensitive data and those with access to it. Unfortunately, implementation has been spotty, slow, and underfunded.

As part of our work to answer the three questions President Obama gave us, we met with the leadership of the NSA and, among other questions, asked: "What do you do to monitor your own staff members and contractors who have access to highly sensitive information (the disclosure of which could cost lives and/or be very damaging to the national security, as Snowden's leaks had been)?" The answer shocked me, because I had for decades assumed that I was being monitored in various ways, given my cumulative access to bizarre, exotic, and highly secret information. It turns out I was not being effectively or systematically checked on, and neither were tens of thousands of Americans who had been granted Top Secret/Special Compartmented Information (SCI), or Special Access Program status of various types.

When I asked the head of the NSA why the agency did not do continuous monitoring of such employee "outside" activity, he said, without a hint of irony, that the NSA did not want to intrude on the privacy of its employees. Given its intrusion on the privacy of millions of other people, I had to do all I could not to laugh out loud. In reality, most government employees and contractors I know who work in the super-secret world assume, as I did, that they had given up most of their privacy when they signed up for the mission.

The truth is that most of the review of a person's fitness for access is conducted when they are initially hired and perhaps again when they are first given access to a special control system. Everyone in such a program fills out an extensive questionnaire, which is used as a guide for security officers to do field visits to verify the applicant's biography, stability, and loyalty. Some agencies also require an entry-level employee to be polygraphed (an activity of very dubious worth, in my opinion, about which more later). After that, employees are essentially unmonitored until they undergo a periodic review, three to five (or more) years later. Often, because of backlogs, the periodic reviews are delayed by years.

I had thought that, surely, my home telephone and internet records were being watched (why did I call Moscow once a month?), my credit card purchases were being examined (why did I buy all of that explosive material?), and some program was scraping court records (why had I filed for bankruptcy, been divorced, had a restraining order placed on me, or been given a DWI citation by the local constabulary?). Nope, not really.

What we discovered was that a government employee or contractor with high-level secret access could do any number of disturbing things and stand a fairly good chance of not being noticed for them by their employer. They could, as in Snowden's case, use another employee's persona to gain access to restricted material for which they themselves were not cleared. They could, as in the case of allegations against another NSA contractor, walk off the property with downloaded copies of some of the government's most advanced hacking tools and then install them on a home computer.[3] (This misuse of classified information, including stolen US cybertools, may have facilitated foreign government agents doing millions of dollars of damage to private corporations through illegal hacking.) Between reviews of their suitability for access to sensitive information, employees could, as in the case against one Coast Guard officer, fail to disclose that they had been active in the white supremacist movement, planned attacks, and amassed a small arsenal.[4]

It should not be a matter of much debate that the government has an obligation to know in a timely manner when someone with access to rarefied government secrets is searching secret databases for information not relevant to their job, or taking such information home, or showing signs of instability, or knowingly associating with terrorist groups or hate groups, or contacting foreign intelligence agencies or their front organizations. Continuously monitoring certain kinds of employee activities, both at work on government information systems and "off the clock" at home, is the only effective way to safeguard against bad intent, careless handling of sensitive information, and changes to an employee's fitness for security clearances. As it stands, the government may not know about dangerous activities in a sufficiently timely manner to prevent costly damage, including the loss of lives.

The Private Sector Is More Advanced

In my private sector consulting practice,[5] I regularly see corporations employing software applications that use data about their customers and employees. The use of customer data has obvious implications for business strategy. The analysis of employee network behavior is critical for organizational security, and private companies use this technology far more effectively than most of the government today in managing employees with access to highly sensitive information. Three kinds of software programs are relevant: insider threat, zero trust, and big data analytics. All are powered by machine learning (ML) algorithms.

First, many corporations in financial services use so-called insider threat programs to identify possible illegal trading, premature or unauthorized disclosure of information, money laundering, or fraud by their employees. The software monitors the metadata or content of their employees' computer use, telephone calls, emails, and texts. In certain regulated industries, hiring can be conditional on a candidate's agreement to continuous monitoring, whereby they may have to disclose and limit all of their personal email accounts, telephones, and encrypted signaling applications.

Finding indicators of unauthorized activity in such a sea of data was once almost impossible until the illegal actions were revealed by other means. Today, however, ML programs can discover patterns in near real time. While insider threat software is now in widespread use in the Intelligence Community (IC), often it is less effectively implemented than the combinations of programs being used in the financial sector. For example, the US Army unit from which Chelsea Manning downloaded and disclosed secret information had reportedly bought a license for an insider threat software program but had failed to install the application.

One regulated sector, the casino industry, has for almost two decades been using software that identifies non-obvious relationships among employees in the above-ground gambling world with organized criminals or "big winners." The non-obvious relationship software accesses public databases to determine, for example, who the employees' relatives (in-laws, cousins) are, who were their fraternity or sorority associates or roommates in college are, who their neighbors across the backyard fence are, and who sold them their car or house. While regulators require this type of in-depth vetting of those who deal out cards at a casino, government agencies will seldom subject their own staff to such scrutiny, despite their access to sensitive data, even if that means gambling with national security.

Second, many companies with valuable intellectual property or restricted data (e.g., drug trial information, engineering designs, chemical formulas, or healthcare material) use what the Forrester Consulting group has called zero trust (ZT) software and network systems. ZT systems are designed to link identity with restricted access to information on a granular level, permitting someone to view restricted data only when they have sufficiently proven their identity in a multifactor manner, only when access is necessary and only for as long as it is necessary to do their assigned task. Typically, these decisions are made by ML algorithms running in real time. Decisions are not just yes or no but allow for gradations based on available information and risk management policies. Active micro-segmentation of a network is usually a prerequisite for implementing a ZT architecture. Audit trails are created and continuously reviewed by threat-hunting ML programs to detect anomalous activities.

Two related kinds of ZT software are privileged access management (PAM) and digital rights management (DRM). PAM software requires greater demonstrations of certainty that the user is who that person says they are as their degree of access expands or moves into more highly sensitive information. DRM software limits what a user can do with access to data (read, edit, copy, transmit, download) and records what they do, as well as where and when they do it.

Few national security agencies have fully implemented state-of-the-art ZT designs on their classified networks, a pattern attributable to organizational roadblocks rather than unsuitable technologies. Government agencies are unable to quickly adopt new technology, and departments depend on a short list of consulting firms with narrow approaches to systems integration. The very name Zero Trust would be anathema to many government managers who think that after their initial security vetting, all government employees and contractors deserve to be trusted. When the bottom line, investors' money, and corporate reputations are on the line, however, many private sector executives believe the ZT approach to information handling and security is far more prudential than relying on a one-time assessment of each employee, supplemented by updates years later.

Equally as deterring as organizational reluctance to employ the ZT approach is the still-prevailing belief across government in the "need to share" philosophy. Following the work of the 9/11 Commission, which (erroneously, in my view) said that the terrorist attacks were the result of governmental agencies not sharing intelligence information more broadly within and among government departments,[6] there was a movement within intelligence agencies to disseminate and grant access to sensitive information widely among those who had a security clearance. "Need to share" replaced the previous mantra of "need to know." As often occurs in government, the pendulum had swung from one bad extreme to another, without resting in the sensible middle ground.

Third, so-called big data software programs access large numbers of databases, many on a nearly continuous basis, to develop and update personas for profiles of billions of customers and potential consumers. By piecing together snippets of information from numerous publicly available records and pay-for-access databases, corporations' ML applications are able to learn an enormous amount about an individual and flag people who are of interest as possible buyers or voters. In the 2016 presidential election, the infamous Cambridge Analytica developed or accessed detailed profiles of millions of US voters. That information, and the software it trained, may have powered Russian micro-targeting of certain groups with erroneous propaganda. Facebook and Google have ML software that does similar micro-targeting every day, perfectly legally. Similar algorithms to those used for consumer and social engineering can be ethically harnessed to better track who has access to what information and assess the risk they pose in having it.

Big data companies already know far more about most individual citizens than any one part of the government does. Regulations and laws prohibit federal agencies from sharing some kinds of government data (tax returns and banking transactions, for example) with each other or accessing some private sector databases to develop profiles or personas. These restrictions are necessary civil liberties safeguards to prevent government abuse, but they should not apply in all cases to federal agency workers or contractors who have access to highly secret data.

Such national security agencies as the Pentagon, the State Department, the FBI, or the CIA, for example, should have continuous monitoring programs for those employees throughout the government with access to their highly sensitive information. These programs should use big data and ML tools to search all government and some private sector databases to identify behavior or patterns of activity that constitute red flags, requiring review and in-person discussions with the employee. Does the employee's pattern of spending indicate a new source of wealth? Have they traveled to foreign locations but not disclosed the trips to their security office as required? Has the employee's right to possess firearms been limited by state red flag laws allowing a court or law enforcement official to temporarily seize the weapons and restrict their ability to buy new ones? (Amazingly, many US national security agencies would not today know in a timely manner if one of their employees with Top Secret access had been subject to a state red flag gun law.)

Suggesting the use of these private sector techniques to better protect government data is likely to create howls of objections that such programs would infringe on civil liberties. As a civil liberties advocate, I disagree. Of course, government employees and contractors, even those with access to highly secret information, have the civil liberties and rights that other citizens enjoy. The people I am suggesting be subject to continuous monitoring with ML programs and the other software programs is only that group of our fellow citizens who have sought the privilege of holding access to extraordinarily secret and potentially damaging information.

Employees in the national security sphere are already led to believe that they trade a degree of privacy for the opportunity to be entrusted with national secrets and security. No one has forced such access upon them, and they have accepted the trade-offs such access demands. As powerful as this culture of sacrifice is, lacking oversight leaves the door open for transgressions, despite the availability of technological solutions to help prevent or detect wrongdoing. To leverage these technologies ethically, the government must make transparent its intent to closely monitor agency staff and contractor behavior as a condition of their employment instead of continued reliance on a tacit contract.

The open question is whether that sacrifice of privacy is producing the outcomes sought and used to justify it. Is the intrusion into their lives being done in such a way as to effectively achieve the goal that justifies it: seeking to discover spies and others whose unauthorized disclosures can cost lives and other significant losses? All too often, I believe, government has failed in, and to some large extent continues to fall short of, utilizing existing software technology to identify those with secret access who are attempting to do harm.

The Dangerous Reliance on the Flutter Box

Many government agencies justify lagging behind the private sector in the use of modern ML-driven security to monitor sensitive data and the people who use it, citing the use of the lie detector machine as a substitute. Far more intrusive than these proposed uses of software is this primitive practice of polygraphy, which is still widespread in national security agencies. It is telling that the polygraph is not commonly trusted in the private sector, in many states is banned by law as a pre-employment screening tool, and is generally inadmissible in US courts of law.

The reason for such legal limits on the polygraph is that the tool is notoriously unreliable, producing both false positives and false negatives with unacceptable frequency. Advocates of the polygraph, mainly US intelligence agencies, generally admit that the accuracy of polygraph results is highly dependent upon the skill of the "examiner." What that really means is that polygraph results are open to interpretation, like tarot cards. Similar to that of the fortune tellers' tool, a polygraph's accuracy varies significantly with the ability of the operator to provide performances that can trick or create a psychological effect in the mind of the subject.

Almost all of the well-known spies who have victimized the US government were polygraphed, but their examinations did not raise sufficient red flags to prompt investigations resulting in the employee being denied access or being arrested. Some governments even train their spies in techniques to successfully evade the polygraph. The deep-seated, prevailing belief across US government security agencies is that the polygraph is the most reliable tool. This complacency breeds a false sense of protection and discourages exploration of potentially more effective, ML-driven access management and insider threat detection practices at work in the private sector. The ignorance of alternative options' potential is particularly troubling when combined with the shortcomings of the other vetting process used in government known as the "field investigation."

The field investigation usually consists of supposed personnel background specialists, often referred to as "agents," who interview an applicant's known associates. Most of the known associates have been identified in the first place by the applicants themselves, giving some reason to believe that the known associates will be unlikely to provide disparaging information. All associates questioned are first informed by the agent that their remarks will be available to the applicant through FOIA procedures. This knowledge also tends to have a dampening effect on the dialogue. ML software algorithms are a far more efficacious method than either the lie detector or the field investigation and should be widely adopted to protect government data.

The Oxymoronic World of "Authorized Leaks"

The second major problem with the ways in which the US government controls access to its secrets is in the area of what is sometimes called the "authorized leak." Some senior government officials create an atmosphere in which lower-level government employees may come to believe that leaking classified information is routine or acceptable, even if it "technically" may break the law.

Few are the days in which no major national newspaper in the United States (*Washington Post, Wall Street Journal,* or *New York Times*) reports information that the US government has classified as Secret or even Top Secret. In the overwhelming majority of these disclosures, select reporters have been provided classified information by a senior government official. CIA directors, FBI directors, national security advisors, and secretaries of defense and state have all done this.

When such a leak occurs, it is often described as an "authorized leak." The person who authorized it, to the extent that it has actually been sanctioned (an issue we will return to shortly), is usually also the very official who conveys the information to the reporter. Despite the information having been leaked, other government officials will typically refuse to confirm the information, in large part because the data is legally still classified. Sometimes a cabinet member will leak the information one afternoon, it will be published overnight, and the leaker's own press secretary will refuse to confirm it to other reporters the next day. They may, however, refuse with a wink or a nod, with body language that suggests the information is true. Outside the press briefing room, the public affairs officer may say to a telephoning reporter, "I wouldn't guide you away from that," which is bureaucratic speak for "Yes, it's true."

Senior officials choose which media outlet to inform in their "authorized leak" by gauging the readership (or viewership) size and makeup. They may also attempt to "cultivate" reporters for good press in the future or reward them for past favorable coverage with access to secret information. Inversely, officials may use their position as a source to compel a journalist not to report on them unfavorably. These top-level leakers engage in this kind of information dissemination sometimes to shape public, congressional, or foreign government perceptions, attitudes, and actions. Telling a reporter a fact may be the quickest and most effective way in which a senior government official can ensure that a group of senators or foreign officials learns about that fact. Because the information was in a news report and not an official diplomatic "démarche" or congressional letter, the leaker has some deniability should reactions to the leak then suggest a different course of action.

One of the problems with all of this commonplace activity is that there is not an adequate system for approving these leaks, and, except for approved statements made in an open press conference, an official press release, or an on-the-record interview, there is no such thing as an "authorized leak." Under regulations for handling classified information, the government official who originated the report containing sensitive data is given the administrative "classifying authority" to label a report as Secret or Top Secret. Only that official can begin the *process* of declassifying that information; the originator alone cannot legally decide to share a classified piece of information with a reporter or other person lacking security clearances and "need to know." That official process for deciding to remove a security classification on some information, a process involving several officials and frequently several agencies, examines risks of disclosure and trade-offs with other government objectives.

Often, that official process may seem unnecessarily time-consuming and cumbersome to senior officials on tight schedules, and so, without checking with others, they create what they believe is an "authorized leak." Unfortunately, these officials may not always be able to perform an accurate disclosure damage assessment on their own. They may not know the damage or risks that the leak could create.

There are numerous examples of unintended consequences. Two such stories relate to the late terrorist Osama bin Laden and his alleged use of satellite telephones during a period when I was heavily involved in US government attempts to locate and capture or kill him. In one case, an unknown official allegedly disclosed in 1998 that the NSA regularly listened to the terrorist on his Iridium satellite telephone, and soon thereafter, bin Laden stopped using that method of communicating. While some dispute the cause and effect involved in this story by noting that bin Laden had made no secret of his use of the satellite telephone, I can attest that the NSA intercepts of the Iridium telephone ceased shortly after the disclosure that the NSA was listening (not after the earlier reports of his use of the device). That cessation made it more difficult to know in real time the exact location of the terrorist and thus made it more difficult to target him for a strike or raid.

The second case occurred during the post-9/11 period when investigators were performing postmortems on the attack and events leading up to it. Even though 9/11 had already happened, al-Qaeda was still very active, and efforts to suppress the organization's attacks continued, often facilitated by communications intelligence. In this instance, as publicly reported, the Senate Select Committee on Intelligence (SSCI) was informed that during the months leading up to the 9/11 attack, the NSA was decrypting al-Qaeda calls on the "secure" Thuraya satellite telephone. Possibly from a senator on the SSCI, that information leaked within hours of the briefing, allegedly because the senator wanted to make clear to the public that the IC could have known about the 9/11 attacks in advance. Unfortunately, prior to that disclosure, it was apparently not widely known that the NSA had the ability to listen in on and to decrypt those encrypted calls. Whoever made that disclosure probably did not realize its intelligence value or understand the high risk that such a leak would prompt al-Qaeda members who had been using the device, thinking it was safe, to cease doing so.

Mid-level officials seeing that their bosses engage in "authorized leaks" without going through the interagency declassification process come to believe that they, too, have that "right" to leak in order to conduct policy. The result is an all-too-common perception that revealing classified information, though "technically" a crime, is tacitly accepted as part of standard information flow. This perception's pernicious effect is that it undermines the government's ability to control its own officials' conduct. While most administrations eventually come to live with this norm, they do so because of what is normally the extreme difficulty of determining the identity of leakers and then disciplining them, not because it is an insignificant transgression. (There have been a few notable exceptions, such as the prosecution of the vice chairman of the Joint Chiefs of Staff, a four-star general and the second-most-senior US military officer, for an unauthorized disclosure of a US intelligence covert activity.)[7]

It is at least worth consideration to address this issue by creating a senior, interagency mechanism for rapid review of declassification requests made by senior officials for policy-related purposes. (Such a mechanism would also have to address the "if one, then all" procedures that now require government agencies to inform all accredited media when a fact is declassified and disclosed. Policymakers will still want to provide information on an unattributable and exclusive basis to just one or two outlets.) Having such a mechanism may not stop the "authorized leak" altogether, but it would make more clear to both senior and mid-level officials that a failure to adhere to policy-related disclosure procedures is a clear and serious violation, rather than, as is the widespread impression, that it is "just something everybody does" and "part of the job."

These two areas for improvement are among a series of steps that the US government could take to clean up its own house. Rather than infringe on the civil liberties of reporters or citizens not employed by the government, those concerned with the issue of leaked classified information should begin with what can be done in-house. There is indeed a lot to be done there, and, if done well, taking such steps could be highly effective in preempting the risk to national security posed by "unauthorized" and "authorized" leaks alike.

PART TWO

THE JOURNALIST PERSPECTIVE

Behind the Scenes with the Snowden Files

How the Washington Post *and National Security Officials Dealt with Conflicts over Government Secrecy*

ELLEN NAKASHIMA

In a conference room ordinarily reserved for foreign visitors at Liberty Crossing—the northern Virginia headquarters of the US Intelligence Community (IC)—two senior *Washington Post* reporters sat opposite more than a dozen stone-faced intelligence officials and subject matter experts. The officials came from the NSA, the CIA, the DIA, and the FBI, among other three-letter organizations. The tension was palpable.

"You could see a lot of expressions around the room of anger, frustration, indignation," recalled Greg Miller, one of the reporters in the room.

It was the summer of 2013, and the *Washington Post* had obtained a vast cache of highly classified documents from a former NSA contractor detailing some of the most sensitive secrets in the IC.

Among them was something that had never before been made public: the "Black Budget." Here was the annual IC budget, a lengthy blueprint that the nation's seventeen spy agencies submit to Congress to justify their request for tens of billions of American tax dollars. It summarized programs, goals and operations, and agencies' successes and failures.

The *Post* was preparing to publish a series of articles based on the document, which revealed how, despite immense funding, intelligence agencies were unable to provide critical data on a range of national security threats. The reporters entered the conference room expecting to outline their reporting and engage with the experts on particular programs and capabilities that raised publication concerns.

But the session became "more like an emotional moment than anything else," recalled Barton Gellman, the other reporter in the room that day and the *Post* journalist who had first received the classified trove. "They kept asking, 'What are you doing with this, and why aren't we taking it back? How is it even legal for you to publish this? How is it up to you?'"

Miller and Gellman tried to convey the *Post*'s reason for publishing. "We explained that writing about how the US government spends tens of billions of taxpayer money and the priorities that it sets in national security are pretty basic to the job of a news organization," Gellman said. "We thought there was strong public interest in knowing these things and debating the priorities and in understanding the extent to which the US government is or isn't satisfied with its understanding of the world. But we understood that we didn't want to be giving adversaries clues that could help them evade US surveillance, or could help them stop US operations. That was the balance we were always looking for."

The encounter at Liberty Crossing reflected the gulf that often exists between journalists' and intelligence officials' views of the role of the press in covering national security programs. It is part of the natural, indeed necessary, tension that permeates the world of national security reporting.

But if there was frosty distrust in the beginning, a wary working relationship of sorts did emerge as the media reported on the material leaked by the former contractor, Edward Snowden. I was a part of the team that delved into the documents and witnessed the efforts of colleagues and editors to grapple with tough questions of whether the public interest in publishing certain information outweighed intelligence and security concerns.

In this essay, I will show that far from simply dumping online thousands of pages of documents that the *Post* obtained from Snowden, our reporters and editors took pains to protect the material, vet it for accuracy, and engage with the IC to gauge the potential harm to national security—all crucial steps taken before the *Post* published its series of articles.

The Snowden case was exceptional. The amount of highly classified material in journalists' hands exceeded all previous leaks, including that of Chelsea Manning, an Army private who had passed to WikiLeaks hundreds of thousands of diplomatic cables and military reports from Afghanistan and Iraq. The impact on intelligence operations was potentially far-reaching and severe. Yet the lessons learned should apply to challenges of much smaller scope. Reporters with a bias for public disclosure voluntarily withheld certain documents and details, and intelligence officials with a bias toward secrecy did not fight every disclosure—though they did with many. What I found is that journalists and government officials did their best to serve their missions and the values they stand for: advancing the public's right to know—in particular, to be made aware of potential government encroachment on civil liberties—and defending the security of the American homeland while respecting civil liberties. I'm a working reporter, and readers should not be surprised that I have a bias in favor of transparency on critical issues. In our coverage of the Snowden leaks, the results were never perfect, but the experience provided a rich opportunity to gain insights into how to better navigate the inevitable conflicts between journalists' desire to inform the public and the government's desire to protect its secrets from foreign powers.

An Olive Branch at Liberty Crossing

Shawn Turner, the top communications official for the Office of the Director of National Intelligence (ODNI), was convinced it was necessary to engage with the *Post* reporters on the Black Budget. He and his boss, DNI James Clapper, knew they could not prevent the *Post* from publishing and that their best hope was to minimize the harm to national security. Clapper "put out the word we're going to do this," Turner recalled, "and that's all there was to it."

Nonetheless, the atmosphere in the room that day was one in which many of the intelligence professionals there were reeling from the initial disclosures, felt uncomfortable discussing sensitive programs with people outside the IC, and believed that "extending an olive branch to bring in the *Washington Post* was over the top," Turner observed.

A key goal for the *Post* reporters was simply to reassure the agency officials that the newspaper was not going to blindside them and would not proceed without talking things through with them first. "We were just trying to impress upon them that we were trying to behave responsibly with this," Miller recalled. "We had to talk through our criteria and explain to them how we were looking at this from the perspective of a news organization trying to discern what was of news value, where there was a legitimate public interest in revealing what's here, and talking about where we think there are meaningful gaps between what the public assumes the government is doing on its authority and what the government is actually doing in this case."

The officials thought that they were going to be "grilled" by the reporters and that the meeting would be "very contentious," Turner said. They were actually relieved when it wasn't. When an analyst commented that she could not say anything more about a particular program or operation or was not comfortable answering a question, the *Post* journalists moved on. Though they did not dissuade the reporters from publishing, Turner said, "the people who walked into the room frustrated or irritated often walked out feeling better because of the interaction that the journalists gave them."

By the spring of 2013, the relationship between the US national security community and the media had been strained by years of reporting on controversies
arising out of the US government's often-secret response to the September
11, 2001, terrorist attacks. When journalists revealed the stretching of legal
boundaries to give the agencies more latitude to gather intelligence that might
prevent the next terrorist attack or the secret detention and torture of suspected
al-Qaeda militants in CIA "black sites" overseas, the government responded
with leak investigations and admonitions that the disclosures would harm national security and undermine allies' cooperation. In 2010, WikiLeaks had
posted hundreds of thousands of sensitive cables, military records, and other
documents obtained from Manning, infuriating the US government.

The government believed it had made the country safer and viewed media
stories as undermining that goal. And while individual reporters had relationships
of trust with some government sources, most officials saw few incentives to engage with reporters, either because they viewed them as adversaries or because
they just thought nothing good could come of it. At the NSA, for instance, press
queries were often met with a standard "no comment," when calls were returned
at all. The joke was that NSA, besides standing for "no such agency," also meant
"never say anything."

The First Story: Phone Records

This was the state of affairs when on June 6, 2013, Glenn Greenwald published
a story in the *Guardian* headlined "NSA Collecting Phone Records of Millions
of Verizon Customers Daily." It was based on an actual court order from the secretive Foreign Intelligence Surveillance Court (FISC) that directed the phone
company to provide "all call detail records" to the NSA on "an ongoing daily
basis." I remember that evening well. I was sitting on my back patio with a glass
of white wine, anticipating a pleasant late-spring dinner al fresco when I saw the
story pop up on my iPhone. I rushed upstairs and called a former national security official, who confirmed the court order indeed was legitimate, and I raced to
write a story matching the *Guardian*'s.

This was a big deal. I realized that *this* was the classified program based on the
"secret law" that US Senator Ron Wyden (D-OR) had been cryptically warning
about for so long. Several national security reporters, including myself, had been
trying for some time to figure out what Wyden was talking about. We knew his
warning had something to do with Section 215 of the Patriot Act, or the business
records provision of the Foreign Intelligence Surveillance Act (FISA), the law
that governs the gathering of foreign intelligence inside the United States. But
we had no idea the law authorized the collection of millions of Americans' call

records every day. That's because it had been secretly authorized by Congress, arguably without a number of lawmakers fully understanding what it was they had voted for, as many had not taken the opportunity to listen to the government's classified briefings.

The records did not include content—what people actually said on the calls. They contained only metadata, such as the date, time, and length of calls and the parties' phone numbers. But analysts can learn a lot about a person's associations and activities from knowing who called whom, how often, and for how long. They can marry this with other data to build profiles of a person and map his or her network of friends, family, and associates in what intelligence officials call chain analysis. In short, this can be highly invasive. And yet the government was obtaining millions of such records each day on a mere assertion that it was "relevant" to an ongoing investigation. That seemed to be flexing the language of the law beyond any reasonable interpretation. That story touched off a wrenching two-year-long national debate, which I covered, that culminated in new legislation, the USA Freedom Act of 2015.

But in that first week of June 2013, officials such as Turner did not realize that Snowden was the source of the leaked court order. Or that they were confronting anything more than one big shocking story. Turner took the first call about the phone records program from a *Guardian* reporter working with Greenwald three days before the article ran. Internally, he said, there were people who wanted the ODNI to do as it had frequently done, which is to say nothing and justify the silence by simply saying the program was classified. In the end, the NSA, the White House, and the DOJ declined to comment to the *Guardian*. Part of the rationale, Turner explained, was that officials believed this was a "one-off," that "this was going to be a big reveal, and we were going to move on."

But they were wrong. The next day, the *Post*'s Gellman published a story about the NSA harvesting emails and other data from nine American tech companies for foreign intelligence purposes under a program code-named PRISM. Shortly thereafter, Snowden came forward and, in separate interviews with Gellman and Greenwald, acknowledged that he was the source of the documents that fueled the *Post* and *Guardian* articles. It was gradually dawning on Turner and other senior IC officials that there were many documents out there, and they were likely in the hands of a number of journalists.

"Internally," recalled Turner, "there was the shock and awe of the fact that they were in possession of the documents." Then, as they realized that Snowden had traveled to Hong Kong and then Moscow, their concerns grew that the information would fall into the hands of adversaries. In any case, it was now clear that the IC was going to be confronted with a series of articles from a variety of news organizations.

The *Post*, meanwhile, was aware of the highly sensitive nature of the material. And Gellman, perhaps more than any national security journalist I know, takes operational security seriously. The measures he and the newspaper took to protect the documents from foreign adversaries and other malicious actors were extraordinary.

Two Rooms and a Manual

The room, even with the lights on, was dim. It was on the seventh floor of the old *Washington Post* building on 15th Street NW, down the hall from the publisher's office. Only a handful of reporters and editors at the *Post* knew about the room, much less had access to it. There was no internet access. No Wi-Fi. Entry required obtaining a special key from a trusted colleague on the national security desk.

This was the room that housed a select portion of highly classified documents provided by Snowden, which Gellman had obtained. It contained two air-gapped computers. One of them held a carefully vetted handful of documents that Gellman selected for colleagues to work on. The other was used to take notes on the documents.

The material was mind-blowing. There were actual intercepts—emails, instant messages, and Facebook chats obtained under wiretap orders authorized by the FISC. There were classified "certifications" issued by the FISC allowing the NSA to spy on more than 190 countries and institutions, including the World Bank, the International Monetary Fund, the European Union, and the International Atomic Energy Agency, under a 2008 law known colloquially as Section 702 after a section of the FISA Amendments Act. There were top-secret documents showing that NSA had secretly been tapping into communication links connecting Yahoo and Google data centers around the world.

This is material that had never been seen in public. And the *Post* had tens of thousands of sensitive documents like these. We were never going to publish all of it or even one percent of it. In the end, the *Post* made public a tiny fraction.

But, Gellman said, "There's no point in congratulating ourselves for holding back information that shouldn't be published if we let the whole thing get stolen," he told me. He drew up a three-page set of "document reading guidelines" for the small group of reporters working on the selected Snowden files. He noted that the risk came from the fact that "we have to decrypt files to work with them" and that "if we don't follow this work flow every time, it is likely that somebody will grab our files while they're unencrypted." He admonished us not to "remove any files from *Washington Post* property or store them on any other device or cloud service . . . even while encrypted." The *Post* provided the reporters with special encrypted IronKey thumb drives. We saved our notes on them.

Eventually, Gellman stopped using the seventh-floor room and set up shop in a room in the basement of the 15th Street building—a room I didn't even know existed. There he kept the entire trove that Snowden had given him (itself only a small part of what Snowden took). That room was windowless, with a special lock and a video camera trained on the door. The encrypted hard drive to the computer was stored in a heavy safe bolted to the floor. To gain access to the file, you would need to obtain the room key, know the safe combination, have a software token, and know the pass phrase. Only three people were allowed in the room: Gellman; Julie Tate, the national security desk research director; and Ashkan Soltani, a computer scientist who brought technical and policy expertise to the reporting and collaborated on stories. Not even the cleaners were allowed in, so the reporters had to try to keep the room from getting cluttered up with notes, water bottles, and candy wrappers. "We spent many, many hours in there together," Gellman said.

Still, these precautions came nowhere close to those the IC used, said Katrina Mulligan, who was part of a four-person directorate set up by the White House to handle the "disclosures response" to the Snowden leaks. "No amount of measures the *Post* could have taken would have been enough for us," she said.

She appreciated the irony that though the IC's measures were stronger, they proved inadequate to prevent major leaks. "Our defenses are designed to protect against external threats," she said. "What we have failed to do pretty profoundly is protect ourselves against each other."

Public Interest versus Harm to National Security

The *Post* does not publish stories simply because it has obtained classified documents. "We have standards on this," Marty Baron, the *Post*'s executive editor, told me. "We publish because of strong public interest." How does the *Post* define public interest? "It sort of defies definition," he said, then echoed the words of former Justice Potter Stewart—"but it's one of these things where you understand it when you see it."

One area of coverage clearly in the public interest is showing how government actions affect "individual privacy," Baron said. In the Snowden documents, the Section 215 "bulk collection" of phone metadata was the marquee example. After the *Guardian* broke the story, the *Post* and scores of other news outlets reported on it and on the ensuing debate. "In this instance, a policy had been implemented without any real public debate," Baron noted. He pointed out that President Obama himself decried that lapse and directed that a new, less invasive approach be taken.

The irony, two former senior intelligence officials told me, is that Snowden's disclosure of bulk collection probably prolonged the program's life. The NSA was ready to end it, as it was not proving useful, they said. But the Snowden disclosure provoked "a great desire to circle the wagons," one former official told me. "If Snowden hadn't revealed it, NSA would have dumped it on their own."

The vast majority of the Snowden documents were either too sensitive to be published or far too technical and esoteric to be meaningful to the average reader. As he reviewed material for his first story—the PRISM piece—Gellman found numerous documents that he knew the *Post* would never disclose publicly. One was a forty-one-page slide deck written by the program manager to persuade NSA analysts of PRISM's value. The *Post* published fewer than ten pages. The slides' message essentially was "If you're not making use of this, you're missing out on something good," Gellman said. They cited specific examples of intelligence obtained, including weapons of mass destruction activity by a particular target in a particular location who was not aware the United States knew about it. "The examples were (a) very cool and (b) obviously super-sensitive," he said.

That kind of material, if published, would tip off the target that the NSA knew what he was up to, the person would change his behavior, and "you would lose that window on him," Gellman said. The *Post* felt it had a duty to protect the United States and not gratuitously reveal information that would undermine that goal. So, he said, "there were categories of stories where it was just obvious to me or to us" that the *Post* would not publish them. "Sometimes I did it by myself and didn't even bring it up with the *Post*. Sometimes it was consensus."

Another category of documents the *Post* was sensitive to involved the physical safety of sources or government personnel overseas. And then there were the many documents for which the potential damage to intelligence collection was not so immediately clear. In both cases, we relied on the IC to make its case to us regarding the concerns it would have if certain documents were to be published. Sometimes we found the case persuasive. Other times we did not. It was a learning process, and in the beginning of the Snowden series, the lines of communication were not yet optimized.

PRISM

The first article the *Post* published based on the Snowden documents was about PRISM, a foreign intelligence collection capability that had grown out of one of the components of a controversial post-9/11 terrorist surveillance program code-named STELLARWIND. Part of it was disclosed by the *New York Times* in December 2005, a disclosure based on leaks that prompted a huge national outcry and lengthy public debate.

The article was written by Gellman and Laura Poitras, a journalist on contract with the *Post* for that piece. It provoked a great deal of consternation and criticism from the NSA. The article stated that "the program, codenamed PRISM, has not been made public until now." In fact, as Gellman reported, it was authorized by Section 702 of the FISA Amendments Act, often just called Section 702. That authority had been publicly debated for more than two years before Congress approved it and President George W. Bush signed it into law in 2008. What Gellman revealed, though, were details about the program's operation and, crucially, the names of nine major tech firms that provided data to the government pursuant to court order. That latter disclosure in particular upset the agency.

"The most highly classified thing in that whole document, *they* claimed, was the names of the nine companies," Gellman recounted. "They didn't want us to publish the story at all. But the thing we fought about the most once I told them I wasn't going to be saying which person was doing which WMD program at some secret location, was the names of the companies."

Naming the companies, argued ODNI general counsel Robert Litt, would chill their cooperation with the NSA. And this program was and is one of the most valuable capabilities the IC has when it comes to collecting foreign intelligence to inform policymakers from the president on down. Gellman discussed this with Baron, and the two agreed that that objection was not a reason to refrain from publishing. Gellman recalled telling Litt, "If the harm you're worried about is the public won't like something and the company will stop doing it because the public disapproves, then that's why we publish it. Any harm that comes that way is the normal operation of the marketplace, or of democracy. If the government is doing something that the public or the market disapproves of, then we're not going to shield them from that."

That was the "accountability purpose" of the story: to make the public aware of how major American tech companies, under court order, were helping the government gather intelligence, Gellman said. First of all, Silicon Valley has long fostered an image of independence from the government, of being renegades and innovators who began their businesses in garages and basements. Second, these firms—even before Snowden—did not want to be linked too closely to spy agencies, lest they be seen as fueling a modern surveillance state, a perception that could jeopardize their billions of dollars in profits.

Litt, however, pointed out that the companies were barred by court order from revealing their cooperation, because that was classified. "The fact is," he told me, "we had reason to believe that the people whose communications we were intercepting were not focusing on the fact that we had the ability to collect them. Once it was spread out in the *Washington Post*, we saw potential targets stay away from a particular platform, because they knew the NSA could look at it" and urge others to stay away from it.

Litt's point raises the question about the extent to which the government should be transparent about how it conducts surveillance in today's wired world, where more data than ever is flowing across more platforms in myriad ways—and often through the servers of American companies. An informed electorate is central to a healthy democracy. As Litt makes clear, disclosure could aid adversaries. Yet as long as US communications platforms are in the hands of the private sector, it should not be a surprise that the government relies on these firms for collection purposes. Americans ought to know under what circumstances this collection happens and with what privacy and civil liberties protections. And they ought to be comfortable with the collection and those constraints.

One could argue—and government officials often do—that the checks placed on the government's use of privately collected data are more stringent than those imposed by the companies themselves. In fact, firms are subject to few limits on how they can collect, use, and store data, whereas the government is subject to many. In a sense, the PRISM story was just as much about the tension faced by Silicon Valley—wanting to preserve an image of independence from the government while fulfilling its obligation to comply with court orders—as it was about the program itself.

Perhaps the most controversial aspect of the story derived from one of the forty-one slides that Gellman and Poitras relied on. This slide characterized the NSA as having "direct access" to the companies' servers. The story's lead paragraph flatly stated: "The National Security Agency and the FBI are tapping directly into the central servers of nine leading US Internet companies, extracting audio and video chats, photographs, e-mails, documents, and connection logs that enable analysts to track foreign targets, according to a top-secret document obtained by The Washington Post."[1]

When the story was posted online, an uproar ensued. The companies, including Facebook and Apple, loudly objected. Within minutes of the article appearing, I got a call from a lawyer for one of the companies, who, quite agitated, told me, "The NSA does not have direct access!" I alerted Gellman, who was also hearing objections from Silicon Valley and the agency. He inserted the firms' denials. Then he found a document that described how the NSA's access was attenuated and updated the article with that information.

"It is possible that the conflict between the PRISM slides and the company spokesmen is the result of imprecision on the part of the NSA author," he stated in the updated article. "In another classified report obtained by The Post, the arrangement is described as allowing 'collection managers [to send] content tasking instructions directly to equipment installed at company-controlled locations,' rather than directly to company servers."

Still, the top of the article went unchanged, dismaying IC officials who felt it was hard to change an impression once it was out there. "There were no scenarios," Turner said, "in which the Intelligence Community was able to gather or touch data and not have the tech companies know that we were doing it."

Gellman told me that he informed Litt, the ODNI lawyer designated to speak for the IC, that he was planning to refer to the direct access slide. Following the *Post*'s standards of due diligence and fairness, he wanted to give the agency an opportunity to respond, clarify, or correct. The problem, Turner said, was that the intelligence officials were not in a position to do more than inform a reporter that his information or interpretation was incorrect. They could not provide the correct information, because doing so would divulge classified information. In this instance, Gellman said, agency officials did not object or alert him that his characterization of direct access was inaccurate.

Litt, for his part, said he does not remember Gellman apprising him of the direct access point—or at least of conveying how prominent it would be in the article. "Had he run that by," Litt said, "somebody would have said, 'That's not right, Bart.'" Turner, who was with Litt during the call with Gellman, said that while he recalls discussion about the direct access slide, he does not remember Gellman saying specifically that he intended to report on it, and he attributes that to the fact that the story "was still coming together as we were talking to him."

Gellman's mention of the slide likely did not provoke a stronger reaction initially from the agency because, in fact, within the NSA, as Gellman later learned, the phrase "direct access" is a term of art that means indirect access, while suggesting the opposite. "I've thought about it numerous times over the years," Turner said. "We probably could have done better with that misleading terminology."

Another issue, Gellman said, was the lack of a secure means to communicate with the intelligence agencies on classified materials. When he first approached them about the PRISM material, which mostly consisted of slides, he did not want to have the conversation on an open phone line. But because of classification rules, there was no other option. So he said things like "Can you please get this document with this title and this author and this date and tell me how you want to talk about it?" Or he'd say, "Everything between pages thirteen and twenty-three we're not even considering publishing, so we don't have to talk about that."

The reporters met with the agency officials in person sometimes. But often there were time constraints, and sometimes the subject matter experts were dispersed around the region and the country. So they made do with conference calls and "a lot of page this, paragraph that," Gellman said. "It was a chronic and longstanding source of frustration for me."

Rick Ledgett, a former NSA senior executive whom the deputy director had tapped to lead a newly created "media leaks" task force, said that in his experience, "in most cases," reporters did not tell the NSA what document they had, even when the agency asked for a title or document number. Instead, he said, "we played 'Go Fish.'" At one point, he said, he had twelve hundred people working for him whose job was solely to comb through massive amounts of material to try to find the documents the reporter was referring to. "Twelve hundred people whose job it was to go dumpster diving," he said.

Black Budget

The series of articles the *Post* ran on the IC's budget provoked perhaps the greatest degree of consternation inside the IC.

In the end, the *Post* ran at least five stories. They covered, among other things, how the money was spent, the NSA's effort to build a quantum computer, details of al-Qaeda's attempts to counter the US drone campaign in South Asia war zones, the US intelligence gap in Pakistan, and the spy agencies' covert insertion of tens of thousands of hardware and software "implants" in adversaries' computers overseas to gather intelligence and system access. But the *Post* held a lot back, including information about a specific intelligence-gathering capability for North Korea.

During the meeting at Liberty Crossing, Litt, the ODNI general counsel, expressed concerns that foreign intelligence services, especially the Russians, would "go to school" on the information the *Post* published. Merely describing the priorities as outlined in the budget would help them gain a deeper understanding of what the United States' blind spots were and where the IC was devoting its resources, he argued.

Miller and Gellman countered that too much secrecy was not justified. "Why is it harmful for the public to know that counterterrorism is listed as the highest priority in the budget?" Gellman said he asked. "Why can't you reveal that? . . . You've got to be kidding me if you don't think there is an epidemic of overclassification and a meaningful public interest in the enormous amount of money that US intelligence agencies have been given post-9/11."

In addition to the session held at Liberty Crossing, Turner set up a meeting between DNI Clapper and the *Post*'s editor Baron in the ODNI's office at the stately Eisenhower Executive Office Building next to the West Wing of the White House. Clapper outlined his concerns about compromising sources and methods and the insights into US capabilities that the stories could give to adversaries, Baron recalled.

"That's actually fairly general," Baron said. "Can you be more specific?"

Clapper replied, in his curt baritone, "I just was."

Clapper told me that publishing any article based on the "congressional justification budget book"—the lengthy document that the intelligence agencies submit to Congress to justify their budget request—would be harmful. For sophisticated intelligence services, such as those of the Russians and the Chinese, any glimpse into the process gives them a leg up in analyzing the US agencies' potential capabilities, even if sources and methods are not disclosed, he said.

Turner, with input from the White House, became a broker of sorts between the IC and the media. Typically, an agency expert would insist that virtually every sensitive detail needed to be withheld from publication. Turner and White House officials knew that would not fly. So, he said, they learned to ask the experts, "Of all the things you're concerned about, what are the most critical?" Then he would have a follow-up call with the reporter to say, "Okay, of the ten things laid out, here are our top three. If these are included, we will have a real problem." Generally, the reporters accommodated the requests when they were accompanied by credible explanations of the harm. That led to a "kind of calming feeling across the agency," Turner said, because although the experts did not get everything they wanted, the most significant items were withheld. "This is as close as we're going to get to a win," he told them.

In Clapper's view, there is no reconciling the differences. "The media's definition of what harms national security and my definition of what harms national security is different."

Then he added, "At least the *Washington Post* was responsible enough to talk to us."

Tapping Google/Yahoo Servers

A major objection from Clapper, Ledgett, and other senior intelligence officials at the time was that Snowden released far more material than warranted. A tiny part, they said, dealt with what might arguably be called domestic surveillance or gathering data on Americans. Vast amounts, they said, dealt with overseas collection and foreigners—not US persons.

It is true that the US Constitution spells out rights accruing to Americans and that US privacy and surveillance laws such as FISA protect US persons here and abroad and govern collection on US soil. But Snowden's leaks ignited a legitimate public policy debate born of the digital era in which collection from internet companies' servers, whether here or overseas, of necessity includes a mix of domestic and foreign bits and bytes.

One story that raised many of those thorny issues was Gellman and Soltani's October 2013 piece reporting that the NSA was secretly tapping into the communications links overseas that connect Yahoo and Google data centers around the world. The collection activity was code-named MUSCULAR.

"By tapping those links, the agency has positioned itself to collect at will from hundreds of millions of user accounts, many of them belonging to Americans," they wrote. "The NSA does not keep everything it collects, but it keeps a lot."[2]

The piece cited a top-secret document stating that the NSA "sends millions of records every day from internal Yahoo and Google networks to data warehouses at the agency's headquarters at Fort Meade, Md." In one thirty-day period, the document said, field collectors had sent back "181,280,466 new records— including 'metadata,' which would indicate who sent or received e-mails and when, as well as content such as text, audio and video."

IC lawyers asserted that the activity was lawful. If it took place on American soil, it would need court approval. But under Executive Order 12333, the NSA is permitted to gather intelligence overseas without court oversight or a warrant as long as it is not targeting an American citizen or permanent resident.[3] James A. Baker, a former FBI general counsel and senior DOJ official who is an expert on FISA, told me it is "a widely accepted" understanding of the law that "as long as you're outside the United States and not targeting a US person," the US government may acquire data in bulk, including from American companies.

According to briefing documents leaked by Snowden, collection from Yahoo and Google servers produced important intelligence leads against hostile foreign governments, Gellman and Soltani reported, without naming the adversaries. Still, the tech companies were irate. And they rushed to encrypt the data flowing between their data centers. Google's chief legal officer, David Drummond, told the *Post*, "We are outraged at the lengths to which the government seems to have gone to intercept data from our private fiber networks, and it underscores the need for urgent reform." This story, more than many others, contributed to the frosty relationship between Silicon Valley and the IC—a relationship that would only grow more strained with the encryption battles that erupted in late 2014.

Afghanistan Program

When asked to provide an example of how national security was harmed by Snowden's revelations, intelligence officials have often lamented that terrorists and other targets adopted greater security measures following the leaks. They moved to encrypted communications, changed methods, or simply went dark.

But it's also arguable that with the rise in encrypted apps, the shift to harder-to-track communications was a natural evolution in tactics.

One specific example of a concrete harm came from Clapper in September 2015, more than two years after the *Guardian*'s and the *Post*'s first stories. Speaking at a Washington, DC, intelligence conference, Clapper revealed that a key program had been shut down in Afghanistan as a result of Snowden's leaks. He didn't give details but said the program "was the single most important source of force protection and warning for our people in Afghanistan."[4]

What was the program, and how did it come to light? It turns out that the revelation came in stages, despite the press's withholding of crucial details and because another party—WikiLeaks—wanted it fully disclosed. In March 2014, the *Post*'s Gellman and Soltani reported on a program called MYSTIC under which the NSA was collecting "every single" phone conversation in a foreign country. The *Post* withheld the country's name following requests by US officials.

Two months later, the online news site the Intercept published a similar story, saying the NSA was "secretly intercepting, recording, and archiving the audio of virtually every cell phone conversation" in two nations. The Intercept named the Bahamas as one country. It refrained from naming the other, citing "specific, credible concerns that doing so could lead to increased violence."

Both the *Post* and the Intercept withheld information to prevent harm to national security. But that stance angered the anti-secrecy site WikiLeaks, which several days later reported that the country in question was Afghanistan. WikiLeaks cofounder Julian Assange, who in April 2019 was arrested in London on a US warrant and is facing prosecution under the Espionage Act for having solicited and disclosed classified material, harshly criticized the *Post* and the Intercept for having "censored" the country's name at the request of the US government. "Such censorship," Assange wrote in a statement published on-line, "strips a nation of its right to self-determination on a matter which affects its whole population. An ongoing crime of mass espionage is being committed against the victim state and its population."[5]

Shortly after WikiLeaks revealed the country, Afghan president Hamid Karzai shut down the program. The disclosure of the intimate cooperation between the Afghan and US governments—especially when framed as a surveillance program—was politically fraught for Karzai, who already had a tense relationship with Washington.

This case shows that even when a news organization seeks to withhold documents that might harm national security, other actors who do not observe a process such as the one followed by the *Post* can disclose material. This is the reality of the digital age, and it places an even greater responsibility upon the IC to protect its material. A series of breaches in the last decade, from Manning to

Snowden to others involving NSA personnel who took massive amounts of material home with them on thumb drives and disks, drives this point home.

"The government has the capacity to control information," Baron said. "It can safeguard its systems so that that information does not get out. They did a poor job, obviously. If it's important for the government to keep that information secret, then it should be especially diligent in keeping the information secret. With Snowden, there were clearly failures in terms of who they hired to handle this information and how people could extract that information without notice."

The Worst-Kept Secret in the World

The IC has cried wolf before, Miller noted. Before Snowden ever came along, the *Post* had learned that the CIA was building a secret drone base in Saudi Arabia to target an al-Qaeda affiliate in Yemen. "The CIA insisted that if you write about this, the Saudis are going to pull the plug on this," Miller recounted. "We'd be kicked out of Saudi Arabia. We would not have the ability to go after AQAP [Al-Qaeda in the Arabian Peninsula], which is the biggest threat to us right now. You will have blood on your hands."

The *Post* capitulated, killing a story that was already written, he said. Several months later, news of the drone base leaked out in a smaller online publication. Then the *Post* learned that the *New York Times* was about to break a story naming the country. "It was the worst-kept secret in the intel world—and it was all exposed," Miller said. "We basically ended up running the story that was in the system. We just did it five months later. And the Saudis didn't care. They didn't kick us out. The base is still there, as far as we know."

For all his displeasure with the disclosure of the Snowden material, Clapper said, "I don't fault the media for reporting that stuff. The fault is with people who leak the data, not with the media." In general, he said, "the reporters—with a couple of notable exceptions—were trying to get the story right. And although I might wish the story did not get published, my job was to make it less harmful than it might have been on some really important dimensions, like avoiding harm to people and to key partnerships, operational partnerships."

In 2017, then-FBI director James Comey testified that he thought WikiLeaks, which had published the Afghan war logs and State Department cables, was not engaging in journalism but trafficking in "intelligence porn," a reference to a prurient desire to know the secrets that lie behind the veil of classification because such secrets—especially the details—are generally in and of themselves sexy.[6] Ledgett said he felt a similar dynamic was at work with the Snowden documents. "My view," Ledgett said, "is there is a legitimate need in a democracy for people to understand the principles that guide intelligence, the controls on intelligence, the broad outlines of what's done, how it's done, why it's done, how well it's done." But going beyond that verges on intelligence porn. "President Obama talked about transparency," he said. "I like translucency better. Transparency is a clear pane of glass. Translucency is a frosted pane of glass. You can see outlines, but you can't see the details."

But a deeper issue is overclassification and the reflexive secrecy that permeates the US IC. "As the guy who often took the call when reporters had obtained classified information," Turner said, "I can say with certainty that there is intelligence information that was revealed by the media that probably should never have been classified in the first place."

The Snowden disclosures forced, for a while, an unprecedented degree of transparency, particularly at the NSA. In a break with standard practice, public affairs officers were now reaching out to offer on-the-record interviews with officials. The ODNI launched a website, IC on the Record, on which the public could read declassified FISC opinions, agency memos, and other material that months earlier officials such as Litt had argued could not be declassified without divulging material harmful to national security. And the disclosures also prompted government reviews and legislative reform, notably the USA Freedom Act.

Since 9/11, every major policy reckoning by the IC—on surveillance and the use of torture in interrogations—has been triggered by the media pulling the curtain back on highly classified programs. The *Post* and the *Guardian* shared the prestigious Pulitzer Prize for public service in 2014 for reporting that drew from the material Snowden disclosed.

Miller reminds us, "Secrecy almost invites abuse. The Snowden documents are like a course correction that happens every ten or twenty years. There is a pent-up internal pressure that leads to these exposures."

And when those exposures occur, there is a need to ensure that they serve to enlighten, not endanger. The system we have is not perfect. As Clapper said, there will never be an accommodation that entirely satisfies both the press and the IC.

In the end, the process is subjective, and at the *Washington Post*, editors and reporters with national security experience made sincere efforts to consult agency stakeholders. National security officials made good-faith efforts to protect information that would have caused particular harms. Where the engagement was frank and two-way, the odds of misunderstandings were lessened. Where the discussions were hurried or nonexistent, the chances of a story containing inaccuracies or revelations harmful to national security increased.

The compromise we reached in this case may not be ideal, and it's likely that this accommodation will not apply to all media in all cases. It certainly does not account for organizations such as WikiLeaks or media outlets that do not feel an obligation to consult national security officials. But in this imperfect world, it seems to me there is no better option than the push-and-pull between the media and the government that I've described. Baron perhaps put it best: "In a way, the tension between the press and government is the answer. We don't want the government to have total control over the information that we have. And we do want the press to gather information on behalf of the public."

Let's Be Practical

A Narrow Post-Publication Leak Law Would Better Protect the Press

STEPHEN J. ADLER AND BRUCE D. BROWN[*]

"The Department of Justice is open for business."
Attorney General Jeff Sessions, 2017[1]

Introduction

In the 233 years of US history before 2009, the prosecution of journalistic sources for the disclosure of national defense secrets to the press was exceedingly rare and, with only one (factually complicated) exception, unsuccessful.[2] For various reasons, pragmatic as well as legal, the government was disinclined to bring these cases, and the press generally believed that journalists themselves enjoyed some immunity from criminal prosecution for reporting based on leaked information.

Beginning with investigations under the George W. Bush administration and continuing with prosecutions under Presidents Obama and Trump, that state of affairs has changed.[3] In the last ten years, the government has brought eighteen cases against journalistic sources[4] and an additional two based on the public disclosure of classified information outside of the news media context.[5] It has won convictions or pleas in fourteen of these twenty.[6] And in 2019, the government secured an indictment based in part on the theory that the act of publishing classified documents alone violates federal spying laws, the first "pure publication" case in this line of precedent.[7]

The legal arguments advanced by the government in these cases do not preclude the worrisome prospect of a case against a journalist or news organization for publishing defense secrets. As such, the press faces a new and stark choice.

Should it continue to trust that the First Amendment provides meaningful protections in a case against a reporter or news organization for publishing secrets, or is it time to embrace a federal law that narrowly defines when such prosecutions would be permissible?

As discussed below, a successful First Amendment defense in a leak prosecution against a reporter is far from certain. The government has consistently claimed the authority to bring leak cases directly against the press—and no court has held that it cannot do so. Just as a federal shield law would provide an imperfect but important safeguard for reporters facing DOJ demands that they identify sources, a well-tailored reform of the Espionage Act should now be considered, even if that reform contemplates cases against the press that First Amendment advocates had previously thought unimaginable.[8]

Much will depend on the details. The proposal discussed below would undercorrect, for example, by still permitting conspiracy charges against a journalist provably hostile to US military operations who publishes secrets to mobilize public sentiment against those operations, and overcorrect, on the other hand, by protecting some good-faith disclosures that could harm national security.

But as with a federal shield statute, which Congress has not yet enacted, we argue that these imperfections are offset by the real protections a narrowed Espionage Act would provide in an environment where administrations of both parties have increasingly been comfortable treating journalistic sources, and now the straight publication of secrets, as akin to spying.

Further, just as a statutory federal shield law would still permit a reporter to argue separately for a privilege based on the First Amendment, passage of a reform package would not eliminate the possibility of First Amendment protections in an Espionage Act prosecution. Indeed, while the success of a constitutional challenge may be uncertain, arguments would remain, under various theories, that putting the press on trial in cases where national security disclosures in the news media promote government accountability would violate the First Amendment.

As Alexander Bickel wrote with respect to the Pentagon Papers case, those "freedoms which are neither challenged nor defined are the most secure."[9] An unchallenged and undefined freedom to publish national defense information is certainly preferable. However, the proliferation of leak cases over the last decade suggests that a "challenge"—a case against the press for publishing government secrets—may be on the horizon. Legislation provides a floor that permits First Amendment defenses but also acts as a backstop if those arguments fail.

Unless we believe that the pendulum of history will swing dramatically back to prosecutorial forbearance in these cases—and that is unlikely—congressional intervention is now imperative. The challenge will be making that intervention as limited and precise as possible so that it doesn't inadvertently create a dangerous new power to prosecute the press for publishing national security secrets in the public interest (or expand the government's authority to prosecute sources, which itself chills newsgathering). But given recent history, that possibility should not dissuade First Amendment advocates from trying to reform the law, and we should support efforts to craft the most effective reform possible.

This essay proceeds in five parts. After the introduction, the next part explores the contours of the Espionage Act reform proposal currently pending in Congress and how it could intersect with the First Amendment. Then the third part argues that the press's reliance on the tacit understanding that it would not be prosecuted for responsibly publishing government secrets is preferable to a new law but that recent events have shaken that understanding. The fourth part surveys the pendulum's swing, in just the last decade, away from government forbearance. The fifth part is the conclusion.

Espionage Act Reform Efforts and the First Amendment

In March 2020, Senator Ron Wyden (D-OR) and Representative Ro Khanna (D-CA) introduced a bill to narrow the Espionage Act.[10] The Espionage Act, read literally, permits the government to prosecute individuals as spies who have sworn no oath of secrecy to the United States and who disclose national defense information.[11] To our knowledge, Wyden-Khanna is only the second narrowing bill to be introduced since passage of the Espionage Act shortly after America's entry into World War I.[12]

The bill would make two major changes to existing law. One, it would limit the direct application of the law to individuals who have a security clearance as part of their work with the government.[13]

Two, and important, it would permit charges under theories of conspiracy, aiding and abetting, or accessory after the fact against an individual who has not pledged to keep secrets *only* if the government can prove that the individual acted with specific intent to cause serious harm to the United States and directly helped acquire the relevant information. (The person must "directly and materially aid[]" or "procure ... for monetary value" the commission of the offense.) The bill envisions a case where, for instance, a non-covered reporter who desires to harm the United States provides a government employee with the key to a government safe, which is not something that an editor or newsroom lawyer would encourage or condone in a journalist.[14]

It is important that, with one exception, the bill would narrow only the Espionage Act, meaning the government could still use other statutes, such as computer crimes or false statement laws, to punish leakers and potentially the press.[15] These statutes pose their own First Amendment risks, and misuse of these laws against journalistic sources or journalists would, of course, still be subject to First Amendment challenge. Wyden-Khanna would not change that.

With respect to the Espionage Act, the question, then, is whether the press in a post-publication prosecution would be better off with a straight First Amendment defense under the law as it exists today or under an amended statute that significantly limits such prosecutions but does not eliminate them. Were a constitutional challenge to an Espionage Act prosecution of the press likely to succeed, it might be better to rely on the First Amendment rather than on a reform law that confirms the power to prosecute the press. Conversely, uncertainty around a constitutional defense counsels in favor of a remedial law, even if it would permit such prosecutions in extraordinary cases.

When it comes to post-publication punishment of the press under the Espionage Act, the First Amendment tea leaves are mixed. At least one judge in the first successful Espionage Act source prosecution prior to 2009 said that the press "probably" could not be prosecuted for publishing national defense information.[16] Additionally, a defendant could point to the various US Supreme Court cases, not in the Espionage Act context, establishing constitutional protections for the publication of truthful newsworthy information when disclosure would otherwise violate the law (including laws criminalizing the disclosure of the names of rape victims, juvenile offenders, or judges subject to disciplinary proceedings).[17]

These cases make clear that any restraint on the publication of truthful information—be it a prior restraint or post hoc punishment—can only stand if it furthers "a state interest of the highest order."[18] And although the Supreme Court has never found an interest sufficiently weighty to justify a pre- or post-publication sanction, the Court has also conspicuously noted that there was no illegality on the part of the news organization when recognizing First Amendment protections for publication. Further, although these cases can be read expansively, the Court's holdings can also be read narrowly and limited to their facts.

For instance, in the *Daily Mail* case, the Court refused to find that the state's interest in protecting the identity of juvenile offenders was sufficient to permit West Virginia to punish the publication of an offender's name, which was gleaned through ordinary newsgathering activities, but it also offered a narrower ground to decide the case: that the relevant law only applied to newspapers, not other forms of media.[19] Justice Rehnquist rested his concurrence on that fact.[20]

This line of cases culminated in *Bartnicki v. Vopper*, which, in 2001, held that the wiretapping laws could not constitutionally be applied to the airing of intercepted conversations so long as the broadcaster had not been involved in the illegal acquisition.[21] In that case, Justice Stevens applied "parallel reasoning" to the logic of *New York Times v. Sullivan*.[22] That is, the commitment to the "principle that debate on public issues should be uninhibited, robust, and wide-open ... requires the conclusion that a stranger's illegal conduct does not suffice to remove the First Amendment shield from speech about a matter of public concern."[23]

And while the majority opinion in *Bartnicki* could be read to suggest a broader rule—that absent any underlying illegality by the news organization or journalist, the publication of intercepted communications may not be punished—it could also be read more narrowly. Justice Breyer wrote a concurrence joined by Justice O'Connor holding that the ruling does not stand for a "broader constitutional immunity."[24] Rather, Justice Breyer applied an explicit balancing of "competing constitutional concerns": privacy and free expression. He would have held that because the broadcaster acted lawfully and because the underlying recording could be considered a physical threat, the free expression interests were high and the privacy interests low.[25] Further, Chief Justice William Rehnquist (elevated since the *Daily Mail* decision), joined by Justices Antonin Scalia and Clarence Thomas, dissented entirely.[26]

Accordingly, while one could argue that Justice Stevens's "parallel reasoning" extending *Sullivan* to *Bartnicki* ought to protect the publication of true, newsworthy government secrets from criminal liability under the Espionage Act, no court has ever addressed the question. Further, with facts like those in the Assange prosecution—where the government has alleged a colorable criminal offense (the password cracking)—a court applying a more explicit balancing approach like the one favored by Justice Breyer could find, for the first time, that the state interest in national security trumps free expression considerations.

Finally, while it is true that what we are calling the three "pure publication" counts do not rest as a legal matter on the password-cracking allegation, a court could find that the underlying illegality somehow "infects"—our word, not a term of art—those counts enough to bring the case outside of the *Bartnicki* protections.

All of that having been said, there are arguments—independent of the *Bartnicki* case—that post-publication punishment of the press would violate the First Amendment. These arguments—including facial vagueness and overbreadth challenges, along with clear indications in the legislative history that the law was never intended to apply to the receipt or publication of defense information by the media—have grown only stronger with the proliferation of leak prosecutions since 2009.[27] Even with the Wyden-Khanna amendment, those arguments would also be available in journalistic source cases, though they have been historically unsuccessful.

By contrast, arguments that the First Amendment would allow the post-publication punishment of the press include the fact that three of the Justices in the Pentagon Papers case expressly said they would permit an Espionage Act prosecution, and two implied that they would.[28] And, as discussed above, the *Bartnicki* line of cases does not expressly cover Espionage Act prosecutions, and no court has ever considered, let alone resolved, the issue.

Further, the DOJ has consistently taken the position that the Espionage Act *does* apply to the publication of defense information by the press, based on the plain terms of the statute. For instance, in a case involving a 1975 *New York Times* story about a submarine surveillance program against the Soviets called Operation Holystone, Attorney General Edward Levi expressly confirmed in a memorandum to President Gerald Ford the DOJ's belief that section 793(e) of the Espionage Act covers the press, and that the term "communicates" in that provision encompasses the act of publication.[29]

Similarly, the administration of Ronald Reagan, in the formal report of the Inter-Agency Group on Unauthorized Disclosure of Classified Information, known informally as the Willard Report after its chair, Deputy Assistant Attorney General Richard K. Willard, found that, "[The Espionage Act] could also be used to prosecute a journalist who knowingly receives and publishes classified documents or information."[30]

Finally, in all of the cases that have analyzed whether the Espionage Act is unconstitutionally vague or overbroad as applied to the dissemination of information *to* the press, the courts have rejected vagueness and overbreadth arguments.[31]

In short, First Amendment law on post-publication punishment of the press is unsettled, perhaps more so than many believe.

An Unwritten Understanding Is Preferable but May No Longer Be Viable

As noted, the rarity of cases before 2009 involving the dissemination of national defense information to or by the press led to a sense on the part of both the government and the press that the former would forbear from prosecutions except in extreme circumstances, and the latter would "consider the responsibilities that its position implies."[32] The dearth of confrontations between the press and prosecutors during this era suggests that this unwritten understanding was, as a practical matter, a more effective protection than that provided by the First Amendment.

Following his praise for undefined and unchallenged freedoms, Bickel continued:

> In this sense, for example, it is true that the American press was freer before it won its battle with the government in *New York Times Company v. United* States . . . in 1971. Before June 15, 1971, through the troubles of 1798, through one civil and two world wars and other wars, there had never been an effort by the federal government to censor a newspaper by attempting to impose a restraint prior to publication, directly or in litigation. The New York Times won its case . . . but that spell was broken, and in a sense freedom was thus diminished. . . .
>
> We are, or at least we feel, freer when we feel no need to extend our freedom. The conflict and contention by which we extend freedom seem to mark, or at least to threaten, a contraction; and in truth they do, for they endanger an assumed freedom which appeared limitless because its limits were untried. Appearance and reality are nearly one. We extend the legal reality of freedom at some cost to its limitless appearance. And the cost is real.[33]

Bickel, counsel for the *New York Times* in the Pentagon Papers case, wrote this passage in his essay crediting our "disorderly system" of checks and balances that pits self-interested parties against other self-interested parties as the ultimate maximizer of individual rights and good government.[34] Bickel recognized that dynamic as also mirroring the adversarial posture of the news media relative to government power: "[The First Amendment] ordains an unruly contest between the press, whose office is freedom of information and whose ambition is joined to that office, and government, whose need is often the privacy of decision-making and whose servants are ambitious to satisfy that need."[35] Bickel called this tug of war between the government's ability to keep secrets and the press's right to report them, absent "immediate harm of the gravest sort," a "disorderly situation."[36]

Ultimately, Bickel said, "The best resolution of this contest lies in an untidy accommodation; like democracy, in Churchill's aphorism, it is the worst possible solution, except for all the other ones."[37] And this "accommodation works well only when there is forbearance and continence on both sides. It threatens to break down when the adversaries turn into enemies, when they break diplomatic relations with each other, gird for and wage war."[38]

Under his framework, this "accommodation" between the press and the government began to erode with the Pentagon Papers case. That erosion continues today, evidenced by growing concern that a case against the press for reporting on government secrets may be near. The press should certainly strive for an accommodation, but it must also acknowledge the possibility, based on recent experience, that future accommodation seems less probable.

Inevitably, critics of a legislative solution to this looming confrontation will make two related arguments, which bear discussion but cannot be resolved in the Wyden-Khanna proposal without real harm to an independent press.

One, many would argue that a bill should define "journalism." That is, only the responsible gathering, receipt, and publication of defense secrets—reported through the filter of established journalistic ethics—should be granted First Amendment protection. (It is arguable that Wyden-Khanna tries to do this indirectly by requiring proof of malicious intent.)

Two, modern technology has increased the potential harm from disclosures. The government is creating the digital equivalent of tens of millions of filing cabinets of classified information every month, and the internet makes it possible to release that information en masse. Critics would argue that any reform legislation should therefore permit charges against an individual or entity that publishes defense secrets online indiscriminately.

As with the first point above, an ideal bill for these critics would delineate and protect "legitimate" journalism while exposing "non-state hostile intelligence agenc[ies]"—as then-CIA director Mike Pompeo put the distinction in 2017 with respect to WikiLeaks—to prosecution.[39]

Ultimately, though, this approach would be a direct threat to a free and independent press, as it allows the government to determine what constitutes "bona fide" journalism. The closest an acceptable law could come to separating the malicious actor from the benign is by requiring prosecutors to prove specific intent to harm the United States. That may result in cases of overcorrection, where some legitimately sensitive information is disclosed but, in the absence of bad faith, the government cannot charge it. Under our political traditions, where the press is specifically named in the Constitution, that is the right result.

The First Amendment errs on the side of protecting the disclosure of truthful information about government activities because the alternative is a less robust public discourse. We shield "bad" speech to insulate the good. That has been our national consensus in cases going back to *Near v. Minnesota*.[40] As Justice O'Connor wrote in *Philadelphia Newspapers v. Hepps*, "[W]here the scales are in such an uncertain balance, we believe that the Constitution requires us to tip them in favor of protecting true speech."[41]

Further, the need to protect truthful information is more acute, not less, in cases involving national security. If a decision to classify a government secret itself automatically triggers potential criminal liability (for the press or for government sources), it turns the classification system into a potent means of censorship. We know from history that such tools will often be used to silence speech critical of or embarrassing to those who wield them. As Justice Stewart wrote in the Pentagon Papers case, "For when everything is classified, then nothing is classified, and the system becomes one to be disregarded by the cynical or the careless, and to be manipulated by those intent on self-protection or self-promotion."[42]

Unfortunately, the scales have tipped today toward the *suppression* of speech in national security reporting. The federal government now sees journalistic sources as spies. That trend began in the years after 9/11, accelerated during the Obama administration, and continues with President Trump. It knows no party or political ideology, and many dedicated public servants believe that the scales should tip further away from protecting fact-driven journalism that potentially threatens national defense.

Transparency and public accountability must be the guiding principles of laws around leaks. Occasionally, tipping the scales in favor of speech might indeed overcorrect and permit ethically questionable publishers to take advantage of the American commitment to expressive freedoms. But that is our risk as an open society. It is because "[m]en feared witches and burnt women" that we have as a country always been tugged back to a belief in free discourse and been dubious of giving the government the power of the censor.[43]

The only question then is: Is the current state of play so bad that it is now time to entertain the notion of opening up the Espionage Act to reform? As surveyed below, we believe circumstances have forced our hand and the answer is yes.

The Modern History of Prosecuting Sources as Spies
World War I to 2009

Many often begin the history of confrontation between journalists, their sources, and the federal spying laws with the unsuccessful criminal prosecution of Daniel Ellsberg and Anthony Russo in the Pentagon Papers case.[44] It is certainly true that this is the most prominent case in modern memory, though there are several others that predate the Ellsberg/Russo Espionage Act prosecution, which ended in dismissal following revelations of government misconduct.

If anything, these earlier cases actually demonstrate the pendulum's swing in the early years of the Espionage Act toward the government's reluctance to prosecute. In other words, these cases show that while the government occasionally gave serious consideration to prosecuting journalistic sources and the press itself, something invariably pulled it off the cliff.

Famously, in 1929, for instance, President Herbert Hoover's secretary of state, Henry Stimson, closed the "American Black Chamber," the peacetime successor to military cryptographic efforts, saying, "Gentlemen do not read each other's mail." Black Chamber chief Herbert Yardley (suddenly out of work) wrote a tell-all book. And prosecution under the 1917 Espionage Act was considered but rejected.

Following Yardley, there were just three other pre–Pentagon Papers journalistic source cases: the empaneling of a grand jury in 1942 to investigate the *Chicago Tribune* and war correspondent Stanley Johnston for the leak of information about the Battle of Midway; the *Amerasia* case in 1945; and the court-martial of John Nickerson in 1957. All were unsuccessful or resulted in a plea on significantly reduced charges.

In 1972, the adventures of President Nixon's "plumbers" and the offer to the trial judge of the FBI directorship doomed the Ellsberg/Russo prosecution. It was only in 1985—almost seventy years after passage of the Espionage Act—that the DOJ finally secured a clean spying conviction against a journalistic source.

In 1984, Navy analyst Samuel Loring Morison sent a British periodical three classified photographs taken by a KH-11 reconnaissance satellite of the Soviet Union's first nuclear-powered aircraft carrier, then under construction. He was indicted, tried, and convicted in federal court in Baltimore. His appeal was denied in 1988, and he served eight months of a two-year sentence.

But, again, the pendulum's position during the *Morison* case still suggested a strong press rights constituency in government. Following Morison's conviction, Senator Daniel Patrick Moynihan, the preeminent expert on government secrecy in Congress, began lobbying for a pardon. Senator Moynihan was not driven by sympathy for Morison but rather objected to the theory and singularity of the case. As Moynihan wrote in a 1998 letter to President Bill Clinton:

> What is remarkable is not the crime, but that he is the only one convicted of an activity which has become a routine aspect of government life: leaking information to the press in order to bring pressure to bear on a policy question.
>
> As President Kennedy has said, "the ship of state leaks from the top." An evenhanded prosecution of leakers could imperil an entire administration. If ever there were to be widespread action taken, it would significantly hamper the ability of the press to function.[45]

In 2001, President Clinton pardoned Morison.

The years between 2001 and 2009 were relatively quiet on the leaks front, with only two exceptions. Indeed, these instances seem particularly exceptional given that the years immediately following the attacks of September 11, 2001, featured anonymous sources confirming CIA black-site secret prisons, the use of enhanced interrogation techniques such as waterboarding, NSA "warrantless wiretapping" and "bulk" metadata collection, and law enforcement targeting of populations based on religion, ethnicity, and national origin.

That the only two cases during that span involved an alleged conspiracy among a Pentagon analyst and two employees of a pro-Israel organization to leak information about Iran, and the *Libby* case, neither of which really fits the mold of the *Morison* prosecution, again suggests an appetite for forbearance.

The Obama Administration: Leibowitz through Cartwright

The first Obama era case was that of Shamai Leibowitz, an FBI linguist who pled guilty before trial in 2009 to violating the signals intelligence provision of the Espionage Act for disclosing to a blogger details of US wiretaps of conversations at the Israeli embassy. Leibowitz received a twenty-month sentence. The case received significant attention in the small world of "leak law"—it was, after all, similar in theory to Morison's prosecution—but it wasn't major national news.

But in 2010, things started to change, and, we would argue, the pendulum started its decade-long swing to where we are today. First was the Espionage Act prosecution against alleged NSA leaker Thomas Drake (which, to be clear, started under President Bush). The Drake case ended in a misdemeanor plea agreement on a computer crime charge.

Then came WikiLeaks. Beginning in mid-2010, the website started publishing tranches of military logs from the Afghanistan and Iraq wars, followed by leaks of State Department cables. In May 2010, military authorities arrested Chelsea Manning at a forward operating base in Iraq in connection with the leaks.

Manning was ultimately court-martialed for the disclosures, facing numerous charges under the Espionage Act and one charge of "aiding the enemy," a death penalty offense (though Army prosecutors told defense lawyers they would not seek the death penalty). While acquitted on that most serious charge, Manning was convicted and sentenced in August 2013 to thirty-five years in prison under the Espionage Act and other provisions, including computer crime laws. As discussed below, the WikiLeaks "War Logs" and "Cablegate" leaks continue to feature in the public debate today—and Manning was imprisoned from March 2019 to March 2020 for refusing to cooperate with a grand jury that is reportedly still investigating the 2010 WikiLeaks disclosures.

That year, 2010, brought two more high-profile cases. In one, that of State Department analyst Stephen Jin-Woo Kim, the government sought and obtained an email search warrant for then–Fox News national security reporter James Rosen. Kim accepted a plea in 2013. Finally, in December 2010, the DOJ charged Jeffrey Sterling, a former CIA officer, in connection with a Clinton administration covert plan to disrupt the Iranian nuclear program. He was convicted at trial.

The *Sterling* case also began during the Bush administration, with a notable subpoena against the press. Prosecutors had sought to compel testimony from reporter James Risen on the identity of his sources for a book about the Clinton program. The Risen subpoena resulted in a major Fourth Circuit decision refusing to recognize a reporter's privilege, though prosecutors ultimately decided not to force Risen to testify about his sources. The Risen subpoena was one of two such efforts to compel a reporter to disclose sources under the Obama administration. The other, against then–Fox News reporter Mike Levine in 2011, also produced a green light in court for the DOJ to demand source information, but as in the Risen case, it did not proceed.

Prosecutors continued to bring these cases in 2012. In April, CIA official John Kiriakou was charged under the Espionage Act in connection with disclosures about the interrogation program; he pled guilty in 2013 to disclosing the identity of an undercover CIA officer. An FBI bomb technician was charged with leaking details of the so-called underwear bomb plot to a reporter. (His case included a controversial subpoena for phone records from numerous lines at the Associated Press.) A contract Navy linguist was charged in part for sending defense information to a public archive at Stanford University.

In June 2013, news outlets began reporting on a cache of NSA documents containing details about two secret post-9/11 surveillance programs. Soon the source, Edward Snowden, revealed his identity publicly. He continues to face Espionage Act charges in absentia.

Finally, in 2015, Obama administration prosecutors sought to try the highest-ranking discloser to date, former CIA director and Army general David Petraeus, for disclosing secrets to his biographer. He accepted a plea agreement on lesser charges and received probation. The last Obama era case was that of Marine general James Cartwright for allegedly making false statements to FBI agents investigating leaks about the Stuxnet computer virus. Cartwright pled guilty and was pardoned before sentencing.

In sum, over the eight years of the Obama administration, the DOJ investigated and prosecuted nine or eleven cases, depending on how one counts, involving the unauthorized disclosure of national defense information to the public.[46] (Some lists omit Petraeus and the Stanford public archive case.) Further, all of these cases, save Snowden's, resulted in conviction, though some on reduced charges.[47]

The Obama administration's record stands in contrast to the mere five attempted leak prosecutions over the entire 230 years of prior American history, of which only one (*Morison*) resulted in a successful conviction under the Espionage Act, and two (*Amerasia* and *Nickerson*) resulted in conviction under lesser charges.

The Trump Administration: Reality Winner
through the Present

As of December 2019, DOJ prosecutors under President Trump have brought charges in nine cases involving the unauthorized disclosure of government secrets to the press, including the Assange indictment, which we discuss below, and two cases for the disclosure of controlled financial information under bank secrecy laws.[48] Of these, prosecutors secured successful plea agreements on Espionage Act charges in two and on a false statement charge in one.[49]

The Trump administration's record on unauthorized disclosures is notable in that it includes the longest sentence to date, that of NSA contractor and former Air Force linguist Reality Winner, at sixty-three months, and the second-longest, that of former FBI agent Terry Albury, at forty-eight months. The actual number of cases doesn't diverge dramatically from the Obama administration in that eight of the eleven Obama administration cases were brought before his second term.[50]

Additionally, the Obama administration featured three high-profile subpoenas to the press—the Associated Press subpoena in *Sachtleben*, the Risen subpoena in *Sterling*, and the Levine subpoena—as well as the Rosen "co-conspirator" email search warrant. As far as the authors are aware, the Trump administration has issued only one subpoena to a member of the press, in the James Wolfe false statement case.

Further, at the time of writing, there are at least two cases under the Trump administration where the defendant has sought to challenge his indictment under the First Amendment. Most notably, federal defenders in Virginia are seeking to dismiss the indictment of Daniel Everette Hale, accused of leaking details of CIA and military drone operations to the press, on First Amendment grounds.

The Reporters Committee filed an amicus brief in that case, arguing that the First Amendment analysis must be considered in light of the proliferation of leak cases since 2009. Specifically, the Reporters Committee argued that to the extent that the law has been used to prosecute sources revealing newsworthy information in the public interest, there is now evidence of "overbreadth"—as these cases suggest the law can be used to criminalize a substantial amount of constitutionally protected expression.

It also argued that given the frequency of leaks—"a routine activity of government life," as Senator Moynihan put it—the uncertainty around when the government will seek to prosecute a leak speaks to the law's "vagueness." An overly vague law also violates the First Amendment.

Further, in the 1988 *Morison* appeal, the two concurring judges rested much of their concurrences on their belief that these cases would be rare and would not impose a chill on newsgathering.[51] The Reporters Committee brief illustrates how the former contention has proven inaccurate and that chill can be demonstrated and perhaps now even quantified.

Finally, as noted, the Assange case involves novel legal arguments that bear special mention. The Australian-born founder of WikiLeaks had been living in the Ecuadorian embassy in London until April 11, 2019, when the Ecuadorian government revoked his asylum and he was arrested at the request of American authorities. That day, the DOJ unsealed a one-count indictment against Assange for conspiracy to violate a section of the primary federal computer crime law, the Computer Fraud and Abuse Act (CFAA). The provision under which he was charged makes it a federal crime to hack into a computer to obtain classified information.

It is important that the agreement that formed the basis for the conspiracy charge was the solicitation, receipt, and publication of classified information exfiltrated by Manning. But there was one aspect to the government's theory that made this initial one-count indictment "a hard model for future prosecutions targeting the press."[52]

That is, because the government charged the crime under the general federal conspiracy statute, it had to allege an "overt act" in service of the conspiracy. One of those acts was an alleged assurance that Assange would use his own computer resources to "crack" a password that would have given Manning access to someone else's account on the military's "secret"-level classified network. That is not conduct that newsroom leaders or media lawyers would ever counsel a reporter to undertake.

But the government then unsealed, on May 23, 2019, an eighteen-count superseding indictment charging Assange with the CFAA conspiracy and adding seventeen counts under the Espionage Act. All of the Espionage Act counts are based on the same theory as the CFAA charge: that the solicitation, receipt, and publication of classified information alone can constitute conspiring to violate, or aiding and abetting a violation of, the Espionage Act. None, save the lone CFAA charge, is reliant on the password-cracking allegation.

Further, three of those counts charge Assange as the principal violator of Section 793(e) of the Espionage Act based exclusively on one fact: that he published classified documents online "to all the world." As discussed above, this is the first time in American history that the government has successfully secured an indictment based on an act of "pure publication."

The government has argued that Assange is "no journalist" and that the Assange case is distinguishable because Assange failed to redact the names of US informants and assets when publishing the Manning documents.

While the failure to redact this information serves to distinguish Assange, as an ethical matter, from news organizations that reported on the same material, it is not a legal distinction. There is nothing in these "pure publication" counts that would preclude the government from bringing charges under the same theory against a reporter or news outlet. The government's legal theory under Section 793(e) of the Espionage Act is that Assange had "unauthorized possession" of national defense information and that he "willfully" communicated it to others not entitled to receive it (to "all the world") by "publishing [it] on the internet." The news organizations that reported on the Manning disclosures did the same thing.

Conclusion: Half a Loaf Is Better Than No Bread

The tension between national security secrecy and transparency is not new. Arguably, the first leak case predated the First Amendment by more than a decade. Thomas Paine resigned as secretary of the Committee of Foreign Affairs in 1779 after being criticized (and physically beaten) for allegedly embarrassing France by publicly disclosing early aid to the American Revolution.[53] Similar controversies occurred—largely in connection with leaks from Congress—throughout the nineteenth and early twentieth centuries.

But through the Civil War, World War I, World War II, Korea, Vietnam, all of the Cold War, the first Gulf War, the Balkans, the Afghanistan invasion, and the Iraq occupation, there were only a handful of national security leak prosecutions, of which only the *Morison* case saw a successful conviction under the spying laws.

And that prosecutorial forbearance was not for lack of opportunity—or desire. Rather, as many of the examples of conscious forbearance in the historical record show, the decision not to prosecute was often driven by a complex mix of concern over further disclosures, fear of public backlash or follow-on scandals for the politicians involved, and even principled adherence to the American ideal of a free and independent press.

On December 30, 1971, for instance, it is well known that the Nixon administration indicted Ellsberg under the Espionage Act for leaking the Pentagon Papers. Less well known is that—on that very day—the "Moorer-Radford" scandal was unfolding in the White House.[54] Yeoman Charles Radford, a Navy stenographer, would ultimately admit that he stole classified documents from the National Security Council, where he was assigned, and leaked them to the Joint Chiefs of Staff (Admiral Thomas Moorer was the chairman).[55]

Crucially, many also suspected that Radford was an anonymous source for "Washington Merry-Go-Round" columnist Jack Anderson, who had repeatedly embarrassed the White House with scoops about foreign policy during the India-Pakistan War and domestic scandal with the "I.T.T. Affair," involving alleged bribes for a favorable merger decision.[56]

Though the Radford affair hit far closer to the Nixon White House than the Pentagon Papers, the president decided to take no action.[57] Part of letting Radford go (in exile to a remote posting in Oregon) was that Admiral Moorer was now more pliable, having been caught.[58] But the White House also discussed and declined to take action against Anderson.[59] An aide wrote a memo for the president confirming that Anderson could likely be prosecuted for the theft of government documents.[60] Nixon, however, demurred: "The only two guys who can prove it are the source and Anderson."[61] Bringing Anderson in to testify against Radford "would be a fatal mistake—you can't bring a newsman in [without generating media backlash]."[62] That didn't stop the Nixon administration from using extralegal tactics to discredit Anderson, including a CIA surveillance operation called Celotex, but it left Ellsberg and Russo as the only leaks-as-spying case under that presidency.

Similarly, the Levi memorandum in the Operation Holystone case mentioned earlier says the government has ample authority to bring a spying case against a newspaper but ultimately recommends: "the most promising course of action, for the moment, would be to discuss the problem of publication of material detrimental to the national security with leading publishers."[63] In other words, despite a feared national security breach so severe that it demanded the attention not just of President Ford's chief of staff, Donald Rumsfeld, but of Rumsfeld's deputy, Richard Cheney, the proffered solution was as it usually was: to talk it out.

The DOJ in the Holystone sequel, Ivy Bells, was even more pithy. Despite threats from the CIA and the NSA, credible enough that the *Washington Post* delayed publication of an article for months, the DOJ simply told *Time* magazine, "We're not hot to trot on this thing."[64]

It is important that inclinations toward forbearance do seem to have survived even into the modern era of leaks prosecutions. Reporting suggests that several federal prosecutors under both the Obama and Trump administrations disagreed with bringing charges against Assange specifically for fear of First Amendment harm, though ultimately, that position was overruled after the renewed focus on leaks led federal prosecutors in Virginia to take another look at the case.[65]

But regardless, even if there are press-friendly elements in government today, the pendulum is indeed swinging. The reasons aren't completely clear but probably include some combination of bureaucratic inertia, political posturing, genuine fear of national security harm, the proliferation of and ease of access to electronic fingerprints, and, most ominously, perhaps a sense that public outcry over these cases is, over time, becoming more muted.

The threat, in any event, is entirely clear. As Matthew Miller, DOJ public affairs lead from 2009 to 2011 told *New York Times* reporter Charlie Savage, "When we took office . . . I don't think bringing a lot of leak cases was high on anyone's agenda. But then they came up one by one, and without realizing it, we had set a record."[66]

That post-2009 record now stands at eighteen cases directly implicating the news media and twenty cases involving the public disclosure of government secrets rather than traditional spying. All of these cases started as spying investigations, and many ended as spying convictions. In one of the most recent cases, the DOJ deployed a legal theory never before approved by a grand jury: that by publishing secrets "to all the world," one acts as a spy.[67]

At the same time, the mainstream press faces significant challenges: to its legitimacy, to its competency, and to its sustainability. Further, while the proliferation of leak prosecutions post-2009 has occurred under presidents of both parties, President Trump has made cracking down on leaks a priority of his administration,[68] and he's done so while calling the press an "enemy of the people"[69] and suggesting that the media commits treason when it publishes national security stories he would prefer to keep secret.[70]

To be sure, the press should not be immune from public scrutiny or criticism. But this confluence of challenges comes at a time when the delicate equipoise between the press and the government, which served as an unwritten, de facto protection for press rights in America, has also eroded.

James Madison opposed the Bill of Rights before he ultimately wrote the First Amendment and the other codicils to our Constitution. He feared written protections in part because he believed the act of definition would invite their challenge and imply that those rights not defined would be assumed not to exist.[71] Madison changed his mind after Thomas Jefferson famously argued, "Half a loaf is better than no bread."[72]

The pendulum of history may swing back the press's way at some point. But right now, the legal and practical realities recounted above suggest that a spying case against a journalist for reporting on a leak is no longer a remote possibility. To the extent that Congress can better define press rights under the Espionage Act, even if it means confirming a government power vis-à-vis the press that to date has remained hypothetical, the press should take that half a loaf.

What We Owe Whistleblowers

JAMEEL JAFFER

In the years since the September 2001 terrorist attacks, the United States has paid a staggering price for excessive secrecy. Time and again, national security policies crafted behind closed doors and shielded from public scrutiny have proved to be deeply flawed, with far-reaching consequences for life, liberty, and security. Mistakes, excesses, and abuses that might have been avoided or quickly corrected had they been subjected to prompt outside review have led to ill-considered war,[1] the gross infringement of human rights,[2] the alienation of our allies,[3] the fortification of our enemies,[4] the misdirection of colossal amounts of money,[5] the erosion of the United States' influence around the world,[6] and the sapping of Americans' confidence in the competence of their government.[7]

And yet the price we have paid for excessive secrecy would have been greater still had it not been for government insiders who disclosed official secrets in order to inform the public about official decisions they believed to be wrong. Americans learned about the abuses at Abu Ghraib only because a soldier, in defiance of orders from superiors, supplied photographs to the *New Yorker* and *60 Minutes*. When we learned about the CIA's network of overseas black sites, it was because intelligence officials uneasy about the legality and morality of the CIA's activities revealed their apprehensions to the *Washington Post*. It was Edward Snowden, a government contractor, who exposed the NSA's dragnet collection of Americans' telephone records and other programs of mass surveillance. Documents and videos furnished to WikiLeaks by Chelsea Manning undermined official narratives about the wars in Afghanistan and Iraq. And when American media organizations reported that official statements about American drone strikes had dramatically understated the number of bystander casualties and grossly mischaracterized the military's rules of engagement, they relied in part on information supplied by Daniel Hale, an NSA analyst; on accounts from drone operators haunted by abuses they had witnessed; and on disclosures by other military personnel and public servants, most of them still anonymous, who shared official secrets without authorization.

One need not believe that these people acted with pure motives, or that all of their disclosures were justified, or that none of their disclosures was harmful, to recognize the pivotal role that they played. Informed public debate about national security policy would have been impossible had these insiders not revealed what the government would have preferred to suppress. It's not simply that the American public would have remained unaware of some of the government's most consequential mistakes and abuses or that we would have learned of them much later than we did. It's also that these mistakes and abuses would have gone uncorrected for much longer than they did. In the wake of insiders' unauthorized disclosures, the government made significant adjustments to policies relating to interrogation, detention, surveillance, and extrajudicial killing. In some instances, unauthorized disclosures provoked executive branch officials to course-correct almost immediately. But even when they did not spur immediate adjustments to government policy, these disclosures fueled investigative journalism and civil litigation and sparked investigations by congressional committees, inspectors general, and the military—investigations and processes that in many instances led eventually to significant reform.

Government officials habitually call for the imposition of harsh penalties on insiders who share official secrets without authorization. The rhetoric has become markedly more heated even as the prosecution of leakers has become more frequent and even as the sentences imposed on leakers have become more severe. In recent years, the government has made aggressive use of the 1917 Espionage Act, which, as the courts have interpreted it, imposes draconian penalties on leakers without regard to the value to the public of the information they disclose. Most significantly, prosecutors have begun to use the Espionage Act against leakers who disclose information to the press. During the twentieth century, only one person was convicted under the Espionage Act for supplying official secrets to the press, but since 9/11, the government's use of the Act against journalists' sources has become routine. It is likely to become even more common. Whatever norms once kept the government from using the Espionage Act against journalists' sources have now been abandoned. New surveillance technologies and new legal authorities allow the government to identify leakers without incurring the political costs that have historically been associated with serving subpoenas on journalists. The Trump administration made no secret of its hostility to press freedom and pursued leakers aggressively.

The proposition that legal protection should be extended to certain national security insiders who share official secrets with the press or public is not new, but it is newly urgent. Developments since 9/11 have made whistleblowing both more necessary and more perilous. To protect the public's ability to understand, evaluate, and influence national security policy—and to maintain the link between national security policy and democratic consent—we need to extend legal protection to insiders who responsibly disclose official secrets in order to inform public debate. We need to establish stronger legal protections for national security whistleblowers.[8]

This essay develops a conceptual case for strengthening whistleblower protections in the national security sphere. Part one identifies some of the features of our system that make whistleblowers indispensable to the proper functioning of our democracy, and, in particular, to preserving democratic control over national security policy. Part two highlights the role that national security whistleblowers have played over the past two decades and argues that establishing new protections for national security whistleblowers is especially imperative right now. Part three argues that we should recognize a "public value" defense to Espionage Act prosecutions, observing that recognizing such a defense would, among other things, reduce the disincentive to socially beneficial leaks, lend legitimacy to Espionage Act prosecutions, more closely align our legal regime with widely shared intuitions about moral responsibility, and restore the courts to an appropriately central role in protecting the public's access to an essential channel of information.

Part One

Informed public deliberation about war and national security sometimes depends on the readiness of government insiders to disclose classified information without authorization. What Max Frankel wrote fifty years ago remains true today: there could be "no adequate diplomatic, military, and political reporting of the kind our people take for granted" if the press did not publish official secrets.[9] It is equally true that the press could not publish official secrets if government insiders did not disclose them. Certain features of our system of regulating national security information make the unauthorized disclosure of official secrets not simply inevitable but vital to the proper functioning of our democracy.

First, Executive Order 13526, which establishes the classification system, allows the government to classify information without regard to whether and to what extent disclosure would aid public deliberation. Under that executive order, an "original classifying authority" may classify government information if the information falls within one of a number of specified categories—for example, "military plans," "intelligence activities," "foreign activities of the United States"—and if disclosure "reasonably could be expected to cause damage to the national security that the original classification authority is able to identify or describe."[10] If an original classifying authority determines that these criteria are satisfied, information can be classified even if it is plain that the benefits of disclosure would outweigh the harms. In practice, it is common for the government to classify the kinds of documents that could be expected to be especially important to the public's ability to understand, evaluate, and influence national security policy—including documents that describe government policy, documents that explain the government's understanding of its legal authorities or obligations, and documents that describe conduct that is unlawful.[11] The executive order gives decisive weight to the security interest and no weight at all to the interest in informed public deliberation.

Second, despite the limiting language in the executive order, the government routinely classifies information whose disclosure could *not* reasonably be expected to cause damage to the national security, as many government studies have found.[12] William Leonard, then director of the Information Security Oversight Office, testified in 2004 that "half of all classified information is overclassified."[13] Former New Jersey governor and 9/11 Commission chairman Thomas Kean said that "three-quarters" of the classified material he had reviewed in connection with the 9/11 Commission "should not have been classified in the first place."[14] The executive branch overclassifies for many different reasons—among them, that officials are rarely sanctioned for overclassifying information,[15] that classifying information can afford the classifier bureaucratic advantage,[16] and that classifying information can shield controversial decisions from scrutiny both inside and outside the government.[17] For these reasons and others, "we overclassify very badly,"[18] as former CIA director Porter Goss once observed, and the mere fact of classification is not a reliable indicator that disclosure could reasonably be expected to cause harm.[19]

Third, the courts have rejected the proposition that the First Amendment guarantees the public or even the press any general right of access to information in the hands of government. Acknowledging the "structural" role that the First Amendment plays in "securing and fostering our republican system of government," the Supreme Court has held that the First Amendment protects the public's right of access to criminal proceedings and certain documents filed in connection with them,[20] and lower courts have held that this right extends to civil proceedings.[21] The courts have declined, however, to recognize a more general right of access to government information.[22] Moreover, even in the narrow circumstances in which a right of access has been recognized to attach, some courts have held that the mere fact of classification is sufficient to overcome the constitutional right.[23]

Fourth, Congress has not afforded the public or the press a meaningful statutory right of access to information relating to national security. While the FOIA allows ordinary citizens to request records from the government on any topic, it does not permit courts to order the disclosure of information that is properly classified, and the courts almost always defer to the government's assertion that the information is properly classified. (Indeed, courts have overturned the executive branch's classification decisions only a small handful of times.)[24] Because the FOIA does not include a public interest "override," courts affirm the government's withholding of classified information under the Act without reference to whether the benefits of disclosure are likely to outweigh the harms. Indeed, courts affirm the government's withholding of classified records even when they believe that the records describe or authorize government conduct that is unlawful.[25]

Fifth, the courts have operationalized the FOIA in a way that accommodates selective disclosure. Congress enacted the FOIA in large part out of concern that the government had distorted debate about the war in Southeast Asia by cherry-picking the information it shared with the public.[26] The way the courts have implemented the FOIA, however, facilitates the very practice that the statute was meant to address. As interpreted by the courts, the FOIA allows the government to disclose classified information unofficially—through unattributed leaks to the media—without waiving its right to withhold that same information in response to FOIA requests.[27] As it has been interpreted by the courts, the statute also permits the government to disclose classified information selectively without waiving its right to withhold closely related information.[28]

Sixth, statutory protections for insiders who use internal channels to report official malfeasance are weak in the national security sphere.[29] The whistleblower protections available to other government employees are not available to employees of the intelligence agencies. Recent legislation protects Intelligence Community (IC) employees from reprisal for certain disclosures to Congress provided they file a complaint first with the IC's inspector general. This channel, however, is more likely to be useful to employees who are concerned about isolated abuses than to employees concerned about failures that are systemic—ones that relate to, for example, the lawfulness of executive branch policy or the failure of institutional oversight mechanisms.[30] And yet these are the complaints that are most vital to ensuring that national security policy does not escape popular control.

It would certainly be possible to design a system in which unauthorized disclosures of classified information would be less necessary.[31] The executive branch could narrow the categories of classifiable information, incorporate consideration of the public interest into the classification process, or subject classifiers' decisions to additional internal review and audit within the executive branch.[32] Congress could expand protection for IC whistleblowers who submit complaints through internal channels, narrow FOIA's national security exemptions, require more robust judicial review in certain classes of FOIA cases,[33] or modify the official-acknowledgment doctrine in ways that might disincentivize selective disclosure. The courts could construe the First Amendment to encompass a general constitutional right to information in the hands of the government and clarify that the mere fact of classification cannot be sufficient to overcome this constitutional right.[34]

In the system we have now, however, unauthorized "disclosure of some national security secrets is not only inevitable but also essential for the proper functioning of our government."[35] Without unauthorized disclosures, the public's ability to understand and evaluate national security policy would be almost entirely dependent on the goodwill of executive officials. There could be "no mature system of communication between the Government and the people," because public debate about national security policy would take place in an information environment controlled almost entirely by the officials most responsible for developing, authorizing, and overseeing that policy.[36] The most significant mistakes and abuses—those that result in unlawful policies (rather than isolated abuses) or that reflect failures of the oversight system—would be insulated from public scrutiny.[37] And public policy would become unmoored from the democratic consent that gives it its legitimacy.

Part Two

Unauthorized disclosures of classified information have always been crucial to our democracy,[38] but developments over the past two decades have made whistleblowing more necessary as well as more perilous. Post-9/11 developments have deepened our dependence on whistleblowers for multiple reasons. The military and the intelligence agencies have grown dramatically in their budgets, personnel, prestige, and influence.[39] They are relying heavily on potent new technologies whose implications for individual freedom and human rights are poorly understood even by their developers. The United States is at war in the Middle East, North Africa, and central Asia,[40] but the increased reliance by the military on remotely piloted aircraft and covert operations has rendered war, and many of its implications, invisible to most Americans.[41] And because of the global nature of the continuing "war on terror," the decisions made by the military and intelligence agencies often have direct implications for Americans and others in the United States.[42]

The record of the past two decades reveals the extent of our new dependence on whistleblowers. Consider the following.

Interrogation. The abuses at Abu Ghraib came to public attention because a soldier, defying orders from superiors, supplied photographs to the *New Yorker* and *60 Minutes*.[43] The public learned of the CIA's network of overseas prisons because officials who were concerned about the lawfulness and morality of the CIA's policies supplied classified information to the *Washington Post*.[44] When the public learned, several years later, that the CIA had destroyed videotapes of prisoners being waterboarded, this, too, was the result of unauthorized disclosures.[45]

These disclosures were inflection points in the public debate about the Bush administration's interrogation policies and about the "war on terror" more generally, and they led, sometimes circuitously but often directly, to institutional reflection and legal reform. At least in part in response to information made public by whistleblowers, the military conducted multiple investigations relating to the abuse of prisoners,[46] the Senate Armed Services Committee undertook a major investigation and held public hearings,[47] and the DOJ launched criminal investigations.[48] Some of these investigations and processes were whitewashes or failures, but others resulted in significant changes to the law and to the practices of the military and intelligence agencies. Congress clarified and strengthened the prohibition against cruel, inhuman, and degrading treatment.[49] The Defense Department narrowed military interrogators' authority to use techniques that had led to abuse. President Bush transferred prisoners out of the CIA's black sites.[50] The Office of Legal Counsel (OLC) withdrew a memo that purported to supply a legal basis for "enhanced interrogation techniques," including waterboarding, a technique that the United States had previously prosecuted as a war crime.[51] When he took office in 2009, President Obama shut down the black sites, rescinded related OLC memos, and declared that the United States would disavow torture.[52] Later, the Senate Intelligence Committee undertook a years-long investigation and wrote a six-thousand-page report meant to ensure that the "system of detention and interrogation described in [the] report is never repeated."[53] These reforms and processes came about for many reasons, but it is inconceivable that they would have come about if government insiders had not disclosed classified information without authorization.

Surveillance. The public learned of the NSA's mass surveillance activities because Snowden, an NSA contractor, leaked classified documents to the *Guardian* and the *Washington Post*. In the months before Snowden did this, government officials who spoke publicly about the government's surveillance practices described them in terms that obscured the scope and implications of those practices,[54] the director of national intelligence (DNI) testified inaccurately to Congress that the NSA was not collecting information about large numbers of Americans,[55] the Supreme Court dismissed a constitutional challenge to the NSA's mass surveillance activities on the grounds that the plaintiffs lacked proof that the government was actually engaged in those activities,[56] and the DOJ systematically failed to notify criminal defendants of its use of evidence derived from the NSA's mass surveillance activities, though the law required it to provide such notice.[57] Public debate about the NSA's activities was not simply impoverished but profoundly distorted.

Snowden's disclosures alerted the public to the scope of the NSA's surveillance activities, the implications of those activities for the rights of people living in the United States, and significant failures on the part of the congressional intelligence committees and the specialized courts tasked with overseeing some of the NSA's surveillance practices. Like the unauthorized disclosures about interrogation, Snowden's disclosures about surveillance led to institutional reflection and legal reform. The FISA court (FISC) gave serious consideration for the first time to whether the NSA's call-records program complied with the Fourth Amendment.[58] A federal appeals court declared the program to be unlawful.[59] The DOJ began to comply with its obligation to notify criminal defendants of the provenance of evidence derived from the NSA's mass surveillance activities, which had the effect of permitting criminal defendants to challenge the constitutionality of those activities in court.[60] Congress passed legislation that dramatically curtailed the call-records program, empowered the FISC to hear from court-appointed amici in certain contexts, and obliged the DNI to declassify and release FISC opinions of broad significance.[61] President Obama instructed the DNI to establish a "review group" to assess the government's use of communications and surveillance technologies,[62] and the review group made a series of recommendations that the executive branch adopted, at least in part.[63] None of this could have taken place if Snowden had not disclosed classified information without authorization.

"Targeted" killing. Like the public debate about the NSA's surveillance practices, public debate about the government's use of armed drones overseas was characterized by selective disclosure and official misdirection.[64] Even as it normalized the practice of extrajudicial killing, the Obama administration refused to disclose statistics on civilian casualties, the legal memos purporting to supply the basis for the government's policies, and the standards and procedures by which suspected enemies, including American citizens, were added to government "kill lists."[65] The ACLU and the *New York Times* brought litigation under FOIA, but the courts proved unwilling to compel the government to publish more than it wanted to, repeatedly deferring to the government's assertion that additional transparency would cause grave damage to national security.[66] At the same time, military and intelligence officials routinely supplied cherry-picked facts to the media under cover of anonymity.[67] Through a veritable flood of officially sanctioned leaks, they painted a picture of a program that was closely supervised, legally sound, and narrowly focused on terrorists believed to be planning imminent attacks.[68]

The officially sanctioned disclosures did not decrease the necessity of unauthorized ones. To the contrary, unauthorized disclosures became especially valuable because they served not merely to inform the public but to correct dis-information as well. Documents supplied by Hale, an NSA analyst, allowed the Intercept to report that many of the government's targets were not terrorists, that most of its strikes were predicated on evidence that was thin and unreli-able, and that its "body counts" were based on the indefensible assumption that bystanders were combatants.[69] The accounts of drone operators who were dis-traught by abuses they had witnessed further complicated the picture of a pro-gram that was supposedly discriminating and, in President Obama's description, "kept on a very tight leash."[70] On the whole, unauthorized disclosures about the drone program were probably less consequential than the ones that shaped public debate about interrogation and surveillance policy, but they nonetheless contributed in important ways to public discussion of the legality, morality, and effectiveness of the program and helped spur significant reforms, including ones that brought US policy into closer alignment with human rights law and almost certainly reduced civilian casualties.[71]

Thus, in each of the areas discussed above—interrogation, surveillance, and targeted killing—whistleblowers played an essential role. Indeed, consider what public debate about the "war on terror" would have looked like if the govern-ment had been able to conceal, for longer than it did, what these whistleblowers disclosed to us. The decisions to hold prisoners in secret black sites, to subject them to cruel treatment and torture, to deploy the NSA's awesome surveillance powers against billions of people, to authorize extrajudicial killings that led to the deaths of hundreds of innocents in half a dozen countries—these decisions were surely among the most morally treacherous and politically consequential our government made in the two decades after 9/11. Would a democracy in which decisions of such moment had been concealed from the people indefi-nitely be worthy of the label? The question would be easy to answer even if one were to stipulate (against the evidence) that the decisions the government made in secret were ones the public would have endorsed. But the question is even easier to answer once it is recognized that in each of the areas addressed above, government policy had escaped democratic control. We needed whistleblowers to narrow the distance between what the public had consented to and what the government was actually doing. Whistleblowers' disclosures enabled a more informed public debate, and ordinary citizens used what whistleblowers disclosed in order to press for reforms that were in many cases adopted. It was whistleblowers' disclosures, in other words, that allowed the democratic process to work.

The essential role that whistleblowers have played over the past two decades is reason enough to doubt the defensibility of our current legal regime. But there is another reason, too: even as post-9/11 developments have made whistleblowers more necessary, whistleblowing has become more difficult and more dangerous.

One reason for this is that new technology has made it easier for the government to identify leakers. Because virtually all government files are now stored electronically, the government usually has a precise record of who accessed the files and when. It also has detailed records of government employees' communications and activities. The government determined that it was Reality Winner who leaked files relating to Russian cyberattacks because the government's digital records showed that Winner was one of six people who had printed the records and that Winner was the only one of the six who had communicated with the Intercept, the media organization that published the files.[72] It is easier to leak information today than it was fifty years ago, but it is more difficult to preserve anonymity.[73] Snowden assumed that the government would be able to identify him quickly, and it did.[74]

New surveillance authorities have also reduced the political costs associated with surveillance of journalists. Through mass surveillance programs, the government collects journalists' communications metadata and (sometimes) content without targeting journalists specifically; the collected data is stored in databases that can be queried secretly.[75] In addition, the USA Patriot Act expanded the government's authority to use "national security letters" to obtain the call records of individuals not themselves suspected of engagement in criminality or espionage. The letters are served on communications providers without prior judicial authorization and typically accompanied with nondisclosure orders that foreclose the providers from alerting the targets of the government's interest in their communications.[76] The letters give the government the ability to identify reporters' sources without paying the high political price sometimes associated with serving subpoenas on journalists and media organizations.[77] During the Obama administration, Attorney General Eric Holder adopted new guidelines that placed new restrictions of the DOJ's use of subpoenas to identify sources. Notably, the new restrictions did not apply to national security letters.[78]

Perhaps most significantly, insiders who share official secrets with the press face a far more hostile legal landscape than they did twenty years ago. To be sure, it has long been the case that government insiders who consider supplying classified information to the public or press must contemplate the possibility of losing their public service employment, being stripped of their security clearances, and being prosecuted under a range of unforgiving criminal statutes, including, most significantly, the Espionage Act, which criminalizes the unlawful retention and communication of "national defense information."[79] The Espionage Act subjects insiders who disclose classified secrets to the possibility of harsh sanctions regardless of the value to the public of the information they disclose.[80] Like the classification system, the Act gives decisive weight to the government's asserted interest in secrecy and no weight at all to the public's interest in informed deliberation about national security policy.

But although the Espionage Act was enacted a century ago, only in recent years has the government begun using the Act against government insiders who disclose information to the press. During the twentieth century, Samuel Loring Morison was the only person convicted under the Espionage Act for sharing classified secrets with the press, and President Clinton pardoned him in 2001.[81] In the years since, however, the government's use of the Espionage Act against journalists' sources has become routine. The Obama administration indicted eight people under the Act for leaking secrets to the press, and the Trump administration indicted another four in only three years.[82] In a sign of the times, James Comey, then the FBI director, told President Trump in 2017 that he "was eager to find leakers and would like to nail one to the door as a message,"[83] and Jeff Sessions, then the attorney general, later told the media that the DOJ was engaged in twenty-seven investigations into classified leaks—a major escalation over previous years.[84] Thanks to decisions by administrations of both major political parties over a period of two decades, whatever norms once dissuaded the government from using the Espionage Act against journalists' sources seem to have evaporated.[85]

Part Three

Legal scholars, press freedom advocates, and others have argued that insiders should be protected in some circumstances for disclosing official secrets without authorization. One proposition common to many of these proposals is that leakers should not be held liable under the Espionage Act without a court first considering the public value of the information they disclosed.[86] In the remainder of this essay, I want to make a case for one version of this proposition— specifically, for allowing Espionage Act defendants to argue, as a defense to liability, that any harms caused by their disclosures were outweighed by the value of the disclosures to the public.[87] At the risk of disappointing the reader, I do not endorse or even describe any particular implementation of this public value defense here, though such a defense could be implemented in many different ways. My aim here is to develop a more conceptual case for recognizing a public value defense in some form. The arguments for recognizing such a defense, as I will explain, are more numerous, diverse, and substantial than commonly appreciated.

The principal argument usually made for affording Espionage Act defendants a public value defense is that doing so would lessen the deterrent to socially beneficial leaks. This is a powerful argument and perhaps reason enough to make such a defense available. In general, of course, we want government insiders to respect their nondisclosure agreements. It would not serve the public interest if security-cleared government employees and contractors subjected every classification decision to their own de novo review. We want government insiders to hesitate, and to think carefully, before disclosing official secrets without authorization.[88] At the same time, though, we need government insiders to inform the public when they learn of significant abuses or systemic failures.

A public value defense would allow us to treat different kinds of leaks in different ways. It would allow us to distinguish socially beneficial leaks from socially harmful ones. While the defense would be unavailable concerning most leaks (because the leaker would not be able to demonstrate that the social benefits of disclosure outweighed the harms), it would, by design, change the calculus for insiders with access to information of most value to the public. Under the new regime, insiders would consider not only the possibility that they would be charged under the Espionage Act but also the likelihood that they would be able to satisfy the public value defense. The Espionage Act would continue to serve as a strong disincentive to most leaks, but the possibility of satisfying the public value defense would reduce the disincentive to the leaks that are most important to the public. An appropriately calibrated defense would accommodate the government's legitimate interest in protecting (most) classified information but also give appropriate weight to the public interest in maintaining democratic control over national security policy.

It might be argued that the current system does not, in fact, prevent the public from learning about controversial national security programs the government would prefer to keep secret. The same evidence I marshal above to establish the indispensability of whistleblowers could be deployed instead to support the argument that the threat of heavy penalties does not dissuade insiders from bringing crucial information to public attention, at least when it really matters. But this argument is ultimately unpersuasive. First, we don't know what we don't know; we know that some abuses were disclosed, but we have no idea what abuses might have been disclosed if we had had something other than a strict liability regime for leaks. In addition, we do not know how the availability of a public value defense might have altered the *timing* of leaks. If a public value defense had been available, perhaps an insider might have leaked the infamous torture memos in 2002, when they were written; perhaps an insider might have disclosed the NSA's call-records program in 2003 rather than a decade later; perhaps the public might have learned of drone strikes' civilian toll early enough to compel changes to government policy in 2010 or 2011 rather than 2013 or 2015. More fundamentally, there is simply no reason to believe that the logic of incentives and disincentives that operates in other spheres would not operate in this one. It seems reasonable to assume that the availability of a public value defense for leaks would have resulted in more leaks and a more informed public.

Another argument sometimes offered in support of the status quo is that a public value defense would *over*-incentivize leaks, perhaps in part because it would erode respect for the classification system by encouraging insiders to treat the government's secrecy decisions as something other than final and binding. It is doubtful, however, that insiders would systematically overestimate the social benefits of disclosure or systematically underestimate the social harms—especially because the disincentive to that kind of miscalculation would be severe, since a leaker who miscalculated in one of these ways would suffer the same consequences she would suffer under the current regime. Indeed, it seems quite likely that whistleblowing would be undersupplied even if we made a public value defense available, because even an insider who is justified in her belief that the social benefits of disclosure would exceed the harms would have to take into account the possibility that a jury might disagree. For this reason, it is unlikely that the recognition of a public value defense would result in a flood of leaks or even an oversupply of them.

Nor is it likely that the recognition of a public value defense would erode respect for the classification system in some more fundamental sense. Consider other contexts in which we recognize analogous "necessity" defenses to general criminal prohibitions. The availability of a self-defense argument is not usually thought to erode respect for the prohibition against deliberate killing. The requirement that military service members refuse orders that are unlawful is not usually thought to erode respect for military discipline. To the contrary, it is frequently suggested that these exceptions are vital to the legitimacy of the general rules.[89]

Thus, the usual argument for extending public value defense to whistleblowers is compelling. Certain kinds of leaks—the ones that are most crucial to our democracy—are almost certainly undersupplied under our current legal regime, and affording leakers a public value defense could go some way toward correcting this. But affording leakers a public value defense would have other important benefits, too, including some that are perhaps less obvious.

For example, recognizing a public value defense could help regularize the treatment of leakers. Even in a broader landscape that is famously "disorderly,"[90] our treatment of leakers stands out as especially irregular. Defendants charged under the Espionage Act often argue that their actions were justified, but they direct those arguments to the executive branch, which has the power to determine whether to offer a plea bargain, how severe a sentence to recommend, what the conditions of confinement should be, and whether to offer a pardon or another form of clemency. Because the executive branch is less concerned about precedent and consistency than the courts and more exposed to political pressure, and also because the executive branch is poorly positioned to assess the value of disclosures relating to misconduct by executive branch officials, these decisions are unprincipled. Allowing a public value defense would make our treatment of whistleblowers more predictable—that is, more orderly.[91] While the executive branch would, of course, still control prosecutorial decisions, and the president would, of course, still control the pardon power, the courtroom would become the principal forum for consideration of the social benefit of the defendants' disclosures, and the question of whether the public value defense was satisfied in any given case would be answered within a consistent analytical framework by actors insulated to some extent from the politics of the moment.

Allowing a public value defense could also incentivize responsible leaking, as Benkler has observed.[92] If the defense entailed a balancing of costs and benefits, the possible availability of the defense would give prospective leakers reason to consider the costs carefully. It would also give them reason to mitigate costs to the extent possible—for example, by limiting the scope of the information disclosed, redacting some information, or disclosing the information to a news organization likely to exercise independent editorial discretion in determining what to publish. With a public value defense, the law would recognize and give weight to these efforts at mitigation, instead of ignoring them, as it does now. It would encourage leakers "to be careful what they leak."[93]

Relatedly, allowing a public value defense would more closely align our regulatory framework with widely shared intuitions about moral responsibility. Most of us share the view that individuals sometimes have a moral duty to break promises, disobey orders from superiors, or violate the law. Many of us believe that there are circumstances in which government insiders who have agreed to guard the government's confidences are morally obliged to betray those confidences instead—though, of course, we may disagree about the circumstances in which this obligation should attach and about whether the obligation attached in a given case. Important social institutions frequently honor whistleblowers and the journalists and media organizations that publish the information they provide.[94] Allowing a public value defense would better align our legal system with the widely shared view that whistleblowing is justified and socially beneficial in some circumstances.

And if allowing a public value defense would legitimize some whistleblowing, it would also have the effect of lending legitimacy to Espionage Act convictions. Because the current regime denies defendants the opportunity to argue that their actions were justified, it allows those convicted under the Espionage Act to claim the mantle of whistleblowers even if the requirements of a public value defense would not have been satisfied in their cases. An insider who discloses official secrets of little value to the public, or with little regard for the harms likely to be caused by the disclosures, can claim the same mantle as one who acted more responsibly. As a result, the unavailability of a public value defense has the effect of tainting even those Espionage Act prosecutions in which the defense would not have been available.

Recognizing a public value defense could have still other benefits. For example, the executive branch might disclose more information of its own accord if government insiders could sometimes expect to receive legal protection for responsibly disclosing official secrets of special value to the public. Under the existing regime, executive branch officials have almost total control over what information the public receives about executive branch policy. Empowering whistleblowers would have the effect of subjecting the executive branch's classification decisions to a kind of public interest override in some narrow contexts. The possibility that a whistleblower might disclose information would incentivize government officials to consider disclosing the information preemptively. An appropriately calibrated public value defense would change the calculus of the executive branch with respect to the withholding and selective disclosure of information of special relevance to the public's ability to understand, evaluate, and influence national security policy.

Allowing a public value defense could also help resolve one of the fundamental tensions of the post–Pentagon Papers legal framework. As others have observed, there is something paradoxical, troubling, and even unseemly about our system's disparate treatment of whistleblowers and journalists.[95] Insiders who disclose classified secrets routinely receive the harshest punishments; the journalists who report the same secrets are more likely to receive Pulitzer Prizes. Allowing a public value defense would close this gap to some extent. There would still be (many) circumstances in which the insiders who disclosed official secrets could be punished but the journalists who published the secrets could not, because the public value defense would apply only to some classes of disclosures, and only where the harms caused by the disclosures were outweighed by their social benefits. (I assume for present purposes that the First Amendment would preclude the government from prosecuting a journalist or publisher under the Espionage Act except in truly extraordinary circumstances.)[96] But with respect to some class of disclosures of special significance to the public's ability to maintain democratic control of national security policy, the new regime would treat leakers and journalists the same way.

Finally, allowing a public value defense would also give the courts an appropriately central role in protecting a channel of information that is crucial to the functioning of our democracy. Given the essential role that whistleblowers play in protecting democratic control over national security policy, the treatment of whistleblowers should not be left entirely to the executive branch. The courts are better positioned than the executive branch to assess the social benefits of whistleblowers' disclosures, because they are relatively insulated from immediate political pressures and accustomed to giving legal effect to democratic values. Moreover, even if the executive branch is better positioned than the courts are to assess the risks associated with disclosure of classified information, as it is sometimes suggested to be,[97] it is not better positioned to assess the risks associated with disclosures relating to malfeasance by the executive branch, and this is the category of information we are most concerned with here.[98]

All of this is to say that there are very good arguments in favor of extending a public value defense to leakers charged under the Espionage Act. How such a defense should be implemented is, again, a question I leave for another day. My modest hope here is simply to highlight that recognizing such a defense would have substantial systemic benefits that go far beyond the ones usually identified, even by whistleblower advocates.

Conclusion

The legal, political, and technological developments of the past twenty years have rendered us more reliant on whistleblowers even as they have made whistleblowing more difficult and more hazardous. To promote informed public debate about national security and to preserve the connection between democratic consent and government policy in this sphere, we should extend legal protection, in some circumstances, to government insiders who responsibly disclose official secrets without authorization. Affording leakers a public value defense against prosecution would have benefits beyond those usually cited. It would, among other things, reduce the disincentive to socially beneficial leaks, lend legitimacy to Espionage Act prosecutions, more closely align our legal regime with widely shared intuitions about moral responsibility, and restore the courts to an appropriately central role in protecting the public's access to an essential channel of information.

The Long (Futile?) Fight for a Federal Shield Law

JUDITH MILLER

This is an anxious time for American journalists and journalism. While the need for a free, independent, and courageous press, however irritating and occasionally infuriating, has never been as vital to the preservation of freedom and democracy, the pressure on reporters to bend to the will and demands of presidential power has never been as deliberate, persistent, and intimidating as it has in recent years.

Though reporters and the government have long engaged in political and legal battles, and some degree of tension between the three branches of government and the so-called fourth estate in American democracy is inevitable, never before was a virtual war on the press so personally led by an American president. Day after day, President Trump used his powerful bully pulpit to denounce reporters he disliked as lazy, biased, corrupt, incompetent, unreliable, purveyors of "fake news," "terrible" people, "human scum," and, in his inimitable and historically incendiary words, "enemies of the people" or traitors to the nation.

President Trump not only assailed his media critics in tweets and at the informal press gaggles that replaced formal news conferences and daily White House briefings, but through direct threats and innuendo, he also blessed physical attacks on reporters covering his rallies and attempted to deny White House press credentials, and thus access to information, to journalists who displeased him. He and top officials forced reporters to sue for what should be public information, denigrated the media's constitutionally designated role as the government's watchdog, and ordered his campaign to file defamation suits against individual journalists and such news organizations as the *Washington Post* and the *New York Times* for publishing embarrassing stories about him and his entourage.[1]

The fact that his anti-media tantrums and tirades resulted in huge audiences and high ratings for broadcast and cable news networks and circulation increases for some of the country's largest newspapers (as smaller local and regional papers continue to close and struggle) should not mask his intent: to undermine and delegitimize one of the few remaining constitutional checks on what has been a steady increase in presidential power since World War II.

A particularly dangerous component of Trump's multifaceted war on the press, though not new, was his use of the DOJ to silence whistleblowers and punish the media for reporting leaks. During the George W. Bush and Obama administrations, journalists were subpoenaed in record numbers in several high-profile cases and also in many less well-known situations by federal judges, special prosecutors, or civil litigants and threatened with jail if they refused to name their confidential sources.

According to reports of such actions collected by the Reporters Committee for Freedom of the Press (RCFP), the Trump administration exceeded even Obama's record.[2] Under Obama, in eight years, there were eight prosecutions involving the leak of government information. There were eight such prosecutions in the first three years of the Trump administration. Ominously, the RCFP also found that the number of subpoenas for the records or testimony of reporters from government and private litigants increased steadily from eight during Trump's first year in office in 2017 to twenty-seven in 2019.

Perhaps even more "troublingly," the RCFP reported that in 2020, several journalists and news outlets told the news advocacy group that they believed they had been subpoenaed "as a form of retaliation or harassment for critical reporting or for filing court access or public records lawsuits." Moreover, Katie Townsend, the RCFP's legal director, reported that the organization was disturbed "by the increasing severity of punishment of and prison sentences for leakers." She noted, for example, that Reality Leigh Winner, a twenty-nine-year-old former Air Force linguist and intelligence contractor who pled guilty in June 2018 to leaking a top-secret government report on Russian hacking to the Intercept, was sentenced to five years and three months in federal prison—the longest sentence in American history for such unauthorized disclosure of classified information. "And that was part of a plea agreement, not a conviction," Townsend added. Nor was Winner's tough sentence unique.

Theodore Boutros, a partner in the Los Angeles office of Gibson, Dunn & Crutcher who specializes in First Amendment issues, said that the growing number of leak investigations by the government and the growing number of subpoenas issued to journalists both by the government and by private litigants has not only intimidated prospective whistleblowers and risked punishing those who disseminate the information but also advanced President Trump's goals of increasing pressure on journalists at a financially vulnerable time and eroding public confidence in the press.

The press has periodically pushed back hard against DOJ excesses when they have been disclosed. President Nixon's DOJ, for example, was pushed into introducing fairly restrictive guidelines limiting when reporters could be subpoenaed. Under those guidelines, prosecutors had to weigh the potential benefit to law enforcement against the public's interest in the disclosure of the information. Before a subpoena could be issued to a reporter, other means of investigation had to have been foreclosed. The information being sought had to be considered "essential" to the case. Finally, the attorney general had to approve all such subpoenas.

In response to public outrage over the Obama DOJ's overzealous surveillance of reporters in an effort to identify national security leakers, Attorney General Eric Holder and media representatives negotiated even tougher guidelines to strike a better balance between the conflicting needs of the government to prevent and investigate leaks of classified information and the press's mandate to investigate and disclose government abuse.[3]

In light of recent developments, particularly in the Trump administration, Boutros, Townsend, and other First Amendment activists argue that some form of statutory protection for journalists is essential. "Congress should enact a federal shield law that would prevent journalists from being forced to testify and identify sources in federal investigations," Boutros said.

Journalists and policymakers have long debated whether a federal shield law to protect reporters and their sources is needed or wise. In considering the merits of the issue, a bit of context is useful. The law generally recognizes a range of privileges, such as the attorney-client privilege, a medical privilege for doctors and therapists, a privilege for spouses, and a privilege for communications with clergy. Such privileges are rooted in the belief that the public interest justifies the exclusion of testimony by some categories of people against others in order to encourage free and open communication in those settings. Thus, in these settings, the law generally protects the privacy of such communications.

Reporters, mandated by the First Amendment to seek information in the public interest and to act as a check on government and private sector abuse, have long sought a similar exemption to encourage sources to disclose instances of government criminality or unethical conduct. Since a reporter's credibility depends upon his or her perceived independence, shield law proponents argue that if journalists are seen as an investigative arm of the government or as the tools of private interests, individuals will be less willing to trust them with confidential information.

In the national security setting, the Supreme Court has held that government employees who leak classified information can be criminally punished but that members of the press who disseminate such information to the public are protected by the First Amendment unless the information they disclose creates a clear and present danger of serious harm, a test that is almost impossible to satisfy. Although that state of affairs might seem somewhat anomalous, it is the accepted outcome of the Pentagon Papers decision. But that still leaves open the critical question of whether journalists can be compelled to disclose to criminal prosecutors and other government officials the identities of those who reveal the classified information to them. This is obviously a central issue, for it directly affects the willingness of government employees to disclose such information to the media, and it directly affects the integrity, independence, and credibility of the press.

One question is whether the First Amendment itself guarantees such a journalists' privilege. In 1972, in *Branzburg v. Hayes*, in a 5–4 decision written by Justice White, the Supreme Court ruled that requiring a reporter to testify does not abridge the constitutional guarantee of freedom of the press. The Court explained, in part, that it would be inappropriate for the Court to decide as a matter of constitutional law which would-be "journalists" would and would not be able to claim such a constitutional privilege. At the same time, though, the Court also warned that "without some protection for seeking out the news, freedom of the press could be eviscerated" and that only a "compelling" state interest in a reporter's testimony might trump First Amendment protection. Justice Powell, ruling with the majority against the privilege, wrote separately to say that a journalist might be considered privileged in future cases. Because his vote was needed to secure a majority, some lower courts have cited his opinion to recognize such a First Amendment privilege for reporters. But that is not the current state of the law, and *Branzburg* still controls the constitutional issue.

On the other hand, states and the federal government remain free to adopt a journalist-source privilege, just as they have adopted the other testimonial privileges. Indeed, as of today, forty-nine states and the District of Columbia have recognized some form of reporters' privilege. Of those, forty states and the District have enacted "shield law" statutes granting journalists an absolute or partial privilege—with varying degrees of protection against being compelled to disclose confidential sources.[4] But the differences in state laws have created a judicial hodgepodge, as well as a conflict over how different states and the federal government perceive reporters' rights. As a result, the Supreme Court has been asked repeatedly—but has consistently refused—to revisit the issue.

In the first three decades after *Branzburg*, the DOJ only rarely issued subpoenas seeking the disclosure of a journalist's confidential sources, and federal courts even more rarely ruled in the government's favor. In testimony before a House subcommittee in 2018, Lee Levine, senior counsel at Ballard Spahr, said that no journalist had been found to be in contempt or imprisoned for refusing to disclose a confidential source in a criminal matter during the last quarter of the twentieth century.[5]

The devastating 9/11 attacks marked a political and judicial turning point. Politicians and the DOJ stepped up efforts to stop the leak of sensitive national security information. Between 2001 and 2007, four federal courts of appeals affirmed contempt citations issued to reporters, each of which imposed longer prison sentences than any previously known to have been experienced by journalists in American history. Mine was among them. Then an investigative reporter for the New York Times, I spent eighty-five days in jail in 2005 for refusing to reveal the identity of a confidential source in response to a grand jury subpoena. (I was released only after my source made clear that he had, in fact, waived the protection of the confidentiality pledge I had given him.) My incarceration received huge publicity, but it was not an isolated case. In 2007, Josh Wolf, a videographer, spent seven months in jail for refusing to give the FBI unpublished video footage of a protest he had covered.

Such actions served to embolden private parties and the federal and state courts hearing their cases. The dam of judicial restraint was broken. According to the RCFP and other lawyers who specialize in First Amendment cases, as many as two dozen reporters were subpoenaed in cases that involved confidential sources around the time I received mine.

As subpoenas and search warrants began proliferating in the aftermath of 9/11, so, too, did calls for Congress to emulate what most states save one (Wyoming) eventually did: enact legislation granting or recognizing a reporter's right not to be coerced into disclosing confidential sources. Many state courts, too, issued rulings establishing a de facto privilege in test cases.

But Congress has continued to resist reporters' pleas for statutory protection. While several versions of a federal shield law that appeared to enjoy bipartisan support were introduced in Congress after the 9/11 attacks—one of them, the Free Flow of Information Act, was co-sponsored by none other than then–Republican representative and now Vice President Mike Pence of Indiana—none has become law.[6] After energetic lobbying, Pence was able to win House approval of the bill co-sponsored by Rick Boucher (D-VA). But a comparable measure failed in the Senate. When Representative Jim Jordan (R-OH) and Representative Jamie Raskin (D-MD) introduced a similar measure in 2018, only a single hearing was held to consider it; no House vote was taken. Neither legislator has reintroduced the measure since. So at this point, no legislative remedy is pending as the number of leak investigations and reporters caught in their crossfires has continued to grow.

The arguments for and against such protection for journalists, and, by extension, reporters' sources, have not changed much since the debate about their merit began. But a few of the most enduring are worth considering, especially in light of the technological advancements that have so profoundly altered our political landscape.

Opponents of a federal shield law have marshaled wide-ranging arguments against a federal statutory shield for journalists, the most important of which are rooted in a central premise, asserted by Gabe Schoenfeld in his attack on the proposal in an essay ten years ago: leaks are very bad, and those who leak and those who publish leaks should be punished by law.[7]

In another essay in *National Affairs*, Schoenfeld argued that at a time when the United States remains under terrorist and other national security threats, a federal shield law "would undermine the government's ability to enforce the law and provide for the common defense, upsetting the delicate balance between freedom and security that we now struggle to maintain."[8]

A version of this argument has been made at different times by every administration since, and even before, the 9/11 attacks, which were a psychological/political turning point in the shield law debate. Public concern about impeding the government's ability to maintain security has helped defeat at least two bipartisan attempts to approve shield legislation. The effort was also dealt a near-death blow by two extraordinary, massive, and in some ways harmful leaks of national security information: Chelsea Manning's downloading of more than 750,000 classified documents from a workstation in Iraq, which Julian Assange posted on WikiLeaks in 2010, and Edward Snowden's theft of tens of thousands of sensitive documents outlining the NSA's secret surveillance methods in 2013. While some of the newspapers to which Snowden sent the material were careful to edit the information so as not to disclose material that could harm intelligence "sources and methods," WikiLeaks published the raw downloaded files, causing what some intelligence experts claimed was incalculable national security damage.[9]

Shield law critics, such as Schoenfeld and Anthony Lewis, the former *New York Times* columnist and advocate of the First Amendment who opposed shield laws, have also argued that granting journalists a privilege, or protection from identifying or testifying about sources, would be tantamount to "institutionalizing" the press.[10] A shield law, or privilege for reporters, they argued, would begin to "integrate the press into the government in a way that is foreign to the Constitution, making the press resemble a formal branch of government." Quoting Lewis, Schoenfeld warned that treating the press as an "institution" aroused "uneasy feelings," in that institutions were usually subject to external check. While the press had traditionally operated as a "freebooter, outside the system," treating it as a veritable fourth branch of government would diminish its perception as independent, undermine its credibility, and give rise to demands that it be made "formally accountable." Thus, legally institutionalizing the press, they warned, "could imperil the very independence that a shield law seeks to bolster."

Another argument against a federal shield law is what has repeatedly been described as the daunting challenge of defining who is a journalist, that is, whom the privilege would cover, a problem cited by Justice White in *Branzburg*. Justice White feared that too narrow a definition would exclude and discriminate against the "lonely pamphleteer" whose voice the nation's founders sought to protect and create a de facto privileged class of "covered" journalists who would have a competitive advantage over those not covered by the law. As Schoenfeld later warned, at a time when digital technology was elevating the status and impact of bloggers and independent writers unaffiliated with "old media" institutions, for Congress to create such a privilege through legislation would give an elevated status to those whom Congress designates as "covered journalists" while "diminishing the rights—and the competitive position—of everyone else."

The flip side of that complaint, of course, is today's reality—concern that a federal shield law would have to cover too many people, given the explosion and growing impact of social media, and thus complicate law enforcement's ability to identify and prosecute criminals. In a world where more than 31 million active bloggers in the United States who post at least once a month can claim the status of journalists entitled to "privilege"—or exemption from identifying or discussing sources—would the government ever be able to prosecute successfully leaks that truly endangered American national security?[11]

Recently, Schoenfeld has expressed a new but related objection. Given that the First Amendment does not stop at the border, would foreign journalists in America be covered by a shield law? While covering British and French reporters might pose no challenge, what about Chinese, Russian, or Turkish journalists, he wrote me, "some or all of whom are state agents"? Would a shield law cover American citizens working for the foreign press? "The foreign press corps is larger than ever," he wrote. "Who gets protection? Who doesn't? Where does one draw the line?"

Another newer argument against a federal shield law is that the digital revolution has made such a law redundant and, hence, unnecessary. After my incarceration, which caused a considerable stir, some First Amendment advocates warned that because the DOJ had succeeded in compelling the testimony of several reporters about their sources, subpoenas to journalists would dramatically increase.

In fact, the opposite occurred in the years immediately following my jailing in 2005, but not because the number of leak investigations declined or the government stopped trying to plug leaks and discover their origin. Under President

Obama, who had promised to run the most open and "transparent" government possible, access to senior officials declined sharply, and the number of leak investigations soared.[12] As of June 2014, six government employees, plus two government contractors, had been the subjects of felony criminal prosecutions under the 1917 Espionage Act for alleged leaks of classified information to the press—more than double the number of such prosecutions in all previous administrations. By the end of Obama's presidency, his administration had prosecuted a total of nine cases involving whistleblowers and leakers, compared with only three by his predecessors. David Sanger, my former colleague at the *New York Times* and a veteran Washington correspondent, called Obama's White House the "most closed, control freak administration I've ever covered."[13]

Despite the Obama administration's passion for secrecy, however, reporters continued getting world-class scoops. While the internet and cybertechnology made it simpler for the government to spy on its citizens without warrants or cause, they also made it easier for Manning to download a ton of classified documents from remote Iraq and post them on WikiLeaks or for Snowden to leak tens of thousands of top-secret NSA documents about its surveillance methods to protest what he called unacceptable invasions of citizens' privacy and civil rights. Given their size and content, both leaks were political dynamite for the shield proposal. Critics, and even some First Amendment advocates, pushed the Obama administration to punish both leakers and the media outlets that disseminated the information. The argument that a federal shield law would encourage others with access to highly classified national secrets to leak them doomed the Free Flow of Information Act and successive versions of the measure. "Julian Assange did our profession no favor," said Lucy Dalglish, RCFP's former executive director and current dean of the Philip Merrill College of Journalism.[14]

Until the Trump administration, while the number of federal leak investigations increased, subpoenas to reporters involved in those investigations declined. Dalglish and others attributed this apparent anomaly partly to advances in the surveillance technology that has enabled Washington to collect, store, and access billions of telephone calls and emails a day. Such capability, they argued, has meant that in many cases, to bring an indictment or win a conviction, the government no longer needs to force reporters to divulge sources or even to testify at criminal proceedings about the content of their interactions with a source. For example, it was enough for prosecutors to see that the *New York Times's* Jim Risen had contacted former CIA official Jeffrey Sterling more than a dozen times in less than a year to identify him as the probable source for a book chapter Risen wrote in 2004 about a failed CIA effort to stop Iran from getting a nuclear weapon. Similarly, it was sufficient for a prosecutor to know that James Rosen of Fox News had sent numerous emails and made numerous calls to a nuclear expert at the State Department to charge and eventually convict him of leaking a story on North Korea's nuclear program.

Increasingly, the government has used technology instead of subpoenas to identify the sources of leaks and to pressure them into pleading guilty. According to Dalglish, "prosecutors have figured out how to build cases simply by seeing whom journalists have been talking to." As one government prosecutor told her at a meeting in 2011, "We don't need you anymore." Indeed, George Freeman, the executive director of the Media Law Resource Center and the chief First Amendment lawyer for the *New York Times* when I was fighting several subpoenas, has also long worried that given the government's ever-growing, almost Orwellian surveillance capabilities, journalists might well have to resort once more to meeting sources "in parks and garages so that their emails and phone numbers can't be traced."

Nonetheless, leaks of government information have continued and, if anything, escalated. The fact that no journalist has followed me to the Alexandria Detention Center in a federal criminal investigation in fifteen years is fodder to critics who see a federal shield law as both unnecessary and unjustified. "While openness is essential to a democratic society," Schoenfeld recently wrote, a democratic society "has a right to safeguard information it deems vital to its self-preservation. The need for freedom of the press must be balanced with the government's responsibility to fight crime and provide security. The press's liberty makes it a useful check on the government, but its liberty does not grant it a right to access governmental information—let alone sensitive classified information."

Proponents of a shield law obviously take issue with such arguments. Perhaps the easiest arguments to counter are those about definition. The issue of who is a journalist in the era of omnipresent social media may seem daunting in specific cases, but forty-nine states and the District of Columbia have managed to resolve it in their respective state statutes and court rulings—albeit in different ways and with different definitions. One can easily overcomplicate the challenge. But most states and a few of the proposed congressional measures have opted for a functional definition by adopting what I call the "if it walks like a duck" test. A person who engages in journalism is a journalist. Does the person work part- or full-time disseminating information that he or she collects and/or analyzes? It should not matter whether the reporters or their publications have a pronounced point of view—most of the nation's earliest scribes and government gadflies surely did. Should a shield cover foreign reporters based in the United States? Yes, if their main occupation is journalism, not spying. If, for example, there is evidence that Assange was coordinating with a foreign nation to harm the United States—as officials allege but for which evidence is not presented in his indictment—he is neither a journalist nor protected by any version of the proposed legislation that Congress has been asked to consider.

That being said, conflicting state definitions have caused some confusion and given rise to the potential for unequal justice. Some states have defined shield coverage tightly—limiting the privilege and the scope of the law's protection to those employed by "old media" or "legacy" publications and to those who hold paid posts at well-established online or broadcast outlets. Other states, such as New York and California, have elected to cover a far broader range of reporters, bloggers, and self-styled reporters, wherever they live or work.

Such differences can aid or imperil journalists. In 2013, a single vote in a 4–3 ruling by New York's highest court kept Jana Winter, a reporter and former colleague of mine at Fox News, from being sent to jail for protecting her sources in Colorado.[15] By one vote, she was freed from having to divulge the sources of her reporting or face jail in the murder trial of James Holmes, the man eventually convicted of murdering twelve and injuring fifty-five people in an attack at an Aurora, Colorado, movie theater in July 2012. By deciding in her favor, the New York court ruled, in effect, that New York's shield law, which broadly protects journalists from being forced to reveal the identities of confidential sources of their reporting, applies to New York reporters no matter where they go to gather news—to any of our fifty states and the District of Columbia, few of which offer reporters comparable protection.

More to the point of this essay, the concern that a shield law might encourage leaks of vital national security information—secrets whose disclosure could seriously damage American interests at home or abroad—should not mask the merits of such protection, not just for journalists and their potential sources but for American national security. As Mark Feldstein, the director of the journalism program at George Washington University, testified several years ago, the Assange imbroglio and that of WikiLeaks are anomalies. The overwhelming majority of federal cases in which a reporter's testimony is being sought do not involve national security. A federal shield law would definitely do much to protect them.

Moreover, over the years, far more damage to national security has been caused by government secrecy, deceit, and incompetence than by the press's reporting of secret information. The most notorious example is that which occurred under President John F. Kennedy, when, at his request, the *New York Times* declined to publish information it had gotten about plans for the Bay of Pigs invasion. Long after the fiasco unfolded, President Kennedy famously asserted that the country would have been better off if the *Times* had disclosed the information.

In fact, Feldstein asserted, American historians would be hard-pressed to find more than a few instances in which national security had been severely compromised by a reporter's publication of government secrets.[16] What most cases show, rather, is a pattern of official leaking when it suits the government's interest and an increase in such leaks in response to government abuses and the overclassification of information that the public has a right and, indeed, a need to know. Whistleblowers usually resort to the press to get the truth out when it is being suppressed. Rather than being a threat to American democracy, Feldstein argued, and I concur, leaking, on balance, is most often a healthy, self-correcting mechanism.

Critics of the proposals also argue that in the post-9/11 era, the balance between secrecy and disclosure was bound to shift as the nation became engaged in a "war against terrorism," a war without an obvious end, in a world increasingly filled with nuclear and other weapons of mass destruction, the use of which could kill or injure thousands, if not hundreds of thousands. But experts who examined the two most important intelligence and security failures in recent history—the failure to appreciate and act on evidence that militant Islamist terrorists were planning to strike the American homeland on September 11, 2001, and the consensus, but erroneous, opinion of the entire US Intelligence Community (IC) that Saddam Hussein was continuing his weapons of mass destruction programs, an opinion that helped justify the 2003 invasion of Iraq—did not conclude that government leaks were responsible for either of those catastrophes. The independent, bipartisan 9/11 Commission and three panels and commissions that investigated the IC's massive failure with respect to Iraq concluded that less government secrecy and greater transparency were needed to prevent another such massive failure.[17]

Since 9/11, however, the government has engaged in an orgy of unwarranted, often dangerous overclassification of information. As I wrote several years ago, and believe even more firmly today, it is hard to imagine a more inimical trend than the government's growing secrecy, except perhaps its growing incompetence in managing national security emergencies. The latest example seems to be President Trump's stubborn refusal to respond to the warnings of government analysts and experts about the devastation that the novel coronavirus from Wuhan, China, might inflict, his indifference to and failure to prepare for such a massive potential pandemic threat, and his mangled efforts to save American lives once the danger could no longer be ignored or downplayed.

The government's secrecy obsession, of course, long precedes President Trump. According to a report on government secrecy by OpenTheGovernment. org, a watchdog group, the federal government classified in fiscal 2004 what was then a record 15.6 million new documents, more than an 80 percent increase over those classified in the year before 9/11. The National Archives and Records Administration has called the practice, which continues to this day, "intimidation through classification."

By 2008, a study by the RCFP concluded that the federal government was classifying government documents at a rate of more than 125 a minute. According to the National Archives, the government continues to limit the disclosure and distribution of millions of documents that were once available to the public through the use of some sixty new categories of secret information, including my personal favorite, "Sensitive, but unclassified." This passion for secrecy does not come cheap. Back in 2004, three years after 9/11 and a year after the invasion of Iraq, the government spent $7.2 billion stamping 15.6 million documents "top secret," "secret," or "confidential." By fiscal 2017, the National Archives estimates, the government was spending $18.39 billion a year on security classification.[18]

In such a climate of official butt-covering paranoia, even conservatives who favor a strong government to protect national security might reconsider the need to boost statutory protection for journalists, whose professional mission is to shed light in such darkness partly through the recruitment of confidential sources and the information they provide. For as then-Congressman Pence said in reintroducing his shield proposal after it failed the first time, "as a conservative who believes in limited government, . . . I believe the only check on government power in real time is a free and independent press." (Of course, that was during the Obama administration.)

Furthermore, few shield law advocates believe that a shield law today would protect reporters from going to jail or being forced to reveal their sources if a compelling national security interest were at stake. The political landscape has shifted too firmly in favor of a priority on collective security for any of the post-9/11 measures once debated on Capitol Hill to win congressional approval today. Most of the earlier proposals, which established a "balancing" test in national security cases between the protection of sources and the government's need for information, leaned more heavily in the government's favor than I or First Amendment purists would have liked. Most of those proposals, for instance, would not have prevented me from going to jail if I had refused to identify my sources or my discussions with them about a prospective story I never wrote. Yet congressional approval of some form of federal shield for journalists and our sources—even if it were what free speech advocates call a "qualified" or limited privilege, as opposed to a total exemption from federal subpoenas—would make it harder for the government to use reporters to bolster evidence and win convictions.

History suggests that federal prosecutors under both Republican and Democratic presidents are occasionally all too willing to cut corners, ignore federal guidelines, and engage in judicial overreach to secure a conviction or expand commonly accepted interpretations of law.

Once again, what happened under President Obama is instructive. As part of its crackdown on leaks, Holder's DOJ took action that trod on press freedom.[19] To help secure a conviction after a four-year investigation against Stephen Jin-Woo Kim, a State Department analyst, prosecutors were willing to name Rosen, then my Fox News colleague, as an unindicted co-conspirator in the unauthorized disclosure of government information. In its affidavit for a search warrant of Rosen's Gmail accounts, the FBI asserted that in collecting information for his story, Rosen had operated "as an aider, abettor and/or co-conspirator of Mr. Kim" and had "solicited and encouraged Mr. Kim to disclose sensitive" material "by employing flattery and playing to Mr. Kim's vanity and ego." In so doing, he had acted "much like an intelligence officer would run an [sic] clandestine intelligence source," or like any reporter in search of a story.[20]

In yet another example of overreach, Obama DOJ prosecutors ignored the spirit of a law requiring them to subpoena records from reporters so that they can be challenged, rather than to secure search warrants for such information that journalists can protest only after the fact. But a year after a suspect's arrest in 2012, federal prosecutors informed the Associated Press that the FBI had used subpoenas to secure two months of telephone toll records from telephone service providers for twenty lines that were used by more than one hundred AP reporters and an editor.

Only after such abuses were disclosed did Attorney General Holder agree to negotiate stricter guidelines on investigations involving reporters. Only then did he and President Obama unenthusiastically agree to support passage of a federal shield law for reporters, legislation that by then stood little chance of approval.

But neither President Bush nor President Obama did what the Trump DOJ did; neither employed the Espionage Act to prosecute journalists for their role in disseminating leaks. Nor did either accuse a person or publication of treason under that law for seeking and disclosing leaked information. That is precisely, however, what happened under President Trump's DOJ and Attorney General William Barr's stewardship—a stunning, unprecedented, and, in the view of First Amendment activists, dangerous action.

In a superseding indictment filed against Assange in May 2019, federal prosecutors for the first time cited Assange's "pure publication" of Manning's leaked trove in its indictment as, in effect, treasonous. In so doing, free speech advocates warn, the Trump DOJ attempted to criminalize journalism.

The DOJ's unprecedented action in the Trump administration brings us full circle back to why the time has clearly come to reconsider the merits of a federal shield law. In some respects, despite his bombast and aggressive style, which give the term *bully pulpit* new meaning, Trump's view of the need to balance the government's desire to protect secrets against the press's desire to protect sources is not much different from that of his predecessors. "I'm a very big believer in freedom of the press," Trump declared. "But I'm also a believer that you cannot leak classified information."[21]

Whether or not the government succeeds in bullying reporters into betraying sources through subpoenas and threats of jail, fighting such demands is an expensive proposition for the press. Some fifteen years ago, my protracted fight to protect my sources cost the *New York Times* well more than a million dollars. With so many newspapers and news outlets struggling to survive, such fights may be financially devastating and, hence, prohibitive, observed Freeman, the former *Times* lawyer, even if the reporters win.

"Most of our earlier battles for press freedom and against government overreach occurred when papers were financially strong and circulations and television audiences were growing. Sadly, that is not the case today," said Dalglish.

Realistically, there is no appetite on Capitol Hill in either party for a federal shield law, even one that would merely codify the DOJ guidelines that the Obama administration accepted under political duress. The growing need for such a measure has tragically collided with ever-mounting financial and political obstacles to it. An economically ailing industry, coupled with the challenge of reporting on a government obsessed with security and secrecy, spells danger for the free press. It may be hyperbole to say that sources are the lifeblood of investigative journalism, but a fearless, independent press willing and able to disclose government and private abuses has surely been one of the pillars upon which our cantankerous republic has depended. Given new technology's obliteration of traditional concepts of privacy and individual rights and growing political polarization, the media should prepare for the numerous battles ahead.

Covering the Cyberwars

The Press versus the Government in a New Age of Global Conflict

DAVID E. SANGER

In the opening weeks of the Trump administration in 2017, the *New York Times* approached a White House immersed in the chaos of its early days to alert it that the paper was preparing to publish a story describing the immensity of the challenge the new president faced in dealing with a longtime American adversary, North Korea.

A lengthy *Times* investigation, begun well before it became clear that Donald Trump had a serious chance of winning the White House, had uncovered a long-running effort by America's newly created cyber force to sabotage North Korea's missile program. The results had been murky. Without question, an overwhelming majority of North Korean missile tests conducted between 2014 and October 2016 had gone awry. Yet even inside Fort Meade, home to the NSA and the new US Cyber Command, it was virtually impossible to tell for sure whether those failures were the result of American-led sabotage, North Korean ineptitude, or bad luck.

What was clear from the investigation, however, is that the United States had turned a new class of offensive weapons—its growing arsenal of exquisite cyberweapons—against North Korean intercontinental ballistic missiles that would likely soon be able to reach Los Angeles, Chicago, and Washington, DC. It was hardly the first time the United States had used these weapons to sabotage an American adversary. In 2012, the *Times* had revealed the inside story of "Olympic Games," the code name for a secret American-Israeli effort to attack Iran's nuclear production capabilities with precisely targeted computer code that would destabilize sensitive nuclear centrifuges.[1] That disclosure led to one of the largest DOJ leak inquiries in modern times and the eventual indictment of the former vice chairman of the Joint Chiefs of Staff on a charge of lying to the

FBI. Later there would be stories about similar American offensive cyber efforts against Iran's missile systems[2] and Russia's power grid.[3]

This is the new frontier in national security reporting. The day-to-day coverage of the escalating cyber conflict among nations has become a staple of serious efforts to measure how well the Pentagon, the intelligence agencies, and private firms—from banks to the utilities that run the electric power grid—are doing at the task of keeping us safe. They involve some of the most sensitive offensive and defensive technologies in the hands of the United States. To cover it right, journalists have to explore the escalating attacks on the United States: the Chinese efforts to steal industrial designs and government secrets, the Russian disruption of elections, the North Korean theft of cryptocurrencies. But they must also cover the immense, often clandestine American program to use cyberweapons to undermine adversaries across the globe. And increasingly, that puts reporters and news organizations at odds with the US government, which has wrapped its offensive cyber programs in more secrecy than surrounded the expansion of its nuclear arsenal in the 1950s, '60s, and '70s.

This new line of reporting doesn't easily fit the mold of the 1971 Pentagon Papers case, the clash with the government that changed the way American news organizations weigh the decisions to publish national security stories. None of the *Times's* articles had emerged from the disclosure of a secret Pentagon history of America's cyberwars, akin to Daniel Ellsberg's revelation of a secret history of the Vietnam conflict. Nor did they come from a huge digital data dump, like the WikiLeaks disclosures or the revelations of Edward Snowden in 2013. Instead, they emerged from the reporting that is now an everyday staple of covering national security in an age of terrorism, drone warfare, and daily cyber conflict. They are more akin to battlefield reporting, the kind that reports on American progress and setbacks on the ground in Iraq or Afghanistan. But this reporting takes place at a distance and tries to explain the murky battle over control of cyberspace. The operations are often covert or clandestine, run by the NSA or US Cyber Command, the NSA's military cousin.

It all bears little resemblance to covering the Vietnam War. Yet the legal and journalistic issues have strong echoes of the legal debate—and journalistic decisions—of the Pentagon Papers era. Much as the Pentagon Papers forced Americans to wonder why we were in Vietnam and why the government was lying about our progress, the coverage of cyberweapons and other technologies is designed to force a debate about how America wants to use its power—and at what price.

When America reaches into its cyber arsenal—which it does frequently—are its new weapons deterring Russia from meddling with elections or threatening American infrastructure? Or is it inviting retaliation against the famously soft targets of the United States, the most wired nation in the world and one of the most vulnerable to massive disruption? Are we triggering a new arms race, with a new class of weapons that are so cheap, so easy to develop, and so widespread that they are far harder to control than the fearsome nuclear weaponry of the Cold War? Under what circumstances should the president or the president's commanders utilize cyberweapons against adversaries—and with what limits?

Not surprisingly, these are questions many in the government say are unsuitable for public discussion, and they say that the more journalists write about the capabilities of America's multi-billion-dollar offensive cyber program, the more we aid potential enemies. I disagree. Like all complex conflicts, this one needs to be covered from all sides, its trade-offs and strategies examined, the public engaged. And that fundamental difference in view has led to a growing number of leak investigations and legal confrontations.

That was the background when my colleague William J. Broad and I were escorted down into the White House Situation Room in February 2017 to talk with officials about what they had learned about the program against North Korea's missiles. We were hardly newcomers to such sessions. For three decades, the two of us had reported extensively on nuclear proliferation, the capabilities of American adversaries, the loss of nuclear secrets, and, more recently, how cyberweapons were being used to sabotage such programs. Many of the officials in the Situation Room that afternoon knew us. And the meeting was part of the now-familiar, post–Pentagon Papers dance between reporters from the major news organizations and the government over the publication of sensitive stories.

We opened the meeting by explaining that some of the story we were getting ready to publish was based on evidence hidden in plain sight. While we had clearly consulted anonymous, confidential sources, there were hints of the effort to undermine North Korea's program littered in budget testimony in Congress and in the PowerPoint presentations prepared by military contractors eager to sweep up some of the billions of dollars now being spent on cyberweapons.

Those documents—which we downloaded before they were swept offline by the contractors—described an effort the Pentagon calls "Left of Launch." That phrase is a benign way of describing a variety of techniques to sabotage missile programs around the world *before* missiles are launched or just as they lift off. Sometimes that involves slipping bad parts into an adversary's supply chain. Sometimes it involves recruiting insiders to undermine launch systems. But in this case, the critical element relied on cyber- and electronic-warfare methods to affect the trajectory of the missiles.

For the United States, the program amounted to an extra insurance policy, atop traditional missile defenses. At best, the interceptors that the United States has deployed in Alaska and California, a $300 billion investment over the past three decades, can knock down a few incoming missiles; as North Korea's arsenal grew in size and sophistication, experts had little confidence that those traditional missile defenses would create the kind of shield President Reagan had dreamed about four decades ago. "Left of Launch" is about boosting America's chances of preventing an attack.

Not surprisingly, the officials were concerned about the specific details we had uncovered. They did not dispute our assertion that Kim Jong-un, the North Korean leader, had already discovered the sabotage program; in the fall of 2016, while the United States was wrapped up in the presidential election, Kim had radically changed the kind of missiles he was launching. The new tactics worked. His subsequent launches were nearly flawless. But the intelligence officials were worried that the revelation would alert other adversaries to the techniques used by the United States and its allies. It was not an unwarranted worry. In a world in which missile arsenals were growing more sophisticated from Iran to Pakistan to China, defeating missile threats was growing more complex.

Anticipating those concerns, we had already deleted some specific details. The story could be told without revealing specific techniques the United States was using without affecting the main storyline. The officials acknowledged those and pressed for a few more. But at the end of the meeting, they asked what always becomes the key question in national security reporting: Why write this story at all? Do the American people need to know? Isn't it enough to simply say the United States is protecting citizens from foreign threats and avoid discussing how?

To the *Times*, the import of the story was clear: The United States was clearly not the only nation using cyber sabotage to undermine their adversaries' launches. As such efforts become widespread, they had huge implications for strategic stability. The concept that kept the peace during the Cold War— mutually assured destruction—was threatened by a new reality in which countries could attempt to undercut each other's ability to launch. And yet there had been little public discussion about whether the use of cyberweapons by the United States—not only in this case but also against Iran's nuclear program and Russian information operations—made Americans safer or less safe. There were good reasons to think that the use of these weapons, while satisfying at first, was ultimately imperiling our own safety and making it more tempting for nations to reach for their nuclear weapons earlier. Hundreds of millions of lives were at stake.

There is a long history in the United States that backed up our rationale to publish. Those were exactly the kinds of stories the *Times* and other news organizations wrote during the nuclear age, as the United States and the Soviet Union stared each other down. The *Times* and other news organizations covered the lengthy debates over what kind of nuclear weapons to build, what rules should govern their use, and how to deter adversaries. Cyber was simply the newest—and in many ways most dangerous—iteration of that arms race.

Not surprisingly, the intelligence officials were not there to debate nuclear strategy or the importance of First Amendment rights. They were there to cut a deal. And as we emerged from the meeting and discussions with H. R. McMaster, the president's national security advisor, we thought we had something of a mutual understanding about what we could publish without tipping off American adversaries.

But before the story was even published, some cryptic tweets came from the newly inaugurated president. "The real story here is why there are so many illegal leaks coming out of Washington?" President Trump, tweeting as @ realDonaldTrump, wrote on Valentine's Day, 2017. "Will these leaks be happening as I deal on N.Korea etc.?"

Two days later, that was followed by another tweet: "Leaking, and even illegal classified leaking, has been a big problem in Washington for years. Failing @nytimes (and others) must apologize!" (By that time, of course, he had forgotten that the previous October, he had hailed the leak of Democratic National Committee documents by WikiLeaks and told his supporters at a rally, "you gotta read it!")

And that was followed by a letter from Donald McGahn, then the White House counsel, who wrote to the *Times* a few days later saying that the article about North Korea "will compromise and/or otherwise negatively impact the national security of the United States." As the *Times*'s lead attorney on national security issues, David McCraw, wrote later, his "verb of choice was 'will,' not 'might,' not 'could.' Was a new administration, with less than a month in office, getting ready to turn its back on history" and begin prosecuting reporters under the century-old Espionage Act?

It was a real possibility, and in the newsroom of the *Times*, reporters and lawyers prepared for it.

In the century since the Espionage Act was first enacted into law by Congress, American news organizations have feared the law would be turned against them. The concern was legitimate, since the statute, as amended, plainly put journalists in its sights. It begins: "Whoever knowingly and willfully communicates, furnishes, transmits, or otherwise makes available to an unauthorized person, *or publishes*, or uses in any manner prejudicial to the safety or interest of the United States or for the benefit of any foreign government to the detriment of the United States any classified information . . ."[4]

Stunningly, the concern has proven premature for a century. While the government has episodically imprisoned reporters for refusing to reveal sources, there have been no prosecutions under the Espionage Act for the publication of information "prejudicial to the safety or interest of the United States," though, in the eyes of many government officials, that happens every day. And information that benefits foreign governments? Rifle through the pages of any newspaper, or thumb through a news organization's home page, and such information is everywhere: disputes over American weapons systems, stories about Pentagon failures, and, of course, news questioning the honesty, the health, or the secret conversations of an American president. All this is possible because of the First Amendment, an oddity even among Western democracies. Two hundred thirty years of case law has held that the First Amendment does not allow criminal punishment for publication of such topics, except in the most extraordinary of conditions.

But while the government has kept its hands off the news organizations, it has been far more aggressive against their sources. During Obama's presidency, the government pursued more leak investigations than under all of his predecessors combined, an effort to chill leakers—and, inevitably, chill newsrooms. Not surprisingly, the DOJ's hunt prompted reporters to go to great lengths in recent years to protect those sources. Notes are not kept on electronic systems for the most sensitive stories. And communications, when they can be, are moved to encrypted apps like Signal, in the hope that there is no record on either side of the conversation for the government to subpoena. Still, in a case involving my former *Times* colleague James Risen, the Supreme Court let stand a lower court ruling that stated that the First Amendment interests in protecting the identity of sources can be easily outweighed by other government interests. That ruling came in response to an Obama administration–initiated prosecution. It was a predictable extension of the 1972 decision in *Branzburg v. Hayes*, where the Supreme Court ruled that the First Amendment did not give reporters a right to protect the confidentiality of sources and that requiring reporters to disclose confidential sources could be a "paramount" state interest[5].

In the Risen case, the government never compelled him to testify. It prosecuted a suspected source of his without Risen's testimony or notes. But the case left reporters with very little legal backup should push come to shove and the government insisted on the names of sources.

All that was before President Trump launched an all-out effort to discredit news organizations that covered him aggressively. It began with Trump's perversion of the phrase *fake news*, an effort to conflate in the public's mind true newsgathering and foreign government propaganda. Trump knew exactly what he was doing. By denigrating news organizations, he was making it easier to deny and ignore their later revelations about him. And by castigating the press as "enemies of the people"—a phrase he was repeatedly warned was triggering violence against newsrooms and reporters—he sought to undermine the central

American concept that the purpose of a free press is to act as a watchdog on the government.

But at least at the time of this writing, the Trump administration seemed comfortable attacking the press, not prosecuting it. It has not pressed, at least yet, the central question of whether a journalist might be criminally charged under the Espionage Act—though it seems to be edging in that direction with the indictment of Julian Assange, the founder of WikiLeaks, the organization that candidate Trump praised so effusively. ("WikiLeaks. I love WikiLeaks!" he famously proclaimed when it was revealing details about the campaign of his 2016 rival, Hillary Clinton.)[6]

It is hardly clear that Assange is a journalist; he doesn't weigh facts, sift evidence, and write or broadcast stories. But in newsrooms around the country, the fear is that if he, or WikiLeaks, is successfully prosecuted for publishing classified data, the precedent will soon be applied to real newsrooms—not just organizations that are accused, as WikiLeaks was, of being more akin to a foreign intelligence agency. Measuring the likelihood of such a possibility is nearly impossible. But the chilling effect would be huge. In my thirty-seven years of reporting on national security issues at the *New York Times*, I've never seen a story withheld because of the fear of government prosecution. But I worry about journalists from other news organizations that might not have the legal budgets, or the resolve, to take on the government.

Those thirty-seven years have given me some sympathy for the plight of government officials, generals, intelligence officers, and others who see their efforts on behalf of the American people hindered by the flood of leaks, large and small. It was that frustration that led the Obama administration to pursue leakers with such ferocity, a tendency that led me to declare in a study by the Committee to Protect Journalists that the Obama White House was the "most closed, control freak administration" I'd ever covered, determined to control every bit of information that flowed out of the government.[7] (Its record has since been surpassed by the Trump administration.)

I understand where those control freak tendencies come from. Even governments that wildly overclassify—as the United States does—need to keep some truly vital secrets. The Manhattan Project was one. Had the operation to kill Osama bin Laden leaked out, the world's most-wanted terrorist, a man with the blood of three thousand Americans on his hands, might easily have escaped. (It was a miracle that it didn't leak, though I remain convinced that most major news organizations would have held the story until after the operation started. As it was, the first public news came not from a news media leak but from a sleepless Twitter user in a nearby compound in Abbottabad.)

But those are the exceptions. The vast majority of leaks are not as consequential as the bin Laden raid. But as Harvard's Graham T. Allison notes, even leaks of debates over policy narrow the government's "decision space," the ability to debate out the consequences of an action and to change one's mind. That is what enraged Obama as details of his Situation Room meetings in 2009 to select a new strategy for dealing with Afghanistan and Pakistan appeared in the *Times* and the *Washington Post*.

So I understand why many government officials—and even some lawyers at news organizations—declare "there should be laws against some types of leaking," even if they are not enforced very often.[8] And of course, we shouldn't pretend that leakers are all high-minded: for every true whistleblower who seeks to expose corruption or wrongdoing or suspects the president may be extorting a foreign power, there are many more who are seeking revenge, bureaucratic victory, partisan advantage, or ego gratification. But every leak investigation comes with a cost. It creates a deterrent to leaking that may satisfy the DOJ and the president, but it also imperils future leaks that the proper operation of a democracy depends upon. One needs to look no further than the torrent of leaks about the Russian interference in the 2016 election or the Trump administration's fumbled handling of the coronavirus outbreak.

And the past few decades have shown that there is no way to write a law or decide a case that permits "good" leaks and prohibits bad or self-interested leaks. Allowing the former means tolerating some of the latter. And the issue is particularly fraught when the branch of government deciding whether to prosecute the leakers, and maybe the reporters they talked to, is the same branch that is being exposed in news articles that are revealing a vital truth: that the war in Afghanistan is not going as well as the government wants you to believe; that the privacy protections on the communications of Americans are not as effective as the government says; that the State Department is denouncing human rights abuses abroad while the Customs and Border Patrol is separating mothers and their children. Or that the president knew a lot about the approach of a deadly virus, even while he was publicly playing down its potential impact.

And in the Trump era, even revelations that do not involve classified secrets are considered grounds for leak-hunts. At the end of 2019, a senior official in the Trump administration called me in to complain about the coverage of his agency and of the White House. As his anger grew, he said that if he could repeal a single law, it would be FOIA. "Every FOIA request we receive will be responded to with pages of black lines," he said, referring to the big, blocky redactions that government censors use to delete classified information—along with whatever embarrassing or inconvenient revelations lay under the black lines.

Of course, FOIA only applies to unclassified information. The Trump administration official was essentially saying that the executive branch should be able to hold back both classified and unclassified data, at will. And that became clear when Covid-19 struck the country. The administration discovered that most health-related information—from the size of stockpiles of masks and ventilators to the number of sick sailors on a Navy aircraft carrier—is unclassified. The publication of that information—which came not from leaks but from public data—was viewed as a political threat to the president.

So as soon as the Coronavirus Task Force began to meet in the Situation Room, White House officials started declaring that the decision-making around vaccine projects and ventilator supplies could be withheld because the subject was being discussed in a classified space. It was a classic case of turning the law on its head: the locale of the meeting, rather than the national security implications of disclosure, became the rationale for secrecy.

News organizations, as one might imagine, were unimpressed with the argument that debate over an issue as fundamental as saving the lives of American citizens became secret because of the room those debates took place in. Not surprisingly, they did not hesitate to base stories on accounts of the meeting provided by participants or their notes. Government complaints that they were violating classification rules did not hold sway.

That experience was instructive. The United States rightly complained that the Chinese government was covering up information about the origins of the virus and detaining scientists who revealed the DNA of the novel coronavirus. They assailed the Chinese—rightly—for revoking the visas of reporters from the *New York Times*, the *Washington Post*, and the *Wall Street Journal*, all of which had vigorously reported on the origins of the virus in China and Xi Jinping's response.[9]

But then the United States edged up to the same line. Even before China's expulsion of the American journalists, the United States had put new restrictions on Chinese journalists, making them register as lobbyists. It demoted or exiled scientists whom it regarded as disloyal to the president's strategy, then expressed shock that many of their accounts of how the government mismanaged the response were "leaked." (In fact, most of the scientists put their names to their complaints, which is hardly the action of a leaker.) All of this demonstrates the fundamental tension in our system. Governments need to keep some number of secrets for the sake of real national security. And without doubt, if every email is made public, in a news article or over the internet, it would be painfully difficult to reach decisions. But at the same time, it is even more dangerous to let the executive branch hold the power to prosecute journalists or their sources. The system is just too prone to abuse. Even unsuccessful attempts at prosecution will have exactly the chilling effect that undercuts the core of our constitutional system. And it is the citizens, not the journalists, who suffer the most. "When people are allowed to know only what the government wants them to know, they become little more than sheep in a fog," McCraw writes in his account of the *Times*'s First Amendment battles with the government. "If you are a lawyer in leak-world, you inevitably find yourself advocating for something that could be best described as a modicum of unlawfulness, which is not the concept they teach you in law school."[10]

In short, to preserve our democracy, we have to allow some speech that undercuts good order, worsens government decision-making, and, undoubtedly, sometimes harms immediate national security interests. To journalists and First Amendment advocates, that doesn't seem like a contradiction; it seems like a reasonable trade-off, accepting some national security risk in order to preserve the core of the American democratic system. To others, it sounds like a suicide pact. And that divide has only widened in recent years.

At the core lies this question: how much risk do we need to bear to preserve the ability of an active, intrusive, sometimes partisan press to act as a check on government?

To answer that question, we must turn to what has become known in recent years as "the WikiLeaks problem."

WikiLeaks is not, in the view of this journalist, a news organization. It does not "report" in the traditional way. It does not collect and assess evidence. It does not have much, if any, editorial process. Instead, it amasses large volumes of information—emails, memorandums, internal documents—and simply makes them available, en masse. Everything is published—the classified and the unclassified and, more concerning to those who worry about personal privacy, addresses and social security numbers and other identifying information. Then WikiLeaks lets the chips fall where they may.

Not only does the public cringe when this happens, but so do real journalists, who know that in the minds of the public, there will be very little differentiation between what WikiLeaks does and what the *New York Times* or CNN does.

To make matters worse, groups like WikiLeaks quickly become the stooges of hostile governments. The Mueller investigation revealed how effectively Russian intelligence agents made use of the WikiLeaks platform. When the Russian agents began posting their stolen trove of data on the internet, they did it on their own sites and through social media. Few paid attention. In relatively short order—a matter of weeks—the Russian agents figured out that their impact would be far greater if they turned the same data over to WikiLeaks and had it published there. It was a brilliant stroke. Suddenly, leaks that would easily be branded, and dismissed, as "Russian disinformation" were given new prominence. WikiLeaks not only served as a cutout for Vladimir Putin, but it also served as a megaphone. As one investigator said later, "if WikiLeaks didn't exist,

Putin would have to go out and create it." (In fact, he and his allies tried—that's part of what the Internet Research Agency in St. Petersburg was trying to do.)

So it is tempting to argue, as the Trump administration has, that WikiLeaks should not have the kinds of protections that "real" news organizations rely on. Mike Pompeo, when he was still CIA director, contended that WikiLeaks was a "hostile intelligence service," whose founder, Assange, used to make "common cause with dictators."[11] Pompeo compared Assange to Philip Agee, a former intelligence agent who left the government, became a public gadfly, and ultimately published the names of American intelligence officers around the world. One of those officers, Richard Welch, the CIA station chief in Athens, was assassinated in December 1975. Agee, Pompeo noted, "settled down as the privileged guest of an authoritarian regime—one that would have put him in front of a firing squad without a second thought had he betrayed their secrets as he betrayed ours."

Pompeo's analogy has some legitimacy. WikiLeaks did act more like a foreign agent in 2016 than like a news organization. It willingly allowed itself to be taken over by a foreign power—an adversary of the United States—and did that power's bidding. So it was little surprise that two years after Pompeo's speech, the United States indicted Assange on seventeen counts of violating the Espionage Act for publishing secret and top-secret American military and diplomatic documents in 2010.[12] (The indictment had nothing to do with Assange's role in the 2016 election; instead, it focused on his publication of military documents and then the State Department's trove of cables, which were also published by the *Times* in the fall of 2010.)[13]

Satisfying as the moment may have been for Pompeo and the prosecutors, the indictment left the DOJ in a quandary. How could it explain why it was indicting Assange—an Australian living in London who held no security clearances— but not indicting the *Times* or other news organizations that published excerpts from the very same trove of documents? What made them different?

"Some say that Assange is a journalist and that he should be immune from prosecution for these actions," John Demers, the head of the DOJ's National Security Division, told reporters on the day of the indictment, which at this writing is mired in a lengthy extradition process in Britain. "The department takes seriously the role of journalists in our democracy and we thank you for it. It is not and has never been the department's policy to target them for reporting."

Yet Demers went on to argue that Assange was "no journalist," because "No responsible actor, journalist or otherwise, would purposefully publish the names of individuals he or she knew to be confidential human sources in a war zone, exposing them to the gravest of dangers."

He was almost certainly right—no responsible journalist would do that. In fact, when the *Times* published some of the State Department cables in 2010, it omitted names and other identifying information for people who had been sources for the State Department or whose mere appearance in a news story could lead hostile governments to exact retribution against them. (I deleted from one set of documents the casual mention of one person who, I learned after consulting with the US government, had been a CIA asset in the Middle East.)

But Demers sidestepped the core problem. In issuing the indictment, the government of the United States was essentially deciding who was a "journalist" and who was not. How did he come to the conclusion that Assange could be indicted but that the old-line news organizations that published the same material could not? In fact, the details of the indictment listed actions by WikiLeaks that closely replicate ordinary, day-to-day national security reporting conducted by real journalists from legitimate news organizations—publishing information of real news value, some of it secret, that was obtained outside ordinary or legal channels.

In short, the Demers distinction—between real news organizations and the WikiLeaks of the world—is useful as a political statement, but it doesn't stand up as a legal distinction. And for that reason, the Trump administration's indictment poses a real threat to legitimate news organizations. Even if you take Demers at his word—that he would not indict real journalists or real news organizations for the kind of activity he indicted Assange for committing—that is a matter of policy, not law. If Assange is extradited to the United States and convicted of violating the Espionage Act, the precedent will almost certainly change the way the government wields a century-old law. And sooner or later, a prosecutor or future attorney general will determine that the precedent set in the Assange case can be used to prosecute a reporter—next time, from a real news organization.

Much as it would be satisfying for the government—and even some journalists—to prosecute Assange, the price to our future freedoms is just too high. Had the government simply indicted Assange for conspiring to hack into government systems, a violation of the Computer Fraud and Abuse Act, there would be little concern. The First Amendment doesn't protect journalists from prosecution for robbing banks, and no one expects it to give them carte blanche to steal State Department documents. But once the DOJ took the next step, accusing Assange of violating the Espionage Act, it veered into dangerous territory. It is only a matter of time before a future government seeking to avoid embarrassment will invoke that same law to chill deep reporting into American operations in Afghanistan or Iraq or arms control negotiations with North Korea, Iran, or Russia.

That is simply too high a price to pay.

Beyond the question of whether WikiLeaks is a news organization lies another legal issue: the differential treatment of the press and the leakers.

Ever since the Pentagon Papers decision, an uneasy status quo has existed, in which the government pursues leakers but—at least until the Assange indictment—not those who publish leaked data. It has never been a very satisfying compromise. That amounted to what my colleague McCraw called "an unspoken bargain of mutual restraint in which the press embraced an ethos of responsibility and the government generally treated leaks as an accepted, if not fully condoned, part of modern democratic dominance."

Alexander Bickel, the noted First Amendment scholar, called it "the disorderly situation," which McCraw and Stephen Gikow, a First Amendment fellow at the *Times*, described this way:

> As Bickel saw it, American law ceded to the government broad powers to keep secrets but afforded news organizations broad freedom to publish secrets once those secrets were in the hands of journalists, largely irrespective of how those secrets got there. At least at a theoretical level, it is a system that both overprotects and underprotects secrets and serves up no legal principle or overarching policy for deciding what should be disclosed and what should not.[14]

Indeed, there is something of an internal logic to this seemingly contradictory approach. The government undoubtedly has the right to prosecute officials and contractors who leak classified information in violation of the oaths they took and the classification rules. The classic case cited by government officials is Snowden, the NSA contractor who used a "sweeper" program to scoop up hundreds of thousands of internal documents from inside the NSA. He fled to Hong Kong, then Russia, where he remains today; seven years later, the government maintains it is still cleaning up the damage.

Snowden triggered the classic massive, digital, unauthorized leak, and if Putin tires of his presence and returns him to the United States, there is an indictment awaiting him. But no one gets prosecuted for the far more common "intentional leaks," organized by the executive branch. I've been the recipient of dozens, from access to satellite photographs of North Korean nuclear activity provided by senior government officials seeking to send a message to an adversary, to military or diplomatic plans leaked as a trial balloon. Naturally, government officials want it both ways; they want both to prosecute unauthorized leakers and to keep themselves free to disclose classified or sensitive data when they consider it in their, or the national, interest.

Of course, going after the leaker, not the reporter, has clear benefits for the government. It is a way of intimidating federal employees to prevent them from talking with the press without running headlong into First Amendment challenges. It is a technique that avoids relitigating the Pentagon Papers case. No wonder the "unspoken bargain" has remained in place for so long.

But in most cases, the motives behind leaks are not so clear-cut. In my experience, there is no clear line between "authorized" and "unauthorized" conversations. Most conversations with current and former government officials take place in the murky waters between those two categories. And often, sources seeking to do the right thing—to explain policy, warn about national dangers, or persuade a reporter that certain information they are preparing to publish could be truly damaging—find themselves at risk. That is why leak investigations, with their interrogations and seizures of emails, can quickly become insidious, and often political, exercises. They are usually designed to send an intimidating message to warn against talking with the press, rather than to protect legitimate government secrets.

I was directly involved in a case that underscored both the "unspoken bargain" and the dangers of such leak investigations. In early 2012, as I was wrapping up the writing of a book titled *Confront and Conceal: Obama's Secret Wars and the Surprising Use of American Power*, I went to see General James Cartwright (Ret.), who had served as vice chairman of the Joint Chiefs of Staff. Cartwright had been a major force in designing the military's cyber strategy and helped launch what later became US Cyber Command.

I had been referred to Cartwright by a senior member of President Obama's national security staff. Key parts of the book dealt with the country's increasing use of cyberweapons. And that included the largest and most sophisticated cyberattack that any nation has launched against another: Operation "Olympic Games," the effort to sabotage Iran's nuclear enrichment program with a cyberweapon that, quite literally, blew up Iran's centrifuges, the machines that spin at supersonic speed to purify uranium gas.

The program had been revealed fourteen months before, in 2010. The computer code that infected the centrifuge plant had gotten out—not by a deliberate leak by some anonymous official but by what appears to have been a technical mistake. By the summer of 2010, copies of the code, quickly dubbed "Stuxnet," were flying around the world. As a result, the Iranians, the Russians, the Chinese, and many others could dissect the code, line by line. So did journalists, with the help of outside experts. And to anyone who knew what they were looking at, the forensic analysis quickly made clear that Iran's Natanz nuclear plant was the target, and it pointed to American and Israeli cyberwarriors as the authors of the code.

When I went to see Cartwright, all of this was known. And my own reporting, based on the code's revelation, had uncovered the decision-making to launch the covert program. It involved two presidents, Bush and Obama. And since the

Iranians already had the code in hand, it was hardly news to them that they were under attack.

I had already taken my findings through official channels to the administration and been sent to the deputy director of the CIA, Michael Morell, to discuss any concerns that the government had about what I had discovered. At his request, I removed from the book some technical details of the operation that the Intelligence Community believed the Iranians may not have discovered or understood.[15]

My separate conversations with Cartwright focused on fact-checking the history of the American offensive cyber program and, ultimately, his own advice about what would be damaging to reveal about the Stuxnet operation. He believed that the White House, by sending me to consult him, had blessed the conversation. And I wanted an independent view of what would be truly damaging to publish and what, based on the revelation of the code, the Iranians already understood.

In short, because Cartwright had already left government, he was neither an "authorized" or "unauthorized" source; he was, as many sources are, in the netherworld somewhere in between. He believed he was acting at the government's request, and I believed so, too. That proved no protection when the book was published. A major leak investigation was launched, and it was not long before the FBI was at his door, with emails proving that the two of us had planned to meet.

It made no difference that the vast majority of the reporting and the writing had been completed before Cartwright and I met. Or that there were sources for "Olympic Games" all over the world—in Europe, in Israel, at the International Atomic Energy Agency. This had been a classic case of a "mosaic" reporting exercise, piecing together the puzzle. But of the scores of interviews I conducted, the FBI focused only on the retired general.

After several years of investigation that damaged Cartwright's financial and physical health, he ultimately pled guilty to lying to FBI agents in his initial interview about his contacts with me and another reporter. He was never charged with leaking anything. Ultimately, President Obama pardoned him.

Curiously, after considerable internal debate, the government never sought my testimony or my notes from the conversations with Cartwright. Perhaps it did not want to touch off a First Amendment fight with the *Times*. Perhaps it feared more revelations about the Stuxnet program if the case went to trial and I was forced to testify. Perhaps it was just following the unspoken bargain: go after the source, not the reporter.

But I emerged from that experience deeply worried about the hidden costs of the unspoken bargain. Reporters have few legal protections; sources have none. The crackdown on government officials that so accelerated in the Obama years had a long-term cost: in a world where governments hoard more and more secrets, it impeded the public's ability to understand even the outlines of vast new activities by the government in the national security sphere, in this case the use of a new weapon, guided by American strategies that are also fueling regular retaliatory strikes on the American public.

None of these trade-offs is easy. Governments will always have secrets to protect. News organizations will always press for more and more information. New media will continue to emerge, forcing hard decisions about who is a reporter, who is a publisher, who is just a partisan in journalistic clothing, and who is acting as an instrument of a foreign power.

But if there is a single lesson from the first Trump term, it is that the need for deep, thorough reporting on national security issues is greater than ever. Rarely has the world, or the national security infrastructure, been in more tumult. Topics that have been written about for decades—arms control, biological threats, the dangers of new technologies—are being declared "classified" and off limits. In such a world, ensuring that the press is free to publish what some in the government would term secrets has never been more important to our democracy. Certainly, there will be mistakes and abuses. But to allow the government to make those decisions—to use the Espionage Act to censor the unflattering, to intimidate sources—would be to undercut one of the few real checks left on executive power.

The uneasy balancing act of the decades since the Pentagon Papers was messy, but it worked. To destroy it now would be a critical mistake.

PART THREE

THE ACADEMIC PERSPECTIVE

Outlawing Leaks

DAVID A. STRAUSS

Several federal statutes make it illegal to disclose, without authorization, information related to national security. The most general prohibition is the Espionage Act, a statute first enacted in 1917. But as the most comprehensive study of the Espionage Act puts it, the "fundamental problem" with the Act is that it "is in many respects incomprehensible."[1] Judges have, not surprisingly, complained about that, and it's become common to say that we need a new statute to determine when leaking or publishing leaked information should be a crime. What should that statute look like?

There is no simple answer; if there were, we would have enacted a new statute by now. But the experience under the Espionage Act, and under other statutes that prohibit unauthorized disclosures of national security information, has at least taught us something about the issues that we would have to confront in drafting such a statute. Three issues, in particular, stand out.

(1) How do we define the category of information, related to national security, the unauthorized disclosure of which should be made a crime? The Espionage Act refers to information and tangible materials "relating to the national defense." But that phrase is vague and potentially too broad. "Classified information" is a more clearly defined alternative, but experience under the Espionage Act and the generally acknowledged problem of overclassification both suggest that simply forbidding leaks of classified information will not solve the problem.

(2) In what ways does the state of mind of the defendant—the individual charged with the unlawful disclosure—matter? Intent has to play some role. Espionage on behalf of a hostile power is different from, for example, an unauthorized but well-intentioned disclosure of information about arguable government misconduct; even assuming the latter should also be illegal, the punishment should not be the same. Beyond that obvious case, it is implausible to say that every accidental disclosure should be treated the same as a deliberate

disclosure. And deliberate disclosures might reflect different states of mind that are arguably not equally culpable.

(3) The third issue concerns the difference between what might be called insiders and outsiders—individuals to whom the government has entrusted sensitive information, which they then disclose without authorization, and individuals or entities that have no connection to the government but have come into the possession of information, without authorization, which they then publicize. The latter category, of course, includes members of the press, and criminalizing the publication of information by the press obviously raises First Amendment problems as well as serious policy issues.

The basic problem, of course, is that while unauthorized disclosures of sensitive national security information can be very damaging to the national interest, we sometimes want there to be such disclosures. They will reveal errors or wrongdoing by the government or will otherwise make important contributions to public debate, and those benefits will sometimes outweigh the harm done by the disclosure. There is general agreement in retrospect that this was true of the Pentagon Papers, for example. Inevitably, it will be harder to reach agreement on more recent instances, partly because it is so difficult to determine the relevant facts, particularly about the harm done (or not) by the disclosure. But unauthorized disclosures, including disclosures of national security information, are regularly the source of some of the most valuable journalism. This is an important difference between an anti-leaking statute and a statute that outlaws ordinary criminal conduct. Ideally, ordinary criminal conduct would never happen. That is not true of leaks. That makes it especially difficult to design an anti-leaking statute.

Nevertheless, one possibility in drafting a new statute would be simply to have a criminal prohibition that banned all unauthorized disclosures, without trying to make any allowance for disclosures that are less culpable or that are, on balance, beneficial. The idea would be that the government would exercise its discretion to prosecute only people who deserved to be prosecuted. The argument for proceeding in this way is that any effort to draft a narrower statute would undermine the deterrent effect that prevents damaging disclosures. Preventing, or even punishing, beneficial disclosures is a price worth paying to make sure that damaging disclosures are deterred, and prosecutors will not bring charges in cases where they are clearly not warranted—that would be the argument for a sweeping prohibition. Government officials who have been responsible for protecting sensitive national security information, in particular, might find this approach attractive.

Prosecutorial discretion is, in fact, a safety valve throughout our criminal justice system: we routinely rely on prosecutorial discretion to deal with criminal statutes that sweep too broadly, impose too harsh a punishment, or involve judgments too complex to be captured in statutory language. But an anti-leaking statute presents special issues that make it less reassuring to rely on prosecutorial discretion. Leaking is often a way of challenging government officials. It performs some of the same functions as public criticism of officials. Sometimes a leak is actually of an internal, confidential dissenting opinion, and in any event, leaks routinely make the government look bad. For that reason, there is a greater risk that a prosecution for an unauthorized disclosure will be an act of political retaliation—at least a greater risk than in the case of an ordinary criminal prosecution. It may be, in the end, that the best we can do is to rely heavily on prosecutorial discretion. But there is good reason to try to avoid that result.

Laws forbidding leaks are different from ordinary criminal statutes in at least one other respect as well. It seems fair to say that the motivations of people who leak will often be less malign. They will often think that they are acting for the greater good. Of course, that does not excuse their conduct. (Assassins and spies might also think they are acting for the greater good.) And even benign motivations may be part of a psychological tangle of narcissism and delusion. But ordinary criminal laws are, in general, directed against antisocial bad actors, and people who leak or who publicize leaked information will often not fit into that category. This complicates the question of defining criminal intent, in particular. It also raises some issues about how to design laws so that they deter conduct that should certainly be deterred but that is not flagrantly culpable so much as it is wrongheaded or misguided. This, too, will make it especially difficult to find answers to the three issues I mentioned.

1. *What information should be protected from disclosure?* The existing law on this question is problematic in several respects. As I said, the provisions of the Espionage Act that are most often used to prosecute leaks forbid the disclosure of information or tangible materials "relating to the national defense."[2] That vague language potentially encompasses matters that may not be very sensitive and the disclosure of which will not be harmful. A World War II–era case, *Gorin v. United States*[3]—which was decided before the current system of classifying national security information was in place—addressed this issue. *Gorin* held that the term "relating to the national defense" (as it appeared in an earlier version of the Espionage Act) was not unconstitutionally vague. But that holding was premised on the Court's understanding that the Espionage Act includes an intent requirement—that the defendant had "reason to believe that the information to be obtained is to be used to the injury of the United States, or to the advantage of any foreign nation."[4] The intent requirement both narrowed the coverage of the Act and mitigated the concern with vagueness, on the theory that individuals who act with bad intent cannot complain about not having been warned that their act was unlawful.

One problem is that the intent requirement itself is not very well defined. To say that the defendant has reason to believe that the information "is to be used" to injure the United States might require only that the defendant have reason to believe that the information could *potentially* be used to injure the United States. Or it might require a showing that the defendant has reason to believe that the information is *very likely* to be used to injure the United States. The first interpretation seems to make the prohibition too broad; lots of information "relating to the national defense" might conceivably be used in some way to injure the United States or to help a foreign nation. But the second interpretation—requiring the government to show a high likelihood that an unauthorized disclosure will, in fact, harm the United States—might make it too difficult for the government to prove a violation.

As mentioned, *Gorin* was decided before the current system of classifying national security information was in place, and today it would be natural to say that information "relating to the national defense" means classified information.[5] In fact, that is roughly how courts have applied the term "relating to the national defense" in more recent Espionage Act prosecutions.[6] Defining a criminal violation as the disclosure of classified information would squarely deal with the vagueness problem, but it would raise two other questions. One is whether other statutes can adequately define, and protect, sensitive national security information that, for one reason or another, is not classified. There are such statutes now;[7] the question would be whether Congress can create a comprehensive enough network of such specific prohibitions to justify limiting a successor to the Espionage Act to classified information.

The second question is whether the government's decision to classify the information that was disclosed will be reviewable in a criminal prosecution. The difficulties with allowing a defendant to raise improper classification as a defense are obvious. Courts are usually not in a good position to determine how important it is to keep national security information secret; that determination will often require a lot of contextual knowledge and a degree of expertise that courts do not have. In addition, the government might not be able to explain why information is classified without revealing sources and methods of intelligence gathering or other sensitive information. That can precipitate a graymail problem: if a defendant can force the government to disclose sensitive information in order to justify its classification decision, the government might decide that an otherwise justified prosecution is not worth it.

On the other hand, there is a persistent concern that the government overclassifies information. While it is, in the nature of things, hard to know just how big a problem overclassification is, it would not be surprising if the kinds of things that the public has an especially strong interest in knowing—evidence of activity that would be politically very controversial if it were disclosed or of activity that is unlawful or embarrassing to government officials—are prone to being unnecessarily classified. And a criminal prosecution that could result in an individual's being sent to prison presents the strongest case for allowing a judge to review a classification decision.

The best solution would probably be robust procedures within the executive branch to review classification decisions, especially when a putative whistleblower claims that the classification system is being used to conceal wrongdoing by the government. Those procedures could be integrated with a criminal statute by means of an exhaustion requirement. Exhaustion requirements, common elsewhere, specify that a would-be litigant must seek relief in a forum that is less intrusive before bringing suit against the government—in an administrative agency before suing in court, for example, or in a state court before proceeding in federal court. But they allow an exception if the litigant can show that it would be futile to exhaust the specified remedies because they are inadequate or too burdensome or are not designed to provide the relief in question. So perhaps a solution would be an exhaustion requirement, according to which defendants charged with disclosing classified material could not assert that the material was improperly classified unless they pursued remedies within the executive branch or showed that those remedies were inadequate. This would give the executive branch an incentive to create good procedures for reviewing classification decisions, and it would put courts in the position of evaluating the adequacy of executive branch procedures, rather than reviewing the nature of national security information itself. This is obviously not a cure-all, but it does play more to courts' institutional strengths.

Gorin and a Second Circuit opinion from the same era written by Judge Learned Hand raise another question about the scope of a prohibition on leaking. Those cases said that the disclosure of national security information could not be made criminal under the Espionage Act unless that information was "closely held" by the government.[8] Thus, an individual who disclosed even classified information might be able to defend against a prosecution on the ground that the information was already publicly available.

On its face, that limitation seems reasonable: it is hard to see why someone should be prosecuted for disclosing information that is already public. Also, a prosecution brought in those circumstances is more likely to reflect some form of political or otherwise illegitimate motivation by the government, rather than a genuine concern about protecting secrets. But even this sensible-seeming limit may be more problematic today than it was in the 1940s or even the 1980s. Given how easy it is today for people to obtain information in a digital form and circulate it widely, it would not be surprising if even highly sensitive information were, fairly often, available in some unauthorized place. The government might have a legitimate interest in preventing the information from being spread even further. To put the point another way, it is not clear that we want a system in which an unauthorized disclosure immunizes further unauthorized disclosures. And even if sensitive national security information was available in the public domain, a leak that confirmed its accuracy could be damaging. So the essentially sound requirement that the information be "closely held" will still have to be defined with care.[9]

2. *How much does the defendant's intent matter?* There are two categories of issues about intent.[10] One set of issues, familiar from tort law, concerns the degree of care that the defendant displayed in dealing with the sensitive information in question: was the unauthorized disclosure intentional, or reckless, or negligent, or just accidental? An unintentional disclosure might be the result of a mistake either about whether information was classified or about whether the act would disclose the information; and the mistake might happen because of recklessness or carelessness, or it might have happened by accident, even though the individual took all reasonable precautions.

Deliberate disclosures would be the core of a criminal prohibition against leaking. Reckless disclosures, and certainly careless disclosures, are less culpable, and strict liability—making individuals liable even when they took all reasonable precautions—is rare in the criminal law; it seems unacceptable to criminalize a truly inadvertent disclosure.[11] But theoretically, if one wanted to follow the model of outlawing a wide range of conduct and relying on prosecutorial discretion to mitigate the harshness, a strict liability regime would have to be considered. That regime would spare the government the need to prove anything other than a causal connection between the defendant's act and the release of information. If we were concerned about, for example, elaborate technical contrivances that could make a deliberate disclosure look accidental, then maybe such an extreme approach would be worth considering. But it would make prosecutorial discretion critical, which, for the reasons I mentioned before, is problematic.

The second set of issues about intent concerns what might be called motivation. Should it matter whether an individual acted out of a good-faith belief that the disclosure advanced the public interest? The problems of making motivation important are obvious. Motivations are complex and multilayered, and fact-finding about motives is often unreliable. But espionage should certainly be punished more harshly than other forms of unauthorized disclosure, and it will be difficult to define espionage without taking motivation into account.[12] That is particularly true today, when someone who wants to aid a hostile power can easily do so by transmitting information through an intermediary that presents itself as, for example, a news aggregator.[13]

There have also been occasional suggestions that there should be a "good faith" defense, of some form, if a person is charged with an unauthorized disclosure.

The Supreme Court's opinion in *Gorin* used that phrase in characterizing the willfulness requirement in the Espionage Act, although the Court's meaning was unclear. One district judge, in a prominent case, suggested that a patriotic motive might be a defense.[14] Commentators have made similar suggestions, for example, that there should be a defense if an individual reasonably believed that he or she was disclosing government wrongdoing. The defense would have to be objective; it would not be enough that an individual believed he or she was exposing wrongdoing, unless that belief was objectively reasonable. But if it were, one might draw an analogy to the doctrine that government officials who violate constitutional rights will not be held liable for damages if they could have reasonably believed that their actions were constitutional.[15] If government officials should have that kind of leeway to make sure that they can effectively do their jobs, why shouldn't government employees who are trying to inform the public about misfeasance have a comparable protection from criminal liability?

Such a "good faith" defense is plausible, and it has many advocates. But there are at least two problems that would have to be considered. One is that the defense as usually defined—an objectively reasonable belief that the disclosure revealed some form of government wrongdoing—addresses only one side of the balance. It does not take into account the possibility that a disclosure, while serving a legitimate purpose, might also be very damaging to important government interests. An individual with access to sensitive information, acting in good faith, might see one side more clearly than the other; he or she might have excellent reasons for believing that the disclosure of the information would provide valuable information to the public but might not be able accurately to assess the damage that the disclosure will do to the national interest. In fact, that seems likely to happen; sensitive national security information is compartmentalized, so relatively few officials will be in a position to assess both the costs and the benefits of keeping it secret. For that reason, a "good faith" defense might immunize damaging disclosures. To deal with this problem, the defense could, in principle, be defined as an objectively reasonable belief that, on balance, disclosure will be more beneficial than harmful. But then it seems to call for a court to make the same kind of decision it would make in deciding if the information was properly classified, with all of the difficulties of judicial competence that entails.

A more subtle problem, related to the first, is the effect that the availability of such a defense will have on people who are considering disclosing sensitive material without authorization. This is a place where the psychology of potential leakers, which I mentioned before, can be a factor. Unlike ordinary criminals, people who engage in unauthorized disclosures are more likely to see themselves as providing a valuable public service; that is to say, they will see themselves as acting in good faith even if, objectively, their belief that they are revealing abuses is unjustified. In other words, they may be especially prone to disclosing information in the mistaken belief that their unauthorized disclosure will be protected by a "good faith" defense. If that is true, then the availability of a "good faith" defense is likely to weaken, excessively, the deterrent effect of a criminal statute and in that way encourage disclosures that should not happen.

3. *Government insiders versus outsiders.* It would be possible to have a statute forbidding unauthorized disclosures of information that applied only to insiders: people, such as employees and contractors, who had access to the information because of their relationship to the government. Certainly, a ban on unauthorized disclosures by such insiders would be the core of such a statute. Even apart from the government's interest in keeping secrets, insiders have voluntarily undertaken an obligation, explicitly or implicitly, not to disclose sensitive information that has been entrusted to them. That is not true of people outside the government who come into the possession of information as the result of a leak—the news media, most conspicuously.

In fact, the current regime, for practical purposes, prohibits disclosures only by insiders, not by outsiders. Insiders are sanctioned for leaking; the press is not. There are plausible arguments that the Espionage Act and other statutes could, by their terms, apply to publications in the news media.[16] But it is pretty clear that under the First Amendment, as it is currently understood, members of the news media cannot be prevented from disclosing sensitive information or punished if they do disclose it, at least in the absence of extraordinary circumstances. This understanding—that the government may prevent leaks, but once the information is leaked, the government generally cannot prevent its further publication—is associated with the Pentagon Papers case.[17] And it is reflected in practice: government employees have been successfully prosecuted under the Espionage Act for unauthorized disclosures, but so far, at least, the government has not tried to prosecute members of the press.

This paradoxical state of affairs—leaking can be forbidden, but once confidential information is leaked, there is usually nothing the government can do to prevent its further spread—might no longer work. The reasons are familiar.[18] Among other things, in the Pentagon Papers era, the major media outlets—principally, a few national newspapers and television networks—acted as gatekeepers. They essentially determined what news would get widespread publicity. And they were—arguably—responsible gatekeepers, because they conceived of themselves as acting in the public interest, and they cooperated to some degree with the government to ensure that truly damaging information was not disclosed. Of course, the extent to which they were truly responsible can be debated. Maybe they were too quick to publish material that was damaging to legitimate government interests; maybe they were too willing to suppress information at the government's behest. But the character of the media gatekeepers was part of the rationale for allowing outsiders freedom to publish information that insiders could be sanctioned for leaking.

It is not clear that there are any gatekeepers anymore, given the ease of publicizing material on the internet. And there is no reason to think that everyone who publicizes leaked information will be responsible in any relevant sense. So that raises the question of whether disclosures of leaked information by individuals or entities outside the government should also be subject to sanctions. The sanctions might not be as severe as those imposed on people who have undertaken an obligation to keep the government's secrets. But if the government has an interest in preventing at least some information from being leaked, it obviously has an interest in preventing that same information from being widely disseminated. If the news media no longer can be counted on to prevent the dissemination of damaging information—it might be argued—then maybe criminal law should.

But, of course, the fundamental dilemma remains: some leaks *should* be widely publicized. Often it is better if the press is not deterred. There seem to be three possible resolutions, each of which has significant problems. One is simply to extend a prohibition against unauthorized disclosures to outsiders, including media outlets, and to rely again on prosecutorial discretion. The argument for relying on prosecutorial discretion in this context—even if doing so is generally problematic in dealing with leaks—is that major media outlets are in a good position to fight back against a criminal prosecution, so the government will be unwilling to incur the political costs of unjustified prosecutions.[19] The fact that the government has never sought to prosecute a member of the press for publicizing classified information suggests that there is something to this argument.

But there are also severe problems with this approach, and those, too, have gotten worse in the time since the Pentagon Papers case. While the major media outlets—the *New York Times* and the *Washington Post*, for example—may be in a position to fight back, others, equally worthy, may not be; journalism is much more financially precarious today than it was a generation ago. Those less established outlets may be more vigorous in attacking the government—this is a version of the idea that the established media are too concerned with being "responsible"—which will make them inviting targets for a government that does not want its mistakes exposed. But even the idea that major media outlets can protect themselves may now be naive. In a polarized political climate, when media outlets tend to be associated with one side or the other, it may be a mistake to assume that the government will always consider the costs of prosecuting even the *Times* and the *Post* to be prohibitive.

The second possible way of dealing with unauthorized disclosures by outsiders would be to allow some form of "good faith" defense for outsiders who publicize leaked information, even if it is not allowed for insiders. Some of the same concerns about a "good faith" defense for individuals who leak—that it might encourage too many damaging disclosures—would be present, but at least conscientious media outlets might be in a position to make a more dispassionate assessment of the harms and benefits of publicizing sensitive information. The bigger problem would again be the costs of litigation, especially for media outlets that are less well established but that might be more inclined to challenge the government when it needs to be challenged. Even a media outlet that was reasonably confident that it would prevail might be deterred by the threat of prosecution, if publishing something meant betting the firm.

The third possibility is to try to differentiate among media outlets—to identify, and exempt, those that might continue to act as more or less responsible gatekeepers, while extending prohibitions against unauthorized disclosures to others. So, to be concrete, the *New York Times* could not be prosecuted, but maybe WikiLeaks could. The obvious problem is that if the government were in the position to decide which media outlets are sufficiently responsible, government officials could abuse their authority, consciously or unconsciously. That's especially true in a media environment in which many firms will not sort easily into one category or another. Aggressive media outlets that occasionally go too far, or even make a point of going too far, may be especially effective in exposing government wrongdoing just because they are willing to venture where more established outlets are not.

Having said that, some such distinction among media outlets may be unavoidable. In various ways, governments already make this kind of distinction. Many states, for example, have laws that protect journalists from having to disclose their sources.[20] Those laws must differentiate between legitimate journalists and people who just want to resist lawful subpoenas. Governments award press credentials that allow special access to certain journalists but not others. And informally, of course, government officials do not treat all media outlets equally.

Possibly, the solution would be for the media itself to try to establish a set of professional norms that could help draw the necessary lines. There might be an analogy to lawyers and the attorney-client privilege. The attorney-client privilege is protected by law, and only actual lawyers—not just anyone who has a website and calls himself a lawyer—can take advantage of it. That requires determining who qualifies as an attorney. The qualifications for determining who will be admitted to the bar are administered according to professional norms. But it remains the case that lawyers are licensed by the state, and government licensing of the press is obviously a chilling prospect; it was exactly the evil at which the First Amendment and its common law antecedents were aimed. De facto, though, something like that already exists in the privileges given to certain journalists over others. Ideally, the process might be formalized so it depends on professional norms rather than the views of government officials.

No doubt, many people, not just journalists, would say that if the choice is between risking large-scale disclosures of damaging national security information, on the one hand, and allowing the government to draw lines between worthy and unworthy media outlets, on the other, we should take a chance on the disclosures. That may be the right answer, or at least it may be too soon to decide that it is the wrong answer. But the dilemma presented by disclosures of sensitive national security information—that they can be both damaging to the nation and indispensable to democracy, sometimes both at once—will not disappear. The changes that have undermined the Pentagon Papers equilibrium—changes in technology and the way the government does its business and the fragmentation of the media industry—also seem to be here to stay. They may require us to consider new kinds of measures to protect the vitally important interests on both sides.

The Growth of Press Freedoms in the United States since 9/11

JACK GOLDSMITH*

The number, frequency, and seriousness of leaks of classified information have grown sharply in the last two decades. The government has reacted to these leaks with several initiatives to stop or deter them. Journalists and their allies, in turn, have complained that these initiatives have narrowed press freedoms and damaged the First Amendment. This essay argues that the journalists are wrong. The last two decades have witnessed an unprecedented growth in press freedoms in the national security context and greater protection for journalists in their reporting of national security secrets. The recent indictment of Julian Assange is no violation of this norm and in many ways confirms it.

The Growth in Leaks

The quantity of leaks of highly classified information has exploded in the last two decades. The Chelsea Manning and Edward Snowden leaks were like nothing that came before—and in Snowden's case, the leaks were unprecedented both in quantity and in the range of very deep secrets about manifold intelligence surveillance programs that he exposed. More broadly, during this period, journalists regularly reported on the details of many covert actions, the identities of covert officers, many signals intelligence and related programs, and even the content of foreign intelligence intercepts.[1] All of these types of secrets (except for the content of foreign intelligence intercepts) were leaked before 9/11, but the quantity and breadth of the leaks after 9/11 are entirely unprecedented.

There are a number of reasons for the growth in leaked secrets. A big one is that the secrecy bureaucracy swelled over the decades. Even after the Snowden revelations, which made it harder to get a security clearance, the number of people with security clearances topped out at about 4 million.[2] The number in 2008 was 2.5 million, and that figure in turn was "substantially" more than the number of clearances extant on September 11, 2001.[3] The growth in clearances mirrors the growth in homeland security and defense and defense contractor jobs since 9/11. As Dana Priest and William Arkin wrote in 2010, "the top-secret world the government created in response to the terrorist attacks of Sept. 11, 2001, has become so large, so unwieldy and so secretive that no one knows how much money it costs, how many people it employs, how many programs exist within it or exactly how many agencies do the same work."[4] This description remains apt in 2020.

The millions of people who possess security clearances create, collect, record, and analyze an unfathomable array of information that is classified. Untold millions of new national security "secrets"—in the form of facts, arguments, programs, policies, analysis, and the like—are created yearly on classified email and other digital systems and in bug-proof rooms known as "Sensitive Compartmented Information Facilities" throughout the government and the contractor community. It is impossible to know for sure how much the secrecy system has grown in the last two decades, but it has grown enormously.

The growth in secrets and security clearances is a major explanation for the growth in leaks. A related reason is that the secrets after 9/11 concerned novel and controversial government actions such as warrantless surveillance, torture, and targeted killing. These actions were controversial inside the government, too, and led to more whistleblowing than before.

Whistleblowing is one reason for increased leaks but far from the only one. Government officials also leak secrets to explain US foreign policy to the public, for advantage in bureaucratic fights, to influence or criticize the formation of government policy, and for self-aggrandizement.[5] Leaks of classified information have grown a lot because the number of secrets and of people with access to them have grown a lot. As former CIA director Richard Helms once noted, "the probability of leaks escalates exponentially each time a classified document is exposed to another person—be it an Agency employee, a member of Congress, a senior official, a typist, or a file clerk."[6]

The digitalization of intelligence has made such leaking much easier. The nation's most important secrets are stored in bits on computer systems. As Manning and Snowden showed, an insider who wants to steal or leak these secrets can in a short time copy hundreds of thousands of pages of classified information onto a small memory device and then can later distribute the information instantaneously around the globe. Moreover, the digitalization of secrets makes it easier for foreign adversaries to penetrate government systems from abroad and extract even the most highly classified secrets. The Shadow Brokers group, for example, stole numerous NSA hacking tools, which would have been much harder to achieve had these secrets not been stored in digital format.

Another reason for the increase in leaks is that US journalists got over their fear of publishing classified secrets. Elite US newspapers that were once the primary outlets for major classified information leaks used to hesitate more than today to publish classified secrets for fear of harming US national security interests. Former *Washington Post* executive editor Leonard Downie Jr. once described the process. "The question is, is it important for the American public to know that its government is acting in its name in this particular way?" he said. "And then you weigh that against the consequences of publication, including national security harm."[7]

This is what former executive editor of the *New York Times* Bill Keller did in 2004 when he considered whether to publish a story about the Bush administration's warrantless wiretapping program, later revealed to be called STELLARWIND by reporters Eric Lichtblau and James Risen. Keller killed the story in 2004 after the White House convinced him that it would harm national security. "I've never had a case where the government raised such strident alarms, at such a high level, as the NSA eavesdropping program," Keller said.[8] But he reversed himself and published the story in December 2005.

One large factor in Keller's decision was that the Bush administration "actively misled us, claiming there was never a doubt that the wiretapping operations were legal."[9] And then, after publication, when the supposed harms never seemed to materialize, the *Times* and other journalists learned to be more skeptical about the government's claims of national security harm. "I think our story broke the fever," Risen said. "We're much better now" about standing up to government pressure.[10] As more and more secrets leaked in the next fifteen years and the sky did not fall, journalists grew much bolder.

Changes in the structure of national security journalism also pushed in favor of publication. The digital revolution led to the rise of dozens of outfits—foreign newspapers, secure digital information collection sources such as WikiLeaks and Cryptome, and even bloggers—that are now competitors and collaborators with elite US news sources that used to have a near-monopoly on national security reporting. American newspapers now sometimes coordinate with foreign newspapers to report on the US government's classified global activities. (Manning's "War Logs," for example, were published by the *Times* in coordination with *Le Monde*, the *Guardian*, and *Der Spiegel*.) Many of the outlets outside the United States do not have the "public interest" filter that made Keller hesitate. They have published US national security secrets that US media traditionally would not. (This is one of the main reasons Snowden gave the bulk of his NSA trove to Glenn Greenwald and Laura Poitras rather than the *Times*.) Competition from these more cosmopolitan outlets in turn has made it yet harder for US journalists to sit on stories out of deference to US national security claims.

The Government's Response

The Bush administration was furious when the *Times* published the warrantless wiretapping story in December 2005. In 2006, it set up a new DOJ task force, led by career officials, to pursue high-level leaks.[11] What followed was a very aggressive investigatory approach to leaks (in which I was personally swept up)[12] and new internal policies to deter leaks but no prosecution for STELLARWIND. The Valerie Plame leak led to an investigation that resulted in vice-presidential aide Scooter Libby's conviction (for lying, not leaking). The Bush administration also prosecuted lobbyists for the American Israel Public Affairs Committee for disseminating secrets leaked by a DOJ official. Many commentators saw this as a step toward prosecuting journalists, but after the trial judge expressed doubt about the case, the DOJ dropped it.[13]

As leaks of classified information ramped up during the Obama administration, the administration created a National Insider Threat Task Force. Established two years before the Snowden leaks, it was a "government-wide program for insider threat detection and prevention to improve protection and reduce potential vulnerabilities of classified information from exploitation, compromise, or other unauthorized disclosure."[14] The Obama administration also disciplined and sought to prosecute government officials and contractors on an unprecedented scale. Specifically, from 2009 to 2016, the DOJ issued indictments against government officials and contractors in ten cases, all of which resulted in convictions.[15]

As classified secrets continued to leak in new and unprecedented ways during the first two years of the Trump administration, the number of Intelligence Community (IC) leak referrals to the DOJ approximately tripled compared to the average over the previous decade.[16] The number of follow-on leak investigations also rose sharply. Attorney General Jeff Sessions testified about the matter in November 2017. He was not entirely clear about when these investigations began, but he was clear that the number had grown a lot under Trump: "We had about nine open investigations of classified leaks in the last 3 years. We have 27 investigations open today."[17] (I believe Sessions was trying to say that he inherited nine investigations and that by November 2017, the number of investigations was at twenty-seven.) As of March 2020, at least eight people had been charged in cases involving unauthorized leaks of national security information.[18] One of these indictments, most notoriously, concerned Assange.

The Bush, Obama, and Trump administrations sought the involuntary assistance of journalists during the course of their national security leak investigations. The Bush administration jailed then–*New York Times* reporter Judith Miller for contempt of court for refusing to testify before a grand jury in the Plame leak investigation. In an effort to find a leaker in one investigation, the Obama administration subpoenaed and seized metadata records for twenty Associated Press telephone lines and switchboards without initially telling the AP. In another investigation, it subpoenaed and seized telephone and email metadata records of the Fox News chief Washington correspondent, James Rosen, and got a search warrant for his emails. And in yet another investigation, it subpoenaed former *New York Times* reporter Risen, who was ordered to testify by the Fourth Circuit, although the government ultimately decided not to call him to testify. In 2018, the FBI seized phone and email records belonging to *New York Times* reporter Ali Watkins in connection with its investigation of James Wolfe, with whom Watkins had a personal relationship, for allegedly leaking national security secrets. (The case concerned Watkins's activities before she arrived at the *Times*.)

Journalists' Response

Journalists have complained very loudly about this government "crackdown." The complaints reached a crescendo during the Obama administration, when the leak prosecutions were most prominent and, compared to expectations, most surprising. A few examples will provide a flavor of the extensive critique.

Former *Washington Post* executive editor Downie described the problem in a report he authored for the Committee to Protect Journalists:

> The [Obama] administration's war on leaks and other efforts to control information are the most aggressive I've seen since the Nixon administration, when I was one of the editors involved in the *Washington Post*'s investigation of Watergate. The 30 experienced Washington journalists at a variety of news organizations whom I interviewed for this report could not remember any precedent.[19]

In the same report, *New York Times* national security reporter Scott Shane said this about the impact of these initiatives:

> I think we have a real problem. . . . Most people are deterred by those leaks prosecutions. They're scared to death. There's a gray zone between classified and unclassified information, and most sources were in that

gray zone. Sources are now afraid to enter that gray zone. It's having a deterrent effect. If we consider aggressive press coverage of government activities being at the core of American democracy, this tips the balance heavily in favor of the government.[20]

Shane's colleague Risen was less restrained:

> The Obama Administration is the greatest enemy of press freedom in a generation. Eric Holder has been the nation's top censorship officer, not the top law enforcement officer. [He] has sent a message to dictators around the world that it is okay to crack down on the press and jail journalists. [He] leaves behind a wrecked First Amendment.[21]

Risen also reportedly said that the Obama administration wanted to "narrow the field of national security reporting [to] create a path for acceptable reporting," that any journalist who exceeded those parameters "will be punished," and that the administration's aggressive prosecutions had created "a de facto Official Secrets Act."[22]

Similarly, David A. Schulz, a First Amendment lawyer and co-director of the Media Freedom and Information Access Clinic at Yale Law School, argued that various actions taken by Attorney General Holder have "undermined reporter-source communications" and "damage[ed] for years to come the media's ability to uncover and report on government missteps."[23]

The Costs and Benefits of Publishing National Security Secrets

Since I will argue below that these and similar journalistic claims are wildly exaggerated, I should first say a word on why national security reporting, including reporting about classified secrets, including secrets that harm our national security on some dimensions, is so vital in our democracy.

The government has a powerful incentive to exaggerate the harms due to leaks of classified information, and it almost certainly does exaggerate. It also massively overclassifies, which, as noted, is a primary reason for leaking. That said, there is also no doubt that the US government suffers many serious losses due to the reporting of classified national security secrets. Massive investments in intelligence techniques (especially electronic surveillance techniques) can be rendered useless, cooperation with intelligence agencies by firms and foreign liaison services become harder, important intelligence streams can dry up, and people can be killed.

These losses are not small things, since intelligence information undergirds every element of US national security and foreign policy—including its extensive military operations around the globe, its pervasive diplomatic engagements, and its numerous economic negotiations and initiatives. Knowledge of what an adversary or other foreign intelligence target is doing or planning gives the United States a huge advantage in its myriad international affairs and is a central pillar of American power.

But, of course, there are many correlative benefits to the published national security secrets over the past two decades. The reporting sometimes (but far from always) exposed illegal or legally doubtful or unwise intelligence programs. It often (but not always) sparked important deliberation that led to reforms, some of which ended some intelligence programs and others of which strengthened and legitimized the programs. The many leaks since 9/11, especially Snowden's, also forced the IC out of its suboptimal and unsustainable obsession with secrecy.

"Before the unauthorized [Snowden] disclosures, we were always, as you know, conservative about discussing specifics of our collection programs, based on the truism that the more adversaries know about what we're doing, the more they can avoid our surveillance," director of national intelligence James Clapper said in 2013.[24] Post-Snowden, the IC operates on the principle that secrecy is not an absolute value but one that needs to be traded off for other values, including domestic legitimacy. As a result of Snowden, the IC got much better at talking to the public and explaining what it does and why it matters. And Congress in turn put NSA collection authorities on a much firmer basis.

As this brief summary suggests, there are costs and benefits to national security from both secrecy and disclosure. We do not have great tools to measure or compare them. The cost-benefit calculus usually depends on where one stands and on contested normative priors. The government and the press tend to see the costs and benefits differently. Both have powerful self-serving incentives to exaggerate costs and benefits, though in different ways. And neither side can always publicly identify and convey the costs and benefits. Many remain hidden or unknowable.

At the end of the day, the press's value in publishing national security secrets does not depend on how this impossible cost-benefit calculus shakes out. Instead, the "freedom . . . of the press" to report on classified national security secrets that is guaranteed by the First Amendment depends on a more fundamental idea: the government must not have the final say about which of its secrets is published. Government action undisclosable to the American public is presumptively illegitimate. We tolerate secrecy to some degree because it is necessary for national security. But such secrecy runs the risk of getting out of control and of fostering illegal or illegitimate action or simply action that the

American people do not approve of. The government, like all institutions, is imperfect—self-interested, myopic, under-informed, biased, prone to mistakes, motivated by glory and power, and the like. If the government had the final say on its secrets, it could define the world of secrecy as broadly as it wanted, in a self-serving way, and shield its actions from a democratic (and judicial) check—an especially dangerous prospect during endless war, where the claims of secrecy are greater.

Of course, journalists, like all individuals and institutions, are biased in some respects. They are self-interested, myopic, under- or ill-informed, often inadequately expert about national security, biased, prone to mistakes, and often motivated in their publication decisions by fame or profit or both. And yet despite these flaws in the reporting corps, our legal system, of which the First Amendment is only a part, gives reporters lots of leeway to report classified national security secrets, even if the harms of doing so outweigh the benefits. It does so, to repeat, because it is intolerable that the government would have the final say on what secrets to disclose. That is the ultimate evil to be avoided. And in the last two decades, contrary to what journalists have claimed, the legal system and the norms that undergird it have strengthened reporters' hands.

Press Freedoms since 9/11

It is entirely unsurprising that three presidential administrations since 9/11 have ramped up leak prosecutions and related anti-leak initiatives in light of the cascade of leaks of deep secrets from the government. US intelligence agencies cannot operate without secrecy, and secrecy cannot be maintained unless there are costs to disclosure. What is remarkable is that the ratio of leak prosecutions to leaks remains tiny. We can assume, as the journalists claim, that the leak investigations have had at least some chilling effect on leakers (i.e., sources) and in that sense made journalists' jobs harder. And yet while the investigations and prosecutions have surely had some impact on leaks, the leaks have continued to pour out of the government at a steady and, on some dimensions, growing pace.

These are the most salient truths about post-9/11 national security journalism: secrets have leaked like never before, the government has done relatively little to stop the barrage, and what little it did was directed mostly at leakers rather than journalists. The government's feints surely chilled some officials from talking and leaking to journalists, but there were countervailing factors as well, and the barrage of leaks continued. Measured by outcomes alone, the balance did not, as Shane claimed, tip "heavily in favor of the government." Holder did not remotely, as Risen claimed, leave behind a wrecked First Amendment or create "a de facto Official Secrets Act." The government did not appear, as Schulz claimed, to "undermine[] reporter-source communications" or "damage . . . the media's ability to uncover and report on government missteps."

Moreover, there were many other developments in the legal and normative space besides leak investigations and prosecutions, and occasional related requests for information from journalists, that journalists obsess about. These other developments are the many ways the government has accepted and acquiesced in national security leaks and given protective space to the press to report on such leaks, even as the number and seriousness of leaks have grown. This is a remarkable and underappreciated development.

Through the Obama administration, it had become much clearer than ever that the government will not prosecute journalists for publishing national security secrets, including for publications that clearly violate extant criminal law. The legally least controversial pertinent criminal prohibition is 18 U.S.C. § 798, a 1950 amendment to the 1917 Espionage Act. In relevant part, it states, "*whoever* knowingly and willfully . . . publishes . . . in any manner prejudicial to the safety or interest of the United States . . . *any classified* information . . . concerning *the communication intelligence activities of the United States*" shall be fined or imprisoned not more than ten years. The law defines "communication intelligence" to mean "all procedures and methods used in the interception of communications." In 1950, it was supported by the American Society of Newspaper Editors as a reasonable national security restriction on the press, and Congress enacted it with little controversy. In their landmark 1973 post–Pentagon Papers article about the Espionage Act that is otherwise very skeptical of the Act's constitutionality, Harold Edgar and Benno Schmidt argued that § 798 was constitutional as applied to the press because it is a "model of precise draftsmanship" that shows "concern for public speech" by limiting its prohibitions "to a narrow category of highly sensitive information."[25]

Although no newspaper has ever been prosecuted under § 798, and although no editor would ever admit to concern about it, fear of prosecution under this section has long been a concern. Justice White stated clearly in the Pentagon Papers case that the government could prosecute ex post under § 798 even if a prior restraint on the same facts were unlawful.[26] Three other Justices signaled their agreement.[27] The statute, the Edgar and Schmidt article, and the opinions in the Pentagon Papers case put the newspapers on clear notice about the potential impact of § 798.

It is impossible to know whether or how often newspapers had information that implicated § 798 but declined to publish because of § 798 or other elements of the Espionage Act. The public can't see decisions not to publish, and journalists have tended not to talk about them. I have talked to journalists who have admitted to worrying about the impact of § 798 and the Espionage Act more generally, but none will go on the record. When editors decline to publish or trim back what they publish, they never acknowledge that they are worried about the law, for to do so would be self-defeating. For example, Ben Bradlee, the storied editor of the *Washington Post* who stood up to the government in the Pentagon Papers case, in 1986 delayed publication of a story about NSA taps on undersea communication cables used by the Kremlin after the government threatened prosecution under § 798. Bradlee later published but only after removing important details. He always suggested that it was fear of national security harm rather than fear of prosecution that informed these actions.[28]

And yet it seems clear that elite newspapers worry less about such legal concerns when publishing today than before 9/11. *New York Times* assistant general counsel David McCraw has acknowledged this truth. In November 2016, he stated:

> There was probably a time when . . . the *Times* would hold back [from publishing classified information due to legal concerns]. I don't think they would make that decision today. . . . Part [of the reason is] that the impact of the WikiLeaks disclosures [and] the Snowden disclosures is that the people on my side of the house have become convinced that there is no legal consequence from publishing leaks.[29]

This is an important point. The *New York Times*'s expert counselor on the law of national security reporting says that the impact of the publication of massive troves of classified information leaked by Manning and Snowden, followed by not a single criminal investigation of the press, much less attempted prosecution, has "convinced" the *Times* that "there are no legal consequences from publishing leaks."[30] (As I discuss below, McCraw later worried about whether this would remain true in the Trump administration.)

The reduced fear of prosecution, even for leaks concerning communications intelligence, has worked hand in glove with editors' diminished trust in the government's claims of harm and their related diminished fear of harmful consequences from publication. Since 9/11, newspapers hesitated less and less to publish classified secrets. As a result, more classified secrets rushed out. But no obvious harms to the public subsequently occurred, and no prosecutions of journalists resulted despite the scale of the leaks and their implication even of § 798. As a result of these developments, editors grew more confident that they could publish more and more secrets, including communications intelligence secrets. They became even more confident after they were awarded Pulitzer Prizes. All the factors pushed in the same direction. And while the government complained and complained about the increase in leaks, it did not use the law to prosecute journalists.

As a result, it is pretty clear that, as McCraw suggested, a new norm has taken hold, and journalists have less to fear from government prosecution for publishing classified secrets even though they publish those secrets like never before. This new norm is reflected in the way the public and the DOJ speak about the press when it publishes classified national security secrets. One hears much less often today than in 2005 that journalists should be punished for disclosing national security secrets. The DOJ goes out of its way now not to step on journalists' toes despite the massive increase in national security leaks. And Congress has taken no material steps to change this state of affairs, even though it could.

Other government actions besides non-prosecution are informing the new norm. Despite attempted government prosecution of a handful of leakers of classified information, and despite its many complaints, the government as a whole has not just acquiesced in (and thus tacitly supported) the new classified information publication norms. It has treated the press gingerly and taken affirmative steps to protect the press despite the massive leaks.

For example, after thrice issuing legal process against journalists, Attorney General Holder later regretted these steps and, working with elite journalists, modified DOJ guidelines twice to raise the bar on the circumstances in which prosecutors can subpoena journalists. Among other things, the new rules presume that prosecutors will give journalists notice before seeking any form of their communications records from third parties.[31] Holder also decided not to force Risen to testify in the Sterling trial even though the Fourth Circuit ruled that he could.

Holder's actions are remarkable, since journalists' claim to possess a legally enforceable reporter's privilege in this context has little basis in the law. In its 1972 decision in *Branzburg v. Hayes*, the Supreme Court ruled that the First Amendment gave reporters no testimonial privilege to refuse to comply with a grand jury subpoena relevant to a criminal investigation.[32] Judge William Byrd Traxler Jr. analyzed *Branzburg* and its progeny and denied Risen's request for a reporter's privilege. Traxler explained: "There is no First Amendment testimonial privilege, absolute or qualified, that protects a reporter from being compelled to testify by the prosecution or the defense in criminal proceedings about criminal conduct that the reporter personally witnessed or participated in, absent a showing of bad faith, harassment, or other such non-legitimate motive, even though the reporter promised confidentiality to his source."[33]

Holder let Risen off the hook, not out of deference to law but rather out of deference to a norm of restraint against the press. He did so following an order from President Obama to review the DOJ's procedures seeking information against reporters. Obama said he was "troubled by the possibility that leak investigations may chill the investigative journalism that holds government accountable."[34] He added: "Journalists should not be at legal risk for doing their jobs. . . . Our focus must be on those who break the law."[35] Holder said similar things in backing up his later actions.[36]

One might think that this "norm" of bowing to the press's prerogatives on national security reporting is limited to the late, legacy-seeking Obama administration and thus not very stable. But I doubt that is so. The Bush administration was overtly more hostile to the press than the Obama administration, and it very aggressively investigated the STELLARWIND leak. In 2006, Attorney General Alberto Gonzales even indicated, in connection with the STELLARWIND investigation, that he believed he had the authority to prosecute journalists. He was almost certainly thinking of § 798.

But the Bush DOJ never indicted anyone, much less journalists, in connection with the STELLARWIND leak. Moreover, Gonzales explained in 2013 that he at the time considered but declined to "go[] after the reporters in order to try to figure out where the source of the leak is"—that is, subpoenaing their notes and related materials.[37] The best explanation for this reticence is that the political costs of doing so outweighed the benefits of figuring out the source of a leak deemed hugely damaging. In other words, it bowed before a norm.

In light of the number and types of leaks during the Trump era and President Trump's unprecedented animosity toward and threats against the press, the Trump administration, too, has been remarkably restrained in its legal *actions* toward the press. Attorney General Sessions in October 2017 declined to make a "blanket commitment" not to put journalists in jail, even as he noted that "we always try to find an alternative way . . . to directly confront[] a media person."[38] But the reality is that the Trump administration has brought no indictments and opened no known investigations against US news outlets for any of the many major leaks since 2017. Nor has it sought to subpoena reporters' records in any of these cases, though, as noted above, it did in the case of a reporter who had a personal relationship with a government source who lied to the government about that relationship. Nor has the Trump DOJ walked back any of the Holder rules on special protections for the press against subpoenas.

New York Times lawyer McCraw's recent account of the Trump administration's reaction to a March 2017 story about how the government had sought to use cyber techniques to sabotage North Korea's nuclear missile program is revealing. The *Times* had gone through the usual ritual of informing the White House in advance and seeking input on possible harm for the newspaper to assess. In the midst of this consultation, White House counsel Donald McGahn wrote a letter to the *Times* that stated that the forthcoming story "will compromise and/or otherwise negatively impact the national security of the United States."[39] McCraw worried about whether the norms of accommodation that had checked the government from prosecuting the press for national security disclosures would hold. But in the end, nothing happened. "If the administration had any legal concerns about the North Korea story post-publication, we never heard about them," he recounted.[40]

It is against this background that one must assess the Trump administration's indictment of Assange, the leader of WikiLeaks, for various activities related to the procurement and publication of hundreds of thousands of classified documents stolen by Manning. The *Washington Post* reported in 2013 that the Obama administration decided not to prosecute Assange because unnamed "government lawyers" said "they could not do so without also prosecuting US news organizations and journalists."[41] This reticence, if real, would be consistent with the post-9/11 norm discussed above.

But then, six years later, the Trump administration indicted Assange in ways that many commentators, including myself, believed could have implications for the press. One concern was that the indictment focused on Assange's encouragement of his sources to "(i) circumvent legal safeguards on information; (ii) provide that protected information to WikiLeaks for public dissemination; and (iii) continue the pattern of illegally procuring and providing protected information to WikiLeaks for distribution to the public."[42] As I and others wrote, this practice has similarities to what contemporary national security reporters do in soliciting sources to provide classified information, especially in an era in which major news outlets use mechanisms such as SecureDrop that accept information from more sources securely and anonymously.[43] Another concern, one even closer to the bone for journalists, was that Assange's acts of acquisition and publication of classified information by themselves were a crime.

The Assange indictment is a response to an extreme act of procurement and publication by a person and institution, Assange and WikiLeaks, that operate outside the United States and that have different and more destructive aims toward the US government and its institutions than does the typical mainstream media outlet that publishes classified information. Unlike US journalists, Assange has threatened to release an "insurance file" of information without "harm minimization" if WikiLeaks is restrained from publishing. WikiLeaks very often does a much poorer job than the US media typically does in curating published information to avoid doing unnecessary harm to individuals and, perhaps, national security. So it is unclear whether Assange's activities are akin in all respects to mainstream journalists' activities.

It is impossible to predict the future. WikiLeaks could have negative legal implications for the norm that supports US journalists' publication of national security secrets. And the indictment might even portend new government pushback against the US press reporting highly classified information.

But I doubt it. It remains significant that the administration, led by a press-despising, norm-indifferent president, has not pursued the press—in known

investigations or subpoenas—for its many publications of leaks, including unprecedented leaks of foreign intelligence intercepts that were deeply damaging
to the president and that pretty clearly violate § 798. It is also noteworthy that
the Trump DOJ went out of its way to deny that the Assange indictment had
implications for American journalists. "Some say that Assange is a journalist, and
that he should be immune from prosecution for these actions," said Assistant
Attorney General John Demers in announcing the indictment. "The department
takes seriously the role of journalists in our democracy. It is not and has never
been the department's policy to target them for reporting. But Julian Assange is
no journalist."[44] This disclaimer is entirely consistent with a firmer norm against
the government prosecuting journalists even in the face of fifteen years of a
truly unprecedented onslaught of very sensitive leaks. Indeed, coming from the
Trump DOJ, it should be viewed as a confirmation of the norm.

Conclusion

The developing norm of enhanced press freedom to publish national security
secrets is just a norm. And we live in a norm-busting era. The norm is no guarantee against a future DOJ trying to prosecute a journalist for publishing a classified national security secret or from ramping up subpoenas in leak investigations.
It raises the costs to such prosecution but is no legal bar to prosecution. And the
norm might have little, if any, impact on courts in either context. There is little
doubt that press freedoms have expanded, in fact, in the last two decades, but
there can be no certainty that these freedoms will persist.

I do not think that this uncertainty is a terrible state of affairs. I have canvassed
the main virtues of a vigorous press reporting national security secrets in a
seemingly endless and super-secretive war. But the American press's extreme
reactions to occasional (and entirely lawful) subpoenas and to enforcement of
the law against leakers sometimes borders on a claim that it should have no legal
accountability at all. Journalists play a vital role in our democracy in reporting
national security secrets. But the value in this reporting is not absolute. There
are other competing values, including national security, secrecy, and the enforcement of duly enacted criminal laws. These competing values have often given
way since 9/11 to the value of reporting secrets to the public, and the norms
and legal constraints on journalists are much more forgiving now than twenty
years ago.

But journalists push the publishing envelope as never before. And such reporting imposes costs and is sometimes hard to justify even under the expanding
criteria under which journalists publish. In this context, the occasional subpoena

against journalists in a national security investigation and the occasional re-
minder that, in fact, the criminal laws prohibit certain forms of national security
reporting are no big deal. Journalists' contention otherwise amounts to a claim
of immunity from all legal accountability in reporting national security secrets—
a position that journalists, of course, would tolerate in no other context.

Edward Snowden, Donald Trump, and the Paradox of National Security Whistleblowing

ALLISON STANGER[*]

What is at stake in honoring legitimate whistleblowers is nothing less than the rule of law itself. In accusing the Intelligence Community (IC) whistleblower who launched the impeachment inquiry of partisanship and treason, President Trump redefined whistleblowing to serve his private interests rather than the Constitution. Dictators may embrace Trump's definition of whistleblowing and his denigration of whistleblowers as spies and partisans, but American history reveals a very different understanding of the concept, one that is shared today by the European Union, which adopted sweeping whistleblower protections that cover both private and public sector employees in October 2019.[1]

Whistleblowing in the national security realm is by definition a delicate balancing act between upholding First Amendment rights and ensuring the national security those rights presuppose. In the national security arena, the threat of retaliation against whistleblowers is always high, because one person's national security whistleblower is another's insider threat. Leaks are justified when the whistle is blown in a manner consistent with the law, but when statute and executive order communicate in different voices, political conflict is the inevitable outcome. The inspector general (IG) system provides an official channel for whistleblowing that keeps government accountable to the Constitution.

Unlawful leaks to tilt the balance in a policy debate should never be celebrated. Unlawful leaks that expose threats to the rule of law should be. Distinguishing between the two requires political rather than partisan judgment, which the IG system is designed to facilitate. Properly constructed and supported, it should protect genuine whistleblowers and see that "urgent concerns" are turned over to Congress. Remember, whistleblowers are individuals who in the eyes of the IG watchdog clear the "urgent concern" bar. They are not anyone who claims to have an urgent concern; they must actually have one.

When perceptions of national security whistleblowing shift based on where one sits on the political spectrum, the concept is transformed from a device to sustain the rule of law to a partisan weapon. It does not need not be this way. Examining the origins and trajectory of national security whistleblower protection in the United States sheds light on formidable obstacles to IC whistleblowing through official channels. The current workaround is leaking to the press. We want whistleblowers to follow the law in reporting injustice, but our laws need to be updated so we can insist on official channels and harness lawbreaking in a rule-based manner to higher constitutional principles.

Whistleblowing: An American Innovation

The tradition of whistleblowing in the New World predates the ratification of the US Constitution. America passed the world's first whistleblower protection law in 1778. America's founders sought to build a new republic that might safeguard both liberty and equality from corruption and hypocrisy in Europe.

In 1777, during the Revolutionary War, a group of ten American sailors aboard the *Warren* revealed that the first commander in chief of the United States Navy, Esek Hopkins, had tortured captured British prisoners of war. They submitted a petition to the Marine Committee on February 19, 1777, asking them to "inquire into his character & conduct, for we suppose that his character is such & that he has been guilty of such crimes as render him quite unfit for the public department he now occupies, which crimes, we the subscribers can sufficiently attest."[2]

Hopkins, the catalyst for the passage of America's first whistleblower law, had acquired his maritime skills as a slave runner in Rhode Island. The collective testimony of the *Warren* officers that accompanied the petition painted a portrait in broad strokes of an egocentric man with a profound sense of entitlement dwelling in a bygone era. One petitioner, Jas Sellers, said that Hopkins repeatedly cursed the Marine Committee as "a pack of damned fools." According to Sellers, Hopkins also said: "If I should follow their directions, the entire country would be ruined. I am not going to follow their directions, by God." In addition, Sellers maintained that Hopkins "treated prisoners in a very unbecoming and barbarous manner." Samuel Shaw testified that he heard Hopkins call the Continental Congress "a pack of damned rascals." John Reed maintained that Hopkins not only "treated prisoners in the most inhuman and barbarous manner" but also believed that "no man yet ever existed who could not be bought." John Grannis detailed Hopkins's mistreatment of prisoners and said his overall conduct was "wild and unsteady." On March 26, 1777, in response to the avalanche of condemnation, Congress suspended Hopkins pending a formal investigation.[3]

In bringing charges against Hopkins, the sailors were upholding principles that had been previously delineated in Congress's original January 5, 1776, "Orders and Directions for the Commander in Chief of the Fleet of the United Colonies." It stipulated that prisoners of war be "well and humanely treated." Congress also urged commanders to promote and protect whistleblowers: "You will . . . very carefully attend to all the just complaints which may be made by any of the People under your Command and see that they are speedily and effectually . . . redressed—for on a careful attention to these important Subjects the good of the service essentially depends."[4]

Several months later, on January 2, 1778, Congress dismissed Hopkins from "the service of the United States."[5] Enraged that his inferiors were giving him a bad name, Hopkins retaliated by filing a criminal libel suit against the ten petitioners. Richard Marven and Shaw had the misfortune of being Rhode Island residents in a colony where the Hopkins family ruled, so they were the only two of the ten who were imprisoned. Marven and Shaw again turned to Congress for justice. Again they were vindicated: Congress ruled that Marven and Shaw should be released from prison.

But the legislators went even further. On July 30, 1778, Congress enacted the first American whistleblower protection law. Its language captures the balance that the makers of the American Revolution sought between upholding whistleblower rights and maintaining the new republic they were bringing into being: "That it is the duty of all persons in the service of the United States, as well as all other inhabitants thereof, to give the earliest information to Congress or any other proper authority of any misconduct, frauds or misdemeanors committed by any officers or persons in the service of these states, which may come to their knowledge."[6] America's public servants were obligated, Congress maintained, to report wrongdoing in their ranks whenever they encountered it.

Congress did not stop at condoning whistleblowing as an expression of American values. It went on to enact legislation to protect whistleblowers from retaliation. Despite being at war and strapped for resources, Congress paid the legal fees of Marven and Shaw, a sum of $1,418.[7] Congress clearly considered it crucial to support whistleblowers, as it also passed a law ensuring that future whistleblowers would have legal counsel to defend themselves. Indeed, Congress authorized all records related to Hopkins's removal to be released to the public, which is the reason this story can today be told.

Whistleblowing in America thus developed as a concept within a rule-of-law tradition. In states that had experienced dictatorship and neighbors being pressed to report transgressions against the regime to the authorities, in contrast, whistleblowing had negative connotations of snitching. A 2013 Transparency International report on whistleblowing in Europe included the original words for whistleblowers in countries across Europe, almost all of which were negative.[8] Whistleblowing had perhaps the worst connotations in post-communist Europe, especially for those who could remember communist show trials.

For a meaningful conversation on whistleblowing to be possible, we have to start with a common definition. A whistleblower cannot be defined as "an advocate for change I'd like to see." That is to confuse whistleblowing with political activism and invite partisan definitions inconsistent with understandings of impartial justice. The usually precise Oxford English Dictionary definition shows an awareness of this confusion and skirts it with what is essentially a circular definition: "One who 'blows the whistle' on a person or activity, especially from *within* an organization."

The Cambridge Dictionary definition is narrower, defining a whistleblower as a "person who tells someone in authority about something they believe to be illegal that is happening, especially in a government department or a company." The Whistleblower Protection Act of 1989, which was strengthened in 2012 through the Whistleblower Protection Enhancement Act, is in keeping with the Cambridge definition. The legislation applies to federal employees who disclose "illegal or improper government activities," protecting them from retaliation for revealing dishonest or illegal activities occurring at a government organization.[9] The US Merit Systems Protection Board (MSPB) elaborates by defining whistleblowing as "disclosing information that you reasonably believe is evidence of a violation of any law, rule, or regulation, or gross mismanagement, a gross waste of funds, an abuse of authority, or a substantial and specific danger to public health or safety."[10]

The MSPB's "reasonable belief" standard depends on an evidence-based, nonideological approach to determining the truth. For our purposes, a whistleblower is an insider who has evidence of illegal or improper conduct and exposes it, either to the authorities or to the press. In government, misconduct is illegality or a violation of constitutional norms. In the corporate world, whistleblowing reveals illegality or the violation of company norms. Whistleblowing is thus the insider exposure of illegal or improper activity. We know something is illegal when it violates the law, as determined by a court. We know something is improper when the relevant community of which the whistleblower is an insider deems it to be so.

Comparing this definition with partisan alternatives brings into fuller relief the vital role truth telling plays in sustaining civil discourse and American constitutional democracy. Whistleblowing is not a mere weapon for advancing partisan or personal interests in a fake-news world. It is not what denigrates others or vindicates our own political biases. The extreme left and right may view any revelation of secret information that serves their political ends as whistleblowing, but that is to blur important lines. Especially in the national security realm, whistleblowing involves political judgment, which, properly understood, does not follow a party line.

All whistleblowers are leakers, but not all leakers are whistleblowers. Leakers expose secrets, but secrets are not always a cover for misconduct, even if their revelation can often embarrass individuals and destroy careers. In contrast, whistleblowers expose wrongdoing, which their perpetrators would like to keep secret.[11]

Could Snowden Have Blown the Whistle through Official Channels?

With a better understanding of what whistleblowing within the American tradition entails, could Edward Snowden have "stayed home and faced the music," as many of his critics in the IC thought he should have done? Here it is important to distinguish between what IC leadership might have said at the time and what it would say today, when its members no longer hold their official positions. As some of them are writing for this volume, it will be interesting to see how their views have or have not evolved over time. But in the immediate aftermath of the Snowden controversy, NSA officials were united in condemning Snowden's failure to report his findings through official NSA IG channels. Given what we know today, however, it seems fair to say that had Snowden tried to report his misgivings from within, they would have never have seen the light of day, in part because of the inherent tensions between whistleblowing (the revealing of secrets) and IC work (the keeping of secrets) and in part because of deficiencies in whistleblower protection in the national security arena.

The statutory taboo on national security whistleblowing first crystallized decades ago, when workers with access to classified information were excluded from the 1978 Civil Service Reform Act that put in place whistleblower protection for all other government employees. Because of the importance of secrecy for keeping Americans safe, the landmark 1989 Whistleblower Protection Act continued to insist that the national security realm must be treated differently.

When the law was updated again, in 2012, the bill that first passed the House protected all government employees, as whistleblower advocates had wanted. Yet the version that President Obama signed into law continued to treat national security workers as a separate category.[12] Explanations of this outcome differ. Some saw the protection of national security workers as legislation Congress could never pass. Others saw it as a casualty of political horse-trading. Regardless, the separate but unequal system continued, and whistleblower advocacy organizations such as the Government Accountability Project supported the compromise in order to save the bill.[13]

While that bill was being debated in Congress, on October 10, 2012, the White House countered the likely national security exclusion with Presidential Policy Directive 19 (PPD-19). It promised whistleblower protection for members of the IC so long as they did not disclose classified information, but it did not explicitly extend that coverage to contractors such as Snowden.[14] Some pointed to the Intelligence Community Whistleblower Protection Act of 1998 as additional support for whistleblowers, but it provides no protection against retaliation.[15] According to Dan Meyer, who led the Whistleblowing and Source Protection Program at the Office of the Intelligence Community Inspector General (IC IG), the act is a "misnomer," since it was concerned only with the rights of employees to transmit classified information to Congress.[16] To codify PPD-19, there were multiple additions to the Intelligence Authorization Act of Fiscal Year 2014, including the following addition to 50 U.S.C. § 3033: "An individual who has submitted a complaint or information to the Inspector General under this section may notify any member of either of the congressional intelligence committees, or a staff member of either of such committees, of the fact that such individual has made a submission to the Inspector General, and of the date on which such submission was made."[17]

President Obama's PPD-19 thus created a potential conflict between statute and executive order, since the former explicitly excludes employees that the latter includes. The national security exemption thus casts a long shadow over any system designed to encourage whistleblowing, especially after the Snowden revelations, when the IC was simultaneously encouraged to identify and eradicate insider threats (those likely to leak classified information).

Speaking in 2015, former NSA general counsel Rajesh De said he believed Snowden had plenty of options for protest that he did not exercise. He could have gone to the leadership and the NSA IG. If that failed, he could have tried the Pentagon or IC IG. If he exhausted those internal options and still got no satisfaction, he could have turned to Congress.[18] As President Obama put it in an August 2013 press conference, "there were other avenues available for somebody whose conscience was stirred and thought that they needed to question government actions."[19]

Yet De himself admitted it is unlikely that the IG would condemn a policy that the NSA leadership had deemed vital. The IG's function is not to mediate policy differences. Since these particular policies had all been reviewed by NSA lawyers and in some instances directly authorized by Congress, the IG would have been unlikely to find them problematic. "If you read the inspector general act, it says 'no one who goes to the IG will be retaliated against,'" explained whistleblower protection lawyer Stephen Kohn. "But there's no law to protect complainants.

To put it bluntly, they left their employees barefoot and frightened. It's as simple as that."[20] Ernest Fitzgerald and Bunnatine Greenhouse are prominent examples of DOD employees who blew the whistle on waste and corruption in Pentagon contracts through legitimate channels, only to be rewarded by being fired and harassed.

Former NSA deputy director Chris Inglis shared De's sense that Snowden did not exhaust the possibilities for lodging an internal complaint, and to his mind this precluded considering Snowden a whistleblower. "If you're a whistleblower, you have insider privilege, which comes with insider responsibility to take the extra care and time to get it right," said Inglis. Snowden told the European Parliament that he complained internally to at least ten NSA officials before taking the course that he did.[21] But as the NSA public affairs department was quick to emphasize, he offered no evidence at the time to support this claim, nor does he do so in his recently published memoir. Snowden's one documented attempt to contact the NSA leadership followed his participation in intelligence oversight training designed to teach NSA employees how to protect and defend the US Constitution while shielding the nation.

In an effort to show that Snowden had made no real effort to file an internal complaint, the NSA released the email Snowden sent to the NSA general counsel on April 5, 2013. In it, Snowden referred to training he had received and asked whether "executive orders have the same precedence as law." The general counsel's office wrote back three days later to say, "Executive Orders (E.O.s) have the 'force and effect of law.' That said, you are correct that E.O.'s cannot override a statute."[22] Snowden was thought to be asking about the hierarchy of laws governing NSA programs.

But there was an alternative explanation. Perhaps Snowden wanted to know if he had any chance of whistleblower protection, since national security employees were explicitly excluded under the 2012 Whistleblower Protection Enhancement Act but given partial yet ambiguous protection under PPD-19. The NSA general counsel's response that an executive order cannot trump a statute would have told him he did not.

I interviewed Snowden both publicly and privately on March 17, 2017, and had the opportunity to float this alternative explanation. I asked Snowden about his motives when he approached the NSA general counsel in April 2013 before his flight. Was he trying to determine whether the more whistleblower-friendly executive order might supersede the distinctly unfriendly statute, which defined national security whistleblowing as a contradiction in terms? He replied, perhaps unsurprisingly, that he had not been aware that any sort of serious whistleblower protection even existed for members of the IC. "I wish I would have been clever enough to have framed my emailed question with that in mind," he said with a smile, but he had not.

Given the sensitivity of the materials, it is hard to argue with Snowden's conclusion that he had to leave the country to get his message to the public, even though Meyer believes he could have reported it through the DOD's intelligence oversight process and received whistleblower protection. "He should have come to me," Meyer said.[23] Speaking at Georgetown University Law Center in February 2014, NSA IG George Ellard also insisted "Snowden could have come to me."[24] Ellard's credibility, however, was rather diminished in 2016, when he was fired from his job for retaliating against whistleblowers.[25] In March 2018, Meyer was also terminated. Meyer was permitted to release a statement by James Clapper's successor, Director of National Intelligence (DNI) Dan Coats, stating that Meyer had blown the whistle the previous summer on the failure of the IC whistleblowing program to protect three whistleblowers, in particular. For the Project on Government Oversight, Meyer's ouster was disturbing, "because whistleblower retaliation concerns are so pervasive in the US intelligence community that they even have infected the offices that are supposed to be a safe haven for those who report abuse."[26]

None of the officials who maintained that Snowden had options articulated a compelling case for how Snowden would have survived the official whistleblower process and sparked reform. Avenues for complaining from within did exist, but the absence of prior successes would have given any thoughtful person pause.

What Did Snowden Reveal?

What Snowden's documents illuminated, taken as whole, was nothing less than a complete transformation in NSA operating procedures after 9/11. Before that date, the NSA's awesome power was explicitly not to be directed at US citizens. But under President George W. Bush's secret executive order of October 2001, dragnet searches were permitted under approved conditions. What began as an emergency measure following an attack on American soil quickly became standard operating procedure, without the American people even knowing that this sea change had taken place. One of Snowden's documents, a 2009 draft NSA IG report, chronicles the parameters of this quiet transformation.[27]

Had Snowden not shared classified information with the press, the sweeping changes in NSA practices following 9/11 regarding the mass collection of both internet and telephone metadata would have remained unknown to the American people. Both in leaking classified information and in writing about it in his subsequent memoir, Snowden violated no fewer than six Secrecy Agreements—three with the CIA from November 2005, August 2006, and April 2009 and three with the NSA from July 2005, May 2009, and March 2013. In December 2019, a federal judge in Virginia ruled that Snowden could not profit from sales of his book, because he did not get approval from the CIA and the NSA to publish the material in it.[28] It is not difficult to understand why Snowden, still charged under the Espionage Act, would not have sought such approval. Despite the unavoidable breach of confidentiality and the great damage his revelations may have caused, the conversation he initiated provided a public service that led to a revision of the Patriot Act. While his place in history has yet to be fully determined, Snowden might one day be seen as America's first traitor-patriot.

In his recent book *Permanent Record*, Snowden finally reveals almost all the details (I say almost all, because he omits full details about how he copied and encrypted the stolen files, in his own words, "so that the NSA will still be standing tomorrow")[29] of how he harvested the data that would reshape the world's understanding of the American IC's operations. There are readboards within the IC's intranet that gather information relevant to those with particular types of security clearances. These are information clearinghouses for those authorized to read. As systems administrator, Snowden's stroke of genius was to produce a readboard of readboards, one that would connect NSA employees possessing the appropriate certification with all relevant documents available to them, given their digital identity badge (PKI certificate). It ran on a server that only Snowden managed, which meant that all harvested documents across the entire IC were directly accessible to him. He called the system Heartbeat, "because it took the pulse of the NSA and wider IC." This was the system that enabled Snowden to consolidate relevant materials in one place and is the source of nearly all the documents he would later disclose to journalists.[30]

Early on in Heartbeat's operation, Snowden got an email that almost stopped Heartbeat cold. An administrator at another node on the internal network, wondering what a system in Hawaii was doing copying every single record in his database, had Snowden blocked as a precaution, pending an explanation. Snowden explained the tech behind his venture and encouraged the administrator to utilize Heartbeat for himself. Over time, as administrators began to value Heartbeat, no one thought twice about it, so it sounded no alarms and was the perfect cover. Snowden could transfer files to old computers under the guise of "compatibility testing," and on those old computers, he could work to search, filter, and organize the files without being detected.[31]

The tricky part was copying the files for transport out of the building. To avoid detection, Snowden used mini and micro Secure Digital (SD) cards (the teeny cards that store files on a digital camera). An SD card could fit underneath a pried-off square of a Rubik's cube, which was how Snowden ushered the cards off NSA premises. Through this process, Snowden "was storing the NSA's storage, making an off-site backup of evidence of the IC's abuses. It could take eight hours or more—entire shifts—to fill a card."[32]

Snowden's technical description of how he encrypted the files is compelling and explains why the journalists who worked with him all believe that he successfully kept the files out of the hands of the Russians or the Chinese.[33]

Thanks to Snowden, we now know that there are basically three authorities baskets for legal surveillance or, put another way, three ways to conduct surveillance while respecting the Fourth Amendment.

The first authorities basket was Section 215 of the Patriot Act, which was revised in 2015. It authorized the collection of telephone and internet metadata. In 2011, the FISA court (FISC) slammed the NSA for improper filtering. In response, the NSA shut down its nascent internet metadata program that deployed "pen registers," because it realized it was just too unwieldy and cumbersome to harvest metadata from US domestic communications in bulk while adequately protecting privacy.[34] The telephone metadata program, however, proceeded full throttle.

The second authorities basket is Section 702 of the 2008 FISA. It established the FISC, which can find that there are no privacy rights for American citizens in certain situations. Section 702 authorized the PRISM program of legal intercept. PRISM collects material directly from the servers of nine US-based internet companies (Microsoft, Yahoo, Google, Facebook, AOL, PalTalk, Skype, YouTube, Apple). It requests materials from companies for security reasons, and the providers have largely complied with NSA requests.

The NSA had long been permitted to vacuum up information on foreigners that was harvested outside the country, but inside the country, it had needed a warrant to monitor any communication that took place on a wire (as opposed to satellite or radio transmission). Section 702 removed that requirement.[35]

The rules for proper collection under Section 702 are not always followed, and mistakes are made. The Cybersecurity Initiative at New America has chronicled all violations of the section since the 2008 amendments, and the most compliance violations occurred in 2014 (sixty-one) and 2015 (seventy-three), the years immediately following the Snowden heist of June 2013. They have since fallen off dramatically (four in 2016), although this may be because of the time lag between when a violation is committed and when it is revealed.[36]

The third and perhaps most wide-ranging basket of authorities is President Reagan's 1981 Executive Order 12333. Promulgated after the Church Committee reforms had reigned in domestic surveillance, the executive order underscored that foreigners were still fair game. It authorizes the UPSTREAM and MUSCULAR programs. UPSTREAM siphons off data from fiber-optic cables as it crosses the US junctions of global voice and data networks. UPSTREAM goes through the backdoor without permission, intercepting data from the fiber-optic cables over which it travels as it bounces around the world, without the knowledge of companies.[37] The vulnerable point for vacuuming data is at the switches and routers, and the overwhelming majority of phone and internet communications pass through switches on American or English territory, regardless of where they originate. The internet architecture itself thus gave the United States unprecedented surveillance power. The revelation of this implicit upper hand was the biggest threat to American national security to emerge from the Snowden leaks. The United States lost a distinctive comparative advantage.

In response to the Snowden disclosures, Apple adopted strong default encryption for its iPhones and iPads, and Google did the same for its Android products and Chromebooks. The private sector replaced Hypertext Transfer Protocol (http) with the encrypted https (the *s* is for *security*), which helps prevent third-party siphoning of web traffic. By 2016, for the first time, more web traffic was encrypted than unencrypted.[38] Privacy rights were bolstered at the expense of a distinctive Anglo-American surveillance advantage.

Warrantless surveillance of foreigners outside the United States, as NSA officials in the wake of the Snowden catastrophe would emphasize, does not violate the Fourth Amendment. However, James Risen's initial disclosures about telephone metadata harvested through STELLARWIND involved American citizens, making this variant of warrantless surveillance an egregious violation of existing law. Even worse, President Bush had told the public that he had ended the program, and in 2007, he signed an emergency gap law called the Protect America Act, which would become institutionalized through the 2008 FISA Amendments. The gap law broke the original warrantless surveillance program into two parts: one about metadata phone records (Risen's discovery) and one about metadata internet collection, which remained concealed until Snowden revealed it.

We now know that on March 12, 2004, Acting Attorney General James Comey and the DOJ's senior leadership threatened to resign if the warrantless surveillance of email metadata and technical records of Skype calls continued, since they believed the president had no lawful authority to harvest this information. Comey had ordered the program stopped, and the president had issued an order renewing it. Comey, Jack Goldsmith of the Office of Legal Counsel, and FBI Director Robert Mueller then began drafting letters of resignation, but when the president learned of their intention to resign, he reversed himself and ended the collection of internet metadata. On July 15, the secret surveillance court allowed the NSA under Director Michael Hayden to resume bulk collection of internet metadata through a legal provision known as pen registers. Pen registers first allowed law enforcement to collect phone numbers of incoming and outgoing calls from a single telephone line but now extended to internet communications.[39]

This general trajectory of expanding permissible surveillance and trusting government to restrain itself is unsurprising. Since it is hard for any politician to be "against" security, the status quo had a compelling logic. Yet the *New York Times* reported that there is no evidence to suggest that any form of warrantless surveillance stopped a single terrorist attack.[40] It is important to keep in mind that the IC has emergency overrides that can be invoked in the presence of clear and undeniable danger, so the default position in peacetime should be to require warrants.

Trump's Misinformation War on Whistleblowing

On the surface, the Obama administration's and the Trump administration's treatment of national security whistleblowers seem similar. The Obama White House charged more individuals under the Espionage Act than had all previous administrations since World War II combined. The Trump White House continued the campaign against leakers of classified information, but it did so in a manner that challenged the very idea of impartial justice itself, placing us in uncharted political and constitutional waters.

Upon his inauguration, Trump immediately dismissed Attorney General Loretta Lynch and appointed the Obama administration's deputy attorney general, Sally Yates, as acting attorney general. Lynch had met informally with President Clinton at Phoenix Sky Harbor International Airport in June 2016, while the DOJ was investigating his wife. The meeting hopelessly compromised Lynch's integrity and forced FBI Director Comey to step in and oversee activities normally in the attorney general's purview.

The firing of Acting Attorney General Sally Yates stands out as a powerful symbol of where the Trump presidency was headed. On January 27, 2017, with none of the customary vetting, the president signed a controversial executive order that banned travelers from seven Muslim-majority countries. As protests swelled nationwide, federal judges in Massachusetts and New York blocked the order.

Yates read over their arguments and found two particularly compelling. The first was that the preferential treatment that the order gave to Syrian Christians was a violation of the First Amendment's establishment clause. Second, in banning entry to both visa holders and legal residents, the order seemed to raise serious problems with due process. Rather than resign to express her objections, Yates chose to speak out in defense of American constitutional democracy and was promptly fired.[41]

The firing of Yates and that of Comey a few months later were salvos launched against the very idea of disinterested standards for evaluating truth and falsehood, the premise on which American constitutional democracy depends. Yates was not alone in believing that we lived in exceptional times. Mainstream media, former members of the IC from both parties, constitutional law and democracy scholars, and the Democratic Party came to embrace her perspective. President Trump and Fox News spun their powerful arguments as transparent partisan maneuvering, hoping to convince voters that the entire matter was one of political spin rather than of the fact-based world on which impartial justice relies.

Like the president of the United States, members of the IC swear an oath to preserve, protect, and defend the Constitution of the United States. Though their job in normal times is to work behind the scenes and transcend politics, when the president of the United States repeatedly impugns the integrity of our law enforcement institutions, fails to defend the electoral system, and undermines the values on which this republic was founded, the IC is left with little choice but to violate its own norms of conduct to defend the Constitution and blow the whistle on Trump's subversion of the rule of law and willful denial of the distinction between truth and falsehood itself. As Hannah Arendt explained in a 1974 interview, "If everybody always lies to you, the consequence is not that you believe the lies, but rather that nobody believes anything any longer. . . . And a people that no longer can believe anything cannot make up its mind. It is deprived not only of its capacity to act but also of its capacity to think and to judge. And with such a people you can then do what you please."[42]

An IC whistleblower who did not leak to the press but instead worked through official channels launched the Trump impeachment investigation. Given the fraught terrain this essay has described—the paradox of national security whistleblowing in America—that the complaint actually rose through the established process and saw the light of day is a miracle. Because of the prominent role whistleblowing has played in keeping government honest over the life of the republic, both Democrats and Republicans in the Senate unanimously endorsed the complaint being turned over to Congress, despite instructions from Trump lackey Attorney General William Barr to do otherwise. Both acting DNI Joseph Maguire, who initially heeded the DOJ in squelching the whistleblower complaint, and IC IG Michael Atkinson, a Trump appointee as well, defended the whistleblower. "I think the whistleblower did the right thing," Maguire told the House Intelligence Committee on September 26, 2019. "I think he followed the law every step of the way."[43] Atkinson's office issued a similar statement on September 30: "The Complainant followed the law in filing the urgent concern complaint, and the IC IG followed the law in transmitting the information to the Acting Director of National Intelligence on August 26, 2019."[44]

To measure the degree of departure from traditional bipartisan public support for whistleblowers, consider the IC whistleblower who launched the Benghazi investigation of Hillary Clinton. The Trump impeachment IC whistleblower's attorney (Mark Zaid) also represented the CIA whistleblowers who initiated the Benghazi proceedings.[45] Why don't most Americans think of whistleblowers when they consider the significance of the Benghazi inquiry? Several possible hypotheses spring immediately to mind. First, there was neither a White House nor a congressional effort to out the whistleblower or incite retaliation against them, so focus centered on the investigation itself, not the person who launched it. Second, there was an entirely different administrative response to each investigation. Hillary Clinton testified endlessly. The Trump White House, in contrast, stonewalled the impeachment investigation.

President Trump's playbook, scrupulously followed by the GOP, was to pursue the Five Ds strategy of whistleblower retaliation: downplay, deny, delay, distract, and discredit.[46] He rejected the very notion of a disinterested national security whistleblower balancing competing concerns and in so doing dismissed the idea of national interests distinct from his personal interests (a dichotomy on which the very concept of national security relies), as well as the possibility of impartial justice on which the rule of law depends.

Understanding how whistleblowing has functioned in American history is thus essential for realizing the grave threat that President Trump posed to the American experiment. When President Trump asserts that the president by virtue of his office is incapable of misconduct or violation of the law, the truth is rendered a matter of perspective and whistleblowing an impossible proposition. Whistleblowing, after all, as we have seen, presupposes fixed notions of right and wrong, of legality and illegality, of truth and falsehood. In the absence of those clear distinctions, whistleblowing cannot exist, save as a partisan ideological weapon rather than a servant of truth and the rule of law. For President Trump, whistleblowing is what denigrates others and elevates him. He intentionally sowed confusion among the American electorate, so that they, too, could confuse loyalty to him with loyalty to their country.

Leaking classified information to uphold the rule of law should be a strategy of last resort. It cannot become standard operating procedure if the constitutional order that makes the delivery of impartial justice possible is to endure.

To stem the tide of illicit leaks, Congress must address the legal ambiguities that have made utilizing the IC IG system a risky proposition for whistleblowers. The 1998 Intelligence Community Whistleblower Protection Act is currently a misnomer, since it provides no protection against retaliation, and the Whistleblower Protection Enhancement Act explicitly excludes members of the IC. Both of these shortcomings need to be addressed in a security-sensitive manner to affirm the importance of internal criticism for healthy democratic institutions. National security must not be pursued in ways that undermine what we are endeavoring to defend. A revitalized IC IG system would enable all government employees to uphold their oath to serve the Constitution. Such reform could be a bipartisan wedge in a currently dysfunctional system from which many other democracy-bolstering benefits might follow. As Fletcher School professor Michael Glennon writes in his book *National Security and Double Government*, "An unrestrained security apparatus has throughout history been one of the principle reasons that free governments have failed."[47]

Some may object that the risks to homeland security are too high to permit the employees of the intelligence communities to be treated as regular government employees, but these risks cannot be assessed in a vacuum. They must be weighed against the enormous damage to American democracy that results from acquiescing in a status quo that treats IC whistleblowers as traitors while sanctioning dragnet data collection. To house the fruits of mass surveillance, whether legally or illegally harvested, Washington built a one-million-square-foot data storehouse in Bluffdale, Utah, called the Mission Data Repository (MDR). The MDR is the NSA's cloud. Even if we assume that rules have been in place to ensure that the MDR's harvested raw data is not accessed without an appropriate warrant, what is to ensure that those rules will be followed under leadership that views the rule of law as a matter of partisan perspective?

To embrace security's demands without questioning their limits is not only to give up on the First Amendment but also to give up on what makes the United States a moral enterprise as well as a political and economic superpower. While they may disrupt and provoke, whistleblowers keep our elites honest and the rule of law sustainable. They take realities that the powerful view as natural or inescapable and show that they are intolerable. They help close the gap between American ideals and reality. In so doing, whistleblowers encourage all of us to think for ourselves. What could be more American than that?

Information Is Power

Exploring a Constitutional Right of Access

MARY-ROSE PAPANDREA

The public demands to know what the government is doing so that it can engage in self-governance and hold the government accountable. At the same time, governmental secrecy is essential to protect our national security and foreign policy interests. The question of how to balance these equally important but sometimes conflicting priorities and, perhaps even more important, who decides how to conduct this balance is a seemingly intractable problem that has occupied scholars for decades.

Our current system of informing the public about some of the most important things the government does—protecting the national security—is mostly a patchwork of customs and norms. The government has no constitutional duty to share national security information with the public and instead selectively reveals information when it suits its purposes. Its tendency to err on the side of nondisclosure and overclassification is well known. Our country relies heavily on unauthorized disclosures and the mediated transmission of this leaked information to the public through third parties. Until recently, the government rarely prosecuted the leakers and never prosecuted the publishers. As Cass Sunstein pointed out years ago, there is absolutely no reason to assume that this system—where the press gets to publish whatever information it can lawfully obtain from government insiders—will strike the correct equilibrium between the protection of legitimate national security secrets and the public's right to know.[1] The revelations the public receives are "rare, haphazard, [and] fortuitous."[2] Secrets that deserve protection may be revealed; things that should be disclosed are not.

In more recent years, the flaws of this system have come into even sharper relief. Just as the national security state has dramatically expanded, the government has made the prosecution of leakers one of its highest priorities. If prosecuted, leakers have very limited defenses, even if they disclosed information to the press and that information reveals government waste, fraud, abuse, or illegal conduct. The government engages in selective prosecution of leakers, most frequently targeting low-level leakers; prosecution of high-ranking individuals is very rare, and the government's position is less aggressive.[3] The prosecutions are high-profile, and the government takes aggressive legal positions.[4] These prosecutions are plainly intended to deter leaks and probably do.

In addition, the United States has brought its first criminal prosecution against a third-party publisher—Julian Assange of WikiLeaks—for newsgathering activities as well as for disclosure of classified information. The government has declared that Assange "is no journalist."[5] This statement inaccurately implies that journalists receive special constitutional protections, perhaps under the Press Clause, or that courts could carve out special First Amendment protections for journalists by defining this profession in such a way that it would exclude Assange but include traditional mainstream media. Unfortunately, the distinction between Assange and the institutional US media is hardly obvious. A successful prosecution against Assange would most certainly upset the "game of leaks." As famous journalist Seymour Hersch has warned, "Today Assange. Tomorrow, perhaps, The New York Times and other media that published so much of the important news and information Assange provided."[6]

One suggestion (among many) for reforming this "trial by battle and cleverness"[7] is to recognize a constitutional right of access to government information. This right to know what the government is doing would support democratic self-governance and allow the public to engage in meaningful oversight. Recognizing this right would permit the public to get access to the information it needs without resorting to the game of leaks. Perhaps more significantly, however, recognizing that the public is entitled to this information could radically refocus the arguments regarding the rights of government employees and contractors ("government insiders") to reveal national security information and of third parties to publish it.

To be sure, recognizing such a right faces a long uphill battle against decades of First Amendment jurisprudence. It would also face innumerable logistical and practical obstacles. Nevertheless, the ongoing collapse of customary press access norms and the government's increasing desire to operate outside of public view may very well warrant a dramatic rethinking of the First Amendment's scope and protections. We just should not fool ourselves into thinking that recognizing this right would end the need to determine when the public, the press, and government insiders can disclose national security information.

The Court's Conflicting Messages about
a Right of Access

Aside from a handful of cases holding that the public's right of access allows attending criminal trials and some criminal pre-trial proceedings, the Supreme Court has not recognized a constitutional right of access to government information or newsgathering activities more generally. As Justice Stewart famously once proclaimed, "The Constitution itself is neither a Freedom of Information Act nor an Official Secrets Act."[8] Instead, the Court has generally held that the First Amendment protects the right to speak but not the right to collect the information that makes that speech capable of serving the important functions of informing our democracy and holding government officials accountable for their actions. It is therefore left to the political process to sort out when the public can obtain information from the government.[9]

This political process has led to state and federal laws such as FOIA creating limited rights to obtain government records and "sunshine laws" that permit access to certain government proceedings. In addition, by statute, regulation, or policy, the press enjoys access to government information through press passes, press rooms, press planes, press galleries, and embedded reporters.[10] Because these access rights are not constitutionally protected, however, they are ephemeral. This is an unnerving state of affairs for a democracy, especially with increasing misinformation problems and a president declaring war on the American press as the "enemy of the American people."[11] This approach limits the effectiveness of public debate; it also establishes a troubling presumption that it is acceptable for the government to keep information from the public.[12]

This state of affairs is a bit strange, given that the Court has emphasized that the First Amendment reflects "a profound national commitment to the principle that debate on public issues should be uninhibited, robust, and wide-open."[13] Time and time again, the Court has declared that the primary purpose of the First Amendment is to provide for "free political discussion to the end that the government may be responsive to the will of the people."[14] The Court has also often mentioned that the First Amendment also has the goal of supporting the "free flow" of information and ideas, especially on matters of public concern.[15] It is not clear how meaningful the "flow" of information can be about public affairs if the government can restrict the acquisition of information at the source.

It turns out that a close examination of the Court's First Amendment jurisprudence reveals mixed messages about whether the First Amendment requires the government to share any information with the people or even whether it protects the right of the people (or the press) to gather information more generally. At the very least, the Court's jurisprudence on these points is theoretically confusing and inconsistent.

To start, the Court has struggled to define what constitutes "the freedom of speech, and of the press." The Court has long since abandoned the notion that these rights are defined solely by history or the Framers' intent, which in Blackstone's view prohibited only prior restraints.[16] In addition to protecting a speaker's right to speak, write, and publish ideas using words or any number of expressive activities, the Court has recognized the right of the audience to receive this expression.[17] This right to receive information has been limited, however, to cases involving "willing" speakers.[18]

The Court has also embraced several "corollary" First Amendment rights, such as the right of association and the right to speak in a public forum.[19] In addition, recognizing that abridgments of the freedom of speech "may occur at various points in the speech process," the Court has held that the right includes the right to contribute money to a political candidate.[20] In recent years, a number of lower courts have protected other types of "speech-facilitating" conduct, such as the videotaping of the police performing their public functions in public places.[21] The idea behind these decisions is that the government could dramatically curtail the freedom of speech if it had the power to restrict the tools used to create that speech and that therefore these activities are themselves entitled to constitutional protection.

The Court has not been so generous with its interpretation of the Press Clause and has instead rendered it a virtual nullity. One of the most famous advocates for a meaningful Press Clause was Justice Stewart, who argued that a free press plays a "structural" role in the Constitution, creating "a fourth institution outside of the Government as an additional check on the other three branches."[22] This view of the Press Clause has not gained traction. The Court has recognized the important role the press plays in informing and educating the public,[23] but it has been very reluctant to give that clause independent meaning. Although the Court expressly rested some of its decisions on the Press Clause in its first few decades of interpreting the provision, over time, the Court's decisions have come to rest squarely on the Speech Clause.[24] The dominant view today is that the Press Clause does not mean anything except that speakers have the right to disseminate their views.[25] Instead, the rights of the press are protected under the Speech Clause, and these rights are enjoyed equally by members of the public.[26]

In rejecting special "press" rights, the Court has explained that "[t]he press does not have a monopoly on the First Amendment or on the ability to enlighten."[27] Furthermore, the Court has also expressed concern about defining "the press," declaring that it was "unwilling to embark the judiciary on a long and difficult journey to an uncertain destination" that "would present practical and conceptual difficulties of the highest order."[28] Long before the internet dramatically changed the media landscape, the Court noted that "the liberty of the press is the right of the lonely pamphleteer . . . just as much as of the large metropolitan publisher." The Court also noted that "[t]he informative function . . . [of the press] is also performed by lecturers, political pollsters, novelists, academic researchers, and dramatists. Almost any author may quite accurately assert that he is contributing to the flow of information to the public."[29]

The Court's decisions relating to constitutional protection for newsgathering—whether by the press or the public—are a hot mess of doctrinal confusion. In its 1965 decision in *Zemel v. Rusk*, the Court rejected a First Amendment challenge to a Cuba travel ban, holding that "[t]he right to speak and publish does not carry with it the unrestrained right to gather information."[30] The Court expressed concern that "[t]here are few restrictions on action which could not be clothed by an ingenious argument in the garb of decreased data flow."[31] By rejecting an "unrestrained" right, however, the Court potentially left open the possibility of a more limited newsgathering right. Indeed, in 1972, when the Court seemingly rejected a First Amendment reporter's privilege in the context of grand jury proceedings, the Court stated in dicta that "newsgathering is not without its First Amendment protections; without some protection for seeking out the news, the freedom of the press could be eviscerated."[32]

But in fact, the Court has not been sympathetic to arguments that the press deserves special protections in order to protect its newsgathering processes. In *Branzburg v. Hayes*, the Court rejected attempts to extend the First Amendment to provide protection for journalists subpoenaed to testify at grand juries.[33] There the journalists claimed that testifying before the grand jury threatened the free flow of information to the public because confidential sources would be less likely to talk to the press.[34] In *Zurcher v. Stanford Daily*, the Court likewise rejected the argument that newsroom searches are unconstitutional because they threaten the press's ability to gather and disseminate information, concluding instead that the usual warrant process should provide sufficient protection.[35] In *Cohen v. Cowles Media Co.*, the Court made clear that the press had to comply with generally applicable laws even if those laws impact its ability to gather and publish the news.[36]

In the 1970s, the Court decided three separate prison access cases that appeared to reject a First Amendment right of access to government information as well as any special rights for the press to obtain such information. In *Saxbe v. Washington Post Co.* and *Pell v. Procunier*, the Court rejected press challenges to policies that did not give the press special access to inmates for interviews. In both cases, the Court stated that the press has no special access right beyond that afforded to the public generally.[37] By equating the press right with the public right, the Court dodged the more fundamental question of what that public right was. A few years later, in another prison access case, a plurality of the Court recognized in *Houchins v. KQED* that the press "can be a powerful and constructive force, contributing to remedial action in the conduct of public business."[38] Nevertheless, the Court rejected claims that journalists should have a right of access to nonpublic areas in prisons in order to conduct face-to-face interviews with inmates of their choosing.[39] The plurality held that the First Amendment protects only the right to communicate information already in its possession and does not provide a right of access to information.[40] Instead, access to information is "a legislative task which the Constitution has left to the political processes."[41] Justice Stewart's outcome-determinative concurrence agreed that there is no newsgathering right to information when the government has not "open[ed] its doors," although he disagreed that the access rights of the press and public were coextensive.[42] Justice Stevens dissented, arguing that the Court had "never intimated that a nondiscriminatory policy of excluding entirely both the public and the press from access to information about prison conditions would avoid constitutional scrutiny."[43]

A short time later, however, the Court recognized a First Amendment right of access to certain criminal proceedings. In *Richmond Newspapers, Inc. v. Virginia*, the Court issued a landmark opinion holding that there is a public right of access to criminal trials under the First and Fourteenth Amendments.[44] Within six years, the Court issued three other opinions recognizing public access to various criminal proceedings.[45] In granting recognition to this newly recognized constitutional right, the *Richmond Newspapers* plurality explained that the expressly guaranteed freedoms of the First Amendment "share a common purpose of assuring freedom of communication on matters relating to the functioning of government."[46] For these rights to be meaningful, the plurality reasoned, the First Amendment must also be interpreted to support a right to gather information.[47] Justice Brennan's concurrence added that the right of access served the First Amendment's "*structural* role in securing and fostering our republican system of self-government."[48] *Richmond Newspapers* did not rely on the Press Clause, even though the claimant was plainly a member of the institutional press, and members of the media are the primary beneficiaries of the right at issue.

In his concurring opinion in *Richmond Newspapers*, Justice Stevens correctly recognized the tension between that case and the prison access cases, proclaiming that *Richmond Newspapers* was "a watershed case" because "[u]ntil today the Court has accorded virtually absolute protection to the dissemination of information or ideas, but never before has it squarely held that the acquisition of newsworthy matter is entitled to any constitutional protection whatsoever."[49]

Justice Stevens's proclamation was correct—*Richmond Newspapers* could have become the foundation for a broader constitutional right of access to government information. That has not come to pass. Since *Richmond Newspapers*, the Court has returned to its mantra that while the government cannot discriminate when it shares information, it could simply decide not to share the information at all.[50] Although the rationale of the *Richmond Newspapers* cases would seem to apply equally as strongly to a broader constitutional right of access to government information, including national security information, the Court has never embraced a broad right of access. In the cases following *Richmond Newspapers*, the Court limited the right of access to judicial proceedings that have enjoyed a history of public access and for which public access would serve important goals.

Possible Approaches to a Constitutional Right

The Court's tangled and confusing history on newsgathering and the right of access to government information leaves open a number of questions. For example, under *Richmond Newspapers* and its progeny, why is a historical tradition of access required for the right to attach? Should the Court breathe life into the Press Clause and locate a right of access there? Or can the Speech Clause do the necessary work?

A constitutional right of access to national security information will fail in most cases if there must be a historical tradition to support it. As the Court has recently noted, there is no right at common law to inspect nonjudicial government documents or records, and while nineteenth-century cases were less categorical, these cases tended to require a personal interest in the records as well as a "specific and legitimate purpose."[51]

But it is hardly clear why a tradition of open public access should be necessary for a right of access to attach. Any inquiry that focuses on history would doom the right of access in many instances outside of the judicial context and is needlessly limiting. The Court has rarely used historical practice as a litmus test for First Amendment rights.[52] Instead, in the First Amendment context, history more frequently plays a supporting role. At best, a historical tradition of openness should be relevant in determining how much weight to give the government's arguments for secrecy.[53] History simply gives the right of access "special force" by undermining any claims that secrecy is necessary, but it does not serve as a meaningful proxy for determining whether the right attaches.[54] In other words, a historical tradition of access should be sufficient but not necessary for the right of access to attach. The Court should instead presume that the public right of access attaches and require the government to meet its burden of demonstrating a compelling interest in continuing secrecy.

This approach also finds support in the Court's developing jurisprudence about what counts as an abridgment of "speech" under the First Amendment. As mentioned above, the Court has not limited the scope of First Amendment protections to the spoken or written word. Instead, the Court has recognized that for the protections of the Speech Clause to be meaningful, its scope must be much broader. Of course, how far these "penumbras" of the First Amendment extend is very unclear, but it is also not entirely clear exactly why newsgathering or even an affirmative right of access would not also fall under this umbrella.

The best (and truly unsatisfying) explanation is that the line has to be drawn somewhere, and a general newsgathering right—never mind an affirmative right of access—is significantly attenuated from the act of communication.[55] But is that correct? The rationale of the lower court decisions extending First Amendment protection to filming the police seems, at bottom, to be protection for newsgathering. The mere act of capturing video footage is not an act of communicating, unless we focus on the symbolic message of a person standing with a cell phone aimed at police ("I am watching you"). It is the sharing of the video footage that constitutes communication about the activities of the police. Images in film are much more visceral and have a much greater impact on the audience. In some ways, taping the police is also a form of newsgathering information from an "unwilling" source. To be sure, an affirmative right of access would be another step away from the act of communicating, but this right of access serves the same values of transparency and accountability supporting the right to videotape. An informed public debate plays an important structural role in checking government power and informing the electorate.

Shoehorning a newsgathering right or right of access to government information into the definition of "speech" is admittedly a stretch. One possible alternative is to focus directly on theories of the First Amendment that usually drive its interpretation. While all of the leading theories could arguably support a right of access, scholars arguing for this right most frequently rely on the self-governance theory to support their position.[56] In order for self-governance to be effective, the public must be engaged and informed. Without information, the people cannot have informed debate.[57] It does not do much good to prohibit government restrictions on speech if the public does not even know what the government is doing. In other words, relying on willing speakers to contribute to public discussions is not sufficient for self-governance if the public must rely on the government's whim for information about its actions (or inactions).

If the constitutional system of checks and balances worked as the Framers hoped, statutory and constitutional rights of access would arguably be unnecessary.[58] Congress has many tools at its disposal to learn how the executive branch is executing the law, including investigations and subpoenas. Occasionally, political pressure will lead the executive branch to promote more transparency. For example, Congress and President Bush created the bipartisan 9/11 Commission to undertake a sweeping investigation into the intelligence failures that permitted a devastating attack on US soil.

But Congress is largely unable to enforce its requests for information when the executive branch refuses to cooperate, which it frequently does, citing national security or foreign policy concerns or concerns that disclosure would interfere with its deliberative privilege or undermine the separation of powers. President Trump's broad assertions of executive privilege and absolute refusal to cooperate with his recent impeachment are exhibit A of Congress's impotence. Even when executive officials agree to testify, there is no guarantee they will be truthful. For example, James Clapper, the former director of national intelligence, told Congress that the NSA does not collect data on millions of Americans; Edward Snowden's leak revealed that this answer was false.[59] Congress's attempts to install inspectors general to receive and process concerns about government wrongdoing are likewise failing spectacularly, as President Trump's removal of five of them illustrates.[60]

Another alternative approach would be to revive the Press Clause as an independent source of the right of access. From an administrability perspective, limiting the right to some subset of the population is potentially desirable to reduce the overall number of claims. Limiting the number of claimants also makes it more likely that the Court will embrace the right.[61] Another potential advantage of limiting the right of access to the press is that it increases the odds that the parties seeking information are doing so for the purposes of contributing to the public debate. After all, individual members of the public who are granted access to government proceedings or government information are not necessarily sharing what they learn and observe with anyone else.

Recognizing special rights under the Press Clause would also be a welcome return to reality. In some of its cases—such as *Richmond Newspapers*—the Court has relied on the Speech Clause and granted a right of access to the public generally even when it might have made more sense to base the decision on the Press Clause. After all, not only was the claimant in that case the press, but the press is also the primary beneficiary of the decision, and the Court recognized that courtrooms could not accommodate the general public and instead might have to grant preferential seating to members of the media.[62]

The problem is that the difficulty inherent in defining the press is one of the primary reasons the Court has not embraced arguments resting on the Press Clause,[63] and these difficulties have grown exponentially with the dramatic changes to the media in the last few decades. This definitional challenge is not insurmountable, but it also might not give rise to a definition that is sufficiently restrictive. In cases where the lower courts have recognized a constitutional reporter's privilege, they have not defined the press by looking at the medium of communication used, whether the claimant has had any sort of journalistic training or abides by certain journalistic norms, the number of audience members, or whether the claimant makes money or spends a certain number of hours a week engaging in newsgathering or public communications.[64] Instead, these courts have focused on whether the claimant had the intent to disseminate the information at the inception of the information collection.[65] This approach suits some of the purposes of the Press Clause by providing a right to people who plan to share the information they gather (rather than keeping it to themselves). One thing the intent to disseminate test does not do, however, is privilege the traditional institutional press.

Limiting access to claimants who are "responsible" or demonstrate a commitment to journalistic ethics is also fraught with problems. It is hardly clear what it means to be a "responsible" journalist. The very best of American publications have been sued for defamation or for revealing information in ways that some people might regard as "irresponsible." Looking to a canon of journalistic ethics offers no more certainty or protection. In order to determine whether this standard is met, courts would first have to figure out what those standards are, which is hardly an easy task. Then the entire publishing history of a given publication would be potentially open to examination and attack. No publication would be guaranteed certification as a "responsible" publisher, not even the members of the institutional media that the proponents of this approach likely have in mind. Limiting access rights to responsible journalists or those who follow certain ethical rules ends up sounding pretty close to "licensing" the press, which would clearly be inconsistent with the First Amendment.

In fact, we can already see this sort of thing at work in the indictment of Assange. Some have argued that editorial review and control of content is one distinguishing feature of journalism. At times, WikiLeaks has simply posted information it received from sources without considering the public value of the information, the harm the information could cause, and the balance between the value and the harm. In contrast, more traditional publications generally will not publish information before engaging in this sort of review. The *Guardian* and the *New York Times* reported that they had "spent weeks cross-checking the information."[66] One fundamental problem with this approach is that WikiLeaks has taken the general position that the public value in information is always greater than the government's interest in secrecy. This approach might seem reckless, but it is a balancing of value and harm, albeit one conducted at a very high level of generality. There is also merit to Floyd Abrams's warning that "[a] press that continually applies to the courts for vindication of its right to gather information cannot credibly be the same press that tells the same courts that what the press prints and why it prints it are not matters that courts may even consider."[67]

The desire to limit the right of access to strong institutional press actors is understandable. After all, it is indeed important to have a vibrant fourth estate that can check government power at every turn. As Lee Bollinger has argued, "[i]t is a serious mistake to assume that a multitude of individual or smaller-scale

Web sites would serve the same purpose as the traditional press."[68] At the same time, however, it is also a serious mistake to think that the traditional press has a monopoly on providing valuable information and perspectives to the public. It is well documented how websites and other nontraditional news sources have uncovered—and published—information that the mainstream media ignored.[69]

If the Court recognized a constitutional right of access under the First Amendment, its next step would be to determine the precise contours of that right. The Court should embrace the presumption that all government information should be information available to the public. The government could then overcome this presumptive right by showing a countervailing compelling interest. These interests most certainly include grave, immediate, and direct harms to national security. Courts might also include serious potential harms to national security that are grave and direct but not immediate. Even if the government can meet this high standard, however, courts should then balance the public's interest in knowing this information against the potential harm. Otherwise, the government might be able to conceal information about illegal and other questionable activities.

Practical and Logistical Obstacles

Even if the Court were willing to recognize a right of access to government information, this new right would face some serious practical and logistical shortcomings. When considering whether and how Congress should provide for a statutory right of access to national security information, a good starting point is an examination of the programs that already exist.[70] The best-known program providing a statutory right of access is FOIA, which was passed after the Nixon impeachment in 1976. More recently, Congress has created other mechanisms providing some rights of access to government information that have produced promising but limited results.

FOIA is intended to "ensure an informed citizenry, vital to the functioning of a democratic society, needed to check against corruption and to hold the governors accountable to the governed."[71] Although FOIA has proven beneficial in some instances,[72] its weaknesses are legendary, particularly in the context of national security information. The biggest reason FOIA does not work—although, of course, there are many issues—is that courts have largely deferred to the executive branch's arguments that national security interests warrant nondisclosure.

At the outset, it is essential to note that the scope of FOIA is relatively narrow. It covers only "agency records" and does not cover the federal courts, Congress, or "the President, his immediate personal staff, or units in the Executive Office whose sole function is to advise and assist the President."[73] Under FOIA, federal agencies are required to turn over requested records "to any person" unless one of nine exceptions applies.[74] FOIA's exceptions recognize countervailing interests such as national security, law enforcement, trade secrets, confidential commercial information, and privacy[75] that agencies frequently invoke, often successfully.[76] Researchers have found that courts affirm agency denials at alarmingly high rates across the board.[77] District courts review agency determinations under a de novo standard rather than the more common "substantial evidence" or "arbitrary and capricious" standards typically used in judicial review of agency decisions.[78]

These affirmance rates are even higher in national security cases. Exemption 1 of FOIA exempts national security documents that have been properly classified pursuant to the criteria established by executive order.[79] The justification for the classification system is obvious: to protect the disclosure of information that could undermine public safety and security. The problem is that the government routinely overclassifies national security information. This state of affairs is roundly condemned but not easily resolved. Indeed, overclassification may, in fact, contribute to the government's inability to control its most sensitive information. Government insiders and outsiders alike realize that the classification of a document does not necessarily mean that it contains sensitive information. Without respect for the classification system, individuals feel more willing to decide for themselves whether disclosure would truly pose a risk to national security.

Because Congress has permitted the executive branch to determine what needs to be kept secret, some have said that Exemption 1 "is not so much an exemption as it is a license to withhold."[80] Even if courts took seriously Congress's instruction to examine whether classification is proper, the classification systems do not take into account the public interest in obtaining information; FOIA similarly does not permit "a judicial weighing of the costs and benefits of disclosure on a case-by-case basis."[81] Furthermore, the national security harm expected from disclosure does not have to be grave, imminent, or even particularly likely. The lowest level of classification—"confidential"—requires merely that disclosure "reasonably could be expected to cause damage to the national security."[82]

Despite Congress's concerted efforts to deter the judiciary from rubber-stamping the government's classification decisions, court review of classification decisions is often extremely deferential. Plaintiffs rarely prevail in FOIA cases in which the government asserts national security interests; they have been even less successful after the 9/11 attacks.[83] Lower courts have extended the deference they have traditionally afforded the government on classification decisions to other cases in which the government asserts national security concerns.[84] Courts allow the government to submit indexes and affidavits shielding the requested information;[85] discovery rarely occurs, and the court frequently rejects the possibility of in camera review.[86] Courts have also embraced the government's questionable mosaic theories[87] and permitted agencies to make a "Glomar" response by which they refuse to admit or deny whether they even have any responsive documents at all.[88] In addition, courts have credited government arguments that secrecy is essential even when the government itself has already made some of the information public. The courts explained that the government must be able to make "strategic disclosures," because the "political reality" is that "our Government may choose to release information deliberately to 'send a message' to allies or adversaries" and that courts "should not second-guess the executive's judgment in this area."[89] Although the Supreme Court has not always deferred to the executive branch when it comes to national security, this profound deference is more common than not.[90]

Agencies are not properly staffed or funded to respond to FOIA requests, leading to long delays, and when production finally occurs, the documents are heavily redacted. One potential problem is that anyone at all can make a FOIA request. As the Supreme Court has made clear, FOIA's "sole concern is with what must be made public or not made public."[91] Requesters do not need to explain why they need the documents, whether the information they seek would serve the public interest, or even that they plan on sharing the information with the public at all. As it turns out, relatively few requests come from concerned citizens and journalists.[92] Instead, the vast majority of requests come from commercial entities, some of which turn around and sell the information they obtain at a profit.[93] Other frequent FOIA users are individuals seeking information relating to their government benefits, immigrants in removal proceedings, or people conducting oppositional research for political purposes.[94] While it is certainly possible that some individual requests will unearth government waste, fraud, or illegality, most FOIA requests are largely divorced from the public interest concerns that drove its enactment.[95]

One bright spot in the current information access regime is the Interagency Security Classification Appeals Panel (ISCAP), which was established by executive order in 1995.[96] Under the order, the ISCAP reviews appeals from government employees as well as members of the public challenging classification policies and classification determinations (as well as exemptions from mandatory declassification after twenty-five years). Unlike FOIA, the ISCAP covers all classified information and not just agency records. Those seeking declassification must first seek relief from the relevant agency; if relief is denied or no answer is received within ninety days, the requester can bring an appeal to ISCAP. Because all of the officials on the ISCAP are executive branch officials from national security agencies,[97] the ISCAP does not defer to government assertions regarding the importance of continuing secrecy for national security reasons and has ordered declassification in a majority of its cases. But limited staff and resources have rendered the ISCAP's reach and impact much more limited than it could be. Requesters often have to wait years for their cases to be heard. Furthermore, although its declassification record is impressive, it has dealt primarily with requests to declassify historical material. It is not clear how well the ISCAP would handle more current classified information, especially because its mandate does not require it to consider the public interest in disclosure.

The existing problems with FOIA suggest that fundamental changes are essential on both the front and back ends to make the right of access effective. Changes on the front end would make FOIA requests less common and necessary. The executive order governing classification should tighten the categories of classifiable information and define "damage to national security" in more detail. Classification should not be permitted unless "disclosure is highly likely to result, either directly or indirectly, in loss of life, serious bodily harm, or significant economic or property damage."[98] Furthermore, documents should be automatically declassified much sooner than twenty-five years (perhaps five to ten years), unless the government can establish that disclosure would still cause this sort of grave harm.[99]

On the back end, litigants would assert constitutional access rights on a case-by-case basis. Over time, this litigation would lead to a body of constitutional common law establishing a right of access to certain types of documents, proceedings, and government places. Consistent with the reason for the right, courts might be able to limit the right to those seeking information for purposes of sharing it with the public and not for private purposes.

Of course, it is important to acknowledge that mandatory disclosure will not help solve all of the problems with FOIA or serve the goal of having an informed electorate and accountable public officials. The government will still have to redact documents in order to protect from disclosure matters that legitimately must remain secret; this takes time and resources. In addition, government actors are unlikely to release proactively any classified information; indeed, they might classify even more documents to avoid automatic disclosure.[100] The government is also likely to continue to conceal documents that reveal corruption, questionable (or even illegal) government activities, and other instances of government malfeasance or incompetence. Furthermore, even if the government disclosed documents, the sheer magnitude of documents would make it difficult for anyone to search for desired information without significant investment in creating databases with useful search capacities. It is therefore not surprising that prior efforts to embrace mandatory disclosure have not been particularly successful.[101]

The right of access is likely to be expensive and time-consuming. As critics have pointed out, we do not have "unlimited federal money to spend, an unlimited number of agency employees to assign, [or] an unlimited number of federal judges to hear and decide cases."[102] Court proceedings can be opened up to the public after minimal judicial review with assistance from the parties. Access to court files can take much longer, at least when confidential or classified information is at issue. But these delays are minor compared to the sorts of delays that would likely accompany any attempts to obtain access to government documents. As with court documents, government documents cannot simply be opened up en masse to the public. There are too many compelling countervailing interests that would have to be considered and protected before release.

Changes on the back end would help make sure that when FOIA requests are necessary, the public obtains the information to which it is entitled. The body reviewing FOIA requests should be a specialized court with national security expertise and security clearances, like the FISA court. At the very least, this would defang arguments that the judges are ill equipped to second-guess the executive branch's national security information, an argument we see the government making (often successfully) in a wide range of cases, not just FOIA cases. The tribunal should offer expedited review for requests involving matters of immediate public concern to avoid the lengthy delays that render our current transparency mechanisms virtually useless. Alternatively, federal district courts could maintain jurisdiction over these actions but exercise their oversight in a meaningful way with the help of in camera review, special masters, or appointed experts. These things could bolster the effectiveness of judicial review.

Ramifications of Recognizing a Right of Access

It is possible that the recognition of an affirmative constitutional right of access would undermine claims that protections for leaking and publishing leaked information are essential for an informed democracy. If the public could obtain access to government information without relying on leaks, both national security and knowledge about the inner workings of the government would arguably improve. The government would disclose more information, either on its own or when forced in litigation to do so. National security would arguably improve, because would-be leakers might leak less. Instead of leaking a flash drive full of top-secret documents, a government insider could instead ask for information to be declassified (or tip off a government outsider, who could ask for information to be declassified).

But it is hard not to be cynical about the likelihood of creating a system that would make the game of leaks unnecessary. Article III judges appear unwilling to second-guess the executive branch when it comes to national security. The creation of a tribunal consisting of individuals with national security backgrounds might eliminate this deference, but these individuals are still likely to give more weight to national security risks than to the public's right to know.

Furthermore, a constitutional right of access simply could never be a sufficient means for checking the executive branch. The government is not likely to turn over every single government document; instead, the press and other interested parties would have to bring lawsuits claiming a right to access particular pieces of government information. The government would vigorously defend its right to keep secrets, leading to long delays and increased litigation costs. And third parties, including the press, increasingly lack the resources to bring these legal challenges. Given that it is seemingly impossible to fix our classification system and that it is unlikely a constitutional right of access will provide meaningful access to all the government information the public has a right to know, leakers—and the third parties that publish leaked information—will continue to play an essential role in ensuring government transparency and accountability.

A right of access could also undermine current First Amendment rights to receive and publish national security information. Although the landscape of these rights remains uncertain, the recognition of a right of access might lead the Court to conclude that pursuing information through the judicial system is the only appropriate method for obtaining information about the government. On the other hand, it is possible that the theoretical basis for protecting the right of the public to obtain and share national security information could bolster the uncertain First Amendment rights of the press and public, as well as government employees and contractors. If the Court embraces arguments that the public has a right to government information, it is more likely to conclude that the press has a right to publish it and that the government insider had a right to disclose it.

Who Said What to Whom

CASS R. SUNSTEIN*

> It was . . . best for the convention for forming the Constitution to sit with closed doors, because opinions were so various and at first so crude that it was necessary they should be long debated before any uniform system of opinion could be formed. Meantime the minds of the members were changing, and much was to be gained by a yielding and accommodating spirit. Had the members committed themselves publicly at first, they would have afterwards supposed consistency required them to maintain their ground, whereas by secret discussion no man felt himself obliged to retain his opinions any longer than he was satisfied of their propriety and truth, and was open to the force of argument. . . . No Constitution would ever have been adopted by the convention if the debates had been public.
>
> James Madison

What Leakers Are Leaking

In domestic and international affairs, there is a distinction between two kinds of transparency: output transparency and input transparency. Leaks might be an effort to create one or the other. Some leakers care only or mostly about outputs. Others focus on inputs. Disclosure of both outputs and inputs can endanger national security. At the same time, such disclosure can serve important public goals, even if it is unauthorized and indeed unlawful.

Suppose that the Department of Transportation has completed a detailed study of what kinds of policies help to reduce deaths on the highways or that the Department of Labor has produced an analysis of the health risks associated with exposure to silica in the workplace. Or suppose that the Environmental Protection Agency produces a regulation to curtail greenhouse gas emissions from motor vehicles or adopts a policy about when it will bring enforcement actions against those who violate its water quality regulations. Or turn to the domain of national security, and suppose that the Department of Homeland

Security has adopted a series of policies to deal with detainees who are suspected to be terrorists or that the president has signed off on a set of policies to govern the use of drones. All these are outputs.

Now suppose that officials within the Department of Energy and the Environmental Protection Agency staffs have exchanged views about what form a greenhouse gas regulation should take or that political appointees within the Department of Labor have had heated debates about the risks associated with silica in the workplace and about how those risks are best handled. Or suppose that the National Security Council has had a series of meetings about whether to kill certain high-level terrorists or even officials in unfriendly nations, such as Iran. The various views are inputs.

My principal focus here is on input transparency. As James Madison's remarks on the Constitutional Convention make clear, that form can be a complicated matter. The costs of disclosure are often high, and the benefits may be low; both are qualitatively different from the costs and benefits of output transparency. There are strong reasons to protect processes of internal deliberation, above all to ensure openness, candor, and trust. These reasons seem all the stronger in the context of national security, where leaks may cost lives, and if the underlying material is classified, there is special reason to protect it. In general, it is often unclear that the public would gain much from seeing inputs, not least because of their massive volume (and usual irrelevance to anything that matters). Sometimes the public would gain little or nothing (except perhaps something like gossip). Another way to put the point is that while those who seek to attract eyeballs or to embarrass their former bosses or political opponents often like input transparency, the public may not much benefit from it.

At the same time, transparency about inputs can be deeply informative, and inputs may have keen historical interest. Leakers can produce significant and desirable change. If the public learns that the deputy secretary of transportation had a different view from that of the secretary on the content of a fuel economy regulation, it knows something; internal disagreement paints a different picture from internal unanimity. If the public learns that the secretary of homeland security and the secretary of state disagreed with the president on whether to engage in a military operation, the public will know something important. It might hold the president accountable for mistakes, emboldened by the views of informed cabinet heads.

But how much, exactly, does the public learn, and why, exactly, is it important for the public to learn it? To be sure, input transparency may be a good idea, especially under circumstances of incompetence or corruption (or something like these) and when relevant inputs have genuine historic importance (and when their disclosure can reduce mistakes). Nations need catalogues. But the argument for input transparency is much different from the argument for output transparency, and it often stands on weaker ground. Would-be leakers, and those who evaluate leaks, need to keep the difference in mind.

These points suggest the inevitable contingency of arguments for or against input transparency and hence *the impossibility of offering conclusions that will stand under all circumstances.* (I put those words in italics because some prescriptions about leaks and leakers purport to be unconditional.) Imagine, for example, that democratic institutions are well-functioning, in the sense that corruption is absent, competence is widespread, and internal processes are both inclusive and deliberative. In such circumstances, the benefits of input transparency are usually unlikely to be high, and their costs are usually unlikely to be low. Leakers might be villains or even traitors (though we need to know what they are leaking). Or imagine, by contrast, that we are dealing with institutions that function very poorly, in the sense that corruption and incompetence are widespread, and internal processes are haphazard and nondeliberative. In such circumstances, input transparency might be indispensable, and leakers might be heroes (though again, we need to know what they are leaking).

The challenge, of course, is that for both outside observers and those inside government, it might not be clear whether existing institutions are at one or another pole. Reasonable people disagree. Leakers take matters into their own hands, and their judgments may be self-serving, ax-grinding, or otherwise unreliable. In a democracy, the right presumption is clear: *do not leak.* Here again, the presumption is strengthened if matters of national security are involved and further strengthened if classified materials are involved. But a presumption is not a rule; it can be rebutted. An obvious case involves a good-faith impeachment inquiry. If a president has done something impeachable, people should leak, even if the issue involves national security. (I bracket potentially difficult questions raised by classified material.)

It should be clear from these general remarks that my approach to this topic is insistently and unabashedly *welfarist.* What are the benefits of transparency, and what are the costs? It is true that the benefits and the costs may not be easy to quantify, but some kind of assessment of both is, I suggest, indispensable to an evaluation of when transparency or leaking is most and least necessary. For those who are not comfortable with talk of costs and benefits in this context, it might be useful to understand those terms not as an effort to create some kind of arithmetic straitjacket but to signal the importance of asking concrete questions about the human consequences of competing approaches. At least for difficult problems, those questions are (I suggest) far more productive than abstractions about "legitimacy" and "the right to know."

Internal Dynamics

For simplicity, let us begin with domestic affairs. When I was clerking for Justice Marshall in 1980, Bob Woodward and Scott Armstrong published a book on the Supreme Court called *The Brethren*. I did not speak with Woodward or Armstrong, and I am also confident that none of my three co-clerks did so. But numerous clerks (largely or perhaps entirely from previous terms) decided to open up to the authors. They leaked. The portrait of Justice Marshall was highly unflattering (and by the way, wildly inaccurate). Justice Marshall was clearly stung and disappointed, much less (I think) because of the unfavorable, unfair, inaccurate portrait than because of what he saw as a breach of loyalty. I do not think it is disloyal to disclose what he said to us, which was roughly this: "I am not going to change how I interact with my clerks, but if you violate my confidence, it's on your conscience."

After I left the White House after working for President Obama, many reporters, and some people outside the world of journalism, asked me questions about internal dynamics. They seemed to have a kind of lust. Who said what to the president? Who disagreed with whom? If something happened, or did not happen, who wanted it not to happen, or to happen? Who won, and who lost? Of course, I did not answer any of these questions, but there was no mistaking the (astounding) persistence with which they were asked. How well I recall a conversation with a superb journalist, working for the *Washington Post*, who was much focused on the who-disagreed-with-whom questions. I finally suggested to her that she should write something on the substance of the issues that most interested her (environmental policy).

As I understand them here (and consistent with the standard parlance), inputs count as both predecisional and deliberative. These are independent requirements. They are predecisional in the sense that they are not themselves official decisions in any respect. They antedate those decisions and are meant to inform them. If an assistant administrator in the Environmental Protection Agency advises the administrator that a new ozone regulation should set a standard of sixty rather than sixty-five parts per billion, the communication is predecisional. If the secretary of state advises the president to adopt a new program for surveillance of suspected terrorists, the communication is also predecisional. Inputs are deliberative in the sense that they are part of a process of ongoing discussion about what to do.

Even with these clarifications, we can imagine difficult cases, as when a report is compiled on (say) the risks associated with silica or the effects of a surveillance program, and that report will be an input into a regulation. But the core should not be obscure. If law clerks are exchanging memoranda on how to handle a dispute over affirmative action, inputs are involved. If people in the White House are discussing the contents of an open government memorandum, we are dealing with inputs. If White House officials are speaking with the Food and Drug Administration about how to handle the risks associated with certain asthma medicines, inputs are involved. If the National Security Council has convened a principals' meeting to discuss the situation in Syria or Iran, the contents of the discussion largely involve inputs. If some members of the president's cabinet have discussed whether to invoke the Twenty-Fifth Amendment to remove the president, we are dealing with inputs.

With respect to inputs, the argument for disclosure, or for leaking, runs into serious problems. First, the benefits of disclosure may be low (not always but usually). Second, the costs of disclosure may be high. These are categorical statements with major qualifications, to which I will turn in due course.

Inputs and More Inputs

From the standpoint of the public, it may not be desirable to obtain inputs. To those who believe in transparency and who focus on particular cases in which leaks have provided important information, that claim might seem controversial, implausible, or even shocking. But the sheer number and range of inputs are daunting, and it defies belief to think that the public would benefit from seeing all of them. An assistant secretary in any cabinet department will have countless conversations in the course of a week, and in many of them, she will be receiving suggestions, venturing possible ideas, requesting more information, joking, offering doubts, and seeking out possible inclinations. Some of the inputs that she receives or offers will not be very interesting. If they are interesting, it might be for a reason that does not exactly argue for disclosure; someone might have ventured an idea, for purposes of discussion, that was or is on reflection a really bad one. The idea was (let us suppose) rejected, and so it never became an output. Is it important, or on balance desirable, for the world to see it?

Now, suppose that public officials are deciding what to do about particulate matter (an air pollutant). The director of the National Economic Council urges caution, emphasizing the overriding importance of economic growth. The Domestic Policy Council urges aggressive action, emphasizing that environmental groups keenly want the US government to reduce particulate matter; invoking international relations, the Department of State does the same. The Office of Information and Regulatory Affairs calls for a middle course, with close attention to costs and benefits. The Office of the Chief of Staff is focused on political considerations. Many memoranda are exchanged, offering various alternatives and competing points of views. It is far from clear how much the public would benefit from seeing this material. What most matters is what the government actually does, not who said what to whom.

The conclusion is not different if the issue involves national security. If the director of the National Security Council is urging caution in responding to a terrorist threat, and if the secretary of state and the director of the CIA disagree, there is a fair question of whether it is important for the public to see, in real time, the nature and the intensity of the disagreement.

It is true that for purposes of my thesis here, these examples may not be the most convincing. The problem of particulate matter and responses to terrorism are exceedingly important, which complicates my argument (for reasons to which I will turn in due course). Consider, then, the general area of federal regulations, the most significant of which must go through the Office of Information and Regulatory Affairs (about five hundred per year). Many of those regulations will never be seriously discussed in the newspapers or online. Some of them involve national security. Their issuance is preceded by a great deal of internal discussion, involving paper documents, electronic documents, and email, often raising questions and doubts. This is the quintessence of a deliberative process. A number of people say a number of things. Much of the time, the benefits of disclosing the content of that process are essentially zero.

Within the federal government, what is true for the regulatory process is true for many discussions—but even more so. The volume of emails is extraordinarily high. As in the case of the hypothetical assistant secretary, they might float ideas, offer tentative reactions, report on what some people appear to think. In general, disclosure would serve no purpose at all, except perhaps to those interested in genuine minutiae or seeking to embarrass, injure, or ruin someone, to create a political uproar, or to uncover some kind of scandal.

Why Input Disclosure Might Make Sense

There are two important qualifications helping to explain the appeal of input transparency for many observers. Both of them play a large role in the domain of national security and help explain the motivation for leaking. Whether they are adequate justifications for leaking depends on the circumstances.

1. *Illegitimate or illicit arguments.* Public disclosure might provide an ex ante deterrent to arguably illegitimate arguments, and it might also provide an ex post corrective. Suppose, for example, that someone favors a decision not because it is a good idea but because it would help the president's electoral prospects, because it would appease a donor or a powerful interest group, or because a prominent senator might like it (with fortunate consequences for the administration). Let us stipulate that the public has a right to know about this, because

it might compromise the pursuit of the public interest. Disclosure could have salutary consequences, and in any case, it will create accountability. In this particular respect, an appealing argument about the beneficial effects of sunlight applies to input transparency as well as output transparency. Recall the case of impeachable conduct, even if it involves national security. Impeachment is the ultimate corrective for grave wrongdoing, and it might not be available without input transparency.

To be sure, disclosure could have the principal effect of shifting the locus of discussion—from email and paper to telephones. Within the federal government, that already happens a great deal. If people do not want their communications to be disclosed to the public or to Congress, they will say, "Call me." (In my own experience, this was always innocent; it does not involve anything illicit, but it does involve issues that are somewhat sensitive, such as strong disagreements that are not best placed in email.) Actually, there is a substantial risk here. If internal discussions are potentially subject to disclosure, the shift from written to oral exchanges may impose losses, in the form of diminished reliance on careful economic, legal, and other analyses. Nonetheless, it is true that disclosure of inputs can have the beneficial effect of "laundering" them.

There is no question that a concern about illegitimate or illicit inputs animates the argument in favor of input transparency. Suppose you believe that some process is "rigged"—that regularly or as a matter of course, powerful private interests are dominating federal processes or that officials, beholden to certain groups, are pushing outcomes in the directions favored by those groups. Of course, you want that to stop. But if you cannot stop it directly, you might insist on input transparency as a way of opening it up to public view. Sunlight might be a disinfectant here as well. True, there is a risk that you will simply drive the relevant influences underground. But in principle, that is a secondary concern. You want to open up internal processes to public scrutiny.

2. *Learning from mistakes.* The second qualification is that journalists and historians can benefit from seeing the give and take, if only because they could give a narrative account of what happened. That might appear to be an abstract, academic benefit, but people (including public officials) do learn from the past, including the recent past, and that learning can provide a valuable corrective. The historical record can be absolutely indispensable for finding out what went wrong, and to understand that record, inputs are necessary. Why did the government make some colossal error in the form of an action or an omission? To answer that question, input transparency might be essential. It can create warning signs about group interactions that work poorly, about institutional blindnesses, about the need for institutional reform. Even in the short term, it can produce corrective action.

Suppose, for example, that the US government has done (too) little to prevent genocide.[1] It may be difficult or even impossible to document the failures without access to inputs. And once the failures are documented, people might take steps to reduce their likelihood in the future. In that sense, the benefits of input disclosure can be high, at least in certain domains.

But there are countervailing points. In many cases, disclosure of inputs has no benefits; it does not reduce the risk of future errors. Disclosure also imposes a risk of distortion. Suppose that people have access to an official's emails—say, the emails of a deputy secretary of state. Suppose that the email has some complaint about the attorney general or about White House officials. The email might reflect a particular day or mood. It might be based on the author's incomplete understanding. It might be a matter of venting. It might reflect a badly distorted perspective.

Because journalists often enjoy and benefit from accusations and scandal-mongering, it might be appealing to give a great deal of publicity to this revelation of internal disagreement. Recall that it is a form of gossip. Readers might enjoy the gossip and in that sense benefit from it, but accusations and scandal-mongering are not necessarily genuine benefits for the public. Of course, a genuine scandal is another matter.

The Costs of Input Transparency

For input transparency, the most obvious problem, of course, is that disclosure could reduce open-mindedness and discourage candor. In a short space, Madison captured some of the essential points. In any deliberative process, people's opinions are various and crude, and much is "to be gained by a yielding and accommodating spirit." Once people commit themselves publicly, they might not be willing to shift. Secrecy can promote openness to the force of the argument. And of course, Madison's knockout punch: "No Constitution would ever have been adopted by the convention if the debates had been public."

What Madison did not emphasize is that input transparency can lead people not to say what they think. It can reduce candor and the free play of ideas. In that sense, it can ensure that groups will have less information than they need. In well-functioning deliberative processes, there is often a sharp separation between an idea-generating phase and a solution-finding phase. In the former phase, many things are on the table, even if they turn out on reflection to be absurd or intolerable. People say yes to getting ideas out there, whether or not there is any chance that they will ultimately be adopted. If inputs are transparent, the idea-generating phase would be far more constrained than it ought to be.

Ensuring candor is, of course, the central idea behind the idea of executive privilege.[2] At best, input transparency would lead people to communicate orally rather than in writing. And in fact, one of the consequences of FOIA is to reduce reliance on email and written documents. In both Republican and Democratic administrations, it is well known that whatever is put in writing might find its way into the *New York Times*—which leads people not to put things in writing. At worst, input transparency can lead certain things not to be said at all.

But reduced candor is not the only problem. In view of the incentives of the media and political opponents, disclosure of inputs can produce extremely unfortunate distractions, destructive to self-government. Instead of focusing on outputs—on how, for example, to reduce premature deaths—a spotlight is placed on comments that seem to make some people into villains or wrongdoers or that put any resulting decisions in the least favorable light. Of course, skeptics might respond, with some passion, that it is paternalistic or worse to deprive members of the public of information on the ground that they will misunderstand it or give it undue salience. On one view, receipt of true information should be subject to the marketplace of ideas. But insofar as the problem lies not in public misunderstanding but in the incentives of those who seek to fuel fires, there is definitely a downside risk.

A Brief Accounting

With respect to input transparency, we seem to have incommensurable values on both sides of the ledger, not easily placed along a single metric. The benefits are often low—but hardly always, especially when there is corruption or incompetence or when the historical record can help to avoid massive or catastrophic mistakes. The costs can be high. But are they always?

It must be acknowledged that those costs diminish over time, and they are certainly lower once the relevant people no longer hold public office. It is one thing to tell the secretary of homeland security that whatever she says will end up in the newspaper that night or the next day. It is quite another to say that at a future date (say, after an administration has ended), there will be a public record of internal communications, subject to safeguards for national security, personal privacy, and other values. And indeed, the Presidential Records Act[3] ventures an approach of this sort (with a five-year gap). With such an approach, the costs of disclosure are significantly reduced. They are not zero, because candor will be chilled and because people's reputations will be wrongly maligned. But in view of the value of obtaining some kind of historical record, that approach is hardly unreasonable. My aim has been not to reach a definitive conclusion about concrete practices and proposals but to outline general concerns to help identify the appropriate trade-offs.

Conclusion

There is a large difference between output transparency and input transparency. For outputs, transparency can be exceedingly important. Formal policies should not be kept secret, at least if there is no reason, founded in national security, to do so. Some materials are overclassified. Sunlight can operate as a disinfectant, and whether the information involves the government's own performance or the performance of the private sector, disclosure can spur better performance.

Inputs belong in a different category. In general, what most matters is what government actually does, not who said what to whom. For the most part, the public is unlikely to benefit if it learns that the assistant secretary of state disagreed with the chief of staff of the secretary of state on some trade agreement or that there was an internal division on how aggressively to regulate greenhouse gases or on the valuation of statistical lives. Disclosure can also have significant costs. Most obviously, it can lead people to silence themselves or to communicate in ways that cannot be recorded. More subtly, it can divert attention from the important question, which involves policy and substance, to less important ones, which involve palace intrigue. At the same time, input transparency can put a spotlight on questionable or illicit practices and can also provide an indispensable historical record. People learn from the past, and for current administrations, it can be essential to have a concrete sense of where past administrations went wrong.

My framework throughout has been welfarist; it asks about the costs and benefits of disclosure. It should be acknowledged that the very idea of welfarism needs to be specified and that many people would start with different foundations—involving, for example, the idea of political legitimacy. It should also be acknowledged that under a welfarist framework, some output transparency does not make much sense, and some input transparency is amply justified, even indispensable. We are speaking of categories, not individual cases. But categories provide orientation. We need much more in the way of output transparency. Input transparency can be important, but it should be treated far more cautiously.

Leaks in the Age of Trump

LOUIS MICHAEL SEIDMAN

From the early 1970s through the middle of this decade, the so-called Pentagon Papers settlement dominated the legal treatment of unauthorized disclosure of government secrets. The Pentagon Papers were the subject of the famous Supreme Court case rejecting the government's efforts to enjoin newspapers from publishing a secret government report critical of American policy toward Vietnam.[1] The terms of the settlement, however, extend beyond the narrow and fractured holding of the case.

The settlement had the following components:

1. Leaking of government secrets to the mainstream press was pervasive and considered part of the ordinary practice of journalism. Some leaks were purely accidental—an indiscreet remark at a dinner party or an overheard conversation at a sporting event. In the case of intentional leaks, the leakers often were disgruntled administration officials or civil service employees who were upset by practices or policy positions that they viewed as unwise or illegal. Other leakers had a variety of different motives, from the settling of scores, to self-aggrandizement, to signaling or getting the attention of other government officials, to floating trial balloons. A fair number of leaks came from higher-level officials, including the president himself.

2. The vast majority of leaks went unpunished. Investigations of leaks were often nonexistent, halfhearted, or ineffectual.

3. On the other hand, the government had more or less untrammeled discretion to prosecute or discipline leakers when it was able to figure out who they were and when it served the interests of government officials to punish the leakers. When government took advantage of this power, leakers had no constitutional and few other defenses to the charges against them.

4. It was also permissible for the government to censor writings by government employees prior to publication when the employees had access to secrets.

There was no legal obstacle to punishing employees who ignored or defied the pre-clearance requirements.

5. As a legal matter, the status of the reporters and news organizations that were the recipients of leaks was more complicated. They had no or little protection against legal action forcing them to reveal their sources.[2] Although they were usually immune from prior restraints, there was ambiguity about whether they could be prosecuted after publication.

6. As a practical matter, though, there were only occasional efforts to force journalists to reveal their sources, and the government almost never tried to discipline the press, even when it published highly classified material.

Despite contradictions and internal tensions, this settlement proved remarkably durable, surviving for half a century through Democratic and Republican administrations. There were predictable grumblings from every administration about leaks, occasional serious investigations designed to discover leakers, and periodic free speech claims made on behalf of both leakers and the press. None of this did much to change the situation on the ground.

Very recently, though, support for the settlement has begun to erode, especially among the sorts of elites who, for example, have been asked to participate in this book project. At this writing, it is unclear whether the settlement will survive and, if it fails to do so, what will replace it. On the one hand, there is growing concern about "irresponsible" leaks, exemplified by the well-publicized disclosures engineered by Edward Snowden and Chelsea Manning. Some commentators have also begun to wonder about the practical immunity enjoyed by the media. The pending prosecution of WikiLeaks founder Julian Assange threatens to unravel this portion of the settlement. On the other hand, there are also growing doubts about the selective prosecution of leakers, especially in cases where they have arguably revealed serious government misconduct, and increasing concern about President Trump's (so far mostly rhetorical) assault on press freedom.

The first section of this essay is descriptive and analytic. It offers a tentative theory that explains the reasons attitudes toward the settlement are beginning to change. I argue that the change results from a shift in the balance of power in the longstanding struggle between populist and establishment forces in American politics.

The settlement was rooted in the assumption that establishment figures would control the levers of power. For these purposes, I offer a concededly loose and unscientific definition of "establishment figures": they are members of the governing elites of both parties who are somewhat insulated from popular "uninformed" opinion, favor only moderate reforms, and pursue "sensible" policies through "sensible" means. As used here, *sensible* is defined in a circular fashion as the policies and procedures favored by government elites.

A series of catastrophic mistakes and external shocks, from Vietnam, to Iraq, to the Great Recession, to the changing demographic character of the country, to growing economic inequality, gradually diminished the prestige of these forces. With the 2016 election, they were displaced by populists, loosely defined here as political outsiders whose legitimacy derives from a supposed closer connection to mass opinion, who favor wholesale disruption of the status quo, and who oppose claims to legitimacy rooted in bureaucratic regularity and expertise. In this radically changed environment, the Pentagon Papers settlement suddenly seemed vulnerable.

The next sections of the essay are normative. The second section suggests ways to think about how to fill the space opened by the erosion of the settlement. It rejects a constitutional framing of the issues as unproductive and unnecessarily divisive. Instead, we need to think in practical terms about how the legitimate claims of both populist and establishment forces might be recognized.

The essay's third section fleshes out this approach with some suggestions for specific reforms. I argue for an end to press immunity, more robust defenses for leakers in criminal prosecutions, and improved whistleblower protection.

The Source of the Problem

Elite attitudes toward the Pentagon Papers settlement did not change suddenly, and the changes that have occurred have more than one cause. In this section, I want to speculate about one particular explanation for changing attitudes: not surprisingly, elite beliefs about the Pentagon Papers settlement changed when elites lost control of both the government and the press.

Throughout the period when the Pentagon Papers settlement prevailed, both government and the press were controlled by individuals who shared mainstream attitudes toward government policy. Of course, there were disagreements, but the arguments played out against a backdrop of widely shared assumptions and values. On the international side, Republican and Democratic administrations and media figures from the moderate left to the moderate right shared a belief in an American-led world order dominated by American views about international law and American support for traditional allies, especially those associated with the Atlantic alliance. On the domestic side, there were more disagreement and persistent tensions over racial, social, and fiscal issues. Still, disagreement was within a fairly narrow range. Establishment figures associated with both parties favored moderate reforms and opposed a large-scale transformation of the status quo. Although elite figures on occasion made more or less subtle efforts to benefit from racial and ethnic divisions, outright race-baiting was off the table.

These substantive values were buttressed by a set of process values. American foreign policy was a product of an orderly exploration of options prepared by an interagency process with the State Department, the Pentagon, and the national security apparatus as key participants and with coordination provided by the national security advisor. This process gave the president choices, but again, the choices were within a fairly narrow range and emerged from a rationalistic, bureaucratic process dominated by regional experts. A similarly orderly process determined domestic policy, with substantive proposals vetted by groups such as the Domestic Policy Council and with the Office of Management and Budget coordinating and rationalizing the budgetary and regulatory processes.

The media was not always happy with presidential decisions and was proud of its role in exposing political misconduct and mistakes. That said, the media that mattered was relatively centralized and, in important ways, was part of the elite coalition. The press also had standards of professionalism that channeled and limited its disagreement with political officials. In general, journalists could be trusted to keep off-the-record conversations secret. They cultivated sources through a web of mutually beneficial interactions. A well-established norm prohibited media publication of information that might harm the national interest. This norm, in turn, was buttressed by the practice of giving the administration a "due process" right to object to publication of stories that arguably invaded a legitimate realm of secrecy.[3]

This constellation provided support for every facet of the Pentagon Papers settlement. Because administration officials were "sensible" and their processes "rational," there was reason to think that secrecy determinations were made in good faith. This presumption was in some tension with the acknowledgment that there was widespread overclassification. But the overclassification phenomenon meant only that government officials were acting wisely when they exercised prosecutorial discretion and failed to investigate or prosecute most leakers. When government officials instead chose to prosecute, it was assumed that they were doing so for good reasons.

The presumption of good faith also meant that when low-level officials observed misconduct, they had at their disposal bureaucratic channels to deal with it. These officials had no excuse for circumventing these channels by going to the press. Instead, they should have relied upon orderly, internal procedures for adjudicating their claims.

In this world, the media was a partner as well as a rival of ruling elites. Of course, exposing government secrets and misconduct was central to the professional identity of journalists. But the mainstream media also saw itself as a responsible filter that eliminated news that was not "fit to print." Most journalists shared elite internationalist views as well as a commitment to the American project. Although journalists could be annoying and disruptive, ruling elites could count on them not to jeopardize national security when the chips were down. For that reason, there was little incentive for the government to attack journalists with criminal prosecutions, especially since journalists had the power to fight back.

There have been other periods in modern American history where populist forces threatened this equilibrium. For example, in the early 1950s, Senator Joseph McCarthy terrified establishment forces in the State Department, the White House, and elsewhere. The fallout from the Vietnam War and from CIA abuses of power caused less dramatic but still important disruptions. But while the establishment consensus was occasionally shaken, until recently, it had always held. The 2016 election changed all that and, for now, at least, put populists in positions of real power.

That change, in turn, dramatically altered the background conditions that produced the Pentagon Papers settlement. On the government side, the "responsible" and "irresponsible" forces have effectively switched places. Under the old regime, the source of concern was the lone official or small group of officials who arrogantly took it upon themselves to go outside regular channels and overrule secrecy determinations. Even if well-meaning, these officials were a threat to bureaucratic rationality and to sensible processes for forming policy. Political officials, who could be relied upon to understand the technical details of American security and separate out damaging from harmless exposures, exercised appropriate control over disclosure.

In the new era, at this writing, it is the remnants of the "deep state" that embody bureaucratic responsibility. Small groups of dissident officials represent battered outposts of rationality and calm and sensible policy formation. In contrast, it is now the top layer of government that is irresponsible, dangerous, impulsive, and uncontrolled. The threat to national security comes not from dissenting civil servants but from political appointees.

There are other role reversals as well. It is now often leaking rather than secrecy that protects national security. Speaking to the press has become a means by which security failures by high-level government officials are exposed and disciplined. Conversely, ordinary bureaucratic channels, such as utilization of whistleblower procedures, have now become a means by which lower-level officials can be threatened with disclosure, retaliation, and discipline.

A parallel change has occurred within the media. The mainstream press retains some loyalty to the professional standards that served as a filter against "irresponsible" leaks, but these standards are changing in response to the Trump disruption. Precisely because the mainstream media remains a part of the establishment, it now sees the Trump administration as an existential threat. Faced with that threat, ordinary journalists now have much more fraught relationships with high-level administration officials even as they cultivate closer relationships with disgruntled lower-level officials. Trust has completely broken down. The press regularly crosses boundaries that were thought impregnable only a short time ago.[4] These changes raise questions about whether the mainstream press will continue to accept government assertions that publication threatens the national interest.

Perhaps more consequentially, in recent years, journalism splintered in dramatic ways. Most Americans now get their news from online and cable media, which often makes no pretense of nonpartisanship or objectivity. Many of these outlets do not adhere to traditional journalistic standards and have no compunction about publishing "secret" information, even in the teeth of plausible claims that publication threatens the national interest.

It is not surprising that this changed environment has led elites to rethink the Pentagon Papers settlement. Now that it is the leakers who are "responsible" and the administration that is erratic and unreliable, there is reason to question the untrammeled power of the government to punish and censor low-level officials who reveal government secrets. At the same time, now that the media can no longer be trusted to adhere to traditional journalistic standards, there is reason to rethink its practical immunity from government control. Put differently, changed circumstances push toward a convergence of the treatment of leakers and the media, with leakers provided more protection than they had in the past and journalists provided less.

How to Think about Solutions

This much more fluid environment opens up space to think about what a new settlement would look like. How should the conversation be structured? There is a natural tendency to view the problem through the lens of constitutional law. On one side, journalists dress themselves in the heavy rhetorical armor of press freedom. On the other, the government relies on what it often characterizes as the weightiest national security imperatives. When phrased this way, the argument fits into a well-established constitutional paradigm, with courts balancing a supposed First Amendment right on one side with a supposed compelling state interest on the other.

In this section, I want to push back on this way of conceptualizing the problem. Treating the question as a problem for constitutional law both raises the rhetorical heat and reduces the chances of finding a sensible resolution.

The first problem with constitutionalizing the dispute is that the standard constitutional sources are remarkably sparse. The constitutional text is unilluminating about what precisely "the freedom . . . of the press" consists of or about what kinds of government actions "abridge" this freedom. Some constitutional scholars think that we should be bound by the original public meaning of the text. But although there can be no doubt that the framing generation valued protection for press freedom, how they would have applied that protection to modern problems concerning the revelation of national security secrets is similarly obscure.

Supreme Court precedent is also uninformative. The Pentagon Papers case itself addressed only the problem of prior restraint against publication of secrets. That focus was unsurprising, given the fact that the Court was asked to rule on such a restraint and that ex ante state licensing of newspapers and magazines was at the heart of—indeed, perhaps the only concern of—the Framers of the First Amendment. The Pentagon Papers Court implicitly recognized, and Justices White and Stewart explicitly stated, that press rights are less extensive when journalists are prosecuted after the fact for disclosing national security secrets.

Moreover, even the protection against prior restraint is more porous than one might think. The Pentagon Papers Court did not hold that prior restraints were always unconstitutional. Instead, it said only that there was a "heavy presumption" against their constitutionality and that the government bore a "heavy burden" in establishing their legitimacy. This language sounds formidable, but in a national security context, it is not hard to imagine circumstances under which judges might find the requirements satisfied. Indeed, a lower court judge did find it satisfied when the *Progressive* magazine threatened to reveal classified information relating to the construction of a hydrogen bomb.[5]

Beyond the Pentagon Papers case itself, Supreme Court precedent does little to answer questions about press liability. The Court has made clear that the press enjoys no broad constitutional exemption from generally applicable laws. Nor does the press enjoy a general right of access.[6] It would seem to follow that there are only a few limits on the government's ability to prevent the press from getting information in the first place, although what those few limits are remains obscure. On the other hand, once the press has the information, the government has only limited but again quite indeterminate power[7] to stop publication.

To make matters worse, the little law that does exist makes very little sense. One might suppose that the Constitution would provide substantive legal rules designed to produce the "right" amount of disclosure of government information or guidance regarding what kinds of information can be disclosed. What constitutional law does instead is to create what amounts to a state of nature where government and press engage in a Darwinian struggle over dissemination against the backdrop of rules that regulate the process but guarantee no particular outcome. The press has some freedom to publish, but the government has reciprocal freedom to discipline its employees who aid in the publication effort. The main thing that the Constitution guarantees is this struggle itself, as if it were an intrinsic good irrespective of the results that it produced. Put differently, no one has made a convincing case for why we should expect this unregulated struggle to automatically produce the right outcome.

For these reasons, there is little ground for hope that constitutional law will produce a sensible resolution of the secrecy dilemma. What constitutional argument does instead is to leave the matter to judges, who possess neither the expertise nor the flexibility to produce a sensible regime. Here, as in many other areas of constitutional law, judges are, at best, partially constrained by determinate text, history, or precedent. They are therefore free to indulge their own prejudices and policy preferences. Because they decide "one case at a time," they are unlikely to put in place systems that get to the right result over the range of cases.

Worse yet, constitutional framing leads to maximalist claims that seem to preclude compromise. On the one hand, journalists would have us believe that the future of the republic depends on affording private actors, elected by no one, untrammeled discretion to determine whether publication is in the national interest. On the other, the government regularly insists that state interests of the highest order are at stake when its often sloppy and self-interested secrecy rules are violated.

Neither side seems prepared to acknowledge what is actually at stake: complex and messy questions of policy that, as important as they are, should not be thought of as matters of inviolate principle. Instead, the questions need to be addressed in the way policy questions are best resolved—that is, humbly, pragmatically, and experimentally, with careful attention to empirical outcomes, a balancing of competing interests, and a recognition that no solution will be perfect or will last forever.[8]

The next section offers some suggestions for what an inquiry along these lines might yield.

Some Tentative Proposals

The fissure Trump has opened between populist and establishment worldviews is unlikely to close anytime soon. No one knows what the shape of our politics will be like a decade from now, but there is at least the possibility that we will see alternating periods when populists and establishment figures hold power.

That fact opens space to think about our security regime behind a veil of ignorance. In a world where the establishment can no longer be assured of hegemonic power, we are forced to think about how things look from both sides. We need legal structures that work when responsible and irresponsible leaders are in control, when leaking bureaucrats are heroic patriots and when they are partisan hacks, when the press informs the public about serious misdeeds and when it is acts out of narrow economic or ideological interest. Beyond that, we need structures that we can agree upon when there is ongoing dispute about who is in one category and who is in the other.

Any legal regime that takes both sides of this dialectic seriously is bound to be imperfect. When one is compromising between competing goods or warding off competing evils, there will be no solution that gives full weight to the values on either side. Any realistic approach is therefore vulnerable to criticism from people who are preoccupied with one risk or the other. Moreover, the answer to these critics is bound to be unsatisfactory. The answer cannot be that they are wrong to worry about one side or the other of the dialectic; it must instead be that something must be sacrificed if we are to take into account the legitimate claims made by both sides.

With these limitations in mind, here are some tentative suggestions for how the balance might be reset.

1. *Ending press immunity.* Whatever the legal status of the press, as a practical matter, the Pentagon Papers settlement provides the media with effective immunity from prior restraint and after-the-fact prosecution. As noted above, the immunity was established when journalistic power was in the hands of establishment figures. The original arguments for it seem less applicable to newly powerful fringe players such as WikiLeaks or Infowars.

One response would be to try to somehow cabin the immunity so that it does not extend to the new, "irresponsible" media. It is far from clear how this cabining could be accomplished. More significantly, even if a distinction between the responsible and irresponsible press could be operationalized, this strategy fails to come to grips with the core problem. What the emergence of the new media really demonstrates is that the settlement was deficient from the very beginning.

The deficiency begins with the fact that much of the mainstream media is controlled by a tiny number of extraordinarily wealthy and powerful individuals who are not subject to meaningful popular control. No one elected the Murdochs, the Sulzbergers, Jeff Bezos, or Mark Zuckerberg to public office. Endless ink has been spilled worrying about unelected Supreme Court Justices making important decisions for the country, but at least the Justices are selected by publicly accountable officials and are subject to a variety of public checks on their power. At best, media executives are responsible only to their shareholders and their customers. The emergence of fringe media outlets that are obviously not operating in the public interest only emphasizes what should have been apparent all along: that it is profoundly undemocratic to grant untrammeled power to make vital decisions affecting the entire nation to a few wealthy, private individuals.

For these reasons, we should end the differential treatment of the originators and recipients of leaks. They are two sides of the same coin, with both equally responsible for the dissemination of the information. The current regime favors people with power who have the ability to use their control of the media to strike back against their opponents. It disfavors isolated and vulnerable government employees with little means to protect themselves. But if the government has a sufficient interest in stopping the leak by punishing vulnerable leakers, then the same interest justifies stopping the leak by punishing powerful media figures.[9]

None of this is to deny the invaluable role that the press has, on occasion, played when it has uncovered government misconduct. Well-functioning republics discipline and regulate private power, but that is something quite different from altogether obliterating a private sphere. What is necessary, then, is a compromise that protects the checking function of a private press while also subjecting it to some democratic control.

What would such a compromise look like? Below I suggest some reforms that would provide additional protection for government leakers. Treating the media and leakers on an equal footing entails not only reciprocal restraints but also reciprocal protection. Immunizing the press from retaliation for publishing leaks that are legal is a natural corollary to ending press immunity for publishing leaks that are not. The protection for leakers that I outline below would therefore also go a long way toward providing the press with protection.

An additional reform might at first seem counterintuitive and even bizarre: we should establish a system of prior restraint with regard to leaked secrets.[10] A traditional and powerful objection to criminal prosecutions aimed at journalists is that it has a profound chilling effect on press freedom. Journalists who risk going to jail for doing their jobs are likely to steer well clear of the line, thereby depriving the public of information that the journalists have a constitutional right to disseminate.

Prior restraint provides a remedy for this problem. Under this system, both a potential leaker and a media outlet contemplating publication of secret material could secure a declaratory judgment from a court that publication was constitutionally protected or not prohibited by law. Conversely, if the government knew that leaking or publication was imminent, it could secure a judgment that the leaking or publication was unprotected. All proceedings, including appeals, would be expedited so as not to delay protected publication, and proceedings would be held in camera so as to protect secrecy. If the private party prevailed in an action brought by either party, it would be immune from subsequent criminal or civil actions against it for publishing the material or providing it to the press. If the government prevailed, reporters and leakers would still have a right to a jury trial before criminal punishment was imposed, but it would be conclusively presumed that the government had a legal right to prevent publication.

Prior review of this kind would free journalists and leakers from uncertainty about criminal prosecution. Would it adequately protect press freedom? That depends in part on the substantive standards the court used, a subject to which I now turn.

2. *Limiting criminal prosecutions.* The government usually initiates criminal prosecutions for leaks under an old and extraordinarily broad and vague statute, passed at a time of war hysteria. The Espionage Act of 1917 prohibits the willful delivery or communication to "a person not entitled to receive it" of "any document, writing, code book, signal book, sketch, photograph, photographic negative, blueprint, plan, map, model, instrument, appliance, or note relating to the national defense." It also prohibits the delivery to such a person of "information relating to the national defense" but only when "the possessor has reason to believe [the information] could be used to the injury of the United States or to the advantage of any foreign nation."[11] A person found guilty under the statute is subject to a prison term of ten years.

The Congress that enacted this measure was primarily concerned with classic espionage, but the courts have (justifiably, given the statutory language and legislative history) interpreted it as applying to press leaks designed to expose government wrongdoing. They have also held that the phrase "relating to national defense" is not unconstitutionally vague and that the classification system itself determines whether the recipient of information is "entitled to receive" it.

Before suggesting ways to reform this statutory framework, it is worth noting that the government need not rely solely on the threat of a ten-year prison sentence to control leaks. The government can use self-help by more carefully guarding secret information. Leakers can be internally disciplined or fired. They can be publicly reprimanded. One might imagine a system under which they could be held civilly liable. The real questions are whether, in addition to these remedies, the government needs the nuclear option of a threatened felony conviction to deter harmful press leaks and whether the marginal increase in deterrence is worth the chilling effect on beneficial leaks.

Even if criminal prosecutions are occasionally necessary, the law should be amended or reinterpreted to provide more recognition of the crucial difference between classic espionage and press leaks. Holding everything else constant, press leaks are at once less harmful and more beneficial. Of course, when material is made public, foreign governments gain access to it. In the case of classic espionage, however, our government will often be unaware that the information has been compromised until it is too late. In contrast, press leaks are, by their nature, public. That means that the government knows that they have occurred and can at least sometimes mitigate the harm. On the other side of the ledger, it will a be rare case when traditional espionage contributes to the national interest of the United States. In contrast, leaks to the media often provide a public benefit in the form of more knowledgeable public debate about important issues.

For these reasons, the law should treat public leaks as a separate violation. What should be different about them?

First, violations should be misdemeanors punishable by no more than a year's imprisonment. Even when misguided and even when they do harm, leakers are typically (although concededly not always) acting for public-spirited reasons. They are usually a far cry from spies who are paid for their treachery or are deliberately disadvantaging their own nation.

Of course, patriotic motivations by themselves should not be a shield against criminal violations. No one thinks that a patriotic assassin should not face punishment. But a misdemeanor conviction is much more than a slap of the wrist, and individuals who tell their fellow citizens what their government is up to are not assassins.

Here as elsewhere, the question is how much punishment is necessary to obtain optimal deterrence. Judgments of this kind require taking into account the efficacy of alternative means to prevent the wrongdoing and the likelihood that the next marginal unit of punishment will deter enough more crime to make up for the marginal cost. For most crime, the latter calculation is simplified by the assumption that the criminal act has no positive value. But that is emphatically not true in the case of leaked information, which often produces a public benefit as well as a cost.

Despite the technocratic rhetoric of deterrence theory, there is no scientific method for reaching these sorts of judgments. Ultimately, there is no escape from making intuitive guesses about costs and benefits. Still, it seems relatively clear that serving a year in prison is enough punishment for conduct that is often undertaken for patriotic reasons and often produces beneficial results. That is especially true in this case, where the government also has non-criminal means to avoid the harm at its disposal.

There is also no reason to punish the release of material that is improperly classified. Lower courts have treated facially valid classifications as proof that the recipient of the information was "not entitled to receive it." This treatment means that completely arbitrary and lawless classification decisions turn otherwise legal activity into a criminal offense. Of course, there are good reasons to worry about uninformed courts and juries second-guessing classification decisions. Those reasons might support a presumption in favor of the validity of those decisions. They do not support altogether insulating from review classification decisions that are lawless, self-interested, or venal.

What about the kinds of material covered by the statute? There is no plausible justification for the statutory distinction between documents and photographs on the one hand and "information" on the other. The statute currently requires the government to prove that "the possessor has reason to believe [that the disclosed material] could be used to the injury of the United States or to the advantage of any foreign nation" with regard to the latter but not the former. Why should release of "documents" that do not injure the United States be punishable, when the release of similar "information," not in the form of "documents," is legal?

Similarly, as the statute is currently written, the government need not prove that the material "could be used to the injury of the United States" if it advantages "any foreign nation." Suppose release of the information advantages a friendly foreign power but could not be "used to the injury of the United States." It is hard to see why it should be punished.

The most serious statutory deficiencies relate to the kind of harm that the government must prove. Under the statute, it is sufficient for the government to demonstrate that the leaker has "reason to believe" that the leaked material "could be used to the injury of the United States." Read literally, this standard covers virtually any information. Under the right circumstances, knowledge of anything that the government does might conceivably be used to harm the country.

Given the good accomplished by the revelation of illegal or otherwise improper government activity, this standard should be tightened. At a minimum, the prosecution should be required to demonstrate that there is good reason to believe that the United States *will* be injured. Moreover, in making that determination, the jury should be instructed that it should reach an all-things-considered judgment about the injury. Where the value of disclosure outweighs the harm, then, on balance, the United States has not suffered an injury. Therefore, the defendant should be acquitted.

This kind of balancing may seem formless and indeterminate, but in principle, it is no different from the task juries regularly perform when they determine whether a defendant's conduct is negligent or, less often, when they evaluate a necessity defense to a criminal prosecution. As a practical matter, in the vast majority of cases, juries are likely to side with the government. But the United States has no legitimate interest in engaging in illegal activity. It follows that when the disclosed activity is illegal, there should be a strong presumption that the value of disclosure outweighs the harm.

An obvious objection to these changes is that they empower untutored judges and juries to make sensitive national security decisions. It might also be argued that forcing the government to prove the likelihood of actual injury creates a burden that is impossible to meet, especially if it is reluctant to reveal more classified information.

These problems are serious and should not be lightly dismissed. Notice, though, that the government would not have to prove actual injury. It could meet its burden by showing that the leaker had *reason to believe* that the United States would be injured. The "reason to believe" qualification permits conviction even in the absence of anything approaching certainty. The current statute grafts the "reason to believe" standard onto a "could be used" standard, thereby piling speculative injury upon speculative injury. Surely one level of speculation is enough.

The drafters of the current statute presumably included the requirement that the prosecution demonstrate the possibility of injury to the United States, because even they recognized that executive branch officials should not be completely trusted with secrecy decisions. That judgment is in accord with how the law treats classified information in other contexts. For example, the government must offer the court evidence "that the withheld information meets the standard for classification" to resist FOIA requests. When courts review claims of state secrets privilege, they go further and weigh government secrecy claims against the need for disclosure.[12]

We allow this review despite the fact that judicial decisions may be less informed than judgments made by insiders. In these contexts, Congress and the courts have decided that price is worth paying in order to check executive branch discretion. If this is true in civil litigation where state secrets or FOIA claims are litigated, then certainly it ought to be true when a leaker's freedom is at stake.

Having said all this, it remains true that juries will sometimes lack the expertise to evaluate the complex issues before them, that the government may be unable to bring some prosecutions because of the need to protect national secrets, and that justice will not always be done. But these problems are hardly new. Almost forty years ago, Congress enacted the Classified Information Procedures Act, designed to deal with the problem of jury and defense access to classified materials in criminal prosecutions.[13] Although the procedures outlined in the Act do not provide a perfect solution, they seem to have put in place a workable compromise.[14]

Similarly, juries are regularly entrusted with complex and technical tasks, such as sorting out esoteric economics in antitrust prosecutions or evaluating disputed scientific evidence in mass tort cases. Doubtless, juries sometimes make mistakes and misunderstand the evidence that they consider, but this is the price we pay for democratic engagement with the criminal justice system. If the government is unwilling to pay that price in cases involving leakers, then it should use the other, non-criminal means at its disposal to deal with the problem.

Finally, we need to do something about the discriminatory prosecution of leakers. Even when the judiciary is unequipped to make substantive judgments about secrecy, it should at least hold the executive branch to its own judgments. Executive branch decisions are entitled to some measure of respect when they are consistently made. As a matter of practice, though, leakers regularly disclose classified information without suffering any adverse consequences. That fact gives rise to a suspicion that prosecutions are based on whose ox is being gored rather than authentic national security concerns.

To deal with this problem, the executive branch should draft regulations subject to notice and comment outlining investigative and prosecutorial priorities in the case of leaks. Defendants, in turn, should be permitted to raise a violation of the regulations as an affirmative defense. If the defendant demonstrates that his or her own prosecution violates the regulations, the judge should dismiss the case. A harder problem arises in cases where the defendant's case comes within the regulations, but the government has ignored other, similar cases that the regulations also cover. In these cases, courts should find that the defendant has made out a prima facie case of discriminatory prosecution, but the government should be allowed to meet its burden by demonstrating special, aggravating circumstances that justify the discriminatory treatment.

Admittedly, this protection against discriminatory prosecution will be of only occasional value to defendants. Executive branch officials have an incentive to write the regulations in an open-ended fashion. Because each case is different, this open texture may well be justified. Still, at a minimum, the requirement serves a signaling function, suggesting to executive branch officials that they should worry about unequal application of the strictures against leaking. It might also serve to root out and avoid egregious cases of discrimination.

3. *Protecting whistleblowers.* If we are to punish leakers who go outside established channels, then we have an obligation to provide safe and effective inside channels to register dissent and complaints about misconduct.

Some of these mechanisms already exist. Since 1971, the State Department has operated a "dissent channel" used to express "responsible dissenting and alternative views on substantive foreign policy issues that cannot be communicated in a full and timely manner through regular operating channels or procedures."[15] Officials using the channel are supposedly protected from retaliation or reprisal. On occasion, the channel has been an effective means of challenging and even changing government policy, and other agencies should establish similar mechanisms. Still, the extent of actual user protection has varied from administration to administration, and it is hard or impossible to police all forms of retaliation.

The Civil Service Reform Act of 1978 prohibits adverse personnel actions against some government employees who reveal unlawful conduct.[16] Even if the information is classified, employees are protected if they refer the matter to the Merit Systems Protection Board or to an inspector general (IG). It is important, however, that the statute does not cover employees of national security agencies such as the FBI and the CIA.

A separate statute permits employees of these agencies who have an "urgent concern" that they wish to convey to Congress to report the matter to their agency's IG.[17] If the IG finds the information credible, the IG must send it to the head of the agency, who forwards it to Congress. These provisions provide an avenue for communication with Congress, but unlike the broader Act, they do not prohibit job-related retaliation or give access to a court or administrative body to challenge the retaliation.

At a minimum, the law should be amended to prohibit retaliation against any employee who goes through approved channels to reveal misconduct. Employees should be permitted to contest alleged retaliation at the administrative level and in federal court.

It would be foolish, though, to suppose that this reform would solve the problem. First, as a practical matter, it is impossible to root out and prove all of the subtle but powerful ways in which an employee's career can be harmed by vengeful superiors. More significantly, even effective protection for whistleblowers provides no assurance that executive branch officials or members of Congress will act on the information. Whistleblower protection can avoid the necessity for some leaks, but it cannot be a full substitute for public disclosure in cases where retaliation remains a threat or where officials refuse to act.

These three proposals should not be interpreted to be more than what they are: tentative suggestions designed to begin a dialogue about reform. I make no claim that the reforms I suggest are the only possible approaches or even that they will necessarily work over the long run. If we are to deal effectively with a new situation where neither populists nor elites are guaranteed supremacy, we need flexibility and a willingness to try out fresh ideas.

I do claim, however, that my proposals do something that the current regime does not do. They attempt to come to grips with the hard, substantive question of how much leaking is in the public interest. Put differently, they do not rely on blind faith that through some mysterious invisible hand, the current struggle between the media and the government will automatically produce optimal results.

My hope is that my suggestions provide a model for how we might balance competing interests once we give up on constitutional posturing and the delusive quest for ideal solutions. If instead we think about the problem as a public policy dilemma that might be ameliorated but not finally resolved by open-minded experimentation, we might actually make some progress.

REPORT OF THE COMMISSION

Introduction

Since the Supreme Court handed down the Pentagon Papers decision in 1971, a revolution in information and communications technology has reshaped the ways in which national security information is compiled, stored, shared, and published. The shift from print to digital media for recordkeeping and communications, the ubiquitous reliance on computers and other digital devices, and the creation and explosive growth of the internet have had far-reaching consequences for the legal and policy framework that should govern the treatment of leaks of national security information.

First, the digitization of government information and the ubiquitous use of computers and other digital devices in the government have (1) greatly expanded the volume of classified and national-security-sensitive information, (2) probably made it more difficult to restrict access to classified information within the government, (3) made it easier for leakers to disclose large quantities of sensitive information, and (4) made it easier for leakers to disclose information to more than one recipient outside the government.[1]

Second, the development of the internet has (1) vastly expanded the number of media outlets and thus diminished the ability of leading newspapers to serve as intermediaries between the government and the public in the handling of leaked national security information;[2] (2) created a broader spectrum of organizations serving or claiming to serve the press's role of informing the public, some with traditional journalistic values and goals, others committed foremost to promoting particular political or policy agendas, and some combining elements of both; (3) facilitated the rapid distribution of leaked information to many recipients, including recipients outside the United States; and (4) enabled recipients to sort through and analyze leaked information more rapidly and more efficiently.[3]

Along with these technology-driven developments, a fundamental shift in the composition of the federal national security workforce has also changed the landscape for leaks. The number of federal employees has not changed substantially since 1950, but the number of employees of federal contractors has risen dramatically. That trend of growing federal reliance on private companies to perform a variety of functions has been particularly pronounced in the defense and intelligence realms. This shift has meant that many more individuals have access to national security information, which may make it more difficult to keep national security information secure.[4]

These changes helped prompt the creation of the "Commission" as part of this book. The recommendations presented by the Commission here represent an effort to advance a constructive dialogue among legislators, executive branch officials, journalists, leaders of media companies, and interested citizens about how, in light of these changes, our society should balance the frequent need for secrecy in national security affairs with the public's need to know, which provides an important check against government misconduct. Reasonable people may disagree about these recommendations, but all can agree that protecting national security and freedom of the press are both compelling interests and need not be in unnecessary conflict. Ultimately, the public is the owner of all government information, including classified information, and how the government treats that information is a matter of vital concern.

Encouraging Helpful Disclosures and Reducing Harmful Leaks

The Pentagon Papers decision focused on the protection the First Amendment affords the press when it comes into possession of national security information that was disclosed unlawfully, that is, "leaked." The recommendations in this section address a pair of antecedent questions: what can be done to enable the publication of national security information through channels other than leaks when the benefits to public debate and democratic decision-making outweigh the harm to national security, and what can be done to reduce such disclosures when the balance tips the other way?

Although the motivations of leakers vary, at least some leaks likely reflect the leakers' belief that the government's determination to shield certain information from public view is misguided.[5] The following proposals aim at reducing the frequency of insiders reaching such judgments by (1) reducing overclassification,

(2) facilitating declassification, and (3) creating meaningful alternatives to leaking for disclosure of national security information.

Reducing Overclassification

Based on the collective experience of its members, the Commission is of the view that overclassification remains widespread, especially at the low end of the classification scale. The distinctions between unclassified and confidential and between confidential and secret, while perhaps clear in theory, have proven difficult to apply in practice, leading often to the classification of information the disclosure of which presents little or no discernible risks to national security. This conclusion is consistent with the views national security experts from both parties have expressed for decades.[6]

The classification system is largely governed by executive order.[7] The most recent of these orders "prescribes a uniform system for classifying, safeguarding, and declassifying national security information."[8] Within this system, information may be classified only if "unauthorized disclosure . . . reasonably could be expected to result in damage to the national security."[9] The classification levels are distinguished by the extent of the "damage to the national security" that disclosure would cause: for top secret, "exceptionally grave damage"; for secret, "serious damage"; and for confidential, "damage" without qualification.[10] Information cannot be classified "[i]f there is significant doubt about the need to classify"[11] or for improper purposes, including "conceal[ing] violations of law, inefficiency, or administrative error"[12] and "prevent[ing] embarrassment to a person, organization, or agency."[13]

Despite these substantive classification standards, there remains a "persistent gap between written regulation and actual practice."[14] According to a review conducted by the Brennan Center, for example, "the primary source of the 'implementation gap' is the skewed incentive structure underlying the current system," which "all but guarantees over-classification."[15] Classification authorities understandably tend to avoid even the slightest risk of revealing sensitive information. On the other side of the ledger, "there are essentially no incentives to refrain from or challenge improper classification."[16]

The Commission agrees that the problem of overclassification is rooted more in practice than in policy. We therefore recommend that the executive branch recalibrate the incentives that inform the day-to-day application of classification standards. Potential procedural reforms include the following:

- To the extent that existing systems do not presently require officials who classify information to actually describe the damage to national security that unauthorized disclosure might cause, require them to make a reasonable effort to do so. At present, as a policy matter, officials do not have to provide such a description; they need only state that they are "*able to* identify or describe" that risk.[17]

- Conduct regular audits to identify chronic overclassifiers, at the individual level and across agencies. For individuals who persistently overclassify, impose remedial measures ranging from training to suspension or revocation of classification authority for egregious patterns of overclassification. For agencies, require management to develop remedial plans and to submit to oversight by the Information Security Oversight Office, the office within the National Archives and Records Administration charged with superintending the classification system.[18]

- As the governing executive order contemplates, impose sanctions on original classification authorities that willfully or knowingly classify information to "conceal violations of law, inefficiency, or administrative error."[19]

- Consult with repeat offenders to identify deficiencies in existing training programs and amend programs to remedy the inadequacies.

Facilitating Declassification

The governing executive order also establishes a system for "automatic declassification." The classifying authority must "establish a specific date or event for declassification," upon which "the information shall be automatically declassified."[20] The default maximum is ten years, and especially sensitive information may remain classified for up to twenty-five years.[21]

The order acknowledges that "[i]n some exceptional cases," a legitimate "need to protect . . . information may be outweighed by the public interest in disclosure of the information, and in these cases the information should be declassified."[22] "When such questions arise," they are directed to the agency head, who "will determine, as an exercise of discretion, whether the public interest in disclosure outweighs the damage to the national security that might reasonably be expected from disclosure."[23]

Others, most notably the congressionally established Public Interest Declassification Board, have suggested comprehensive reforms to the declassification system.[24] While an overhaul of the declassification framework is beyond the scope of the Commission's work, the modest recommendations outlined below would help ensure the declassification of information for which "the public interest in disclosure outweighs the damage to the national security."[25] Either the president or Congress should:

- Direct each agency to adopt policies for determining, upon request, when the value of disclosing classified information outweighs the damage from disclosure.[26]
- In considering such questions, require the agency head to consult with the National Archives' Information Security Oversight Office on whether the information should be declassified.

Adoption of these proposals would help ensure that information essential to the project of self-governance is not improperly shielded from public view.

Creating Meaningful Alternatives to Leaking

The governing executive order requires each agency to establish procedures allowing "authorized holders of information . . . to challenge the classification of information that they believe is improperly classified."[27] Each challenge is reviewed by "an impartial official or panel," and the challenger may appeal an adverse decision to the Interagency Security Classification Appeals Panel (ISCAP).[28]

Although the order prohibits retaliation for raising a classification challenge,[29] government insiders might reasonably be concerned about the risk of adverse consequences. To alleviate this concern, the Commission recommends that government employees and employees of contractors be permitted to challenge classification decisions on an anonymous basis.[30] The identity of the challenger should be irrelevant to the classification decision; requiring the challenger to disclose his or her identity serves largely to deter insiders from using this pathway to declassification and encourages illegal leaking.

A more fundamental weakness in the current classification challenge system is that decisional power rests exclusively within the Intelligence Community (IC). The Commission recommends the creation of an independent government board within the executive branch akin to the Privacy and Civil Liberties Oversight Board composed of representatives from the intelligence agencies and other government agencies. This board could serve as a decision maker on whether specific challenged information should remain classified. Such questions might be raised not only by government employees and employees of contractors but also by stakeholders from outside the government, such as members of the press or representatives from the privacy and civil liberties community. Although a number of standards could be adopted for purposes of informing the board's exercise of its authority, the Commission proposes for consideration the standard set forth in the governing executive order with respect to "exceptional cases" involving "the public interest": declassification is appropriate when "the public interest in disclosure outweighs the damage to the national security that might reasonably be expected from disclosure."[31]

At minimum, if the ISCAP retains authority to decide appeals in classification challenges, the panel ought to be required to consult with stakeholders outside the government prior to issuing a decision on a classification challenge. Even if stakeholders external to the IC are not accorded the power to make final decisions, allowing them a voice in the process would introduce a valuable measure of independence into declassification decisions regarding information of substantial public interest.[32]

Finally, it is the Commission's judgment that the IC whistleblower system does not adequately protect whistleblowers or ensure effective democratic oversight of the intelligence agencies.[33] As a consequence, would-be whistleblowers are deterred from using the whistleblower pathway. The whistleblower system warrants serious study and careful reform.[34]

Deterring and Punishing Leakers of Classified Information

No matter what the government does to prevent leaks of classified information in the first place—and especially if it does nothing to reform the current system of classification—unauthorized disclosures will occur. Leaks emanate from sources high and low; sources leak for many reasons, benign, malignant, and in between; some leaks vitally advance public understanding of the government, while others do not; and in terms of damage to national security, leaks run the gamut from trivial to devastating.

The Commission believes that government employees and contractors should have no "right to leak" classified information, as a matter either of policy or of constitutional law. A system of secrecy preventing indiscriminate disclosure of sensitive national security information is necessary to protect important national interests, even if the current system allows excessive confidentiality. Individuals voluntarily undertake an obligation not to disclose classified information when they join government service, and in return, they are trusted with access to sensitive information. Moreover, individual employees and contractors are rarely positioned to make informed judgments about the potential damage to national security if they leak classified information. Thus, to reiterate, they should have no right to do so.

But the Commission also concludes that the current system for punishing leakers is ineffective, resulting in both excessive punishment and underdeterrence. Government employees and contractors can, of course, be disciplined or terminated from service if they leak classified information. But the government's other principal tool for punishing leakers—criminal prosecution, usually under the Espionage Act and related statutes—is in need of reform. The prospect of criminal punishment for government sources of information to the media, particularly those who disclose information that informs public debate and helps the public hold government accountable, can have an adverse effect on the vital function of the press to inform the public. And the prospect of criminal prosecution of members of the media for publishing classified information that they receive from government sources not authorized to disclose it—which (with one arguable exception) has never been attempted but remains a theoretical possibility under the Espionage Act and other statutes—is also worrisome and should be eliminated or significantly constrained.

Drafted in a moment of national emergency more than a century ago and long criticized as less than a model of clarity, the Espionage Act nonetheless remains the government's principal tool to punish unauthorized disclosures of classified information (aside from termination of service).[35] Section 793 of Title 18, the provision principally used, reaches far beyond "classic spying" and covers a broad array of unauthorized disclosures and communications of national-security-related information, including, potentially, publication by organs of the press. Judicial construction has done little to resolve the statute's ambiguities. Several courts, citing the statute's purportedly plain meaning and the need to deter leaks, have rejected more temperate constructions in favor of more far-reaching ones, even while recognizing that a broad reading could unnecessarily diminish the flow of information relevant to public understanding of the operations of government.[36] Punishments under § 793 may be harsh—up to ten years of imprisonment.[37]

Felony prosecutions for leaks are a blunt tool, and while they are often justified—particularly when the leaker intends his leaks to harm the national security of the United States—there may be circumstances in which such harsh punishment is unwarranted. The Espionage Act could therefore be reformed to provide for a graduated system of sanctions, as many other criminal statutes do.[38] In some circumstances, the prospect of termination of service will likely be sufficient to deter leaking. But where additional sanctions are necessary, a civil fine may sometimes be sufficient to punish and deter leaks of classified information. And when a criminal prosecution is warranted, the Espionage Act could be reformed to divide the offenses into misdemeanors and felonies, with felony prosecution reserved for especially damaging and unjustified disclosures.

The Espionage Act could be modified, for example, in ways that will retain the government's ability to punish damaging and purposeful leaks most severely while employing more tempered measures to punish less culpable conduct.[39] For example:

- The most severe punishment could be reserved for leakers who communicate classified documents or information not to the media but to foreign powers, or who act with a purpose to harm the United States or to aid a foreign power, or who act for the purpose of pecuniary gain (e.g., those who sell classified information).[40] Serious criminal punishment in these circumstances is warranted, because there is no possible justification for the source's conduct. To be sure, requiring proof of a defendant's intent may make it more difficult to secure a conviction in some cases, but requiring proof of intent is commonplace in our criminal justice system, and adjudicating a defendant's intent is well within the province of the traditional jury function. And even if that proof of intent could not be secured, the defendant could be convicted on a lesser-included offense, as described below.
- More moderate but still serious punishment might be appropriate for government employees or contractors who leak documents or information without such specific intent (or where such specific intent cannot be proven beyond a reasonable doubt to a jury) but who should reasonably have understood that their leak might cause harm to the national security.
- Another possibly mitigating factor, either to reduce the degree of the offense or to be taken into account in sentencing, might be if the defendant could prove that the information or documents in question were inappropriately classified.[41]
- The distinction in current law between leaking of documents and leaking of information should be eliminated.[42] That distinction appears to be the result of imprecise drafting and has little justification. Some have suggested that a higher showing of intent for leaking of information may be justified because information, unlike documents, does not have classification markings, and so the leaker may not necessarily know whether the information is classified. But the more appropriate focus for criminal punishment is the damage to national security—whether such damage would result from the leak and whether the leaker acted with intent, knowledge, or expectation that such damage would result.
- The government should not be able to circumvent these limits under an amended Espionage Act by using other, broadly worded statutes such as 18 U.S.C. § 641 (punishing theft of government property).

One possible consequence of reforming the Espionage Act in these ways is that it could make the government more, not less, willing to pursue sanctions against leakers. Under the current regime, the only arrow in the government's quiver, except for employment sanctions, is felony prosecution, and the DOJ likely declines to pursue many prosecutions because it views that sanction as excessive or because it thinks juries may be unwilling to convict in some cases. If the potential sanction is less severe, such as a misdemeanor or a civil penalty, the DOJ may be more willing to act. That is a legitimate concern, but it has to be balanced against the concern that the statute as currently drafted is both imprecise and excessively broad and imposes severe punishment for conduct that, even if not justifiable, is disproportionate to the offense. Moreover, just as unauthorized disclosures of properly classified information should not be over-deterred, they also should not be undeterred, and it may well be that many sources—especially high-ranking government officials—leak with impunity, reasonably expecting that they are unlikely to be subject to criminal prosecution and severe punishment.

Balancing Press Freedoms and National Security

Related to, but separate from, the question of prosecution of leakers is the question of prosecution of the press for publishing classified information that was disclosed without authorization. The constitutionality of such prosecutions under the First Amendment remains uncertain. Although the Supreme Court, in the Pentagon Papers decision, ruled that the government could not obtain a prior restraint against the publication of leaked classified information in that case, the Court did not reach, and certainly did not rule out, prosecutions of the press after publication, and several Justices suggested that such prosecutions would be permissible. In addition, although the Supreme Court has ruled in a series of cases that the press may not be punished for publishing unlawfully obtained information, as long as the press did not participate in the unlawful acquisition of the information, it has never addressed that question in the context of classified information. To be sure, the federal government has never—at least, until the recent indictment of Julian Assange, whom the government claims is not a legitimate member of the press[43]—prosecuted a member of the press for publishing classified information, and the prospect of such prosecutions may seem remote. But the pending prosecution of Assange suggests at least the *possibility* that under current law, there may be no statutory or constitutional impediment to prosecutions of the press for publishing leaked classified information. That prospect threatens to chill the press's legitimate—and absolutely essential—pursuit and publication of information about the government.[44] Congress should therefore consider dispelling that prospect through legislative action.[45]

The Espionage Act Should Be Clarified to Prevent Its Inappropriate Application to the Press

Read literally, provisions of the Espionage Act could be applied not just to leaking of classified documents and information to the press by government sources but also to the publication of those documents and information by the press. Section 793(e) reaches anyone who has "unauthorized possession" of documents or information "relating to the national defense" and punishes "communicat[ing]" the same.[46] Since reporters are unlikely to have authorized possession of classified information, this statute could theoretically reach their "communicating" (i.e., publishing) that information.[47]

In addition, although § 793(d) reaches only unauthorized disclosures by persons who *lawfully* have possession of classified documents and information, it could be used to reach journalists who allegedly facilitate or participate in leaking by government sources, through theories such as solicitation, conspiracy, or accessory after the fact. Although the government has never employed these secondary liability theories to pursue criminal prosecutions against the institutional media, this issue has never been resolved, and this uncertainty poses a potential danger both to the ability of the press to inform the public and the ability of the public to hold government accountable.

Although the Supreme Court has held, in a series of cases, that the First Amendment does not permit the government to punish the press for publishing unlawfully disclosed classified information where the press did not engage in illegal conduct to obtain that information,[48] it remains uncertain whether the First Amendment would pose an obstacle to punishment of the press for encouraging or otherwise facilitating the unauthorized disclosure of such information. Yet "encouraging" or "facilitating" disclosures by government officials could describe much of the work that the press is supposed to do under our system, where the press acts to ensure that government officials are accountable to the public; the press's role is to prod the government for information and explanations. To avoid the chilling effect on the press of possible criminal prosecution of core journalistic functions, the Commission believes that, regardless of how First Amendment law develops in the future, the law should draw a clearer line than is currently reflected in the Espionage Act and related statutes. Congress should amend the laws to make clear that they cannot be used against the press, at least absent conduct by reporters that is independently criminal. This revision would still leave the press, and all other members of the public, entitled to whatever constitutional protection might emerge as First Amendment case law develops.

This protection could be realized in several different ways. For example:

- Under current law, a journalist who asked or suggested that a source leak classified information could conceivably be prosecuted for "inducing" the unauthorized disclosure, under the federal aiding-and-abetting statute, 18 U.S.C. § 2, even if the journalist did not actively participate in the disclosure. Similarly, in some circumstances, a journalist could conceivably be prosecuted for conspiracy under federal conspiracy law or as an accessory after the fact under the federal accessory statute. The possibility of such prosecutions could seriously chill the core of journalists' work, which is seeking information. Journalists constantly engage in a back-and-forth with their government sources, urging the sources to provide more information; that is exactly what our society expects the press to do. The Espionage Act should be amended to make clear that the press cannot be prosecuted under such theories for core journalistic activity.

- On the other hand, journalists could appropriately be subject to prosecution, as they are now, if they engage in separate criminal activity punishable by generally applicable laws with no First Amendment implications, such as hacking computer equipment or trespassing onto government property or bribing government sources to disclose classified information.[49] In addition, and going a step further, the Espionage Act could be amended to make clear that journalists can be prosecuted even for such acts only if they specifically intended to harm the United States or damage the national security.

Congress Should Consider Broader Protection for the Press

In addition to the revisions suggested above, Congress should consider reforming the Espionage Act further, to make clear that members of the press cannot be prosecuted under that statute for publishing leaked classified information, at least when the press is performing its role of informing the public about government operations, rather than acting with intent inconsistent with that role, such as intending to aid foreign powers. Although the First Amendment presumably prohibits prosecutions of the press for publishing classified information unless the government can prove, as the Supreme Court declared in *Brandenburg v. Ohio*, that the speech was "directed to inciting or producing imminent" harm and is "likely to incite or produce such" harm,[50] the Court has never directly addressed this question in the context of the press and classified information. To eliminate the chilling effect created by this uncertainty, Congress should clarify the law in this respect by enacting legislation that expressly recognizes the vital role that the press plays in informing the public of government operations, even (perhaps especially) when those operations concern national security. One possibility would be not only to incorporate the *Brandenburg* standard expressly in legislation but also to make clear that members of the press could not be prosecuted for publishing classified information unless they did so with the intent of aiding foreign powers, damaging the national security, or otherwise intending to harm the United States.

Any such revision will raise questions about how to define "the press" or "the media" for purposes of statutory protection. Although the First Amendment separately protects freedom of speech and freedom of the press,[51] the Supreme Court has generally been loath to extend constitutional protections to "the press" that are not available to the public at large. When the Supreme Court rejected a constitutionally based journalist's privilege to refuse to reveal confidential sources to a grand jury, the Court noted the difficulty of defining a reporter and stressed that the freedom of the press was enjoyed equally by "the lonely pamphleteer" and a "large metropolitan newspaper."[52] That difficulty is even greater now, given the vast expansion of media outlets that can credibly claim to be part of "the press."

Some take the position that the government should play no role in defining who or what is "the press" or "the media" and that for the government (including the judiciary) to do so—or to afford special privileges to the press beyond those that all citizens enjoy—itself raises First Amendment concerns and may impair the independence of the press. These are substantial arguments. On the other hand, the government does afford special protections and privileges to "the press" or "the media" in several ways, and while there may be close cases, the definitional difficulties do not appear to be insuperable. The DOJ, recognizing that "freedom of the press can be no broader than the freedom of the news media to investigate and report the news," requires by regulation that any attempt to seek information from "the news media" through compulsory means such as subpoenas and search warrants meet heightened standards during internal agency review, at least when those means concern "newsgathering activities"—but the regulation does not define either "news media" or "newsgathering activities," evidently leaving its application to common sense.[53] That regulation affords the press a special protection that citizens at large do not enjoy.

Moreover, although the Supreme Court has declined to recognize a reporter's privilege, forty-eight states and the District of Columbia do so in some fashion.[54] Those protections—some adopted by statute, some derived from state constitutional or common law principles—vary widely in both coverage and degree of protection afforded,[55] but they all necessarily raise, and in some cases provide an answer to, the question of who or what qualifies as "the press" or "the media." They often do so in functional terms. The New Jersey shield law, for example, covers any "person engaged on, engaged in, connected with, or employed by news media for the purpose of gathering, procuring, transmitting, compiling, editing or disseminating news for the general public."[56] A proposed federal shield law, which was considered but not ultimately adopted by Congress, would have afforded qualified protection to any "covered journalist" engaged in "gathering the news" but would have excluded anyone "whose principal function, as demonstrated by the totality of such person or entity's work, is to publish primary source documents that have been disclosed to such person or entity without authorization" and anyone who "is or is reasonably likely to be an agent of a foreign power" or is "aiding, abetting, or conspiring in illegal activity with" an agent of a foreign power or a terrorist group.[57] Canada and the United Kingdom also provide statutory protections to members of the press.[58]

Even if First Amendment law does not evolve in a way that affords special leeway to "the press," as contrasted with the general public, to publish classified information, Congress can make the judgment that the special and vital role played by the press in informing the public warrants removing the prospect of prosecution for publishing classified information by the press,[59] even if that shield does not cover the public at large—just as the public at large does not have access to White House briefings and does not have the protection of a shield law for confidential sources. Congress can, of course, limit the reach of such protection, as is currently the case in the DOJ regulation and would have been the case in the federal shield law, excluding purported press outlets that are agents of foreign powers or terrorist or criminal organizations.[60] Should one of those excluded organizations or a member of the general public not covered by a statutory definition of "the press" face prosecution for disseminating leaked classified information, they would be free to argue that the First Amendment prohibited prosecution in the particular circumstances of their case, and that claim would be adjudicated by the courts through the customary development of First Amendment doctrine.

Appendix: Summary List of Recommendations
Encouraging Helpful Disclosures and Reducing Harmful Leaks

Reducing Overclassification

- To the extent that existing systems do not presently require officials who classify information to actually describe the damage to national security that unauthorized disclosure might cause, require them to make a reasonable effort to do so.
- Conduct regular audits to identify chronic overclassifiers, at the individual level and across agencies.
  For individuals who persistently overclassify, impose remedial measures ranging from training to suspension or revocation of classification authority for egregious patterns of overclassification.
  For agencies, require management to develop remedial plans and to submit to oversight by the National Archives' Information Security Oversight Office.
- Impose sanctions on original classification authorities who willfully or knowingly classify information to "conceal violations of law, inefficiency, or administrative error."

- Consult with repeat offenders to identify deficiencies in existing training programs and amend programs to remedy the inadequacies.

Facilitating Declassification

- Direct each agency to adopt policies for determining, upon request, when the value of disclosing classified information outweighs the damage from disclosure.
- In considering such questions, require the agency head to consult with the Information Security Oversight Office on whether the information should be declassified.

Creating Meaningful Alternatives to Leaking

- Permit government employees and employees of contractors to challenge classification decisions on an anonymous basis.
- Create an independent board within the executive branch composed of representatives with security clearances from the intelligence agencies and other government agencies to serve as a decision maker on whether challenged information should remain classified. Allow classification challenges to be submitted by government employees, employees of contractors, and stakeholders from outside the government.
- Allow the board to declassify information when it determines "the public interest in disclosure outweighs the damage to the national security that might reasonably be expected from disclosure."

Deterring and Punishing Leakers of Classified Information

- Reform the Espionage Act to provide for a graduated system of sanctions, including civil fines, misdemeanors, and felonies.

  Reserve the most severe punishment for leakers who (1) communicate classified documents or information to foreign powers, not the press; (2) act with a purpose to harm the United States or to aid a foreign power; or (3) act for the purpose of pecuniary gain.

  Provide for moderate punishment for government employees or contractors who leak without an intent to harm the United States but who should reasonably have understood that the leak might cause damage to the national security.

- Allow the defendant to prove as a mitigating factor that the information was inappropriately classified.
- Eliminate the distinction between leaking of documents versus information.
- Prohibit the government from circumventing these limits by using other broadly worded statutes such as 18 U.S.C. § 641 (theft of government property).

Balancing Press Freedoms and National Security

The Espionage Act Should Be Clarified to Prevent Its Inappropriate Application to the Press

- Amend the Espionage Act to make clear that the press cannot be prosecuted for core journalistic activity under theories of secondary liability, such as solicitation, conspiracy, or accessory after the fact.
- Prosecution should be permitted when the press engages in independently criminal activity that is prohibited by generally applicable laws with no First Amendment implications, such as hacking computer systems or trespassing on government property. The Espionage Act could be amended to make clear that journalists can be prosecuted for such acts only if they specifically intended to harm the United States or damage the national security.

Congress Should Consider Broader Protection for the Press

- Amend the Espionage Act to make clear that members of the press cannot be prosecuted for publishing leaked classified information unless (1) the *Brandenburg* standard is satisfied and (2) the press acted with intent to aid a foreign power, damage the national security, or otherwise harm the United States.
- Recognize "the press" in functional terms that acknowledge the increasingly broad range of individuals and organizations that seek to provide news and information in the public interest.

CLOSING STATEMENT

LEE C. BOLLINGER AND GEOFFREY R. STONE

When we first conceived of this book, we knew that the Pentagon Papers regime had survived intact, and had been more or less successful, for half a century. It has provided a uniquely American response to the classic question every democracy must face: how should we balance the legitimate needs of the government to operate in secret, especially in the realm of national security, against the equally legitimate needs of citizens to know what their government is doing? When power corrupts, as it frequently does, secrecy is often its abettor. On the other hand, no one has elected the press to make critically important decisions for the nation, and the rush to publish—sometimes carelessly and for profit— may inflict lasting damage on a nation in peril.

The Pentagon Papers case came at a moment in American history when the Supreme Court had created the most speech-protective constitutional jurisprudence in the history of the world. It was a stunning victory for the press, and it established the principle that the press has a First Amendment right to publish even illegally leaked classified documents unless the government can prove that the publication would create a clear and present danger of grave harm to the nation.[1] It was an answer to the classic question, but it did two additional vital things: it added gravitas to the whole body of speech-protective First Amendment decisions of that era, and it implicitly reinforced the notion that the press has a semiofficial role to perform in American democracy.

Supreme Court decisions, especially landmark decisions such as *Brown v. Board of Education*,[2] *New York Times v. Sullivan*,[3] and the Pentagon Papers case,[4] often announce general legal principles without providing a lot of detail or answers to the many possible follow-up questions. That was certainly true of the Pentagon Papers case. The multiple opinions did cohere around the holding that courts cannot constitutionally issue injunctions against the publication of purloined classified information, absent proof of a clear and present danger of grave and irreparable harm to the nation.[5] But what was not said was at least as important as what was said: What if the government seeks criminal punishments after publication? What kinds of potential harms to the nation constitute a "clear and present danger"? Does this degree of First Amendment protection apply only to the press or to citizens generally? What rights, if any, do government employees have to disclose classified information to the press? Does the press have a constitutional right to instigate or encourage such leaks without being held criminally responsible for its actions? And if members of the public want access to classified information that the government has in its possession, do they have a First Amendment right to go to court to obtain a court order demanding its disclosure if they can prove that the public interest in having access to the information exceeds the government's interest in keeping it secret?

As we know from the essays in this volume, many of these ambiguities have continued to this day and, not surprisingly, have played a significant role in shaping the impact—both good and bad—of the Pentagon Papers regime. Subsequent decisions and developments, however, have made at least some things clear. First, it now seems evident that the standard for a criminal prosecution of the press for publishing leaked classified information would be essentially the same as the standard for a prior restraint: clear and present danger.[6] Second, it now seems clear that to constitute a clear and present danger, the harms caused by the publication must be at the level of significant loss of life—a standard that is very difficult for the government to establish. Third, the Court has resisted the notion that "the press" has a special status in constitutional law.[7] Rather, partly to avoid having to decide who "the press" is, the Court has inclined toward the view that individuals and the press have equal First Amendment rights, though this has been actively contested in recent decades, and some cases have at least implicitly suggested the contrary.[8] Fourth, although the question has not been resolved by the Supreme Court, lower courts have generally taken the view that government employees do not have a First Amendment right to leak classified information, without regard to its value to the public.[9] Finally, it seems clear under existing law that neither the press nor citizens have a First Amendment right to compel the government to disclose classified information, even if they can demonstrate that the public's need to know outweighs the government's need to keep the information secret.[10]

As is made clear in this volume, over time, this highly complex, exceedingly disorderly, often ambiguous, and just plain messy system has spawned an elaborate set of customs, practices, policies, and laws within this broad framework. And then things changed. The advent of computers, the digitization of information, and the presence of the internet, together with the increasingly perceived threats to the national security following 9/11 and other developments on the international stage, have all contributed to an altered reality, including an exponential increase in secrecy and in the classification of information thought to be even potentially dangerous to the national security, a much greater ability on the part of government employees to leak unprecedentedly large quantities of information, a serious weakening of the financial underpinnings of traditional journalistic institutions, the proliferation and unprecedented capacity of nonmainstream and often untrustworthy organizations to disclose massive amounts of leaked information to worldwide audiences, the rise of an increasingly authoritarian attitude in our national government, and the emergence of actors and organizations eager to challenge our traditional assumption that government officials try in good faith to make responsible judgments about the public disclosure of national secrets. All of these changes in recent years have cast the Pentagon Papers regime in a new light and called into question its fundamental wisdom.

Perhaps the most important upshot of the essays in this volume is the overall judgment that it is too early to call for the abandonment of the system we have created and lived with for half a century. There are myriad reforms that could be instituted to improve the system, to reduce the risks of bad things happening to the nation, and to increase the flow of valuable information to the public. But, while there are major overhauls that one might consider (for example, empowering the courts to strike the balance on a case-by-case basis between secrecy and disclosure), we are not yet at a point in history where we can be confident that we would be better off by radically transforming the Pentagon Papers system than by maintaining its central premises and cautiously reforming what now exists. What these essays reveal, most profoundly, is that although each community of participants in the system is wary of the other, worried about the risks they are most attentive to and responsible for avoiding (too much secrecy or too much disclosure), and always suspicious about possible bad motives and bad judgment infecting their counterparts' decisions to withhold or to publish certain information, at the end of the day, they all seem to believe that the current system has worked reasonably well, even though they think it can be made to work better—but with clear differences over what "work better" means in practice. Despite those differences, this is a profoundly important collective judgment.

And yet we are left with a central conundrum—one that the Supreme Court will have to confront in the decades to come. The Court has traditionally indicated that it is reluctant to be in the position of overseeing the government's judgments about the importance of secrecy in the realm of national security.[11] In short, the Court lacks both experience in dealing with such matters and access to the complex considerations involved in these controversies to have confidence in its capacity to make wise and informed decisions in this realm. Moreover, the Court has been understandably reluctant to create a special set of First Amendment rights for "the press" in this context because of the daunting challenge of defining as a constitutional matter who or what is and is not "the press." As circumstances evolve, though, these judgments can change over time. We, as First Amendment scholars, have somewhat different views about these issues ourselves. But if the conditions of the current world remain in place and continue to provide a backdrop against which new cases will be decided, what can be done to preserve the Pentagon Papers "solution" without running the ever-increasing risk of government employees and contractors leaking ever-increasing amounts of classified information and of ever-more-irresponsible "publishers" doing ever-greater harm to our nation's security?

The plain and simple fact is that we do not have a good answer to that question at this time. It has long been recognized that experience, more than logic, has defined the course of the law. We will only know the true magnitude of the risks we face as actual cases arise. Even then, there are many times in the history of constitutional law when the Court has avoided trying to bring complete logical coherence to an area of the law and, instead, allowed ambiguity, and even inconsistencies, to exist while the Justices, the broader legal community, and the society at large try to absorb the problem and reflect on the proper course. One of the most important elements of wise constitutional decision-making is time. And in the case of the Pentagon Papers "solution," only time will tell.

NOTES

Opening Statement

1. Schenck v. United States, 249 U.S. 47 (1919); Abrams v. United States, 250 U.S. 616 (1919); Debs v. United States, 249 U.S. 211 (1919); Daniel Baracskay, *Bill of Rights*, THE FIRST AMENDMENT ENCYCLOPEDIA (2009, updated 2018), https://www.mtsu.edu/first-amendment/article/1448/bill-of-rights.

2. THE FREE SPEECH CENTURY, Lee C. Bollinger & Geoffrey R. Stone eds. (New York: Oxford University Press, 2018).

3. New York Times Co. v. United States, 403 U.S. 713 (1971).

4. *See* United States v. New York Times Co., 328 F. Supp. 324 (S.D.N.Y. 1971); Bruce Altschuler, *Pentagon Papers*, THE FIRST AMENDMENT ENCYCLOPEDIA (2009), https://www.mtsu.edu/first-amendment/article/873/pentagon-papers.

5. Altschuler, *supra* note 4.

6. *Id.*

7. *Id.*

8. New York Times Co., 403 U.S. at 714.

9. *Id.* at 732.

10. *Id.* at 714.

11. *See* Peter Osnos, *Pentagon Papers: The Glory Days of Journalism*, ATLANTIC (Mar. 23, 2010), https://www.theatlantic.com/entertainment/archive/2010/03/pentagon-papers-the-glory-days-of-journalism/37874/ (calling the decision a "glorious victory for a robust press").

12. *See* Richmond Newspapers, Inc. v. Virginia, 448 U.S. 555 (1980); Houchins v. KQED, 438 U.S. 1 (1978).

13. *See* Snepp v. United States, 444 U.S. 507 (1980); *The Chelsea Manning Case: A Timeline*, AM. CIVIL LIBERTIES UNION (May 9, 2017), https://www.aclu.org/blog/free-speech/employee-speech-and-whistleblowers/chelsea-manning-case-timeline.

14. *See* AM. CIVIL LIBERTIES UNION, *supra* note 13.

15. New York Times Co., 403 U.S. 713.

16. *Cf.* Bart Jansen, *Who Has Security Clearance? More Than 4.3M People*, USA TODAY (June 6, 2017), https://www.usatoday.com/story/news/2017/06/06/who-has-security-clearance/102549298/. Compared to Ellsberg, for example, Edward Snowden is estimated to have stolen more than 1.7 million documents and leaked at least 200,000. Michael B. Kelley, *NSA: Snowden Stole 1.7 Million Classified Documents and Still Has Access to Most of Them*, BUS. INSIDER (Dec. 13, 2013), https://www.businessinsider.com/how-many-docs-did-snowden-take-2013-12.

Introduction

1. 403 U.S. 713 (1971).
2. *Id.* at 728 (Stewart, J., concurring).
3. *Id.* at 717 (Black, J., concurring).
4. Geoffrey R. Stone, *Government Secrecy vs. Freedom of the Press*, 1 HARV. L. & POL'Y REV. 185, 194 (2007).
5. 403 U.S. at 714.
6. The Reporters Committee for Freedom of the Press maintains a list of leak prosecutions, available at https://www.rcfp.org/resources/leak-investigations-chart/.
7. Patricia L. Bellia, *WikiLeaks and the Institutional Framework for National Security Disclosures*, 121 YALE L.J. 1448, 1507 (2012).
8. United States v. Progressive, Inc., 467 F. Supp. 990 (W.D. Wis. 1979). The article, titled "The H-Bomb Secret: How We Got It, Why We're Telling It," apparently "explain[ed] the technical processes of thermonuclear weapons." *Id.* at 991, 993.
9. *Id.* at 994. Indeed, in an earlier hearing granting a temporary restraining order, the court observed from the bench that it could not "help feeling that somehow or another to put together the recipe for a do-it-yourself hydrogen bomb is somewhat different than revealing that certain members of our military establishment have very poor ideas about how to conduct a national effort in Vietnam." Ian M. Dumain, *No Secret, No Defense:* United States v. Progressive, 26 CARDOZO L. REV. 1323, 1327–28 (2005).
10. *United States v. Progressive*, 467 F. Supp. at 995.
11. *Id.* at 994.
12. *Id.* at 994, 996.
13. *Id.* at 992 (citing New York Times v. United States, 403 U.S. 713 (1971)).
14. *Id.* at 996.
15. Near v. Minnesota ex rel. Olson, 283 U.S. 697, 716 (1931) ("No one would question but that a government might prevent actual obstruction to its recruiting service or the publication of the sailing dates of transports or the number and location of troops.").
16. *United States v. Progressive*, 467 F. Supp. at 996.
17. United States v. Progressive, Inc., 610 F.2d 819 (7th Cir. 1979).
18. Richard Parker, *United States v. The Progressive (W.D. Wisc.) (1979)*, THE FIRST AMENDMENT ENCYCLOPEDIA, https://mtsu.edu/first-amendment/article/512/united-states-v-the-progressive-w-d-wis.
19. *Id.*
20. Nebraska Press Ass'n v. Stuart, 427 U.S. 539, 542 (1976).
21. *Id.* at 542.
22. *Id.* at 545.
23. *Id.* at 555, 563–64.
24. *Id.* at 566–67, 569.
25. *Id.* at 558, 570; James L. Oakes, *The Doctrine of Prior Restraint since the Pentagon Papers*, 15 U. MICH. J. L. REFORM 497, 511 (1982) ("The most notable feature of the Burger opinion is that it does not state a general rule, but instead applies an ad hoc balancing test to decide first amendment cases, even in the prior restraint area.").
26. *See also* United States v. Aguilar, 515 U.S. 593, 606 (1995) ("As to one who voluntarily assumed a duty of confidentiality, governmental restrictions on disclosure are not subject to the same stringent standards that would apply to efforts to impose restrictions on unwilling members of the public."); Wilson v. CIA, 586 F.3d 171, 183 (2d Cir. 2009) ("[O]nce a government employee signs an agreement not to disclose information properly classified pursuant to executive order, that employee 'simply has no first amendment right to publish' such information." (quoting Stillman v. CIA, 319 F.3d 546, 548 (D.C. Cir. 2003)); United States v. Pappas, 94 F.3d 795, 801 (2d Cir. 1996) ("The Government is entitled to enforce its agreements to maintain the confidentiality of classified information."); McGehee v. Casey, 718 F.2d 1137, 1143 (D.C. Cir. 1983) ("We hold that the CIA censorship of 'secret' information contained in former agents' writings and obtained by former agents during the course of CIA employment does not violate the first amendment.").

27. United States v. Marchetti, 466 F.2d 1309, 1312 & n.1 (4th Cir. 1972).

28. *Id.* at 1313.

29. *Id.* at 1316.

30. *Id.* at 1313.

31. *Id.* at 1317.

32. *Id.*

33. *Id.*

34. Alfred A. Knopf Inc. v. Colby, 509 F.2d 1362, 1365 (4th Cir. 1975).

35. *Id.* at 1370.

36. *Id.*

37. *Id.* at 1368, 1369–70.

38. *Id.* at 1368.

39. *See* Wilson v. CIA, 586 F.3d 171, 185–86 (2d Cir. 2009) (A court must satisfy itself "from the record, in camera or otherwise, that the CIA in fact had good reason to classify, and therefore censor, the materials at issue." *McGehee v. Casey*, 718 F.2d at 1149. To that end, a court may "require that CIA explanations justify censorship with reasonable specificity, demonstrating a logical connection between the deleted information and the reasons for classification." (quoting Gutierrez de Martinez v. Lamagno, 515 U.S. 417, 426 (1995)); *McGehee*, 718 F.2d at 1148–49 ("While we believe courts in securing such determinations should defer to CIA judgment as to the harmful results of publication, they must nevertheless satisfy themselves from the record, in camera or otherwise, that the CIA in fact had good reason to classify, and therefore censor, the materials at issue. Accordingly, the courts should require that CIA explanations justify censorship with reasonable specificity, demonstrating a logical connection between the deleted information and the reasons for classification.").

40. 444 U.S. 507 (1980) (per curiam).

41. *Compare* United States v. Marchetti, 466 F.2d 1309, 1312 & n.1 (4th Cir. 1972), *with Snepp*, 444 U.S. at 508.

42. *Snepp*, 444 U.S. at 507.

43. *Id.*; *see also* JOHN PRADOS & MARGARET PRATT PORTER, INSIDE THE PENTAGON PAPERS 207 (Lawrence: University Press of Kansas, 2004) (describing Snepp's book as "a critical and scathing account of the mismanaged American evacuation in South Vietnam").

44. *Snepp*, 444 U.S. at 524 (Stevens, J., dissenting) (describing procedural history and asserting that "[t]he Court's decision to dispose of this case summarily on the Government's conditional cross-petition for certiorari is just as unprecedented as its disposition of the merits").

45. *Id.* at 509 n.3.

46. *Id.* at 511.

47. *Id.*

48. *Id.* at 511–13.

49. *Id.* at 515–16. The *Snepp* decision was controversial, and several scholars have argued that it should be overruled or, at the least, not extended further. *See* Mary-Rose Papandrea, *Leaker Traitor Whistleblower Spy: National Security Leaks and the First Amendment*, 94 B.U. L. REV. 449, 530 (2014); Heidi Kitrosser, *Leak Prosecutions and the First Amendment: New Developments and a Closer Look at the Feasibility of Prosecuting Leakers*, 56 WM. & MARY L. REV. 1221, 1234 (2015) ("There are persuasive arguments against extending *Snepp* to the context of leaker prosecutions or otherwise applying it beyond its facts. The most obvious reason is the virtual absence of attention paid by the *Snepp* Court to the First Amendment.").

50. Agee v. CIA, 500 F. Supp. 506, 507–08 (D.D.C. 1980).

51. *Id.* at 508.

52. *Id.* at 509–10.

53. Haig v. Agee, 453 U.S. 280 (1981).

54. *Id.* at 308–9. In addition, the Court dismissed Agee's argument that the government's only remedy against Agee's admittedly damaging disclosures was an order for Agee to comply with his secrecy agreement. The Court noted that such an order would be unenforceable against Agee while he lived outside of the United States. *Id.* at 308 n.60.

55. *Id.* at 308–9.

56. United States v. Marchetti, 466 F.2d 1309, 1313 & n.1 (4th Cir. 1972).

57. *Oakes, supra* note 25, at 515; *Snepp*, 444 U.S. at 509 n.3.

58. Jack Goldsmith of Harvard Law School and Oona Hathaway of Yale Law School have written a series of informative blog posts about the pre-publication review process and have called for its reform. *See* Jack Goldsmith & Oona A. Hathaway, *The Government's Prepublication Review Process Is Broken*, WASH. POST (Dec. 25, 2015), https://www.washingtonpost.com/opinions/ the-governments-prepublication-review-process-is-broken/2015/12/25/edd943a8-a349-11e5-b53d-972e2751f433_story.html; Jack Goldsmith & Oona Hathaway, *Path Dependence and the Prepublication Review Process*, JUST SECURITY (Dec. 28, 2015), https://www. justsecurity.org/28552/path-dependence-prepublication-review-process/; Jack Goldsmith & Oona A. Hathaway, *More Problems with Prepublication Review*, JUST SECURITY (Dec. 28, 2015), https://www.justsecurity.org/28548/problems-prepublication-review/; *see also* Katrin Marquez, *The Unreasonableness of "Reasonable" Prepublication Review, Part 1*, YALE LAW SCH. MEDIA FREEDOM & INFO. ACCESS CLINIC (Feb. 11, 2019), https://law.yale.edu/ mfia/case-disclosed/unreasonableness-reasonable-prepublication-review-part-1.

59. *See* Maggie Haberman & Michael S. Schmidt, *Trump Told Bolton to Help His Ukraine Pressure Campaign, Book Says*, N.Y. TIMES (Jan. 31, 2020), https://www.nytimes.com/2020/01/31/ us/politics/trump-bolton-ukraine.html; letter from Charles J. Cooper, Attorney, Cooper & Kirk, to Ellen J. Knight, Senior Director, National Security Council, Executive Office of the President (Dec. 30, 2019), https://int.nyt.com/data/documenthelper/6727-bolton-lawyer-letter/6ec64dfab61cecc9ac2b/optimized/full.pdf; letter from Ellen J. Knight, Senior Director, National Security Council, Executive Office of the President, to Charles J. Cooper, Attorney, Cooper & Kirk (Jan. 23, 2020), https://www.scribd.com/embeds/444786869/content?start_ page=1&view_mode=scroll&access_key=key-D6nFrbtLkymRceOzcqJZ&show_ recommendations=true; Brett Samuels, *Bolton Lawyer Slams "Corrupted" White House Review Process after Book Leak*, THE HILL (Jan. 26, 2020), https://thehill.com/homenews/adminis-tration/480027-bolton-lawyer-slams-corrupted-white-house-review-process-after-book.

60. Complaint, United States v. Bolton, No. 20-1580 (D.D.C. June 16, 2020), ECF No. 1 at 2; *see also* Emergency Application for Temporary Restraining Order and Motion for Preliminary Injunction, United States v. Bolton, No. 20-1580 (D.D.C. June 17, 2020), ECF No. 3.

61. Emergency Application for Temporary Restraining Order and Motion for Preliminary Injunction, United States v. Bolton, No. 20-1580 (D.D.C. June 17, 2020), ECF No. 3 at 8.

62. Memorandum Order, United States v. Bolton, No. 12-1580 (D.D.C. June 20, 2020), ECF No. 1.

63. *Id.* at 9.

64. Snodgrass v. Dep't of Defense, No. 1:19-cv-02607-EGS (D.D.C.) (complaint filed Aug. 29, 2019).

65. Dan Lamothe, *Defense Department Clears Navy Officer's Book about Former Pentagon Chief Mattis after Facing Lawsuit*, WASH. POST (Sept. 12, 2019), https://www.washingtonpost. com/national-security/2019/09/12/defense-department-clears-navy-officers-book-about-former-pentagon-chief-mattis-after-facing-lawsuit.

66. Edgar v. Coats, No. 8:19-cv-00985-GJH (D. Md.) (complaint filed Apr. 2, 2019). The plaintiffs are represented by the Knight First Amendment Institute at Columbia University.

67. Edgar v. Coats, No. GJH-19-985, 2020 WL 1890509, at *20 (D. Md.) (Apr. 16, 2020).

68. *Id.* at *25–*27. Other recent cases challenging pre-publication review of manuscripts by former government employees include Bakos v. CIA, Civ. No. 18-743 (RMC) (D.D.C.) (complaint filed April 2018), which was resolved by the parties through negotiation before the CIA had to answer the complaint; and Bonner v. CIA, No. 18-cv-11256 (S.D.N.Y.) (complaint filed December 2018), which was voluntarily dismissed, apparently because the parties reached an agreement.

69. United States v. Snowden, Civ. Action No. l:19-cv-1197 (E.D. Va.), Dkt 63, at 9.

70. *Id.* at 9–10.

71. Branzburg v. Hayes, 408 U.S. 665 (1972).

72. *Id.* at 683, 690.

73. Landmark Commc'ns, Inc. v. Virginia, 435 U.S. 829, 831 (1978).

74. *Id.* at 832.

75. *Id.* at 834.

76. *Id.* at 838.
77. *Id.* at 849 (Stewart, J., concurring).
78. 443 U.S. 97, 98 (1979).
79. *Id.* at 104.
80. 491 U.S. 524, 526 (1989).
81. *Id.* at 532.
82. *Id.* at 535 n.8 (emphasis added).
83. *Id.* (citing 403 U.S. 713 (1971)).
84. 532 U.S. 514, 528 (2001).
85. *Id.* (citation omitted).
86. *Id.* at 518.
87. *Id.* at 524–25.
88. *Id.* at 525. Justice Breyer, in a concurrence joined by Justice O'Connor, would have further limited the Court's holding to circumstances where the "information publicized involved a matter of unusual public concern, namely, a threat of potential physical harm to others." *Id.* at 535–36 (Breyer, J., concurring).
89. *Id.* at 528.
90. *Id.* at 529–30.
91. *Id.* at 531.
92. New York Times Co. v. United States, 403 U.S. 713, 730 (1971) (Stewart, J., concurring) (noting Congress has passed criminal laws designed to protect government secrets, and several "are of very colorable relevance to the apparent circumstances of these cases"); *id.* at 737 (White, J., concurring) ("I would have no difficulty in sustaining convictions under these sections on facts that would not justify the intervention of equity and the imposition of a prior restraint."); *id.* at 745 (Marshall, J., concurring) (noting that the Espionage Act appears relevant to the alleged conduct by the newspapers).
93. The seminal work analyzing the Espionage Act is Harold Edgar and Benno C. Schmidt Jr., *The Espionage Statutes and Publication of Defense Information*, 73 COLUM. L. REV. 929 (1973).
94. 18 U.S.C. § 793(d).
95. *Id.* at § 793(e). Section 793(e) thus potentially reaches a journalist who receives leaked information and fails to return it, even if he or she was not personally involved in orchestrating or aiding the leak.
96. 844 F.2d 1057 (4th Cir.), *cert. denied*, 488 U.S. 908 (1988).
97. The government sought to prosecute Daniel Ellsberg and Anthony Russo for leaking the Pentagon Papers. The 1971 indictment included multiple counts under the Espionage Act, as well as counts of theft and conspiracy. The court dismissed the indictment in 1973 due to prosecutorial misconduct. *Ellsberg Case: Defendants Freed, Government Convicted*, N.Y. TIMES (May 13, 1973), https://www.nytimes.com/1973/05/13/archives/ellsberg-case-defendants-freed-government-convicted.html.
98. *Morison*, 844 F.2d at 1061.
99. *Id.* at 1062.
100. *Id.* at 1063–67.
101. *Id.* at 1067–68.
102. *Id.* at 1068.
103. 408 U.S. 665 (1972).
104. *Morison*, 844 F.2d at 1069–70 ("Nor do we find any authority for the proposition that Congress could not validly prohibit a government employee having possession of secret military intelligence material from transmitting that material to 'one not entitled to receive it,' whether that recipient was in the press or not, without infringing the employee's rights under the First Amendment.").
105. *Id.* at 1069.
106. *Id.* at 1071–72.
107. *Id.* at 1072.
108. *Morison*, 844 F.2d at 1081 (Wilkinson, J., concurring).
109. *Id.* at 1082 (Wilkinson, J., concurring) (quoting *Haig*, 453 U.S. at 307 (ellipsis in original)).

110. *Morison*, 844 F.2d at 1084 (Wilkinson, J., concurring).

111. *Id.* at 1085 (Phillips, J., concurring).

112. *Id.* at 1086 (Phillips, J., concurring). Judge Phillips noted that—were he "writing on a clean slate"—the requirement "that information relating to the national defense merely have the 'potential' for damage or usefulness still sweeps extremely broadly." *Id.* He indicated, however, that he felt constrained by Fourth Circuit precedent with respect to the constitutional validity of the jury instructions regarding "national defense." *Id.*

113. United States v. Kiriakou, No. 1:12-CR-127 (LMB), 2012 WL 3263854, at *6 (E.D. Va. Aug. 8, 2012); United States v. Rosen, 445 F. Supp. 2d 602, 618–22 (E.D. Va. 2006); *see also* Stephen P. Mulligan & Jennifer K. Elsea, *Criminal Prohibitions on Leaks and Other Disclosures of Classified Defense Information*, CONG. RES. SERV. 16 (Mar. 7, 2017) (noting requirement that information be "closely held" and suggesting classification "will likely serve as strong evidence" that information was closely held); United States v. Drake, 818 F. Supp. 2d 909, 916 (D. Md. 2011) ("[T]hough Section 793(e) does not define its terms, the meaning of its essential terms—including all those challenged by Mr. Drake—have been well-settled within the Fourth Circuit since the United States Court of Appeals for the Fourth Circuit issued its opinion in *United States v. Morison*.").

A notable exception is *United States v. Kim*, in which the district court rejected *Morison's* requirement that the information be "potentially damaging," deeming that limiting construction inconsistent with the Supreme Court's 1941 decision in *Gorin v. United States*, 312 U.S. 19, 29 (1941), which gave a broad construction to the term "information relating to the national defense." Memorandum Opinion, United States v. Kim, No. 10-225(CKK) (D.D.C. July 24, 2013), ECF No. 137.

114. *See, e.g.*, United States v. Kim, 808 F. Supp. 2d 44, 54 (D.D.C. 2011); *Rosen*, 445 F. Supp. 2d at 622–23; *see also* Kitrosser, *supra* note 49, at 1232 ("Courts have read the 'not entitled to receive it' language in light of the classification system.").

115. *Drake*, 818 F. Supp. 2d at 919, 921.

116. *Rosen*, 445 F. Supp. 2d at 610.

117. *Id.* at 625–26.

118. *Id.* The *Drake* and *Kiriakou* courts subsequently adopted *Rosen's* reasoning. *Drake*, 818 F. Supp. 2d at 916–18; *Kiriakou*, 2012 WL 3263854, at *6 n.4 (citing *Rosen* when holding that the "reason to believe" language applies only to "intangible communication"); *see also* Mulligan & Elsea, *supra* note 113 (describing the "reason to believe" clause's application to information disclosures as settled law). *Cf. Kim*, 808 F. Supp. 2d at 51 (noting the "reason to believe" clause and finding that Congress decided "to impose a *mens rea* requirement for the communication, delivery, or transmission of 'information' but not for tangible items"). The *Drake* court suggested that such a distinction between tangible and intangible communication makes sense because "a defendant will more readily recognize a document relating to the national defense based on its content, markings or design than it would intangible or oral 'information' that may not share such attributes." *Drake*, 818 F. Supp. 2d at 917.

119. Several recent works have catalogued the possible criminal prohibitions against disclosure. *See* GARY ROSS, WHO WATCHES THE WATCHMEN? THE CONFLICT BETWEEN NATIONAL SECURITY AND FREEDOM OF THE PRESS 28, 152–54 (Washington, DC: NI Press, 2011), https://fas.org/sgp/eprint/ross.pdf; Papandrea, *Leaker Traitor Whistleblower Spy*, *supra* note 49, at 511–12; Mulligan & Elsea, *supra* note 113.

In addition to criminal sanctions, the government has civil and administrative sanctions available to punish leakers, including loss of security clearance and dismissal. *See* Papandrea, *Leaker Traitor Whistleblower Spy*, *supra* note 49, at 537; *see also* Letter from John Ashcroft, Attorney General, to J. Dennis Hastert, Speaker of the House of Representatives, *Report to Congress on Unauthorized Disclosures of Classified Information* 3 (Oct. 15, 2002), https://fas.org/sgp/othergov/dojleaks.html ("Department and agency heads have substantial authority to address the problem of persons who engage in the unauthorized disclosure of classified information within their own organizations through suspension or revocation of clearances and procedures to terminate employees in the national security interests of the United States.").

120. Papandrea, *Leaker Traitor Whistleblower Spy*, *supra* note 49, at 511.

121. *See, e.g.,* United States v. Fowler, 932 F.2d 306, 309–10 (4th Cir. 1991); United States v. Girard, 601 F.2d 69, 70–71 (2d Cir. 1979). Morison, the Navy analyst who provided classified photographs to *Jane's*, was convicted of violating § 641. The Fourth Circuit upheld his conviction. *See also* Jessica Lutkenhaus, *Prosecuting Leakers the Easy Way: 18 U.S.C. § 641*, 114 COLUM. L. REV. 1167, 1186–97 (2014). By contrast, the Ninth Circuit has ruled § 641 inapplicable to disclosures of intangible information. United States v. Tobias, 836 F.2d 449, 451 (9th Cir. 1988).

122. *See* Lutkenhaus, *supra* note 121, at 1188–97 (cataloguing court decisions applying § 641 to information and describing their analyses of the First Amendment); United States v. Jeter, 775 F.2d 670, 682 (6th Cir. 1985) ("We do not attempt to determine the constitutionality of Section 641 in a 'Pentagon Papers' kind of situation."); United States v. Jones, 677 F. Supp. 238, 242 n.5 (S.D.N.Y. 1988); United States v. Truong Dinh Hung, 629 F.2d 908, 911 (4th Cir. 1980).

123. 438 U.S. 1 (1978).

124. *Id.* at 3 (plurality op.).

125. *Id.* at 6 (plurality op.).

126. Justices Marshall and Blackmun did not participate in the decision.

127. *Id.* at 9, 15–16 (plurality op.) ("The public importance of conditions in penal facilities and the media's role of providing information afford no basis for reading into the Constitution a right of the public or the media to enter these institutions, with camera equipment, and take moving and still pictures of inmates for broadcast purposes. This Court has never intimated a First Amendment guarantee of a right of access to all sources of information within government control."); *id.* at 16 (Stewart, J., concurring) ("The First and Fourteenth Amendments do not guarantee the public a right of access to information generated or controlled by government, nor do they guarantee the press any basic right of access superior to that of the public generally.").

128. *Id.* at 16 (Stewart, J., concurring).

129. *Id.* at 17 (Stewart, J., concurring).

130. *Id.* at 17–18 (Stewart, J., concurring).

131. *Id.* at 32 (Stevens, J., dissenting).

132. Richmond Newspapers, Inc. v. Virginia, 448 U.S. 555, 576, 580 (1980) (plurality op.) ("What this means in the context of trials is that the First Amendment guarantees of speech and press, standing alone, prohibit government from summarily closing courtroom doors which had long been open to the public at the time that Amendment was adopted. . . . We hold that the right to attend criminal trials is implicit in the guarantees of the First Amendment.").

133. *Richmond Newspapers* included a plurality opinion, five concurrences, and a dissent. Justice Powell did not participate in the case.

134. *Richmond Newspapers*, 448 U.S. at 565–71 (plurality op.) (noting openness in criminal trials had "community therapeutic value" and "gave assurance that the proceedings were conducted fairly to all concerned, and it discouraged perjury, the misconduct of participants, and decisions based on secret bias or partiality"). For a more detailed analysis of the plurality's reasoning, *see generally* George W. Kelly, *Richmond Newspapers and the First Amendment Right of Access*, 18 AKRON L. REV. 33 (1984).

135. Center for Nat'l Sec. Studies v. U.S. Dep't of Justice, 331 F.3d 918 (D.C. Cir. 2003).

136. *Id.* at 934–35.

137. *Id.* at 934 (citing Houchins v. KQED, 438 U.S. 1, 14–15 (1978)).

138. ARTHUR M. SCHLESINGER JR., THE IMPERIAL PRESIDENCY 362 (New York: First Mariner, 1973); *see also* Margaret Sullivan, *Daniel Ellsberg, Who Leaked the Pentagon Papers, Asks: Who Will Be the Next Snowden*, WASH. POST (Feb. 26, 2017) (Ellsberg states that "something like the Pentagon Papers should come out every year"), https://www.washingtonpost.com/lifestyle/style/daniel-ellsberg-who-leaked-the-pentagon-papers-asks-who-will-be-the-next-snowden/2017/02/26/a35ba940-f87c-11e6-be05-1a3817ac21a5_story.html.

139. *See, e.g.,* James B. Bruce, *The Consequences of Permissive Neglect: Laws and Leaks of Classified Intelligence*, CENT. INTELLIGENCE AGENCY (2007), https://www.cia.gov/library/center-for-the-study-of-intelligence/csi-publications/csi-studies/studies/vol47no1/article04.html.

140. *Id.* (finding that "[n]early all of the compelling evidence in support of the argument that leaks are causing serious damage is available only in the classified domain").

141. David A. Strauss, *Keeping Secrets, in* THE FREE SPEECH CENTURY, Lee C. Bollinger & Geoffrey R. Stone eds. (New York: Oxford University Press, 2018); Jason Leopold, *Official Reports on the Damage Caused by Edward Snowden's Leaks Are Totally Redacted,* VICE NEWS (Feb. 25, 2015), https://news.vice.com/en_us/article/438jmw/ official-reports-on-the-damage-caused-by-edward-snowdens-leaks-are-totally-redacted.

142. Leopold, *supra* note 141.

143. Shane Harris, *Congressmen Reveal Secret Report's Findings to Discredit Snowden,* FOREIGN POLICY (Jan. 9, 2014), https://foreignpolicy.com/2014/01/09/congressmen-reveal-secret-reports-findings-to-discredit-snowden/ (Congressmen Mike Rogers and Dutch Ruppersberger argue Snowden leaks have harmed national security after reviewing classified report).

144. Deb Riechmann, *Costs of Snowden Leak Still Mounting 5 Years Later,* ASSOCIATED PRESS (June 4, 2018), https://www.apnews.com/797f390ee28b4bfbb0e1b13cfedf0593.

145. David V. Gioe, *Tinker, Tailor, Leaker, Spy: The Future Costs of Mass Leaks,* NATIONAL INTEREST (Jan./Feb. 2014), https://nationalinterest.org/print/article/ tinker-tailor-leaker-spy-the-future-costs-mass-leaks-9644.

146. Jack Shafer, *Live and Let Leak: State Secrets in the Snowden Era,* FOREIGN AFFAIRS (Mar./ Apr. 2014), 136–42, https://www.foreignaffairs.com/reviews/review-essay/2014-02-12/ live-and-let-leak (reviewing *Secrets and Leaks: The Dilemma of State Secrecy* by Rahul Sagar).

147. *See* TRANSPARENCY INT'L, GOVERNMENT DEFENCE ANTI-CORRUPTION INDEX (GI) (2015), http://government.defenceindex.org/#close.

148. *Examining the Costs of Overclassification on Transparency and Security: Hearing before the H. Comm. on Oversight & Gov't Reform,* 114th Cong. (2016).

149. *Id.* at 2.

150. *Id.* at 57 (Witness Statement by Tom Blanton).

151. DANIEL PATRICK MOYNIHAN, SECRECY 227 (New Haven, CT: Yale University Press, 1998).

152. Steven Aftergood, *An Inquiry into the Dynamics of Government Secrecy,* 48 HARV. C.R.–C.L. L. REV. 511, 512–13 (2013) (noting that the relevant guidance documents from Richard Nixon to Barack Obama have become increasingly ambiguous, leading insiders to unintentionally exacerbate the problem).

153. *Id.* at 513.

154. Pub. L. No. 111–258 (2010).

155. Steven Aftergood, *Telling Secrets,* FOREIGN POLICY (Oct. 18, 2010), https://foreignpolicy. com/2010/10/18/telling-secrets/.

156. NAT'L ARCHIVES & RECORDS ADMIN., INFO. SEC. OVERSIGHT OFFICE (ISOO), 2017 REPORT TO THE PRESIDENT (May 2018), https://www.archives.gov/files/isoo/reports/ 2017-annual-report.pdf; Christina E. Wells, *Restoring the Balance between Secrecy and Transparency: The Prosecution of National Security Leaks under the Espionage Act,* AMERICAN CONSTITUTION SOC'Y (Oct. 2017), https://www.acslaw.org/wp-content/uploads/2017/ 10/Espionage_Act_ACS_Issue_Brief.pdf; *Examining the Costs of Overclassification, supra* note 148.

157. Elizabeth Goitein & David M. Shapiro, *Reducing Overclassification through Accountability,* BRENNAN CTR. FOR JUSTICE (2011), https://www.brennancenter.org/sites/default/files/ legacy/Justice/LNS/Brennan_Overclassification_Final.pdf. As the 9/11 Commission found in 2004, "each agency's incentive structure opposes sharing, with risks . . . but few rewards for sharing information." *See* NAT'L COMM'N ON TERRORIST ATTACKS UPON THE U.S., 9/11 COMMISSION REPORT 417 (2004), http://govinfo.library.unt.edu/911/report/ 911Report.pdf.

158. MOYNIHAN, *supra* note 151, at 222–23.

159. ISOO, *supra* note 156, at 4.

160. NOAH DEMPSEY, HOUSE OF COMMONS LIBRARY, UK DEFENCE EXPENDITURE 4 (Nov. 8, 2018), https://researchbriefings.files.parliament.uk/documents/CBP-8175/CBP-8175.pdf.

161. *Cf.* MOYNIHAN, *supra* note 151 (describing how excessive secrecy has heightened public distrust, leading to an uptick in conspiracy theories over time).

162. New York Times Co. v. United States, 403 U.S. 713, 729 (1971) (Stewart, J., concurring).

163. *See, e.g.,* OPEN SOC'Y JUSTICE INITIATIVE, PENALTIES FOR UNAUTHORIZED DISCLOSURE OF NATIONAL SECURITY-RELATED SECRETS: COMPARATIVE LAW AND PRACTICE (Nov. 2013), https://www.right2info.org/resources/publications/national-security-page/ national-security-expert-papers/penalties-for-unauthorized-disclosure-of-national-security-secrets-2013; UNESCO, FREEDOM OF INFORMATION: A COMPARATIVE LEGAL SURVEY (2008); *see also* LEE C. BOLLINGER, UNINHIBITED, ROBUST, AND WIDE-OPEN: A FREE PRESS FOR A NEW CENTURY 117 (New York: Oxford University Press, 2010) (noting that Britain has historically had "a strict policy against the press publishing state secrets").

164. G. Bartlett & M. Everett (2017), *The Official Secrets Act and Official Secrecy.* House of Commons Library Briefing Paper No. CBP07422, House of Commons Library, London, https://researchbriefings.parliament.uk/ResearchBriefing/Summary/CBP-7422#fullreport. Where a disclosure is made by a civil servant ("Crown servant") or government contractors, it must be shown to be "damaging" to constitute a legal offense. *Id.*

165. Papandrea, *Leaker Traitor Whistleblower Spy, supra* note 49, at 510; *see also* United States v. Morison, 844 F.2d 1057, 1071–72 (4th Cir.), *cert. denied,* 488 U.S. 908 (1988) (affirming jury instruction that defined "related to the national defense" as including the requirement the disclosure would be "potentially damaging to the United States or might be useful to an enemy of the United States"); United States v. Rosen, 445 F. Supp. 2d 602, 621 (E.D. Va. 2006).

166. Bartlett & Everett, *supra* note 164, at 6; *see also* Adam Taylor, *Why Britain's Government Doesn't Leak the Way America's Does,* WASH. POST (May 26, 2017), https://www.washingtonpost.com/news/worldviews/wp/2017/05/26/why-britains-government-doesnt-leak-the-way-americas-does/?utm_term=.7b705aac0163. While some argue that a plain reading of the Espionage Act would also permit the prosecution of publishers, it is a minority view. *See, e.g.,* Katherine Feuer, *Protecting Government Secrets: A Comparison of the Espionage Act and the Official Secrets Act,* 38 B.C. INT'L & COMP. L. REV. 91 (2015).

167. Benjamin Cooper & Mason Boycott-Owen, *What Is the Official Secrets Act and Who Has Been Guilty of Breaking It,* INDEPENDENT (July 13, 2019), https://www.independent.co.uk/news/uk/politics/official-secrets-act-what-penalty-leak-kim-darroch-trump-a9003206.html; David E. Pozen, *The Leaky Leviathan: Why the Government Condemns and Condones Unlawful Disclosures of Information,* 127 HARV. L. REV. 512, 627–28 (noting the United Kingdom's "permissive enforcement practices" and identifying twelve individuals prosecuted under the Official Secrets Act for leaking since 1990).

168. Cooper & Boycott-Owen, *supra* note 167.

169. UK Defence and Security Media Advisory (DSMA) Committee, The DSMA Notice System, *How the System Works,* https://dsma.uk/how-the-system-works/.

170. Ross, *supra* note 119, at 143–45.

171. *Id.* at 144.

172. *Id.* at 143–45.

173. Feuer, *supra* note 166; Pozen, *supra* note 167, at 629 ("Compliance with the DA-Notice system is optional, but reportedly regular."). *But see* David McCraw & Stephen Gikow, *The End to an Unspoken Bargain? National Security and Leaks in a Post-Pentagon Papers World,* 48 HARV. C.R.–C.L. L. REV. 473, 505 & n. 191 (2013) (claiming the DA notice system "has been met with widespread press skepticism and little apparent success in striking the right balance").

174. Taylor, *supra* note 166.

175. Intel, *The Story of the Intel© 4004: Intel's First Microprocessor,* https://www.intel.com/content/www/us/en/history/museum-story-of-intel-4004.html.

176. *Id.*

177. Jeremy Reimer, *Total Share: 30 Years of Personal Computer Market Share Figures,* ARS TECHNICA (Dec. 15, 2005), https://arstechnica.com/features/2005/12/total-share/3/.

178. Larry Greenemeier, *Remembering the Day the World Wide Web Was Born,* SCI. AM. (March 12, 2009), https://www.scientificamerican.com/article/day-the-web-was-born/.

179. Patrick McCurdy, *From the Pentagon Papers to Cablegate: How the Network Society Has Changed Leaking, in* BEYOND WIKILEAKS: IMPLICATIONS FOR THE FUTURE OF COMMUNICATIONS,

JOURNALISM AND SOCIETY, Benedetta Brevini et al. eds. 123, 134 (New York: Palgrave Macmillan, 2013); *see also* Mark Fenster, *Disclosure's Effects: WikiLeaks and Transparency*, 97 IOWA L. REV. 753, 796 (2012).

180. In contrast to the Pentagon Papers, with which Ellsberg was deeply familiar, leaks today "encompass vast quantities of records that the leaker likely knows nothing about, if he or she has even read them." Margaret B. Kwoka, *Leaking and Legitimacy*, 48 U.C. DAVIS L. REV. 1387, 1390 (2015); *see also* Strauss, *supra* note 141, at 123, 128 ("[T]he people who have access to [those] records today are more likely to have only a vague sense of what is in those records and how significant their disclosure would be."). Indeed, "[t]he common thread of leaked records in recent high profile cases is simply that the leaker has access to them." Kwoka, *Leaking and Legitimacy*, at 1390.

181. McCurdy, *supra* note 179, at 134.

182. Strauss, *supra* note 141, at 123, 128.

183. Fenster, *supra* note 179, at 796 ("In the wake of the WikiLeaks disclosures, many both within and outside the government charged that the effort to share information had left data networks insecure and classified information vulnerable to theft and leaking.").

184. *See* Nathan Alexander Sales, *Can Technology Prevent Leaks?* 8 J. NAT'L SEC. L. & POL'Y 73, 74 (2015) ("[A]uthorities should make greater use of technological measures that block leaks from happening. . . . For instance, computer systems should be built with more stringent access controls that limit which employees may access what information for which purposes."); *see* Emily Bell, *The Unintentional Press*, in THE FREE SPEECH CENTURY, Lee C. Bollinger & Geoffrey R. Stone eds. 235, 245 (New York: Oxford University Press, 2018) ("Manning and Snowden, along with Daniel Ellsberg's release of the Pentagon Papers, showed to what degree the centralization and digitization of government data had expanded the amount of information stored, and how the analysis needed far more people and therefore much wider access given to civilians."); Patrick McCurdy, *From the Pentagon Papers to Cablegate: How the Network Society Has Changed Leaking*, in BEYOND WIKILEAKS: IMPLICATIONS FOR THE FUTURE OF COMMUNICATIONS, JOURNALISM AND SOCIETY Benedetta Brevini et al. eds. 123, 134 (New York: Palgrave Macmillan, 2013) (explaining that after the September 11 attacks, the government "balloon[ed] personnel and resources dedicated to generating, gathering and sharing" sensitive information).

185. *See, e.g.*, Daniel Wirls, *Eisenhower Called It the 'Military-Industrial Complex'; It's Vastly Bigger Now*, WASH. POST (June 26, 2019); Deborah Charles & Ben Berkowitz, *NSA Leak Prompts Questions over U.S. Reliance on Contractors*, REUTERS (June 10, 2013) ("The government workforce has pretty much stayed the same over the last 30 to 40 years but we've supplemented that with a contractor workforce that has grown dramatically." (quoting Scott Amey, general counsel of the Project on Government Oversight)); Max Fisher, *What's in the Washington Post Story Terrifying the Intelligence Community?* ATLANTIC (July 18, 2010) ("Officially, according to a 2008 [Office of the Director of National Intelligence] study of human capital within the [Intelligence Community], nearly 40,000 private contractors are working for intelligence agencies, bringing the total number of [Intelligence Community] employees to more than 135,000." (quoting national security reporter Tim Shorrock)); Marc Ambinder, *Previewing Priest: Inside the Semi-Secret World of Intelligence Contractors*, ATLANTIC (July 16, 2010) ("Since 9/11, the intelligence community has welcomed a surge in contractors while building a larger civilian counterterrorism workforce—a larger national security state.").

186. *See* McCurdy, *supra* note 179, at 135 (arguing that modern leaks can "be seen as a function of the volume of data available and the ease with which it can be spread around and shared"); Mary-Rose Papandrea, *The Publication of National Security Information in the Digital Age*, 5 J. NAT'L SEC. L. & POL'Y 119, 119 (2011) ("New technology has made it much easier to leak and otherwise disseminate national security information.").

187. *See* Strauss, *supra* note 141, at 123, 127; Kwoka, *supra* note 180, at 1391 ("Technology has also eased the process of leaking. Long gone are [Ellsberg's] dark nights with photocopy machines; hard copy records have been replaced by easily stored, saved, replicated, and disseminated digital records."); David E. Sanger & Eric Schmitt, *Snowden Used Low-Cost Tool to Best N.S.A.*, N.Y. TIMES (Feb. 8, 2014), https://www.nytimes.com/2014/02/

09/us/snowden-used-low-cost-tool-to-best-nsa.html?pagewanted=all&_r=0 ("Using 'web crawler' software designed to search, index and back up a website, Mr. Snowden 'scraped data out of our systems' while he went about his day job, according to a senior intelligence official."). *See also* McCurdy, *supra* note 179, at 136; Papandrea, *Leaker Traitor Whistleblower Spy*, *supra* note 49, at 459 ("The digital age has led to the collection of incredible amounts of data, much of which is accessible in digital form (and thus more easily copied and disseminated).").

188. *See* Bell, *supra* note 184, at 245 ("An important new phenomenon resulting from large-scale digitization of information has been the 'deluge leak': the release of vast caches of documents too numerous for humans to parse efficiently, easily circulated on thumb drives and CDs.").

189. Kwoka, *supra* note 180, at 1410.

190. Even post-publication, news outlets today struggle to analyze leaked information. Bell, *supra* note 184, at 245 (arguing that the centralization and digitization of so much sensitive information "challenged news organizations working with these new types of deluge leaks to analyze such vast troves that even the leakers themselves had little idea of the contents").

191. Kwoka, *supra* note 180, at 1403–4.

192. *See* Papandrea, *Publication of National Security Information*, *supra* note 188, at 123–24 ("Technology has developed to make it possible for individuals to exchange information anonymously, making it impossible for the government to subpoena the identity of leakers from the website that received the information.").

193. *See* Kwoka, *supra* note 180, at 1410 ("The anonymity of the leaker may also pose practical difficulties verifying the authenticity of leaked records, thereby increasing the risk of misinformation.").

194. Ursula M. Wilder, *Why Spy Now? The Psychology of Espionage and Leaking in the Digital Age*, STUDIES IN INTELLIGENCE 61, no. 2 (June 2017), https://www.cia.gov/library/center-for-the-study-of-intelligence/csi-publications/csi-studies/studies/vol-61-no-2/pdfs/why-spy-why-leak.pdf. In analyzing the psychology behind espionage, Wilder has explained that individuals are motivated to commit espionage, including through acts like leaking, by "personality pathology or vulnerabilities, a precipitating life crisis, and opportunity (finding a safe customer for the spy's espionage services)." *Id.* at 1.

195. *See* Kwoka, *supra* note 180, at 1390–91 ("In a sense, the Pentagon Papers leak was a classic whistleblower leak in which an insider publicly announces secret government conduct believed to be illegal or immoral. [Recent] leakers go beyond protesting a single government policy as whistleblowers do; instead, they also describe themselves as transparency advocates.").

196. Papandrea, *Publication of National Security Information*, *supra* note 306, at 119 ("As the gathering and distribution of news and information becomes more widely dispersed, and the act of informing the public more participatory and collaborative . . . determining who is engaging in journalism and what constitutes the press has become increasingly difficult.").

197. Bell, *supra* note 177, at 240 ("[p]eople who do not routinely have access to mainstream media can benefit from the egalitarian nature of modern social publishing tools"); McCurdy, *supra* note 172, at 124 (explaining that platforms like WikiLeaks are capable of exerting "counter-power" that tries to alter power dynamics within society, including by "harnessing the communicative capabilities of the [internet] to produce and distribute its message to a global audience"); Tim Wu, *Is the First Amendment Obsolete?* in THE FREE SPEECH CENTURY, Lee C. Bollinger & Geoffrey R. Stone eds. 272, 273 (New York: Oxford University Press, 2018) ("The massive decline in barriers to publishing makes information abundant, especially when speakers congregate on brightly lit matters of public controversy."); Yochai Benkler, *A Free Irresponsible Press: Wikileaks and the Battle over the Soul of the Networked Fourth Estate*, 46 HARV. C.R.-C.L. L. REV. 311, 366 (2011) ("What makes the networked public sphere generally, and the networked fourth estate in particular, especially democratic, open, and diverse, is the relatively large role that decentralized, nontraditional speakers and journalists can play. These online media and citizen speakers are newly enabled by the widespread availability of low-cost machines and platforms for speech.").

198. Papandrea, *Leaker Traitor Whistleblower Spy*, *supra* note 46, at 456.

199. *See* Papandrea, *Publication of National Security Information, supra* note 188, at 123 ("Prior to the Internet, those in possession of national security information who wanted to reveal it to the public had to go through a traditional media outlet to accomplish that goal. Thus, when Daniel Ellsberg was in possession of the Pentagon Papers, he went to several major newspapers as well as the three major television networks in an effort to find an outlet. Today's leakers can deposit a treasure trove of information on any number of websites around the world designed to receive confidential information.").

200. Papandrea, *Leaker Traitor Whistleblower Spy, supra* note 49, at 456.

201. McCraw & Gikow, *supra* note 173, at 473, 488.

202. *See* BOLLINGER, *supra* note 163, at 82–83 ("[T]he extraordinary proliferation of voices on the Internet has also led to a dispiriting and sharp decline in the traditional media's audience share and, even more alarmingly, in their advertising revenues, both classified and commercial, which had been the principal financial base for American private media. . . . The simple fact is that the Internet is undermining the business model of the traditional press.").

203. *Id.* at 487–90.

204. Strauss, *supra* note 141, at 123, 128; *see also* Papandrea, *Leaker Traitor Whistleblower Spy, supra* note 49, at 456 ("From the government's perspective, foreign intermediaries like WikiLeaks are particularly dangerous because they operate outside the conventional Beltway atmosphere in which the media and government's mutually beneficial relationship exists.").

205. Bellia, *supra* note 7, at 1454. WikiLeaks also partnered with different entities across the world, leading some to question whether "entities with less significant U.S. connections would take the same guarded approach to the materials" as a domestic publisher sensitive to American national security interests would. *Id.* at 1500.

206. *See* Papandrea, *Publication of National Security Information, supra* note 188, at 124–25.

207. *See* McCraw & Gikow, *supra* note 173, at 473, 488–89.

208. Bellia, *supra* note 7, at 1479. *See id.* at 1482 ("[E]ven if the materials WikiLeaks planned to disclose contained information that could have caused grave, immediate harm to national security, thereby satisfying the standard that some Justices in the *Pentagon Papers* assumed could justify injunctive relief, it is difficult to see how the United States could have enforced an injunction against a far-flung web of redundant servers before the information was disseminated."). Indeed, the district court in *Bank Julius Baer & Co. v. WikiLeaks*, 535 F. Supp. 2d 980 (N.D. Cal. 2008), realized that it "could not confidently impose any judgment on [WikiLeaks], given the fact that the information had already been circulated globally and the site could simply evade any order to take down the documents by mirroring its site on servers around the world."

209. *See* Bellia, *supra* note 7, at 1483 ("[W]hatever force the Espionage Act might exert ex ante upon U.S. media entities or others with a significant U.S. presence to avoid publishing information that would cause grave, immediate harm, it does not necessarily shape or constrain WikiLeaks' actions in the same way."); Fenster, *supra* note 179, at 767 ("[T]he WikiLeaks model of decentralized digital distribution of illegally obtained classified information thus appears resistant—if not impervious—to efforts to contain it.").

210. Lisa O'Carroll, *Guardian Partners with New York Times over Snowden GCHQ Files,* GUARDIAN (Aug. 23, 2013), https://www.theguardian.com/uk-news/2013/aug/23/guardian-news-york-times-partnership.

211. *Id.*

212. *Id.*

Chapter 1

1. *See, e.g.,* MAJ. STAFF OF S. COMM. ON HOMELAND SEC. & GOVERNMENTAL AFFAIRS, 115TH CONG., REP. ON STATE SECRETS: HOW AN AVALANCHE OF MEDIA LEAKS IS HARMING NATIONAL SECURITY (2017); *Congressman Calls for Execution of Wikileaks*

Whistleblower, Fox News (Aug. 3, 2010), https://www.foxnews.com/politics/congressman-calls-for-execution-of-wikileaks-whistleblower.

2. *See, e.g.,* Elizabeth Goitein, *Rescuing History (and Accountability) from Secrecy*, Brennan Ctr. for Justice (Sept. 14, 2018), https://www.brennancenter.org/our-work/analysis-opinion/rescuing-history-and-accountability-secrecy; Michael M. Grynbaum & Marc Tracy, *"Frightening": Charges against Julian Assange Alarm Press Advocates*, N.Y. Times (May 23, 2019), https://www.nytimes.com/2019/05/23/business/media/assange-first-amendment-wikileaks.html; Adelia Henderson & Gabe Rottman, *As the Government Uses Spying Laws to Prosecute Leakers, the Problem of Overclassification Takes on New Urgency*, Reporters Comm. for Freedom of the Press (Aug. 26, 2019), https://www.rcfp.org/overclassification-bigger-problem-leak-hunting/.

3. *See* Letter from Eric Holder, US Att'y Gen., to Sen. Patrick Leahy, Chairman, Comm. on the Judiciary (May 22, 2013), https://www.justice.gov/slideshow/AG-letter-5-22-13.pdf.

4. The disclosure of such information might be damaging because it could, for example, put at risk a relationship with another nation where a strike might have taken place, if that country did not wish it to be known publicly that the United States acted with that country's consent.

5. The current framework for classification and declassification explicitly provides for this option, though it is rarely deployed. *See* Exec. Order No. 13526, 75 Fed. Reg. 707 (Dec. 29, 2009) (stating that "[i]n some exceptional cases . . . the need to protect such information may be outweighed by the public interest in disclosure, and in these cases the information should be declassified").

6. New York Times Co. v. United States, 403 U.S. 713 (1971).

7. Such pressure can also be brought through Freedom of Information Act (FOIA) litigation, but where the purpose is to put pressure on the government to release classified information, there is often an unauthorized disclosure that leads to such lawsuits. *See, e.g.,* Complaint, New York Times Co. v. U.S. Dep't of Justice, 915 F. Supp. 2d 508 (S.D.N.Y. 2013) (No. 12 Civ. 794).

8. *See New York Times Co.*, 403 U.S. at 717 (Black, J., concurring); *see id.* at 720 (Douglas, J., concurring).

9. *See id.* at 730 (Stewart, J., concurring).

10. *See id.* at 717 (Black, J., concurring); *see id.* at 724 (Douglas, J., concurring).

11. *See, e.g.,* Cass R. Sunstein, *Pornography and the First Amendment*, 1986 Duke L.J. 589, 602 (1986).

12. *See, e.g.,* Bruce Ackerman, The Decline and Fall of the American Republic (Cambridge, MA: Harvard University Press, 2010); Clement Fatovic, Outside the Law: Emergency and Executive Power (Baltimore: Johns Hopkins University Press, 2009); Eric A. Posner & Adrian Vermeule, The Executive Unbound: After the Madisonian Republic (New York: Oxford University Press, 2010).

13. *See* Andrew Rudalevige, The New Imperial Presidency: Renewing Presidential Power after Watergate 19–57 (Ann Arbor: University of Michigan Press, 2005).

14. This is a reference to the classic "ambition counteracting ambition" theory articulated in the *Federalist Papers*, in which Congress and the president are intended to stand in structural opposition to each other, with each side alert to "dangerous encroachments" by the other that would threaten, in addition to individual liberties, the prerogatives and the power of the opposing branch. *See* The Federalist No. 51, at 319 (James Madison), Clinton Rossiter ed. (New York: Penguin, 1961).

15. *See generally* Michael E. DeVine, Cong. Res. Serv., R45421, Congressional Oversight of Intelligence: Background and Selected Options for Further Reform (2018).

16. Congressional power over the purse has largely devolved into an up-or-down vote on comprehensive "omnibus" appropriation bills, which makes it particularly challenging to shape specific executive branch behavior. Any member interested in trying, for example, to cut off funds for a war can do so only by voting such a bill down, which may result in shutting down the federal government or at the very least will be seen as not funding US soldiers engaged in protecting the country. *See generally* Elizabeth Garrett, *Attention to Context in Statutory Interpretation: Applying the Lessons of Dynamic Statutory Interpretation to Omnibus Legislation*, 2 Issues in Legal Scholarship 1 (2002) (describing the advent of omnibus lawmaking and describing its costs and benefits).

17. *See, e.g.*, Clapper v. Amnesty Int'l USA, 568 U.S. 398 (2013).
18. *See* Robert M. Chesney, *National Security Fact Deference*, 95 Va. L. Rev. 1361 (2009).
19. *See* Thomas M. Frank, Political Questions/Judicial Answers: Does the Rule of Law Apply to Foreign Affairs? (Princeton, NJ: Princeton University Press, 1992) (criticizing the judiciary's special treatment of foreign-relations cases); Michael Glennon, Constitutional Diplomacy 314–21 (Princeton, NJ: Princeton University Press, 1990) (examining the political question doctrine).
20. *See generally* William E. Scheuerman, *Emergencies, Executive Power, and the Uncertain Future of U.S. Presidential Democracy*, 37 Law & Soc. Inquiry 743 (2012); *Emergency Powers*, Brennan Ctr. for Justice, https://www.brennancenter.org/issues/bolster-checks-balances/executive-power/emergency-powers.
21. We have been at war in Afghanistan since 2001, which is the longest war in American history—outlasting the Civil War, the Spanish-American War, World War I, World War II, and the Korean War combined. *See* Doug Bandow, *Afghanistan, the Longest War in American History*, Am. Conservative (Jan. 2, 2019), https://www.theamericanconservative.com/articles/afghanistan-the-longest-war-in-american-history-trump-withdrawal/. Moreover, it is not clear that any end is in sight.
22. *See, e.g.*, David E. Pozen, *Deep Secrecy*, 62 Stan. L. Rev. 257 (2010).
23. *See* New York Times Co. v. United States, 403 U.S. 713, 727 (1971) (Stewart, J., concurring).
24. Consider, for example, the Church hearings and the disclosure of the CIA's detainee program. There are times when the public's knowledge of certain intelligence activities has resulted in major reforms, demonstrating that there can be a meaningful difference between Congress knowing and the public knowing about such activities.
25. One might additionally argue that with the increasing distrust in government, the clear disconnect that occurs between what the government is doing and what it is saying, which sometimes occurs when classified information is not acknowledged despite widespread discussion of it, undermines the trust in government that is so critical to democracies.
26. *See* James Barron, *At Age 13, Creating the Pentagon Papers; Photocopies, at Least.*, N.Y. Times (Jan. 28, 2018), https://www.nytimes.com/2018/01/28/nyregion/pentagon-papers-robert-ellsberg.html; Niraj Chokshi, *Behind the Race to Publish the Top-Secret Pentagon Papers*, N.Y. Times (Dec. 20, 2017), https://www.nytimes.com/2017/12/20/us/pentagon-papers-post.html.
27. *See* Katherine L. Herbig, Def. Pers. & Sec. Res. Ctr., The Expanding Spectrum of Espionage by Americans, 1947–2015, at 162–63 (2017).
28. For example, when Snowden exposed how the United States tracks terrorists via emails, social media, and cell phones, Matt Olsen, then director of the National Counter-terrorism Center, noted that "[w]e've lost ability to intercept the communications of the key terrorists, operatives, and leaders. . . . We have specific examples of terrorists who have adopted greater security measures in the last year including various types of encryption." Matthew Olsen, Dir., Nat'l Counter-terrorism Ctr., Speech at the American Political Science Association Discussion on NSA Surveillance: NSA Surveillance and Its Consequences (Aug. 28, 2014). Furthermore, based on Snowden's revelations, al-Qaeda published a video guide on the internet on how to avoid detection. *See* Peter C. Oleson, *Assessing Edward Snowden: Whistleblower, Traitor, or Spy?* 21 Intelligencer 15, 18 (2015).
29. *See* Ellen Nakashima, *Weighing the Damage of the WikiLeaks Disclosure*, Wash. Post (May 8, 2011), https://www.washingtonpost.com/lifestyle/magazine/weighing-the-damage-of-the-wikileaks-disclosure/2011/05/02/AFJoBmrF_story.html (noting views of prominent officials on the WikiLeaks leaks).
30. Although the amount of classified information has increased considerably in the last fifty years, the numbers of classification decisions have fluctuated, sometimes even going down. *See* Steven Aftergood, *Number of New Secrets Hit Record Low in 2014*, Fed'n Am. Sci.: Secrecy News (June 4, 2015), https://fas.org/blogs/secrecy/2015/06/isoo-2014/. Nevertheless, there is broad agreement regarding the problem of overclassification. *See, e.g.*, James B. Bruce, Sina Beaghley & W. George Jameson, Rand Corp., Secrecy in U.S. National Security: Why a Paradigm Shift Is Needed (RAND Corporation, 2018); Mike Giglio, *The U.S. Government Keeps Too Many Secrets*, Atlantic (Oct. 3, 2019),

https://www.theatlantic.com/politics/archive/2019/10/us-government-has-secrecy-problem/599380/.

31. *See* Rep. of the Comm'n on Protecting and Reducing Gov't Secrecy, S. Doc. No. 105-2, at 8 (1997) (arguing that when the public is left "uninformed of decisions of great consequence . . . there may be a heightened degree of cynicism and distrust of government").

32. More than a dozen US government committees or commissions have been established to address these challenges since World War II, and each of them concluded that overclassification is a problem. *See* Elizabeth Goitein & David M. Shapiro, Brennan Ctr. for Justice, Reducing Overclassification through Accountability 4–5 (2011).

33. There was an attempt to counter such bias by President Obama in Executive Order 13,526, which included a requirement that records not be classified "[i]f there is significant doubt about the appropriate level of classification." 75 Fed. Reg. 707 (Dec. 29, 2009). It is not clear to what extent this requirement made a difference.

34. *See* Info. Sec. Oversight Off., 2017 Report to the President 17 (2017) (finding, on review of ten agencies, that approximately 64 percent of documents reviewed were marked improperly). This is not surprising to any of us who have served in jobs that required us to deal with a significant volume of classified information from different agencies. For example, note that this same report had identified almost three thousand active security classification guides across the various agencies. *See id.* at 12.

35. *See, e.g.,* Geoffrey R. Stone, *Free Speech in the Twenty-First Century: Ten Lessons from the Twentieth Century,* 36 Pepp. L. Rev. 273, 277 (2009) (explaining "pretext effect").

36. The exact contours of First Amendment rights have shifted over time. *See generally* Jud Campbell, *Natural Rights and the First Amendment,* 127 Yale L.J. 246 (2017) (highlighting the influence that individual Justices have on First Amendment analysis).

37. *See* DeVine, *supra* note 15.

38. *See* 5 U.S.C. § 552(a)(3)(A) (2018).

Chapter 2

1. *See, e.g.,* Niraj Choksi, *Behind the Race to Publish the Top-Secret Pentagon Papers,* N.Y. Times (Dec. 20, 2017), https://www.nytimes.com/2017/12/20/us/pentagon-papers-post.html.

2. *See* Glenn Greenwald, *NSA Collecting Phone Records of Millions of Verizon Customers Daily,* Guardian (June 6, 2013), https://www.theguardian.com/world/2013/jun/06/nsa-phone-records-verizon-court-order.

3. *See* Choksi, *supra* note 1.

4. *See* New York Times Co. v. United States, 403 U.S. 713, 714 (1971).

5. *See* Patricia L. Bellia, *WikiLeaks and the Institutional Framework for National Security Disclosures,* 121 Yale L.J. 1448, 1506 (2012) ("The Pentagon Papers case foreclosed injunctive relief to prevent further disclosure of national security information, at least absent a showing that disclosure would cause grave and immediate harm. Justice Black and Justice Douglas would have held that injunctive relief to block publication is never available, and Justice Brennan's position was not a great distance from that categorical approach. The remaining Justices, however, acknowledged the possibility of injunctive relief in narrow circumstances.").

6. *See, e.g.,* United States v. Marchetti, 466 F.2d 1309, 1312 n.1, 1315–18 (4th Cir. 1972) ("Although the First Amendment protects criticism of the government, nothing in the Constitution requires the government to divulge information . . . [and] the Government's need for secrecy in this area lends justification to a system of prior restraint against disclosure by employees and former employees of classified information obtained during the course of employment. . . . For the stated reasons, our conclusion is that the secrecy agreement executed by Marchetti at the commencement of his employment was not in derogation of Marchetti's constitutional rights. Its provision for submission of material to the CIA for approval prior to publication is enforceable, provided the CIA acts promptly upon such submissions and withholds approval of publication only of information which is classified and which has not been placed in the public domain by prior disclosure."); Alfred A. Knopf, Inc. v. Colby, 509 F.2d 1362, 1370 (4th Cir. 1975) ("We decline to modify our previous holding that the First Amendment is no bar against an injunction forbidding the disclosure of classifiable

information . . . when (1) the classified information was acquired, during the course of his employment, by an employee of a United States agency or department in which such information is handled and (2) its disclosure would violate a solemn agreement made by the employee at the commencement of his employment. With respect to such information, by his execution of the secrecy agreement and his entry into the confidential employment relationship, he effectively relinquished his First Amendment rights.").

7. *See, e.g.,* United States v. Morison, 844 F.2d 1057, 1069–70 (4th Cir. 1988) ("[I]t seems beyond controversy that a recreant intelligence department employee who had abstracted from the government files secret intelligence information and had willfully transmitted or given it to one 'not entitled to receive it' as did the defendant in this case, is not entitled to invoke the First Amendment as a shield to immunize his act of thievery. To permit the thief thus to misuse the Amendment would be to prostitute the salutary purposes of the First Amendment. . . . In summary, we conclude that there is no basis in the legislative record for finding that Congress intended to limit the applicability of sections 793(d) and (e) to 'classic spying' or to exempt transmittal by a governmental employee, who entrusted with secret national defense material, had in violation of the rules of his intelligence unit, leaked to the press. Nor do we find any authority for the proposition that Congress could not validly prohibit a government employee having possession of secret military intelligence material from transmitting that material to 'one not entitled to receive it,' whether that recipient was the press or not, without infringing the employee's rights under the First Amendment."); *id.* at 1077 ("The mere fact that one has stolen a document in order that he may deliver it to the press, whether for money or for other personal gain, will not immunize him from responsibility for his criminal act. To use the first amendment for such a purpose would be to convert the first amendment into a warrant for thievery. As the Supreme Court made clear in *Branzburg,* [] the First Amendment may not be used for such a sordid purpose, either to enable the governmental employee to excuse his act of theft or to excuse him, as in *Snepp* and *Marchetti,* from his contractual obligation.").

8. *Cf.* Branzburg v. Hayes, 408 U.S. 665, 691–92 (1972) (stating, in the context of rejecting a constitutionally based reporter's privilege to not testify against a source, that "[i]t would be frivolous to assert—and no one does in these cases—that the First Amendment, in the interest of securing news or otherwise, confers a license on either the reporter or his news sources to violate valid criminal laws. Although stealing documents or private wiretapping could provide newsworthy information, neither reporter nor source is immune from conviction for such conduct, whatever the impact on the flow of news").

9. *See, e.g.,* Bartnicki v. Vopper, 532 U.S. 514, 528–30 (2001) (noting that "[i]n *New York Times Co. v. United States* . . . the Court upheld the right of the press to publish information of great public concern obtained from documents stolen by a third party. . . . However, *New York Times v. United States* raised, but did not resolve the question whether, in cases where information has been acquired unlawfully by a newspaper or by a source, government may ever punish not only the unlawful acquisition, but the ensuing publication as well. . . . The question here, however, is a narrower version of that still-open question. Simply put, the issue here is this: Where the punished publisher of information has obtained the information in question in a manner lawful in itself but from a source who has obtained it unlawfully, may the government punish the ensuing publication of that information based on the defect in a chain? . . . The normal method of deterring unlawful conduct is to impose an appropriate punishment on the person who engages in it. . . . [I]t would be quite remarkable to hold that speech by a law-abiding possessor of information can be suppressed in order to deter conduct by a non-law-abiding third party. Although there are some rare occasions in which a law suppressing one party's speech may be justified by an interest in deterring criminal conduct by another . . . this is not such a case") (internal quotation marks and citations omitted).

10. *Compare, e.g., Morison,* 844 F.2d at 1077 (upholding a conviction under 18 U.S.C. § 641) *with* United States v. Jeter, 775 F.2d 670, 682 (6th Cir. 1985) ("We do not attempt to determine the constitutionality of Section 641 in a 'Pentagon Papers' kind of situation.").

11. *See* Bellia, *supra* note 5, at 1507 ("To date, *United States v. Progressive,* a case involving an injunction prohibiting the Progressive magazine from publishing certain technical information about the construction of nuclear weapons, remains the sole instance in which a court granted injunctive relief prohibiting publication based on a claim that disclosure threatened national

security."); *see also* United States v. Progressive, Inc., 467 F. Supp. 990 (W.D. Wisc. 1979), *dismissed*, 610 F.2d 819 (7th Cir. 1979).

12. *See, e.g.*, Adam Liptak, *Reporter Jailed after Refusing to Name Source*, N.Y. TIMES (July 7, 2005), https://www.nytimes.com/2005/07/07/politics/reporter-jailed-after-refusing-to-name-source.html.

13. *See* PRESIDENT'S REVIEW GRP. ON INTELLIGENCE AND COMMC'NS TECH., LIBERTY AND SECURITY IN A CHANGING WORLD 75–77 (Dec. 12, 2013), https://obamawhitehouse. archives.gov/sites/default/files/docs/2013-12-12_rg_final_report.pdf ("[A]lthough recent disclosures and commentary have created the impression in some quarters that NSA surveillance is indiscriminate and pervasive across the globe, that is not the case. NSA focuses on collecting foreign intelligence information that is relevant to protecting the national security of the United States and its allies. Moreover, much of what NSA collects is shared with the governments of many other nations for the purpose of enhancing their national security and the personal security of their citizens. . . . Significantly, and in stark contrast to the pre-FISA era, the Review Group found no evidence of illegality or other abuse of authority for the purpose of targeting domestic political activity."); *see also* PRIVACY AND CIVIL LIBERTIES OVERSIGHT BD., REPORT ON THE TELEPHONE RECORDS PROGRAM CONDUCTED UNDER SECTION 215 OF THE USA PATRIOT ACT AND ON THE OPERATIONS OF THE FOREIGN INTELLIGENCE SURVEILLANCE COURT 9–10 (Jan. 23, 2014), https://www.pclob.gov/library/215-Report_ on_the_Telephone_Records_Program.pdf ("Over the years, a series of compliance issues were brought to the attention of the FISA court by the government. However, none of these compliance issues involved significant intentional misuse of the system. Nor has the Board seen any evidence of bad faith or misconduct on the part of any government officials or agents involved with the program. Rather, the compliance issues were recognized by the FISC—and are recognized by the Board—as a product of the program's technological complexity and vast scope, illustrating the risks inherent in such a program.") (footnote omitted).

14. *See* James R. Clapper, *Remarks as Delivered: Worldwide Threat Assessment to the House Permanent Select Committee on Intelligence*, OFFICE OF THE DIR. OF NAT'L INTELLIGENCE (Feb. 4, 2014), https://fas.org/irp/congress/2014_hr/020414clapper-del.pdf.

15. *Id.*

16. *Id.*

17. *Id.*

18. *See* Kevin Liptak, *Ex-Counterterror Chief: U.S. Lost Track of Terrorists after Snowden*, CNN (Oct. 21, 2014), https://www.cnn.com/2014/10/21/politics/olsen-nsa/index.html.

19. *See* Deb Richman, *Costs of Snowden Leak Still Mounting 5 Years Later*, ASSOCIATED PRESS (June 4, 2018), https://apnews.com/797f390ee28b4bfbb0e1b13cfedf0593/ Costs-of-Snowden-leak-still-mounting-5-years-later.

20. *See Snowden Leaks "Worst Ever Loss to British Intelligence,"* BBC (Oct. 11, 2013), https://www. bbc.com/news/uk-24486649.

21. *See, e.g.*, Claire Cain Miller, *Revelations of N.S.A. Spying Cost U.S. Tech Companies*, N.Y. TIMES (Mar. 21, 2014), https://www.nytimes.com/2014/03/22/business/fallout-from-snowden-hurting-bottom-line-of-tech-companies.html (citing two studies estimating losses at up to $35 billion and $180 billion); Elizabeth Dwoskin, *New Report: Snowden Revelations Hurt U.S. Companies*, WALL ST. J. (July 30, 2014), https://www.wsj.com/articles/BL-DGB-36772/ (citing a study reviewing other studies and estimating losses of between $22 billion and $180 billion).

22. *See* HOUSE PERMANENT SELECT COMM. ON INTELLIGENCE, REVIEW OF THE UNAUTHORIZED DISCLOSURES OF FORMER NATIONAL SECURITY AGENCY CONTRACTOR EDWARD SNOWDEN, H.R. REP. NO. 114-891, at 20–21 (2016).

23. *Id.* at 22.

24. *Id.*

25. *Id.* at 24.

26. *Id.* at 20, 23–28.

27. *See* Geoffrey R. Stone, *What I Told the NSA*, HUFFINGTON POST (May 31, 2014), https:// www.huffpost.com/entry/what-i-told-the-nsa_b_5065447 ("I am a long-time civil libertarian, a member of the National Advisory Council of the ACLU, and a former Chair of the

Board of the American Constitution Society. To say I was skeptical about the NSA is, in truth, an understatement. I came away from my work on the Review Group with a view of the NSA that I found quite surprising. Not only did I find that the NSA had helped to thwart numerous terrorist plots against the United States and its allies in the years since 9/11, but I also found that it is an organization that operates with a high degree of integrity and a deep commitment to the rule of law. . . . The Review Group found no evidence that the NSA had knowingly or intentionally engaged in unlawful or unauthorized activity. To the contrary, it has put in place carefully-crafted internal procedures to ensure that it operates within the bounds of its lawful authority. It gradually became apparent to me that in the months after Edward Snowden began releasing information about the government's foreign intelligence surveillance activities, the NSA was being severely—and unfairly—demonized by its critics. Rather than being a rogue agency that was running amok in disregard of the Constitution and laws of the United States, the NSA was doing its job. It pained me to realize that the hard-working, dedicated, patriotic employees of the NSA, who were often working for far less pay than they could have earned in the private sector because they were determined to help protect their nation from attack, were being castigated in the press for the serious mistakes made, not by them, but by presidents, the Congress, and the courts."); *see also* PRESIDENT'S REVIEW GRP. ON INTELLIGENCE AND COMMC'NS TECH., *supra* note 13, at 75.

28. *See* Terminiello v. City of Chicago, 337 U.S. 1, 37 (1949) (Jackson, J., dissenting) ("This Court has gone far toward accepting the doctrine that civil liberty means the removal of all restraints from these crowds and that all local attempts to maintain order are impairments of the liberty of the citizen. The choice is not between order and liberty. It is between liberty with order and anarchy without either. There is danger that, if the Court does not temper its doctrinaire logic with a little practical wisdom, it will convert the constitutional Bill of Rights into a suicide pact.").

29. *See Examining the Costs of Overclassification Transparency and Security: Hearing before the H. Comm. on Oversight and Gov't Reform*, 114th Cong. (2016).

30. *See* DEFENCE AND SECURITY MEDIA ADVISORY COMM., *How the System Works*, https://dsma.uk/how-the-system-works/; *see also* GARY ROSS, WHO WATCHES THE WATCHMEN? THE CONFLICT BETWEEN NATIONAL SECURITY AND THE FREEDOM OF THE PRESS 143–45 (Washington, DC: National Intelligence Press, 2011).

Chapter 3

1. I served as the CIA's chief operating officer from 2006 to 2008, as its head of analysis from 2008 to 2010, and as its deputy director—and twice acting director—from 2010 to 2013.

2. *See* Exec. Order No. 13526, 75 Fed. Reg. 707 (Dec. 29, 2009), for a full discussion of classification and declassification authorities.

3. Presidential Memorandum of May 23, 2019, *Agency Cooperation with Attorney General's Review of Intelligence Activities Relating to the 2016 Presidential Campaigns*, 2019 WL 2241656 (White House).

4. MICHAEL MORELL & BILL HARLOW, THE GREAT WAR OF OUR TIME: CIA'S FIGHT AGAINST TERRORISM FROM AL-QAIDA TO ISIS 295–297 (New York: Twelve, 2015).

5. Ames is a former CIA officer who spied for the Soviet Union from 1985 to 1993. Convicted of espionage in 1994, Ames is serving a life sentence, without the possibility of parole. Hanssen is a former FBI agent who spied for both the Soviet Union and Russia from 1979 to 2001. His espionage was described by the DOJ as "possibly the worst intelligence disaster in US history." He is currently serving fifteen life sentences.

6. *1971 The Year in Review: The Pentagon Papers*, transcript of audio story, United Press International (1971), https://www.upi.com/Archives/Audio/Events-of-1971/The-Pentagon-Papers/.

7. English transcript of interview by Hubert Siebel with Edward Snowden, German Channel ARD (Jan. 26, 2014).

8. Tom Ramstack, *WikiLeaks Case Harms US Diplomacy, Manning Sentencing Told*, REUTERS WORLD NEWS, Aug. 5, 2013.

9. REVIEW OF THE UNAUTHORIZED DISCLOSURES OF FORMER NATIONAL SECURITY AGENCY CONTRACTOR EDWARD SNOWDEN, H.R. REP. NO. 114-891 (2016).

10. *Snowden "Did More Damage to the Private Sector" Than Government, Says Former Intelligence Lead*, CNBC (Nov. 5, 2019, updated Dec. 11, 2019), https://www.cnbc.com/2019/11/05/edward-snowden-hurt-private-sector-more-than-government-sue-gordon.html.

11. NAT'L COMM'N ON TERRORIST ATTACKS UPON THE UNITED STATES, THE 9/11 COMMISSION REPORT: FINAL REPORT OF THE NATIONAL COMMISSION ON TERRORIST ATTACKS UPON THE UNITED STATES 127–128 (New York: W. W. Norton, 2004).

12. RICHARD A. CLARKE, MICHAEL MORELL, GEOFFREY R. STONE, CASS R. SUNSTEIN & PETER SWIRE, THE NSA REPORT: LIBERTY AND SECURITY IN A CHANGING WORLD: THE PRESIDENT'S REVIEW GROUP ON INTELLIGENCE AND COMMUNICATIONS (Princeton, NJ: Princeton University Press, 2014).

Chapter 4

1. *See Verizon Forced to Hand over Telephone Data: Full Court Ruling*, GUARDIAN (June 5, 2013), https://www.theguardian.com/world/interactive/2013/jun/06/verizon-telephone-data-court-order; *see also* Glenn Greenwald, *NSA Collecting Phone Records of Millions of Verizon Customers Daily*, GUARDIAN (June 6, 2013), https://www.theguardian.com/world/2013/jun/06/nsa-phone-records-verizon-court-order.

2. 50 U.S.C. § 1861 (2001).

3. The 215 Program was summarized by the Privacy and Civil Liberties Oversight Board (PCLOB) as follows:

> The NSA's telephone records program is operated under an order issued by the FISA court pursuant to Section 215 of the Patriot Act, an order that is renewed approximately every ninety days. The program is intended to identify communications among known and unknown terrorism suspects, particularly those located inside the United States. When the NSA identifies communications that may be associated with terrorism, it issues intelligence reports to other federal agencies, such as the FBI, that work to prevent terrorist attacks. The FISC order authorizes the NSA to collect nearly all detail records generated by certain telephone companies in the United States, and specifies detailed rules for the use and retention of these records. Call detail records typically include much of the information that appears on a customer's telephone bill: the date and time of a call, its duration, and the participating telephone numbers. Such information is commonly referred to as a type of "metadata." The records collected by NSA under this program do not, however, include the content of any telephone conversation.

> PRIVACY AND CIVIL LIBERTIES OVERSIGHT BOARD, REPORT ON THE TELEPHONE RECORDS PROGRAM CONDUCTED UNDER SECTION 215 OF THE USA PATRIOT ACT AND ON THE OPERATIONS OF THE FOREIGN INTELLIGENCE SURVEILLANCE COURT, at 8 (Jan. 23, 2014) [hereafter PCLOB 215 REPORT].

4. *Edward Snowden: The Whistleblower behind the NSA Surveillance Revelations*, GUARDIAN (June 11, 2013), https://www.theguardian.com/world/2013/jun/09/edward-snowden-nsa-whistleblower-surveillance.

5. *See* Andy Greenberg, *Snowden: I Left the NSA Clues, but They Couldn't Find Them*, WIRED (Aug. 13, 2014), https://www.wired.com/2014/08/snowden-breadcrumbs/; *but see* Glenn Greenwald, *Keith Alexander Unplugged: On Bush/Obama, 1.7 Million Stolen Documents and Other Matters*, INTERCEPT (May 8, 2014), https://theintercept.com/2014/05/08/keith-alexander-unplugged-bushobama-matters/ (disputing the 1.7 million number).

6. *See* Kim Zetter, *Snowden Smuggled Documents from NSA on a Thumb Drive*, WIRED (June 13, 2013), https://www.wired.com/2013/06/snowden-thumb-drive/.

7. *Id.*

8. *See* James Barron, *At Age 13, Creating the Pentagon Papers; Photocopies, at Least.*, N.Y. TIMES (Jan. 28, 2018), https://www.nytimes.com/2018/01/28/nyregion/pentagon-papers-robert-ellsberg.html.

9. *See* James L. Greenfield, *How the* New York Times *Published the Pentagon Papers*, SALON (Dec. 17, 2017), https://www.salon.com/2017/12/17/how-the-new-york-times-published-the-pentagon-papers/.

10. *See id.*

11. Presidential Policy Directive 28: Signals Intelligence Activities (Jan. 17, 2014) [hereafter PPD-28], https://obamawhitehouse.archives.gov/the-press-office/2014/01/17/presidential-policy-directive-signals-intelligence-activities.

12. *See generally* Barack Obama, Remarks at the Department of Justice Regarding NSA Reforms (Jan. 17, 2014) [hereafter Obama DOJ speech], transcript available at https://www.washingtonpost.com/politics/full-text-of-president-obamas-jan-17-speech-on-nsa-reforms/2014/01/17/fa33590a-7f8c-11e3-9556-4a4bf7bcbd84_story.html.

13. *See* Andy Greenberg, *After Six Years in Exile, Edward Snowden Explains Himself*, WIRED (Sept. 16, 2019), https://www.wired.com/story/after-six-years-in-exile-edward-snowden-explains-himself/.

14. *See* Criminal Complaint, United States v. Edward J. Snowden, No. 1:13 CR 265 (E.D. Va. June 14, 2013) (citing 18 U.S.C. § 793(d) ("unauthorized communication of national defense information") and 18 U.S.C. § 798(a)(3) ("willful communication of classified communications intelligence information to an unauthorized person")).

15. An important potential caveat to this media/non-media distinction is the 2018 indictment of WikiLeaks founder Julian Assange for conspiring to violate anti-hacking laws by helping Manning hack government systems to procure classified files for publication by WikiLeaks. *See* Indictment, United States v. Assange, No. 1:18-CR-00111-CMH (E.D. Va. Mar. 6, 2018); Charlie Savage et al., *Julian Assange Arrested in London as U.S. Unseals Hacking Conspiracy Indictment*, N.Y. TIMES (Apr. 11, 2019), https://www.nytimes.com/2019/04/11/world/europe/julian-assange-wikileaks-ecuador-embassy.html. A superseding indictment added charges for soliciting classified information from Manning. *See* Superseding Indictment, United States v. Assange, No. 1:18-CR-00111-CMH (E.D. Va. May 23, 2019); *see also* Charlie Savage, *Assange Indicted under Espionage Act, Raising First Amendment Issues*, N.Y. TIMES (May 23, 2019), https://www.nytimes.com/2019/05/23/us/politics/assange-indictment.html (for the First Amendment concerns raised). DOJ sought to distinguish Assange and WikiLeaks from the traditional press ("Julian Assange is no journalist"), emphasizing that "[i]t is not and has never been the Department's policy to target the press for reporting," and pointing to WikiLeaks' publication of names of sources in a war zone as something legitimate journalists would not do. Assistant Attorney Gen. for Nat'l Sec. John C. Demers, Remarks as Prepared for Delivery from the Briefing Announcing the Superseding Indictment of Julian Assange (May 23, 2019).

16. 403 U.S. 713 (per curiam).

17. *Id.* at 714.

18. *See id.* at 723 n.3 (Douglas, J., concurring).

19. *See id.* at 741 (Marshall, J., concurring); *see also* United States v. Russo, Crim. No. 9373-(WMB)-CD (filed Dec. 29, 1971) (C.D. Cal. May 11, 1973) (C.D. Cal. dismissed May 11, 1973) (later prosecution of Ellsberg, ultimately dismissed for governmental misconduct, not First Amendment reasons, as discussed in Ellsberg v. Mitchell, 709 F.2d 51, 52–53 (D.C. Cir. 1983)).

20. The case did not explicitly *reject* a First Amendment "right to know," but it also never recognized one. As later jurisprudence clarified, "[t]he Constitution is not a Freedom of Information Act . . . and it permits legislative bodies or executive officials to fashion public access policies regarding government information according to their respective visions of the public interest." Bruce E. Fein, *Access to Classified Information: Constitutional and Statutory Dimensions*, 26 WM. & MARY L. REV. 805, 820 (1985) (discussing Houchins v. KQED, 438 U.S. 1 (1978)); *see* Dhiab v. Trump, 852 F.3d 1087, 1091–95 (D.C. Cir. 2017).

21. *See* United States v. Marchetti, 466 F.2d 1309 (4th Cir. 1972); Alfred A. Knopf, Inc. v. Colby, 509 F.2d 1362 (4th Cir. 1975); Snepp v. United States, 444 U.S. 507 (1980); Haig v. Agee, 453 U.S. 280 (1981).

22. *See* Marchetti, 466 F.2d at 1317; Colby, 509 F.2d at 1370; Snepp, 444 U.S. at 509–10.

23. *See* Marchetti, 466 F.2d at 1317–18. Similarly, in a context with the opposite outcome but harmonious logic, the Supreme Court rejected prior restraints on the press except in circumstances involving "direct, immediate and irreparable damage to our Nation or its people." Nebraska Press Ass'n v. Stuart, 427 U.S. 539, 593 (1976) (Powell, J., concurring) (quoting New York Times, Co. v. United States, 403 U.S. at 730 (Stewart, J., concurring)). The Court recognized that judges should not act as "judicial censors" making merits-based decisions about the net value of different speech acts. Nebraska Press Ass'n, 427 U.S. at 573.

24. This essay does not address the important debate about the use of the Espionage Act to address unauthorized disclosures of classified information by government employees and others.

25. Obama DOJ speech, *supra* note 12.

26. *See* CHARLIE SAVAGE, POWER WARS: INSIDE OBAMA'S POST-9/11 PRESIDENCY, 358–68 (New York: Back Bay, 2015) (arguing that anti-leak prosecutions under the Espionage Act chill socially beneficial speech and create a de facto "official secrets" law); *id.* at 362 ("[L]eaks serve as a pressure-release valve for a particular classified fact . . . for which there was an overriding public interest in disclosure notwithstanding the intelligence bureaucracy's insistence on keeping it secret. But the leak crackdown jammed the valve shut.").

27. To be clear, this essay only addresses classified speech by government employees and not other forms of speech protected by the First Amendment, and it does not advocate for prior restraint on nonclassified speech by government employees.

28. Nebraska Press Ass'n, 427 U.S. at 605.

29. In FOIA litigation, courts have historically deferred to the executive branch to avoid making determinations about whether properly classified material in fact implicates the national security interest. *See* DEP'T OF JUSTICE, DEPARTMENT OF JUSTICE GUIDE TO THE FREEDOM OF INFORMATION ACT: EXEMPTION 1, at 141–42 & 141 n.4 (2009), https://www.justice.gov/archive/oip/foia_guide09/exemption1.pdf (collecting cases). However, the protracted litigation about government documents dealing with a drone strike on a US citizen suggests that trend could be changing. *See* New York Times Co. v. U.S. Dep't of Justice, 752 F.3d 123, 140–41 (2d Cir. 2014), *opinion revised and superseded*, 756 F.3d 100 (2d Cir. 2014), *opinion amended on denial of reh'g*, 758 F.3d 436 (2d Cir. 2013), *supplemented*, 762 F.3d 233 (2d Cir. 2014).

30. *See* Greenberg, *After Six Years in Exile*, *supra* note 13.

31. United States v. Morison, 844 F.2d 1057, 1077 (4th Cir. 1988).

32. *See* Jack Goldsmith et al., *Bombshell: Initial Thoughts on the* Washington Post's *Game-Changing Story*, LAWFARE (May 15, 2017), https://www.lawfareblog.com/bombshell-initial-thoughts-washington-posts-game-changing-story (citing Dep't of the Navy v. Egan, 484 U.S. 518 (1988)).

33. *See The Law of Leaks*, LAWFARE (Feb. 15, 2017), https://www.lawfareblog.com/law-leaks.

34. Jack Goldsmith & Ben Wittes, *The "Grand Bargain" at Risk: What's at Stake When the President Alleges Politics in Intelligence*, LAWFARE (Apr. 4, 2017) [hereafter *Grand Bargain*], https://www.lawfareblog.com/grand-bargain-risk-whats-stake-when-president-alleges-politics-intelligence (arguing that post-Watergate bipartisan reforms conferred much-needed legitimacy on the IC and that anti-Trump leaks from within the IC risk involving it in a political back-and-forth that could undo the hard-won perception of neutrality central to the public legitimacy of intelligence activities).

35. *See, e.g.,* Mark Hosenball, *Russia Used Social Media for Widespread Meddling in U.S. Politics: Reports*, ASSOCIATED PRESS (Dec. 17, 2018), https://www.reuters.com/article/us-usa-trump-russia-socialmedia/russia-used-social-media-for-widespread-meddling-in-u-s-politics-reports-idUSKBN1OG257; Ellen Nakashima, *With a Series of Major Hacks, China Builds a Database on Americans*, WASH. POST (June 5, 2015), https://www.washingtonpost.com/world/national-security/in-a-series-of-hacks-china-appears-to-building-a-database-on-americans/2015/06/05/d2af51fa-0ba3-11e5-95fd-d580f1c5d44e_story.html.

36. *See* Andy Greenberg, *The Untold Story of NotPetya, the Most Devastating Cyberattack in History*, WIRED (Aug. 22, 2018), https://www.wired.com/story/notpetya-cyberattack-ukraine-russia-code-crashed-the-world/.

37. *See, e.g.*, Barton Gellman et al., *In NSA-Intercepted Data, Those Not Targeted Far Outnumber the Foreigners Who Are*, Wash. Post. (July 5, 2014), https://www.washingtonpost.com/world/national-security/in-nsa-intercepted-data-those-not-targeted-far-outnumber-the-foreigners-who-are/2014/07/05/8139adf8-045a-11e4-8572-4b1b969b6322_story.html (withholding certain details "*to avoid interfering with ongoing operations*").

38. *See* Zachary K. Goldman, *The Emergence of Intelligence Governance, in* GLOBAL INTELLIGENCE OVERSIGHT: GOVERNING SECURITY IN THE 21ST CENTURY 209, Zachary K. Goldman & Samuel Rascoff eds. (New York: Oxford University Press, 2016) [hereafter *Intelligence Governance*].

39. *See Grand Bargain, supra* note 34.

40. *See Intelligence Governance, supra* note 38, for an excellent discussion of the history of intelligence reforms.

41. *See Grand Bargain, supra* note 34.

42. Reform followed the decision in United States v. U.S. District Court (*Keith*), 407 U.S. 297 (1972), which held that a warrant was required for domestic security surveillance but declined to extend its ruling to foreign persons and agents of foreign powers. This gap was addressed in 1978 with FISA and the creation of the FISC. *See* DAVID KRIS & J. DOUGLAS WILSON, NATIONAL SECURITY INVESTIGATIONS AND PROSECUTIONS §§ 3.6–3.7 (3d. ed. Eagan: Thomson West 2019).

43. *See Intelligence Governance, supra* note 38, at 213 & n.37. For further, excellent discussion of the FISC's superintendent function, *see* David Kris, *Further Thoughts on the Crossfire Hurricane Report*, LAWFARE (Dec. 23, 2019), https://www.lawfareblog.com/further-thoughts-crossfire-hurricane-report. Kris analyzes a series of incidents in which the FISC expressed frustration and lack of confidence in representations by the FBI.

44. 50 U.S.C. § 1803(i)(2)(A).

45. *See* James Risen & Eric Lichtblau, *Bush Lets U.S. Spy on Callers without Courts*, N.Y. TIMES (Dec. 16, 2005), https://www.nytimes.com/2005/12/16/politics/bush-lets-us-spy-on-callers-without-courts.html (exposing the president's Terrorist Surveillance Program authorizing interception of Americans' international communications outside the FISA process). After these revelations, the executive branch sought congressional approval of a statutory framework authorizing this program. The public debate and reform process yielded what ultimately became known as the 702 Program. *See* PRIVACY AND CIVIL LIBERTIES OVERSIGHT BOARD, REPORT ON THE SURVEILLANCE PROGRAM OPERATED PURSUANT TO SECTION 702 OF THE FOREIGN INTELLIGENCE SURVEILLANCE ACT, at 5–6 (July 2, 2014).

46. *See* PCLOB 215 REPORT, *supra* note 3, at 9 (citing Opinion and Order, *In re Application of the Federal Bureau of Investigation for an Order Requiring the Production of Tangible Things from [redacted]*, No. BR 06-05 (FISA Ct. May 24, 2006), and Opinion and Order, No. PR/TT [redacted] (FISA Ct.), as the basis for bulk metadata collection generally).

47. *See* Letter from Assistant Attorney General Ronald Weich to Senator Ron Wyden & Senator Mark Udall 2 (Oct. 9, 2011), https://www.scribd.com/doc/146110942/Letter-to-Sen-Wyden.

48. The government relied on a novel interpretation of Section 215 of the Patriot Act, which permits the FBI to obtain business records that are "relevant" to an investigation. 50 U.S.C. § 1861(a)(1); *see* PCLOB 215 REPORT, *supra* note 3, at 9. It had first obtained FISC authority to collect metadata in bulk after making a classified, ex parte application to the court urging a broad definition of "relevant." *See* Opinion and Order, No. PR/TT [redacted] 72–76 (FISA Ct.); Amended Memorandum Opinion, In Re Application of the FBI for an Order Requiring the Production of Tangible Things from [redacted], No. BR 13-109, at 18–21 (FISA Ct. Oct. 11, 2013), https://fas.org/irp/agency/doj/fisa/fisc-082913.pdf.

49. *See* PCLOB 215 REPORT, *supra* note 3, at 57–81 (disagreeing with the government's interpretations of Section 215, including its understanding of "relevance"); ACLU v. Clapper, 785 F.3d 787, 818 (2d Cir. 2015) (citing the PCLOB Report and holding that "[t]he interpretation urged by the government would require a drastic expansion of the term 'relevance' "); *see also* Klayman v. Obama, 142 F. Supp. 3d 172, 190–95 (D.D.C. 2015).

50. *See* Letter from Weich to Wyden & Udall, *supra* note 47, at 1.

51. *See Bulk Collection of Telephony Metadata under Section 215 of the USA PATRIOT Act,* ADMINISTRATION WHITE PAPER (Obama Administration), Aug. 9, 2013, at 17 [hereafter ADMINISTRATION WHITE PAPER], https://fas.org/irp/nsa/bulk-215.pdf (quoting 50 U.S.C. § 1871(a)).

52. *See* PCLOB 215 REPORT, *supra* note 3, at 95–102, for a comprehensive discussion of congressional consideration of the 215 Program and rejection of the government's argument rooting its legitimacy in the re-enactment doctrine. *See also* the dissenting views of two PCLOB members, *id.* at 209–10 (statement of Rachel Brand); *id.* at 214–15 (statement of Elisebeth Collins Cook).

53. *See* ADMINISTRATION WHITE PAPER, *supra* note 51, at 18 & n.14. *See* PCLOB 215 REPORT, *supra* note 3, at 97.

54. *See* Letter from Assistant Attorney General Ronald Weich to Rep. Silvestre Reyes (Dec. 14, 2009), https://www.dni.gov/files/documents/2009_CoverLetter_Report_Collection.pdf (attaching briefing paper for 2010 reauthorization); ADMINISTRATION WHITE PAPER, *supra* note 51, at 18 & n.14; PCLOB 215 REPORT, *supra* note 3, at 97. The paper was made available to all members of Congress in 2010, but in 2011, access was narrowed in the House to only certain representatives. *See* PCLOB REPORT, *supra* note 3, at 97–98; William Bendix & Paul J. Quirk, *Secrecy and Negligence: How Congress Lost Control of Domestic Surveillance,* 68 BROOKINGS: ISSUES IN GOVERNANCE STUDIES 6 n.12 (Mar. 2015), https://www.brookings.edu/wp-content/uploads/2016/06/CTIBendixQuirkSecrecyv3.pdf.

55. *See* PCLOB 215 REPORT, *supra* note 3, at 97–98.

56. *See* Letter from Sens. Ron Wyden & Tom Udall to Attorney General Eric Holder (Mar. 15, 2012) ("[T]hese documents are so highly classified that most members of Congress do not have any staff who are cleared to read them. . . . [M]ost of our colleagues in the House and Senate are unfamiliar with these documents, and [] many of them would be surprised and angry to learn how the Patriot Act has been interpreted in secret."); Bendix & Quirk, *supra* note 54, at 12–13.

57. PCLOB 215 REPORT, *supra* note 3, at 197 n.672 (quoting *Preserving the Rule of Law in the Fight against Terrorism, Hearing before the Sen. Comm. on the Judiciary* (Oct. 2, 2007) (statement of Jack Landman Goldsmith)).

58. PCLOB 215 REPORT, *supra* note 3, at 10. *But see* separate statements of dissenting PCLOB members, *id.* at 209–10, 214–15.

59. Fact Sheet: Review of U.S. Signals Intelligence (Jan. 17, 2014), https://obamawhitehouse.archives.gov/the-press-office/2014/01/17/fact-sheet-review-us-signals-intelligence. *See also* The White House, Office of the Press Sec'y, Barack Obama, Presidential Memorandum: Reviewing Our Global Signals Intelligence Collection and Communications Technologies (Aug. 12, 2013) [hereafter Obama Review Memorandum] (charge given to Review Group on Intelligence and Communications Technologies in August 2013).

60. Acknowledging the *potential* for abuse if the government houses large quantities of data, the president directed the transition of the program to one that "preserves the capabilities we need without the government holding the data." *See* Obama DOJ Speech, *supra* note 12. The USA Freedom Act ultimately implemented this idea. *See* 50 U.S.C. § 1861; David Kris, *The NSA and the USA Freedom Act,* LAWFARE (July 2, 2018), https://www.lawfareblog.com/nsa-and-usa-freedom-act.

61. *See* Obama DOJ Speech, *supra* note 12.

62. *See* PCLOB 215 REPORT, *supra* note 3, at 2 & n.5 (quoting President Obama's request to review "where our counterterrorism efforts and our values come into tension"); Obama Review Memorandum, *supra* note 12 (directing the DNI to establish the Review Group). Both groups issued lengthy reports critiquing the 215 Program while highlighting the challenges of evolving technology and threats.

63. *See* PCLOB 215 REPORT, *supra* note 3, at 17–18. *See also* PRESIDENT'S REVIEW GROUP ON INTELLIGENCE & COMMUNICATIONS TECHNOLOGIES, LIBERTY & SECURITY IN A CHANGING WORLD, at 21, 36 (Dec. 12, 2013) [hereafter REVIEW GROUP REPORT], https://obamawhitehouse.archives.gov/sites/default/files/docs/2013-12-12_rg_final_report.pdf.

64. 50 U.S.C. § 1803(i)(2)(A), (3)(A) directs the FISC to designate a panel of amici curiae with "expertise in privacy and civil liberties, intelligence collection, communications technology, or any other area that may lend legal or technical expertise to . . ." the FISC.

65. *See* Elizabeth Goitein, *The FISA Court's 702 Opinions, Part I: A History of Non-Compliance Repeats Itself*, JUST SECURITY (Oct. 15, 2019), https://www.justsecurity.org/66595/the-fisa-courts-702-opinions-part-i-a-history-of-non-compliance-repeats-itself/.

66. *See Intelligence Governance, supra* note 38, at 213 ("In the post-9/11 era . . . the FISC shifted to superintending surveillance programs, which represented a fundamentally new role for the institution.").

67. David Kris, *On the Bulk Collection of Tangible Things*, 1 LAWFARE RESEARCH PAPER SERIES, no. 4, Sept. 29, 2013, at 38–39, https://jnslp.com/wp-content/uploads/2014/05/On-the-Bulk-Collection-of-Tangible-Things.pdf.

68. *Cf.* Kris, *Further Thoughts, supra* note 43 (noting "slippage" in which reforms to improve the accuracy and reliability of government testimony before the FISC lose potency and diminish over time).

69. *Compare* Bendix & Quirk, *supra* note 54, at 12–13, *with* ADMINISTRATION WHITE PAPER, *supra* note 51, at 17–19 ("Congress was on notice of this program and the legal authority for it when the statute was reauthorized.").

70. *See* Press Briefing by Press Secretary Jay Carney (June 10, 2013), https://obamawhitehouse.archives.gov/the-press-office/2013/06/10/press-briefing-press-secretary-jay-carney-6102013 ("[T]hese programs are legal. They are subject to the appropriate oversight from three branches of government.").

71. *See* Hayes Brown, *Senator Slams Domestic Spying: "Secret Law Has No Place in America,"* THINKPROGRESS (July 23, 2013) (discussing remarks of Senator Ron Wyden at the Center for American Progress (July 23, 2013) (transcript available at https://www.scribd.com/document/155530126/Wyden-Speech-on-NSA-Domestic-Surveillance-at-Center-for-American-Progress)).

72. PCLOB 215 REPORT, *supra* note 3, at 198.

73. *See id.* at 206. The PCLOB was divided on the issue of public debate and legal authority of the program.

74. *See id.* at 197–198; *id.* at 198.

75. *See Grand Bargain, supra* note 34 ("[The IC's] legitimacy is inherently fraught. So it is crucial not merely that the entire process be above board politically but that it be seen to be above board.").

76. REVIEW GROUP REPORT, *supra* note 63, at 124.

77. *Id.* at 16, 20; PPD-28, *supra* note 11.

78. *See* PPD-28, *supra* note 11, at § 4(a); Intelligence Community Standard 107-01: Continued Retention of SIGINT under PPD-28 (Feb. 2, 2015), https://www.dni.gov/files/documents/ppd-28/ICS%20107-1.pdf.

79. *See* PPD-28, *supra* note 11, at § 2; Fact Sheet: Review of U.S. Signals Intelligence, *supra* note 59.

80. *See* OFFICE OF CIVIL LIBERTIES, PRIVACY & TRANSPARENCY, GUIDE TO POSTED DOCUMENTS REGARDING USE OF NATIONAL SECURITY AUTHORITIES (June 19, 2019), https://www.dni.gov/files/CLPT/documents/Guide_to_Posted_Documents_June__19_2019.pdf (suggesting the DNI's January 2017 Signals Intelligence Progress Report (for 2016) was the last).

81. *See* REVIEW GROUP REPORT, *supra* note 63, at 32.

82. *See* PCLOB 215 REPORT, *supra* note 3, at 2.

83. The existing oversight process has identified numerous compliance issues over the years. *See* PCLOB 215 REPORT, *supra* note 3, at 46–55. FISA requires the DOJ to notify Congress of failures to follow statutorily required targeting and minimization procedures. *See* 50 U.S.C. § 1881a(m); Dep't of Justice Nat'l Security Division, *About the Division*, https://www.justice.gov/nsd/office-intelligence (describing the role of the Oversight Section of the National Security Division). Of course, reasonable concerns could be raised about oversight effectiveness given the recurrence of problems. While oversight does not guarantee perfection,

especially with respect to complex programs, it nevertheless serves a valuable function and can keep problems from metastasizing.

84. *See* PCLOB 215 REPORT, *supra* note 3, at 9–10.

85. *See* David Pozen, *Edward Snowden, National Security Whistleblowing and Civil Disobedience*, LAWFARE (Mar. 26, 2019), https://www.lawfareblog.com/edward-snowden-national-security-whistleblowing-and-civil-disobedience. In 2013, the anti-reprisal protections for intelligence whistleblowers implemented by presidential directive did not reference contractors. Congress addressed this gap after the Snowden disclosures. *See* 10 U.S.C. § 1034.

86. *See* Michael German, *The Law Is Designed to Punish Whistleblowers Like Me*, WASH. POST (Oct. 10, 2019), https://www.washingtonpost.com/outlook/the-law-is-designed-to-punish-whistleblowers-like-me/2019/10/10/9eefe4da-eb71-11e9-9c6d-436a0df4f31d_story.html.

87. REVIEW GROUP REPORT, *supra* note 63, at 126.

88. *See, e.g.*, Brian Barrett, *The Ukraine Whistle-Blower Did Everything Right*, WIRED (Oct. 3, 2019), https://www.wired.com/story/whistle-blower-did-it-right/.

89. 50 U.S.C. § 3033 (k)(5)(G); *see* Letter from Jason Klitenic, General Counsel to the DNI, to Richard Burr, Adam Schiff, Mark Warner, and Devin Nunes, at 2 (Sept. 13, 2019), https://assets.documentcloud.org/documents/6419391/Sept-13-Letter.pdf; Robert S. Litt, *What the Latest Reports Say about the Whistleblower Complaint*, LAWFARE (Sept. 20, 2019), https://www.lawfareblog.com/what-latest-reports-say-about-whistleblower-complaint.

90. Litt, *supra*, note 89.

91. *See* Anna Kaplan, *Trump Retweets Name of Alleged Whistleblower*, DAILY BEAST (Dec. 28, 2019), https://www.thedailybeast.com/trump-retweets-name-of-alleged-whistleblower.

92. *See* Michael Morell & David Kris, *How the DNI-Congress Feud Puts Intelligence and Democracy in Danger*, WASH. POST (Sept. 19, 2019), https://www.washingtonpost.com/opinions/2019/09/20/how-dni-congress-feud-puts-intelligence-democracy-danger/.

93. *See* Margaret Garnett & Preet Bharara, *Remaining Silent about Corruption Should Not Be an Option*, N.Y. TIMES (Oct. 17, 2019), https://www.nytimes.com/2019/10/17/opinion/whistle-blower-trump.html.

94. *See* Gordon Ahl, *Whistleblower's Counsel Signals Intent to Contact Congress Directly*, LAWFARE (Sept. 25, 2019), https://www.lawfareblog.com/whistleblowers-counsel-signals-intent-contact-congress-directly (discussing Ukraine whistleblower's attempt to go directly to Congress); Charlie Savage, *Intelligence Whistle-Blower Law, Explained*, N.Y. TIMES (Sept. 25, 2019), https://www.nytimes.com/2019/09/20/us/whistleblower-law-explained.html (discussing the current regime in which a whistleblower can go to Congress only under the direction of the DNI).

95. REVIEW GROUP REPORT, *supra* note 63, at 35. While the PCLOB could use more full-time staff and other support, making the PCLOB a recipient of such reports suffers from the same deficiencies as the existing process, namely, distinguishing between policy disputes regarding properly authorized programs and waste, fraud, and abuse claims.

96. *See* German, *supra* note 86; *Intelligence Community Whistleblower Protections*, CONG. RES. SERV. REPORT No. 45345, at 6 n.25 (updated Sept. 23, 2019) [hereafter CRS REPORT], https://fas.org/sgp/crs/intel/R45345.pdf. Congress did enact intelligence whistleblower protections shortly after Snowden, but protections for contractors were not included until 2018. *See* CRS REPORT 10–11; 10 U.S.C. § 1034.

97. 50 U.S.C. § 3033 (k)(5)(G).

98. *See* Obama DOJ Speech, *supra* note 12.

99. *See id.* This policy was codified in the USA Freedom Act, 50 U.S.C. § 1861. The statute requires the DNI to review any FISC decision "that includes a significant construction or interpretation of any provision of law … and … make [it] publicly available to the greatest extent practicable." 50 U.S.C. § 1861; *see Declassified Documents*, IC ON THE RECORD, https://icontherecord.tumblr.com/tagged/declassified.

100. *See* 50 U.S.C. § 1861; OFFICE OF THE DNI, *ODNI Releases Annual Intelligence Community Transparency Report*, IC ON THE RECORD (Apr. 30, 2019), https://icontherecord.tumblr.com/post/184553467393/odni-releases-annual-intelligence-community.

101. *See* PCLOB 215 REPORT, *supra* note 3, at 195–96 (discussing the National Counter-terrorism Center's [NCTC's] issuance of public guidelines in 2012 and the attention generated from media and public interest organizations).

102. *See* Elizabeth Goitein, *There's No Reason to Hide the Amount of Secret Law*, JUST SECURITY (June 30, 2015), https://www.justsecurity.org/24306/no-reason-hide-amount-secret-law/.

103. Exec. Order No. 13698, 80 Fed. Reg. 37, 131 (June 29, 2015); Presidential Policy Directive 30: Hostage Recovery Activities (June 24, 2015), https://www.federalregister.gov/documents/2015/06/29/2015-16122/hostage-recovery-activities.

104. *See* Exec. Order No. 13698, *supra* note 103, at § 5(b).

105. *Report on the Legal and Policy Frameworks Guiding the United States' use of Military Force and Related to National Security Operations*, https://www.state.gov/wp-content/uploads/2019/10/Report-to-Congress-on-legal-and-policy-frameworks-guiding-use-of-military-force-.pdf.

106. *See* Obama DOJ Speech, *supra* note 12.

107. *Id.*

108. *See, e.g.,* PCLOB 215 REPORT, *supra* note 3, at 18–19.

109. The government ended the original 215 Program with the USA Freedom Act despite defending its importance after Snowden's revelations; *see, e.g.,* Mattathias Schwartz, *"We're at Greater Risk": Q. & A. with General Keith Alexander*, NEW YORKER (May 15, 2014), https://www.newyorker.com/news/news-desk/were-at-greater-risk-q-a-with-general-keith-alexander (interview with then-NSA chief). *See also* Dustin Volz & Warren Strobel, *NSA Recommends Dropping Phone Surveillance Program*, WALL ST. J. (Apr. 24, 2019), https://www.wsj.com/articles/nsa-recommends-dropping-phone-surveillance-program-11556138247 (discussing recent debates about ending the revised program).

110. *Compare* Eric Schmitt & Michael S. Schmidt, *Qaeda Plot Leak Has Undermined U.S. Intelligence*, N.Y. TIMES (Sept. 29, 2013), https://www.nytimes.com/2013/09/30/us/qaeda-plot-leak-has-undermined-us-intelligence.html, *with* Mike Brunker, *Snowden Leaks Didn't Make Al Qaeda Change Tactics, Says Report*, NBC NEWS (Sept. 16, 2014), https://www.nbcnews.com/storyline/nsa-snooping/snowden-leaks-didn-t-make-al-qaeda-change-tactics-says-n203731; *see* Jason Leopold, *Pentagon Report: Scope of Intelligence Compromised by Snowden "Staggering,"* GUARDIAN (May 22, 2014), https://www.theguardian.com/world/2014/may/22/pentagon-report-snowden-leaks-national-security?view=desktop (discussing DOD INFORMATION REVIEW TASK FORCE-2: INITIAL ASSESSMENT, IMPACTS RESULTING FROM THE COMPROMISE OF CLASSIFIED MATERIAL BY A FORMER NSA CONTRACTOR (2013), https://www.theguardian.com/world/interactive/2014/may/22/pentagon-report-snowden-leaks-damage-report); POWER WARS, *supra* note 26, at 370, 374.

111. REVIEW GROUP REPORT, *supra* note 63, at 45–46 (quoting U.S. CONST. amend. IV).

Chapter 5

1. Deputy Assistant Secretary of State for Intelligence (1985–1989); Assistant Secretary of State for Political-Military Affairs (1989–1992); Special Assistant to the President for Global Affairs (1992–1998); National Coordinator for Security, Critical Infrastructure Protection and Counter-terrorism (1998–2001); Special Advisor to the President on Cybersecurity (2001–2003); Member, Director of National Intelligence Review Group on Intelligence and Communications Technologies (2013).

2. *See* RICHARD A. CLARKE, MICHAEL MORELL, GEOFFREY R. STONE, CASS SUNSTEIN & PETER SWIRE, LIBERTY AND SECURITY IN A CHANGING WORLD (Princeton, NJ: Princeton University Press, 2013).

3. Scott Shane, *N.S.A. Contractor Arrested in Biggest Breach of U.S. Secrets Pleads Guilty*, N.Y. TIMES, Mar. 28, 2019.

4. Lynh Bui, *Self-Proclaimed White Nationalist Planned a Mass Terrorist Attack, the Government Says*, WASH. POST, Feb. 20, 2019.

5. Good Harbor Security Risk Management, http://goodharbor.net.

6. Nat'l Comm'n on Terrorist Attacks upon the United States, The 9/11 Commission Report: Final Report of the National Commission on Terrorist Attacks upon the United States 394, 417 (New York: W. W. Norton, 2004).

7. Press Release, U.S. Dep't of Justice, Office of Pub. Affairs, *Former Vice Chairman of the Joint Chiefs of Staff Pleads Guilty to Federal Felony in Leak Investigation* (Oct. 17, 2016), https://www.justice.gov/opa/pr/former-vice-chairman-joint-chiefs-staff-pleads-guilty-federal-felony-leak-investigation.

Chapter 6

1. Barton Gellman & Laura Poitras, *U.S., British Intelligence Mining Data from Nine U.S. Internet Companies in Broad Secret Program*, Wash. Post, June 7, 2013.

2. Barton Gellman & Ashkan Soltani, *NSA Infiltrates Links to Yahoo, Google Data Centers Worldwide, Snowden Documents Say*, Wash. Post, Oct. 30, 2013.

3. The White House, Exec. Order No. 12333, 40 Fed. Reg. 59941 (1981), *as amended by* Exec. Order No. 13284, 68 Fed. Reg. 4077 (2003), *and by* Exec. Order No. 13355, *and further amended by* Exec. Order No. 13470, 73 Fed. Reg. 45328 (2008).

4. Ellen Nakashima, *Top Spy Bemoans Loss of Key Information-Gathering Program*, Wash. Post, Sept. 9, 2015.

5. Julian Assange, *WikiLeaks Statement on the Mass Recording of Afghan Telephone Calls by the NSA*, WikiLeaks (May 23, 2014), https://wikileaks.org/WikiLeaks-statement-on-the-mass.html.

6. *Oversight of the Fed. Bureau of Investigation: Hearing before the Senate Comm. on the Judiciary*, 115th Cong. (2017) (testimony of James Comey, Dir. of the Fed. Bureau of Investigation), https://www.washingtonpost.com/news/post-politics/wp/2017/05/03/read-the-full-testimony-of-fbi-director-james-comey-in-which-he-discusses-clinton-email-investigation/.

Chapter 7

* The authors gratefully acknowledge the invaluable contributions of their colleague Gabe Rottman, Director of the Technology and Press Freedom Project of the Reporters Committee for Freedom of the Press, to this essay, and thank Gail Gove, Heidi Kitrosser, and David McCraw for their generous reviews and comments.

1. Press Release, Dep't of Justice, Attorney General Jeff Sessions Delivers Remarks at Briefing on Leaks of Classified Materials Threatening National Security (Aug. 4, 2017), https://perma.cc/EAH3-L89B.

2. As discussed further below, that exception is Samuel Loring Morison, a Navy intelligence analyst who was successfully prosecuted under the Espionage Act for theft of government property in 1985 for leaking satellite photographs of Soviet naval facilities and ships. Unlike subsequent cases, Morison had an off-duty, paid arrangement to supply information to the news organization, and the prosecution argued that there was evidence from which one could infer that his desire to secure full-time employment may have prompted the classified leak. *See* United States v. Morison, 844 F.2d 1057, 1060–62 (4th Cir. 1988).

3. Much of the history recounted in this essay is based on research conducted by the Reporters Committee for Freedom of the Press into the history of investigations and prosecutions of the unauthorized disclosure of government information to or from the news media. The Reporters Committee maintains a comprehensive chart listing all of these cases. *See Federal Cases Involving Unauthorized Disclosures to the News Media, 1778 to the Present*, Reporters Comm. for Freedom of the Press, https://www.rcfp.org/resources/leak-investigations-chart/ [hereafter Rottman Chart]. This chart should be consulted for sourcing information on the specific cases, unless we include a citation of another source in an endnote here.

4. *See id.* at 62–107. These eighteen are (1) *Leibowitz*, (2) *Drake*, (3) *Manning*, (4) *Kim*, (5) *Sterling*, (6) *Kiriakou*, (7) *Sachtleben*, (8) *Snowden*, (9) *Petraeus*, (10) *Cartwright*, (11) *Winner*, (12) *Albury*, (13) *Schulte*, (14) *Wolfe*, (15) *Edwards*, (16) *Fry*, (17) *Hale*, and (18) *Frese*.

5. *See id.* These are (1) *Hitselberger* and (2) *Assange.*
6. *See id.* These are (1) *Leibowitz,* (2) *Drake,* (3) *Manning,* (4) *Kim,* (5) *Sterling,* (6) *Kiriakou,* (7) *Sachtleben,* (8) *Hitselberger,* (9) *Petraeus,* (10) *Cartwright,* (11) *Winner,* (12) *Albury,* (13) *Wolfe,* and (14) *Edwards.*
7. These are counts 15 through 17 in the Julian Assange superseding indictment, discussed further below. The authors take no position on whether the WikiLeaks founder is a "journalist" or whether WikiLeaks is a news organization. As the Reporters Committee for Freedom of the Press has argued, there are important "practical and ethical differences between Assange and national security reporters, and they should not be minimized." Gabe Rottman, *Special Analysis of the May 2019 Superseding Indictment of Julian Assange,* Reporters Comm. for Freedom of the Press (May 30, 2019), https://www.rcfp.org/may-2019-assange-indictment-analysis/. It is important, however, that the legal theory advanced in the "pure publication" counts does not turn on one's status as a journalist or a news organization. It also does not rely on Assange's alleged activity in the case that went beyond the solicitation, receipt, and publication of classified information, namely, the government's claim that Assange agreed to use WikiLeaks' own computer resources to decrypt a hashed password, which, if true, would be a crime under federal computer crime law. *Id.*
8. *See, e.g.,* Eric Newton, *Paying Attention to the Shield Law's Critics,* COLUM. JOURNALISM REV. (Sept. 24, 2013), https://archives.cjr.org/behind_the_news/paying_more_attention_to_the_s.php.
9. ALEXANDER M. BICKEL, THE MORALITY OF CONSENT 60 (New Haven, CT: Yale University Press, 1975).
10. *See* Espionage Act Reform Act of 2020, S. 3402, 116th Cong. (2020); H.R. 6114, 116th Cong. (2020).
11. Espionage Act of 1917, ch. 30, 40 Stat. 217 (codified as amended at 18 U.S.C. §§ 793–798 (2018)). The Internal Security Act of 1950, ch. 1024, Pub. L. No. 81-831, 64 Stat. 987, created the two main provisions of concern for journalists and journalistic sources: § 793(d) (covering "insiders," those with authorized access to defense information) and § 793(e) (covering those with unauthorized access). It also created § 798, which covers certain categories of classified information (not just defense information) related to communications intelligence. *See also* GEOFFREY R. STONE, PERILOUS TIMES: FREE SPEECH IN WARTIME 146–53 (New York: W. W. Norton, 2004).
12. H.R. 3468, 96th Cong. (1979).
13. Notably, the Wyden-Khanna bill would make modest improvements to the Espionage Act provisions applicable to individuals who have agreed to maintain the secrecy of national defense information ("covered persons" in the bill). It would, for instance, clarify the intent requirement in 18 U.S.C. § 793, the general unauthorized-disclosure statute, and improve whistleblower protections in 18 U.S.C. § 798, the 1951 Espionage Act amendment governing signals intelligence. Nonetheless, it is important to realize that the Wyden-Khanna bill is focused on strengthening protections for non-covered individuals, such as the press, and would not resolve many longstanding concerns over the use of the spying laws against journalistic sources. As noted below, it is decidedly "half a loaf," but it would improve the law with respect to both journalists and their sources in government.
14. *See* GEOFFREY R. STONE, TOP SECRET: WHEN OUR GOVERNMENT KEEPS US IN THE DARK 29–45 (Lanham, MD: Rowman & Littlefield, 2007) (describing how journalists interact with sources and how those interactions could implicate various criminal laws).
15. Section 4 of the bill as introduced would limit the application of 18 U.S.C. § 641, the theft of government property statute, to "tangible" property. The change would preclude the use of the statute to punish leakers who disclose government information orally to a third party, though most of the leak cases with a theft of government property count involve the disclosure of tangible material.
16. United States v. Morison, 844 F.2d 1057, 1081 (4th Cir. 1988) (Wilkinson, J., concurring) ("[P]ress organizations . . . are not being, and probably could not be, prosecuted under the espionage statute.").
17. *See* Florida Star v. B.J.F., 491 U.S. 524 (1989); Smith v. Daily Mail Publ'g Co., 443 U.S. 97 (1979); Landmark Commc'ns, Inc. v. Virginia, 435 U.S. 829 (1978).

18. *Daily Mail*, 443 U.S. at 103.
19. *Id.* at 104–5.
20. *Id.* at 110.
21. 532 U.S. 514, 535 (2001).
22. 376 U.S. 254 (1964).
23. *Bartnicki*, 532 U.S. at 535.
24. *Id.* at 535–36.
25. *Id.*
26. *Id.* at 541–56.
27. *See* Brief of the Washington Post et al., as Amici Curiae, In Support of Reversal at 26–27, United States v. Morison, 844 F.2d 1057 (4th Cir. 1988) (No. 86-5008) (reviewing First Amendment arguments against the application of the Espionage Act to the press for the dissemination of defense information to the public); *see also* Unopposed Brief of Amicus Curiae Reporters Committee for Freedom of the Press Supporting Defendant's Motion to Dismiss the Indictment at 19–23, United States v. Hale, No. 1:19-cr-00059-LO (E.D. Va. Sept. 23, 2019).
28. *See* New York Times Co. v. United States, 403 U.S. 713 (1971) (per curiam); *id.* at 731 (White, J., with Stewart, J., concurring); *id.* at 752 (Burger, C.J., dissenting); *id.* at 745 (Marshall, J., concurring); *id.* at 759 (Blackmun, J., concurring).
29. Mem. from Edward H. Levi, Att'y Gen., to President Gerald Ford 5 (May 29, 1975), https://perma.cc/9X38-L3SE [hereafter Levi Memorandum].
30. *Presidential Directive on the Use of Polygraphs and Prepublication Review: Hearings before the Subcomm. on Civil and Constitutional Rights of the H. Comm. on the Judiciary*, 98th Cong. 166–80 (1985) (Appendix 2: The Willard Report, Report of the Interdepartmental Group on Unauthorized Disclosures of Classified Information).
31. *See* United States v. Kim, 808 F. Supp. 2d 44, 53–55 (D.D.C. 2011); United States v. Drake, 818 F. Supp. 2d 909, 910, 922 (D. Md. 2011); United States v. Rosen, 445 F. Supp. 2d 602, 643 (E.D. Va. 2006), *aff'd*, 557 F.3d 192 (4th Cir. 2009); United States v. Morison, 604 F. Supp. 655, 658–59 (D. Md. 1985), *aff'd*, 844 F.2d 1057 (4th Cir. 1988), *cert. denied*, 488 U.S. 908 (1988).
32. BICKEL, *supra* note 9, at 81.
33. *Id.* at 60–61.
34. *Id.* at 86.
35. *Id.* at 87.
36. *Id.* at 80.
37. *Id.* at 87.
38. *Id.*
39. Mike Pompeo, Director, Central Intelligence Agency, Remarks at Ctr. for Strategic and Int'l Studies (Apr. 13, 2017) (transcript available at https://www.cia.gov/news-information/speeches-testimony/2017-speeches-testimony/pompeo-delivers-remarks-at-csis.html).
40. 283 U.S. 697 (1931).
41. 475 U.S. 767 (1986).
42. New York Times Co. v. United States, 403 U.S. 713, 729 (1971) (Stewart, J., with White, J., concurring).
43. Whitney v. California, 274 U.S. 357, 376 (1927) (Brandeis, J., concurring).
44. Unless otherwise indicated, sourcing for the historical discussion of the cases can all be found in the Rottman Chart, *supra* note 3.
45. Letter from Daniel Patrick Moynihan, U.S. Senate, to President William Jefferson Clinton (Sept. 29, 1998), https://perma.cc/FTL7-HRHL.
46. *See* Rottman Chart, *supra* note 3, at 62–80. These are (1) *Leibowitz*, (2) *Drake*, (3) *Manning*, (4) *Kim*, (5) *Sterling*, (6) *Kiriakou*, (7) *Sachtleben*, (8) *Hitselberger*, (9) *Snowden*, (10) *Petraeus*, and (11) *Cartwright*.
47. *Leibowitz, Manning, Kim, Sterling,* and *Sachtleben* all ended in convictions under the Espionage Act (all were pleas except for *Manning* and *Sterling*).
48. *See* Rottman Chart, *supra* note 3, at 81–107. The Trump administration cases are: (1) *Winner*, (2) *Albury*, (3) *Schulte*, (4) *Wolfe*, (5) *Edwards*, (6) *Fry*, (7) *Hale*, (8) *Assange*, and (9) *Frese*.

All are under the Espionage Act save *Edwards* and *Fry*, which are under bank secrecy laws, and *Wolfe*, which was a false statement case.

49. *See id.* at 82–83, 85–87. *Winner* and *Albury* are the two plea agreements under the Espionage Act; *Wolfe* is the plea for making false statements to the FBI. Edwards has pled guilty and is awaiting sentencing.

50. Only Snowden (indicted May 2013), Petraeus (pled guilty in 2015), and Cartwright (pled guilty and pardoned in 2016) arose during President Obama's second term.

51. United States v. Morison, 844 F.2d 1057, 1084 (4th Cir. 1988) (Wilkinson, J., concurring). Judge Phillips, in a special concurrence, rested his entire affirmance of Morison's conviction on his crediting Wilkinson's belief that the conviction would not "significantly inhibit needed investigative reporting about the workings of government in matters of national defense and security." *Id.* at 1086 (Phillips, J., concurring, specially).

52. Gabe Rottman, *Special Analysis of the May 2019 Superseding Indictment of Julian Assange*, REPORTERS COMM. FOR FREEDOM OF THE PRESS (May 30, 2019), https://www.rcfp.org/may-2019-assange-indictment-analysis/.

53. *See* Rottman Chart, *supra* note 3, at 3–5; ELIE ABEL, LEAKING: WHO DOES IT? WHO BENEFITS? AT WHAT COST? 11–15 (New York: Priority, 1987).

54. *See* SEYMOUR HERSH, THE PRICE OF POWER: KISSINGER IN THE WHITE HOUSE 477 (New York: Summit, 1984).

55. *See* MARK FELDSTEIN, POISONING THE PRESS: RICHARD NIXON, JACK ANDERSON, AND THE RISE OF WASHINGTON'S SCANDAL CULTURE 186 (New York: Farrar, Straus and Giroux, 2010).

56. *Id.* at 186–87.

57. *Id.* at 191; HERSH, *supra* note 54, at 476.

58. HERSH, *supra* note 54, at 476.

59. FELDSTEIN, *supra* note 55, at 190–91.

60. *Id.* at 191.

61. *Id.*

62. *Id.*

63. Levi Memorandum, *supra* note 29.

64. Jay Peterzell, *Can the CIA Spook the Press?* COLUM. JOURNALISM REV., Sept.–Oct. 1986, at 29.

65. Devlin Barrett et al., *Some Federal Prosecutors Disagreed with Decision to Charge Assange under Espionage Act*, WASH. POST (May 24, 2019), https://www.washingtonpost.com/world/national-security/some-federal-prosecutors-disagreed-with-decision-to-charge-assange-under-espionage-act/2019/05/24/ce9271bc-7e4d-11e9-8bb7-0fc796cf2ec0_story.html.

66. *See* CHARLIE SAVAGE, POWER WARS 362 (New York: Back Bay, 2015).

67. *See supra.*

68. *See* Sessions Speech, *supra* note 1.

69. David Remnick, *Trump and the Enemies of the People*, NEW YORKER (Aug. 15, 2018), https://perma.cc/2DZM-RV8E.

70. *See* A. G. Sulzberger, *Accusing the* New York Times *of "Treason," Trump Crosses a Line*, WALL ST. J. (June 19, 2019), https://perma.cc/P9FB-U77M.

71. *See* JAMES MADISON, *The Federalist No. 48*, in JAMES MADISON: WRITINGS 281, 281 Jack N. Rakove ed. (New York: Literary Classics of the United States, 1999) (questioning whether mere "parchment barriers" will suffice to prevent the encroachment of government power).

72. THOMAS JEFFERSON, *Letter: A Bill of Rights*, in THOMAS JEFFERSON: WRITINGS 942, 944, Merrill D. Peterson ed. (New York: Literary Classics of the United States, 2011).

Chapter 8

1. S. SELECT COMM. ON INTELLIGENCE, 108TH CONG., REPORT ON THE U.S. INTELLIGENCE COMMUNITY'S PREWAR INTELLIGENCE ASSESSMENTS ON IRAQ (2004), https://perma.cc/AZE2-W29B (concluding that excessive secrecy impeded information sharing within the Intelligence Community, interfered with external oversight, and made it more difficult to detect analytical errors and policymakers' exaggerations after they had occurred).

2. Peter Finn & Julie Tate, *Justice Department to Investigate Deaths of Two Detainees in CIA Custody*, WASH. POST (June 30, 2011), https://perma.cc/V9SN-4SFM; HUMAN RIGHTS CLINIC AT COLUMBIA UNIV. & CTR. FOR CIVILIANS IN CONFLICT, THE CIVILIAN IMPACT OF DRONES: UNEXAMINED COSTS, UNANSWERED QUESTIONS (2012), https://perma.cc/ EBM6-XKNG.

3. S. SELECT COMM. ON INTELLIGENCE, COMMITTEE STUDY OF THE CENTRAL INTELLIGENCE AGENCY'S DETENTION AND INTERROGATION PROGRAM, S. REP. NO. 113-288 (2014) [hereafter S. SELECT COMM. ON INTELLIGENCE, CIA PROGRAM], https://perma.cc/X9XC-BRP9 (stating that CIA's detention and interrogation program created tensions with US partners and allies and complicated bilateral relationships).

4. Douglas A. Johnson, Alberto Mora, & Averell Schmidt, *The Strategic Costs of Torture*, FOREIGN AFFAIRS (Sept./Oct. 2016), https://perma.cc/UKQ4-6NB3.

5. *See, e.g.*, S. SELECT COMM. ON INTELLIGENCE, CIA PROGRAM, *supra* note 3, at xx (stating that CIA contractors who helped develop "enhanced interrogation techniques" were paid $81 million despite lacking specialized knowledge of al-Qaeda, a background in counter-terrorism, or any relevant cultural or linguistic experience).

6. Tom Malinowski, *Restoring Moral Authority: Ending Torture, Secret Detention, and the Prison at Guantanamo Bay*, 618 ANNALS AM. ACAD. POL. & SOC. SCI. 148 (2008), https://perma. cc/GK9T-CFFF; S. SELECT COMM. ON INTELLIGENCE, CIA PROGRAM, *supra* note 3 ("the program caused immeasurable damage to the United States' public standing").

7. *Public Trust in Government: 1958–2019*, PEW RESEARCH CTR. (Apr. 11, 2019), https:// perma.cc/E9AL-R84L.

8. The word *whistleblower* does not have a settled definition. In this essay, I use the word to refer to government insiders—that is, government employees or contractors—who responsibly share classified secrets with the press to inform the public about official malfeasance or other official action that is unsupported by democratic consent.

9. Transcript of Deposition of Max Frankel, United States v. New York Times Co., 328 F. Supp. 324 (S.D.N.Y. June 15, 1971) (No. 71 Civ. 2662).

10. Exec. Order No. 13526, 75 F.R. 705 (2009).

11. *See, e.g.*, ACLU v. U.S. Dep't of Justice, 681 F.3d 61, 73–75 (2d. Cir. 2012) (holding that the CIA could withhold records relating to the use of unlawful interrogation method); New York Times Co. v. U.S. Dep't. of Justice, 872 F. Supp. 2d 309, 317 (S.D.N.Y. 2012) (holding that the DOJ could withhold surveillance-related records even if the records described or contained the agency's procedural or substantive law).

12. Brief of Amici Curiae Scholars of Constitutional Law, First Amendment Law, and Media Law at 7 n.9, United States v. Albury, No. 18 Crim. 00067 (D. Minn. Oct. 4, 2018).

13. *See* HEIDI KITROSSER, RECLAIMING ACCOUNTABILITY: TRANSPARENCY, EXECUTIVE POWER, AND THE U.S. CONSTITUTION 63 (Chicago: University of Chicago Press, 2015).

14. Ron Wyden, *Statement on the Intelligence Declassification Provision in the Intelligence Reform Bill* (Dec. 8, 2004), https://perma.cc/VV2F-22LM.

15. Executive Order 13526 contemplates the possibility of sanctions, Section 5.5, but in practice, sanctions are almost never imposed. Exec. Order No. 13526, 75 Fed.Reg. 705 (2009), https://perma.cc/NZ3X-UTYJ; J. William Leonard, *When Secrecy Gets Out of Hand*, L.A. TIMES (Aug. 10, 2011), https://perma.cc/8KFU-Y7M2.

16. Daniel P. Moynihan, *The Culture of Secrecy*, THE PUB. INT., Summer 1997, at 67.

17. Erwin N. Griswold, *Secrets Not Worth Keeping*, WASH. POST (Feb. 15, 1989), https://perma. cc/TD9W-ZW3R ("It quickly becomes apparent to any person who has considerable experience with classified material . . . that the principal concern of the classifiers is not with national security, but rather with governmental embarrassment of one sort or another.").

18. *National Commission on Terrorist Attacks upon the United States*, FED'N AM. SCI. (May 22, 2003), https://govinfo.library.unt.edu/911/archive/hearing2/9-11Commission_Hearing_ 2003-05-22.htm (quoting former CIA director Porter Goss).

19. President Obama acknowledged this himself when he was asked about Secretary of State Hillary Clinton's use of a private email server to store emails that may have contained classified information. *See Obama on Clinton's Emails: "There's Classified, and Then There's Classified,"* CBSN (Apr. 10, 2016), https://perma.cc/ES7C-XNXX ("What I also know, because

I handle a lot of classified information, is that there are—there's classified, and then there's classified," Obama told Fox News. "There's stuff that is really top-secret, top-secret, and there's stuff that is being presented to the president or the secretary of state, that you might not want on the transom, or going out over the wire, but is basically stuff that you could get in open-source."); *see also* GEOFFREY STONE, TOP SECRET: WHEN OUR GOVERNMENT KEEPS US IN THE DARK 192 (Lanham, MD: Rowman & Littlefield, 2007) (classification is a "highly imperfect guide to the need for confidentiality").

20. Press-Enter. Co. v. Superior Ct., 478 U.S. 1, 13 (1986) (recognizing First Amendment right of access to preliminary hearings); Press-Enter. Co. v. Superior Ct., 464 U.S. 501 (1984) (recognizing First Amendment right of access to voir dire); Globe Newspaper Co. v. Superior Ct., 457 U.S. 596 (1982) (recognizing First Amendment right of access to criminal trials); Richmond Newspapers v. Virginia, 448 U.S. 555, 576 (1980) (recognizing First Amendment right of access to criminal trials).

21. *See, e.g.,* Rushford v. New Yorker Magazine, Inc., 846 F.2d 249, 253 (4th Cir. 1988); Westmoreland v. Columbia Broad. Sys., Inc., 752 F.2d 16, 23 (2d Cir. 1984).

22. Houchins v. KQED, 438 U.S. 1, 9 (1978) ("This court has never intimated a First Amendment guarantee of a right of access to all sources of information within government control.").

23. Ctr. for Nat'l Sec. Studies v. Dep't of Justice, 331 F.3d 918, 934 (D.C. Cir. 2003) (stating that the Constitution "is not a Freedom of Information Act" and observing that, in our system, "disclosure of government information generally is left to the political forces"); United States v. Hasbajrami, Nos. 15 Civ. 2684, 17 Civ. 2669, 2019 WL 6888567 (2d Cir. 2019). *But see* In re Washington Post Co., 807 F.2d 383, 390 (4th Cir. 1986); Doe v. Gonzales, 386 F. Supp. 2d 66 (D. Conn. 2005), *appeal dismissed as moot*, 449 F.3d 415 (2nd Cir. 2006).

24. ACLU v. CIA, 710 F.3d 422 (D.C. Cir. 2013); N.Y. Times Co. v. Dep't of Defense, 499 F. Supp. 2d 501 (S.D.N.Y. 2007); Ctr. for Int'l Envtl. Law v. Office of U.S. Trade Representative, 777 F. Supp. 2d 77 (D.D.C. 2011); Cable News Network, Inc. v. FBI, 384 F. Supp. 3d 19 (D.D.C. 2019).

25. *See, e.g.,* N.Y. Times Co., 915 F. Supp. 2d at 515–16, https://perma.cc/J8DQ-FJ7W ("I can find no way around the thicket of laws and precedents that effectively allow the [government] to proclaim as perfectly lawful certain actions that seem on their face incompatible with our Constitution and laws, while keeping the reasons for its conclusion a secret."). Executive Order 13526 bars the government from classifying information "*in order* to . . . conceal violations of law," but this narrow prohibition turns on the reasons why the records are being withheld, not on the content of the records, and the courts almost never question the government's proffered reasons. Exec. Order No. 13526, 75 F.R. 705 (2009).

26. Jameel Jaffer, *Selective Disclosure about Targeted Killing*, JUST SECURITY (Oct. 7, 2013), https://perma.cc/7HRC-6V4Y. Thus, the Republican Policy Committee's statement in support of the proposed legislation declared that "[i]n this period of selective disclosures, managed news, half-truths, and admitted distortions, the need for this legislation is abundantly clear." *Id.*

27. *Id.*

28. Jameel Jaffer, *Known Unknowns*, 48 HARV. C.R.–C.L. L. REV. 457 (2013), https://perma.cc/FXG4-B6FM.

29. *See National Security Whistleblowing: A Gap in the Law*, BRENNAN CTR. FOR JUSTICE (Aug. 21, 2013), https://perma.cc/6ZRY-73UW.

30. Benkler calls these "accountability leaks"—"those that expose substantial instances of illegality or gross incompetence or error in certain classes of particularly important matters associated with the activities of the national security system." Yochai Benkler, *A Public Accountability Defense for National Security Leakers and Whistleblowers*, 8 HARV. L. & POL'Y REV. 281, 303 (2014).

31. For thoughtful attempts to imagine such a system, *see, e.g.,* David A. Strauss, *Keeping Secrets*, in THE FREE SPEECH CENTURY, Lee C. Bollinger & Geoffrey R. Stone eds. (New York: Oxford University Press, 2018); David McCraw & Stephen Gikow, *The End to an Unspoken Bargain? National Security and Leaks in a Post-Pentagon Papers World*, 48 HARV. C.R.–C.L. L. REV. 473 (2013), https://perma.cc/8739-TCRY; LEE BOLLINGER, UNINHIBITED, ROBUST, AND WIDE-OPEN 121 (New York: Oxford University Press, 2010).

32. Elizabeth Goitein & J. William Leonard, *America's Unnecessary Secrets*, N.Y. TIMES (Nov. 7, 2011), https://perma.cc/NH2W-KACJ.

33. McCraw & Gikow, *supra* note 31, at 498–501.

34. BOLLINGER, *supra* note 31, at 120–26.

35. Mary-Rose Papandrea, *National Security Information Disclosures and the Role of Intent*, 56 WM. & MARY L. REV. 1381, 1435 (2015).

36. Transcript of Deposition of Max Frankel, United States v. New York Times Co., 328 F. Supp. 324 (S.D.N.Y. June 15, 1971) (No. 71 Civ. 2662).

37. *See* Benkler, *supra* note 30, at 303.

38. *See* Moynihan, *supra* note 16.

39. DANA PRIEST & WILLIAM ARKIN, TOP SECRET AMERICA (New York: Little, Brown, 2011); Jack Shafer, *The Spies Who Came in to the TV Studio*, POLITICO (Feb. 6, 2018), https://perma.cc/E8G9-HSAZ.

40. Ben Watson & Bradley Peniston, *US at War in 7 Countries*, DEFENSE ONE (Mar. 15, 2018), https://perma.cc/QK22-AXNW.

41. Dana Priest & William M. Arkin, *"Top Secret America": A Look at the Military's Joint Special Operations Command*, WASH. POST (Sept. 2, 2011), https://perma.cc/98NG-LSK3.

42. Benkler, *supra* note 30, at 288 ("The actual leak cases of the past half century reveal that the secrecy protected in those cases was intended to project power into the American public sphere, although always defended as protecting power projection onto legitimate targets.").

43. Seymour Hersh, *Torture at Abu Ghraib*, NEW YORKER (Apr. 30, 2004), https://perma.cc/Z6SU-8CX9 (noting that the photographs were first broadcast on *60 Minutes* a week prior).

44. Dana Priest, *CIA Holds Terror Suspects in Secret Prisons*, WASH. POST (Nov. 2, 2005), https://perma.cc/29KT-93T5.

45. Mark Mazetti, *C.I.A. Destroyed 2 Tapes Showing Interrogations*, N.Y. TIMES (Dec. 7, 2007), https://perma.cc/J59N-Z5PS.

46. *United States Military Medicine in War on Terror Prisons*, UNIV. OF MINN. HUMAN RIGHTS LIBRARY, https://perma.cc/3LZS-FDFC (listing some of the investigations).

47. S. COMM. ON THE ARMED FORCES, 110TH CONG., INQUIRY INTO THE TREATMENT OF DETAINEES IN U.S. CUSTODY (Comm. Print 2008).

48. Josh Meyer & Greg Miller, *Holder Opens Inquiry of CIA Interrogations*, L.A. TIMES (Aug. 25, 2009), https://perma.cc/Y8SB-ETZL.

49. MICHAEL JOHN GARCIA, CONG. RES. SERV., RL33655, INTERROGATION OF DETAINEES: REQUIREMENTS OF THE DETAINEE TREATMENT ACT (2009), https://perma.cc/Q4UD-2R2X.

50. David Stout, *C.I.A. Detainees Sent to Guantánamo*, N.Y. TIMES (Sept. 6, 2006), https://perma.cc/T7PD-7JLM.

51. JACK GOLDSMITH, THE TERROR PRESIDENCY 152–60 (New York: W. W. Norton, 2007).

52. *Obama Orders CIA Prisons, Guantanamo Shut*, NBC (Jan. 22, 2009), https://perma.cc/N2S7-JB5H.

53. S. SELECT COMM. ON INTELLIGENCE, CIA PROGRAM *supra* note 3, at i.

54. Jameel Jaffer & Brett Max Kaufman, *How to Decode the True Meaning of What NSA Officials Say*, SLATE (July 12, 2013), https://perma.cc/D8DH-6G2A.

55. Nomorcocktails, *DNI James Clapper Says That the NSA Does Not Collect Data on Millions of Americans*, YOUTUBE (June 6, 2013), https://perma.cc/4XRU-745S. Clapper later apologized for the statement, acknowledging that it was "clearly erroneous." Bill Chappell, *Clapper Apologizes for Answer on NSA's Data Collection*, NPR (July 2, 2013), https://perma.cc/93KC-6VHP.

56. Clapper v. Amnesty Int'l USA, 568 U.S. 398 (2013).

57. Jameel Jaffer & Patrick C. Toomey, *The Solicitor General Should Correct the Record in Clapper*, JUST SECURITY (Oct. 18, 2013), https://perma.cc/F2XG-RSBB.

58. *See* Jameel Jaffer, *Obama Is Cancelling the NSA Dragnet. So Why Did All Three Branches Sign Off?* GUARDIAN (Mar. 25, 2014), https://perma.cc/DRP6-S5NF.

59. ACLU v. Clapper, 785 F.3d 787 (2nd Cir. 2015).

60. Charlie Savage, *Warrantless Surveillance Challenged by Defendant*, N.Y. TIMES (Jan. 29, 2014), https://perma.cc/L2WM-ENL7.

61. USA Freedom Act, 129 Stat. 268 (2015).

62. *Statement by the Press Secretary on the Review Group on Intelligence and Communications Technology*, WHITE HOUSE ARCHIVES (Aug. 27, 2013), https://perma.cc/4WXG-5KQ8.

63. Geoffrey R. Stone, *The View from Inside the NSA Review Group*, 63 DRAKE L. REV. 1033 (2015), https://perma.cc/ZYG7-Y886.

64. *See generally* JAMEEL JAFFER, THE DRONE MEMOS 24–36 (New York: New Press, 2010).

65. *Id.* at 25.

66. Two appeals courts eventually ordered "disclosures" but only after concluding that the government had already "officially acknowledged" the information that the litigants had sought. N.Y. Times Co. v. Dep't of Justice, 756 F.3d 100 (2nd Cir. 2014) (requiring publication of OLC memo after concluding that DOJ had officially acknowledged its contents); ACLU v. CIA, 710 F.3d 422 (D.C. Cir. 2013) (rejecting CIA's "Glomar" response after concluding that CIA had officially acknowledged an intelligence interest in targeted killings).

67. Because the leaks were authorized or tolerated by the administration and designed to marshal public support for the government's policies, these disclosures are perhaps more accurately labeled "plants" or "pleaks." *See* David Pozen, *The Leaky Leviathan*, 127 HARV. L. REV. 512, 567 (2013).

68. As Jack Goldsmith later wrote, "the global picture [was] one of a concerted and indeed official effort by the [U.S. government] to talk publicly about and explain the CIA drone program—almost always in a light favorable to the administration, or at least to the person or interest[s] of the person who [was] speaking to the reporter." Jack Goldsmith, *Drone Stories, the Secrecy System, and Public Accountability*, LAWFARE (May 31, 2012), https://perma.cc/423C-HELS.

69. Cora Currier, *The Drone Papers*, INTERCEPT (Oct. 15, 2015), https://perma.cc/E8WU-RKJ3; *see also* Jameel Jaffer, *The Espionage Act and a Growing Threat to Press Freedom*, NEW YORKER (June 25, 2019), https://perma.cc/9RWH-ZG9Z.

70. Mark Landler, *Civilian Deaths Due to Drones Are Not Many, Obama Says*, N.Y. TIMES (Jan. 30, 2012), https://perma.cc/98WU-7734.

71. Press Release, President Obama Outlines Counterterrorism Approach Rooted in Human Rights, HUMAN RIGHTS FIRST (Dec. 6, 2016), https://perma.cc/F6YR-XWRT.

72. Affidavit in Support of Application for Arrest Warrant, United States v. Winner, No. 17-024 (S.D. Ga. 2017), https://perma.cc/93AS-ALQS.

73. Benkler, *supra* note 30; McCraw & Gikow, *supra* note 31.

74. Edward Snowden, PERMANENT RECORD 262–63 (New York: Metropolitan, 2019).

75. *See* Charlie Savage, *Fight Brews over Push to Shield Americans in Warrantless Surveillance*, N.Y. TIMES (May 6, 2017), https://perma.cc/B4DB-M47U.

76. *See, e.g.*, 18 U.S.C. § 2709(c) (2018).

77. McCraw & Gikow, *supra* note 31.

78. Charlie Savage, *Holder Tightens Rules on Getting Reporters' Data*, N.Y. TIMES (July 12, 2013), https://perma.cc/Y2YQ-DQYA.

79. 18 U.S.C. § 793(d) (2018).

80. Following the Fourth Circuit in *Morison*, federal courts have limited the scope of "national defense information" in two ways, requiring prosecutors to show, first, that the information in question was "closely held" and, second, that its disclosure could "potentially" damage the United States or be valuable to its enemies. United States v. Morison, 844 F. 2d 1057, 1071–72 (4th Cir. 1988). The courts have viewed classification as "strong evidence" that information was closely held. *See* STEPHEN P. MULLIGAN & JENNIFER K. ELSEA, CONG. RES. SERV., R41404, CRIMINAL PROHIBITIONS ON LEAKS AND OTHER DISCLOSURES OF CLASSIFIED DEFENSE INFORMATION 16 (2017), https://fas.org/sgp/crs/secrecy/R41404.pdf.

81. Steven Aftergood, *When the President Pardoned a Leaker*, FED'N AM. SCI. (Sept. 21, 2016), https://perma.cc/AVY7-PR87.

82. Gabe Rottman, *A Typology of Federal News Media "Leak" Cases*, 93 TULANE L. REV. 1147, 1181–86 (2019); Alex Emmons, *The Espionage Act Is Again Deployed against a Government Official Leaking to the Media*, INTERCEPT (Oct. 9, 2019) (describing the October 2019 indictment of counter-terrorism analyst Henry Frese); Adam Goldman, *Ex-Intelligence Analyst*

Charged with Leaking Information to a Reporter, N.Y. TIMES (May 9, 2019) (describing the May 2019 indictment of former intelligence analyst Daniel Hale).

83. Nicholas Fandos, *Comey Memos Provide Intimate Look into Trump Presidency*, N.Y. TIMES (Apr. 19, 2018), https://perma.cc/R86J-NMXQ.

84. Betsy Swan, *Leak Investigations Rise 800% under Jeff Sessions*, DAILY BEAST (Nov. 14, 2017), https://perma.cc/X7K9-55AJ.

85. For a discussion of why these norms have evaporated, *see* Mary-Rose Papandrea, *Leaker Traitor Whistleblower Spy: National Security Leaks and the First Amendment*, 94 B.U. L. REV. 449, 454–64 (2014).

86. *See, e.g.*, Brief of Amici Curiae Scholars of Constitutional Law, First Amendment Law, and Media Law, *supra* note 12, at 29–35 (arguing that sentences imposed on leakers convicted under the Espionage Act should take into account the "public value" of the defendant's disclosures); Benkler, *supra* note 30, at 286 (arguing that Congress should extend a general criminal law defense to leakers who disclose government secrets "on the reasonable belief that by doing so they will expose to public scrutiny substantial violations of law or substantial systemic error, incompetence, or malfeasance"); Papandrea, *supra* note 85, at 539 (arguing that the First Amendment should be understood to bar the government from imposing criminal liability on leakers who intend to inform the public (as opposed to the enemy) except where the government can demonstrate that the leaks pose a "direct and grave danger to the nation's security that is not outweighed by the public's interest in the information"); Heidi Kitrosser, *Leak Prosecutions and the First Amendment: New Developments and a Closer Look at the Feasibility of Protecting Leakers*, 56 WM. & MARY L. REV. 1221, 1264 (2015) (arguing that the First Amendment should be understood to preclude the government from imposing criminal or other severe sanctions on leakers except where the government can show that the leaker lacked an "objectively reasonable basis to believe that the public interest in disclosure outweighed the identifiable national security harms").

87. There are many other ways, of course, that our legal regime could account for the public value of leaks. For example, we could preclude liability under the Espionage Act except where the defendant intended to aid the enemy rather than inform the public, or we could afford defendants the opportunity to point to the public value of their disclosures at the sentencing stage. But the idea of a public value defense can be used here as a stand-in for the broader category of reforms that would, in one way or another, give weight to the public value of the information disclosed.

88. Strauss, *supra* note 31, at 135 ("It would be a mistake to suggest that a government employee or contractor, no matter how knowledgeable or expert, should routinely appoint himself or herself the ultimate judge about what government secrets should be disclosed.").

89. *See, e.g.*, Christopher Fonzone, *What the Law of Military Obedience Can (and Can't) Do— What Happens If a President's Orders Are Unlawful*, JUST SECURITY (May 4, 2018), https://perma.cc/J5D9-RCYM.

90. ALEXANDER BICKEL, THE MORALITY OF CONSENT 80 (New Haven, CT: Yale University Press, 1977).

91. LEE BOLLINGER, *supra* note 31, at 123 (noting that "an orderly system is preferable").

92. Benkler, *supra* note 30.

93. Strauss, *supra* note 31, at 135.

94. *Joseph Darby*, JOHN F. KENNEDY PRESIDENTIAL LIBRARY & MUSEUM, https://perma.cc/LL7D-MM9B; *The Ridenhour Prize for Truth-Telling 2014: Edward Snowden*, RIDENHOUR PRIZES, https://perma.cc/M93C-CAQ2; *Dana Priest of the Washington Post*, PULITZER PRIZES, https://perma.cc/QT86-SA4H; Ed Pilkington, *Guardian and Washington Post Win Pulitzer Prize for NSA Revelations*, GUARDIAN (Apr. 14, 2014), https://perma.cc/K3K2-LDBS (NSA reporting at the *Guardian* was led by Glenn Greenwald).

95. BOLLINGER, *supra* note 31.

96. The government's indictment of Julian Assange may test this proposition. Charlie Savage, *Assange Indicted under Espionage Act, Raising First Amendment Issues*, N.Y. TIMES (May 23, 2019), https://perma.cc/C3T7-N8AL.

97. Deborah Pearlstein, *After Deference*, 159 U. PA. L. REV. 783 (2011).

98. STONE, *supra* note 19, at 193 n.27.

Chapter 9

1. David Folkenflik, *Trump 2020 Sues "Washington Post," Days after "N.Y. Times" Defamation Suit*, NPR (Mar. 3, 2020), https://www.npr.org/2020/03/03/811735554/trump-2020-sues-washington-post-days-after-ny-times-defamation-suit.

2. SARAH MATTHEWS, REPORTERS COMM. FOR FREEDOM OF THE PRESS, PRESS FREEDOMS IN THE UNITED STATES 2019: A REVIEW OF THE U.S. PRESS FREEDOM TRACKER (2020), https://www.rcfp.org/wp-content/uploads/2020/03/2020-Press-Freedom-Tracker-Report.pdf.

3. Press Release, U.S. Dep't of Justice, Office of Pub. Affairs, Attorney General Holder Announces Updates to Justice Department Media Guidelines (Jan. 14, 2015), https://www.justice.gov/opa/pr/attorney-general-holder-announces-updates-justice-department-media-guidelines.

4. *Reporter's Privilege Compendium*, REPORTERS COMM. FOR FREEDOM OF THE PRESS, https://www.rcfp.org/reporters-privilege/.

5. *Shielding Sources: Safeguarding the Public's Right to Know: Joint Hearing before the Subcomm. on Intergovernmental Affairs & the Subcomm. on Healthcare, Benefits, and Admin. Rules of the H. Comm. on Oversight and Gov't Reform*, 115th Cong. (2018) (testimony of Lee Levine), https://docs.house.gov/meetings/GO/GO27/20180724/108595/HHRG-115-GO27-Wstate-LevineL-20180724.pdf.

6. *Federal Shield Law Efforts*, REPORTERS COMM. FOR FREEDOM OF THE PRESS, https://www.rcfp.org/federal-shield-law/ (last updated Sept. 12, 2013).

7. Gabriel Schoenfeld, *Rethinking the Pentagon Papers*, NATIONAL AFFAIRS (2010), https://www.nationalaffairs.com/publications/detail/rethinking-the-pentagon-papers.

8. Gabriel Schoenfeld, *Time for a Shield Law?* NATIONAL AFFAIRS (2014), https://www.nationalaffairs.com/publications/detail/time-for-a-shield-law.

9. REVIEW OF THE UNAUTHORIZED DISCLOSURES OF FORMER NATIONAL SECURITY AGENCY CONTRACTOR EDWARD SNOWDEN, H.R. REP. NO. 114–891 (2016), https://www.congress.gov/114/crpt/hrpt891/CRPT-114hrpt891.pdf.

10. Gabriel Schoenfeld, *Time for a Shield Law?* NATIONAL AFFAIRS (2014), https://www.nationalaffairs.com/publications/detail/time-for-a-shield-law.

11. Kyle Byers, *How Many Blogs Are There? (And 141 Other Blogging Stats)*, GROWTHBADGER (Jan. 2, 2019), https://growthbadger.com/blog-stats/.

12. James Risen, *If Donald Trump Targets Journalists, Thank Obama*, N.Y. TIMES (Dec. 30, 2016), https://www.nytimes.com/2016/12/30/opinion/sunday/if-donald-trump-targets-journalists-thank-obama.html?mcubz=1.

13. *The Obama Administration and the Press*, COMM. TO PROTECT JOURNALISTS (Oct. 10, 2013), https://cpj.org/reports/2013/10/obama-and-the-press-us-leaks-surveillance-post-911.php.

14. Interview, April 5, 2020.

15. Judith Miller, *Court's Ruling in Favor of Fox News' Jana Winter a Victory for All Journalists*, FOX NEWS (Dec. 10, 2013), https://www.foxnews.com/opinion/courts-ruling-in-favor-of-fox-news-jana-winter-a-victory-for-all-journalists.

16. *Examining DOJ's Investigation of Journalists Who Publish Classified Information: Lessons from the Jack Anderson Case: Hearing before the S. Comm. on the Judiciary*, 109th Cong. (2006) (testimony of Mark Feldstein), https://fas.org/irp/congress/2006_hr/060606feldstein.html.

17. COMM'N ON THE INTELLIGENCE CAPABILITIES OF THE U.S. REGARDING WEAPONS OF MASS DESTRUCTION, REPORT TO THE PRESIDENT OF THE U.S. (2005), https://www.govinfo.gov/content/pkg/GPO-WMD/pdf/GPO-WMD.pdf; NAT'L COMM'N ON TERRORIST ATTACKS UPON THE U.S., THE 9/11 COMMISSION REPORT (2004), https://www.9-11commission.gov/report/911Report.pdf.

18. INFO. SEC. OVERSIGHT OFFICE, 2017 REPORT TO THE PRESIDENT (2018), https://www.archives.gov/files/isoo/reports/2017-annual-report.pdf.

19. Erik Wemple, *Seizing Journalists' Records: An Outrage That Obama "Normalized" for Trump*, WASH. POST (June 8, 2018), https://www.washingtonpost.com/blogs/erik-wemple/wp/2018/06/08/seizing-journalists-records-an-outrage-that-obama-normalized-for-trump/.

20. Appl. for Search Warrant for E-mail Account [redacted]@gmail.com, No. 1:10-mj-00291 (AK) (D.D.C. Nov. 7, 2011), https://fas.org/sgp/jud/kim/warrant.pdf.

21. Remarks by President Trump before Marine One Departure (June 8, 2018), https://www.whitehouse.gov/briefings-statements/remarks-president-trump-marine-one-departure-8/.

Chapter 10

1. David E. Sanger, *Obama Ordered Sped Up Wave of Cyberattacks against Iran*, N.Y. TIMES (June 1, 2012), https://www.nytimes.com/2012/06/01/world/middleeast/obama-ordered-wave-of-cyberattacks-against-iran.html. *See also* DAVID E. SANGER, CONFRONT AND CONCEAL: OBAMA'S SECRET WARS AND SURPRISING USE OF AMERICAN POWER, prologue, ch. 8 (New York: Crown, 2012).

2. David E. Sanger & William J. Broad, *U.S. Revives Secret Program to Sabotage Iranian Missile and Rockets*, N.Y. TIMES (Feb. 13, 2019), https://www.nytimes.com/2019/02/13/us/politics/iran-missile-launch-failures.html.

3. David E. Sanger & Nicole Perlroth, *U.S. Escalates Online Attacks on Russia's Power Grid*, N.Y. TIMES (June 15, 2019), https://www.nytimes.com/2019/06/15/us/politics/trump-cyber-russia-grid.html.

4. 18 U.S.C. § 798(a) (italics added).

5. *Branzburg v. Hayes*, 408 U.S. 665 (1972).

6. During the campaign, Trump praised WikiLeaks at least five times. David Choi & John Haltiwanger, *5 Times Trump Praised WikiLeaks during His 2016 Election Campaign*, BUS. INSIDER (Apr. 11, 2019), https://www.businessinsider.com/trump-wikileaks-campaign-speeches-julian-assange-2017-11.

7. *The Obama Administration and the Press*, COMM. TO PROTECT JOURNALISTS (Oct. 10, 2013), https://cpj.org/reports/2013/10/obama-and-the-press-us-leaks-surveillance-post-911.php.

8. My *Times* colleague and our in-house lawyer, McCraw, made this argument in his brilliantly composed book. DAVID E. MCCRAW, TRUTH IN OUR TIMES: INSIDE THE FIGHT FOR PRESS FREEDOM IN THE AGE OF ALTERNATIVE FACTS 112 (New York: Macmillan, 2019).

9. Marc Tracy, Edward Wong, & Lara Jakes, *China Announces That It Will Expel American Journalists*, N.Y. TIMES (Mar. 17, 2020), https://www.nytimes.com/2020/03/17/business/media/china-expels-american-journalists.html.

10. DAVID E. MCCRAW, TRUTH IN OUR TIMES: INSIDE THE FIGHT FOR PRESS FREEDOM IN THE AGE OF ALTERNATIVE FACTS 112 (2019).

11. *CIA Director Pompeo Calls WikiLeaks a "Hostile Intelligence Service,"* NBC NEWS (Apr. 13, 2017), https://www.nbcnews.com/news/us-news/cia-director-pompeo-calls-wikileaks-hostile-intelligence-service-n746311.

12. Charlie Savage, *Assange Indicted under Espionage Act, Raising First Amendment Issues*, N.Y. TIMES (May 23, 2019, https://www.nytimes.com/2019/05/23/us/politics/assange-indictment.html.

13. The *Times's* collection of those works—edited to remove identifying information—was published in a series called "State's Secrets." *State's Secrets*, N.Y. TIMES, https://archive.nytimes.com/www.nytimes.com/interactive/world/statessecrets.html.

14. David McCraw & Stephen Gikow, *The End to an Unspoken Bargain? National Security and Leaks in a Post-Pentagon Papers World*, 48 HARV. C.R.–C.L. L. REV. 473, 478–509 (2013).

15. I detailed these interactions in my book, DAVID E. SANGER, THE PERFECT WEAPON: WAR, SABOTAGE AND FEAR IN THE CYBER AGE (New York: Crown, 2018).

Chapter 11

1. Harold Edgar & Benno C. Schmidt Jr., *The Espionage Statutes and Publication of Defense Information*, 73 COLUM. L. REV. 929, 934 (1973).

2. 18 U.S.C. §§ 793(d–e).

3. 312 U.S. 19 (1941).

4. *Id.* at 27–28.

5. 18 U.S.C. § 798, for example, criminalizes certain unauthorized disclosures of classified information concerning communications intelligence.

6. *See, e.g.*, United States v. Hitselberger, 991 F. Supp. 101, 106 (D.D.C. 2013); United States v. Rosen, 445 F. Supp. 602, 623 (E.D. Va. 2006) ("[A]lthough evidence that the information was classified is neither strictly necessary nor always sufficient to obtain a prosecution under [the Espionage Act], the classification of the information by the executive branch is highly probative of whether the information at issue is 'information relating to the national defense.'").

7. For example, the Intelligence Identities Protection Act, 50 U.S.C. § 3121, and a provision of the Atomic Energy Act of 1954, 42 U.S.C. §2274, extend to the disclosure of nonclassified information.

8. *See Gorin*, 312 U.S. at 28; United States v. Heine, 151 F.2d 813, 816 (2d Cir. 1945).

9. One possibility, suggested by United States v. Squillacote, 221 F.3d 542, 577–80 (4th Cir. 2000), would be to say that the information is "closely held" as long as the government itself has not officially disclosed it. But unofficial disclosures—deliberate leaks by high-ranking government officials, for example—should surely count as making information available. More generally, the government's tolerating of extensive unauthorized leaking of a piece of information also seems as if it should be treated as showing that it is not closely held and therefore cannot be the basis for a prosecution.

10. For the most thorough discussion of the role of intent in dealing with disclosures of national security information, *see* Mary-Rose Papandrea, *National Security Information Disclosures and the Role of Intent*, 56 WM. & MARY L. REV. 1381 (2015). *See id.* at 1384 n.8 for a summary of views of other commentators.

11. 18 U.S.C. § 1924 makes it a crime for a person who has been entrusted with documents containing classified information "knowingly [to] remove[] such documents or materials without authority and with the intent to retain such documents or materials at an unauthorized location." Agencies also have internal rules governing the handling of classified information—rules that are designed to prevent unintentional as well as intentional disclosures—and they can be enforced by non-criminal disciplinary sanctions. For a summary, *see* JENNIFER K. ELSEA, CONG. RES. SERV., RS21900, THE PROTECTION OF CLASSIFIED INFORMATION: THE LEGAL FRAMEWORK (2017).

12. For example, the Supreme Court has said that treason "requires . . . the mental element of disloyalty or adherence to the enemy." Cramer v. United States, 325 U.S. 1, 265 (1945). Some similar intent seems to be needed to establish that an individual has engaged in espionage, as opposed to a less culpable form of unauthorized disclosure.

The provision of the Espionage Act that is directed toward actual espionage, 18 U.S.C. § 794(a), uses a definition that is surely too broad. It provides for a possible sentence of life imprisonment, or in certain circumstances the death penalty, for anyone who communicates information "relating to the national defense" to any foreign government "or to any representative, officer, agent, employee, subject, or citizen thereof, either directly or indirectly" if the act is taken "with intent or reason to believe that it is to be used to the injury of the United States or to the advantage of a foreign nation." For example, this would seem to cover—but should not cover—the defendants in the high-profile case of United States v. Rosen, 445 F. Supp. 2d 602 (E.D. Va. 2006), who were officials of the American Israeli Public Affairs Committee, a pro-Israel lobbying group. They allegedly transmitted to an Israeli official classified information about US policy in the Mideast that they had obtained without authorization from a US government employee. They were charged with a violation of the Espionage Act but not with a violation of § 794(a), even though they very likely had reason to believe that the information would be used to the advantage of a foreign nation. The prosecution was ultimately dismissed.

13. In fact, this concern may not be new. *See* Papandrea, *supra* note 10, at 1404 ("Congress has been aware for over a century that it is possible for a news organization to have the specific intent to aid the enemy.").

14. *See Rosen*, 445 F. Supp. 2d at 626 (requiring the government to prove, in an Espionage Act prosecution, that the defendant had "a bad faith purpose to either harm the United States or to aid a foreign government" and suggesting that this requirement would not be satisfied if the defendant "viewed the disclosure as an act of patriotism").

15. *See* Harlow v. Fitzgerald, 457 U.S. 800 (1982).

16. *See, e.g.,* Stephen I. Vladeck, *Inchoate Liability and the Espionage Act: The Statutory Framework and Freedom of the Press,* 1 HARV. L. & POL'Y REV. 220 (2007).

17. New York Times Co. v. United States, 403 U.S. 713 (1971).

18. For discussion, *see, e.g.,* David A. Strauss, *Keeping Secrets,* in THE FREE SPEECH CENTURY 123, 123–39, Lee C. Bollinger & Geoffrey R. Stone eds. (New York: Oxford University Press, 2018).

19. *Cf.* United States v. Morison, 844 F. 2d 1057, 1084 (4th Cir. 1988) (Wilkinson, J., concurring) ("Even if juries could be found that would convict those who truly expose governmental waste and misconduct, the political firestorm that would follow prosecution of one who exposed an administration's own ineptitude would make such prosecutions a rare and unrealistic prospect.").

20. See the treatment of this issue in Mary-Rose Papandrea, *Citizen Journalism and the Reporter's Privilege,* 91 MINN. L. REV. 515 (2008).

Chapter 12

* This essay draws on but extends and qualifies my prior writings on this topic. For valuable comments, I thank Bart Gellman, Harry Graver, Shane Harris, Don Herzog, Nicholas Lemann, Charlie Savage, Geof Stone, and Oren Tamir, none of whom should be assumed to agree with one word in this essay. I also thank Alexander Khan, Julia Solomon-Strauss, and Jack You for research assistance.

1. Of course, we don't really know the denominator of overall government secrets, which has also grown significantly during the period. It is possible that the *percentage* of leaked secrets has fallen. But the raw numbers of classified secrets exposed have clearly grown.

2. NAT'L COUNTERINTELLIGENCE & SEC. CTR., FISCAL YEAR 2017 ANNUAL REPORT ON SECURITY CLEARANCE DETERMINATIONS 5 (2018). The number got as high as 5.1 million by 2013. Steven Aftergood, *Security-Cleared Population Rises to 5.1 Million,* FED'N AM. SCI. (Mar. 24, 2014), https://fas.org/blogs/secrecy/2014/03/security-cleared/. The number of original classification authorities has dropped since 2009, however. INFO. SEC. OVERSIGHT OFFICE, 2018 REPORT TO THE PRESIDENT 4 (2019). But the aggregate number of secrets has increased, as creation of classified information annually has "quickly outpace[d] the amount of information the Government has declassified in the total." *See* PUB. INTEREST DECLASSIFICATION BD., REPORT TO THE PRESIDENT FROM THE PUBLIC INTEREST DECLASSIFICATION BOARD ON TRANSFORMING THE SECURITY CLASSIFICATION SYSTEM 3 (2012).

3. H.R. REP. No. 110-916, at 5 (2008).

4. Dana Priest & William M. Arkin, *Top Secret America: A Hidden World, Growing beyond Control,* WASH. POST, July 19, 2010, at A1.

5. *See* David E. Pozen, *The Leaky Leviathan: Why the Government Condemns and Condones Unlawful Disclosures of Information,* 127 HARV. L. REV. 512, 559–86 (2013).

6. RICHARD HELMS, A LOOK OVER MY SHOULDER: A LIFE IN THE CENTRAL INTELLIGENCE AGENCY 184–85 (New York: Random House, 2003).

7. JACK GOLDSMITH, POWER AND CONSTRAINT: THE ACCOUNTABLE PRESIDENCY AFTER 9/11 52 (New York: W. W. Norton, 2012).

8. Jack Goldsmith, *Secrecy and Safety,* NEW REPUBLIC (Aug. 13, 2008), https://newrepublic.com/article/64747/secrecy-and-safety.

9. Margaret Sullivan, *Lessons in a Surveillance Drama Redux,* N.Y. TIMES (Nov. 9, 2013), https://www.nytimes.com/2013/11/10/public-editor/sullivan-lessons-in-a-surveillance-drama-redux.html.

10. *Id.*

11. *See* CHARLIE SAVAGE, POWER WARS: INSIDE OBAMA'S POST-9/11 PRESIDENCY 351 (New York: Little, Brown, 2015).

12. *See* JACK GOLDSMITH, THE TERROR PRESIDENCY: LAW AND JUDGMENT INSIDE THE BUSH ADMINISTRATION 177–80 ((New York: W. W. Norton & Company, 2007).

13. *Id.* at 367.

14. Press Release, White House, Office of the Press Sec'y, Fact Sheet: Safeguarding the U.S. Government's Classified Information and Networks (Oct. 7, 2011),

https://obamawhitehouse.archives.gov/the-press-office/2011/10/07/
fact-sheet-safeguarding-us-governments-classified-information-and-networ.

15. Charlie Savage & Eileen Sullivan, *Leak Investigations Triple under Trump, Sessions Says*, N.Y. Times (Aug. 4, 2017), https://www.nytimes.com/2017/08/04/us/politics/jeff-sessions-trump-leaks-attorney-general.html.

16. Steven Aftergood, *Leaks of Classified Info Surge under Trump*, Fed'n Am. Sci. (Apr. 8, 2019), https://fas.org/blogs/secrecy/2019/04/leaks-surge/.

17. *Oversight of the Department of Justice: Hearing before the H. Comm. on the Judiciary*, 115th Cong. 11 (2017) (statement of Jefferson B. Sessions III, Att'y Gen. of the United States).

18. *Leak Case*, U.S. Press Freedom Tracker (Mar. 16, 2020), https://pressfreedomtracker.us/leak-case/.

19. Comm. to Protect Journalists, The Obama Administration and the Press: Leak Investigations and Surveillance in Post-9/11 America 3 (2013).

20. *Id.* at 2.

21. David Graham, *"The Greatest Enemy of Press Freedom in a Generation,"* Atlantic (Feb. 21, 2015), https://www.theatlantic.com/politics/archive/2015/02/freedom-of-the-press-obama-first-amendment-James-Risen/385699/.

22. Jack Goldsmith, *James Risen Needs to Read the NYT*, Lawfare (Mar. 26, 2014), https://www.lawfareblog.com/james-risen-needs-read-nyt.

23. David A. Schulz, *Eric Holder Still Has Wrongs to Right before He Leaves Office*, Wash. Post (Oct. 29, 2014), https://www.washingtonpost.com/opinions/eric-holder-still-has-wrongs-to-right-before-he-leaves-office/2014/10/29/607982ca-5e08-11e4-8b9e-2ccdac31a031_story.html.

24. James R. Clapper, *Remarks as Delivered: Open Hearing on Foreign Intelligence Surveillance Authorities to the U.S. Senate Select Committee on Intelligence*, Office of the Dir. of Nat'l Intelligence (Sep. 26, 2013), https://www.dni.gov/files/documents/DNI%20Clapper%20as%20delivered%20to%20SSCI_26%20Sept_13.pdf.

25. Harold Edgar & Benno C. Schmidt Jr., *The Espionage Statutes and Publication of Defense Information*, 73 Colum. L. Rev. 929, 1065, 1069 (1973).

26. New York Times Co. v. United States, 403 U.S. 713, 735–37 (1971).

27. Justice Stewart joined White's opinion, and Chief Justice Burger stated that he was "in general agreement with much of what Mr. Justice White has expressed with respect to penal sanctions concerning communication or retention of documents or information relating to the national defense." *Id.* at 752. Justice Blackmun stated that he was "in substantial accord with much that Mr. Justice White says, by way of admonition, in the later part of his opinion." *Id.* at 759. Justice Harlan did not state a view on Justice White's point, but he dissented in the case. Justice Marshall joined the majority but viewed Justice White's more controversial claim that the newspapers could be prosecuted under § 793 as "plausible." *Id.* at 745.

28. Ben Bradlee, A Good Life: Newspapering and Other Adventures 468 (New York: Simon & Schuster, 2017).

29. *Video: National Security and Transparency in this Administration and the Next*, Just Security, at 47:30 (Nov. 4, 2016), https://www.justsecurity.org/34123/video-national-security-transparency-administration/.

30. *Id.*

31. Reporters Comm. for Freedom of the Press, Summary of Changes to the Attorney General Guidelines in January 2015, at 3 (2015). Some journalists have told me that this particular rule has been honored in the breach—for example, Watkins never received notice.

32. 408 U.S. 665 (1972).

33. Brief for Thomas Jefferson Center for the Protection of Free Expression et al. as Amici Curiae Supporting Intervenor, United States v. Sterling, 724 F.3d 482 (4th Cir. 2013) (No. 11-5028).

34. Mark Landler, *Obama, in Nod to Press, Orders Review of Inquiries*, N.Y. Times (May 23, 2013), https://www.nytimes.com/2013/05/24/us/politics/obama-offering-support-for-press-freedom-orders-review-of-leak-investigations.html.

35. *Id.*

36. Charlie Savage, *Holder Hints Reporter May Be Spared Jail in Leak*, N.Y. TIMES (May 27, 2014), https://www.nytimes.com/2014/05/28/us/holder-hints-reporter-may-be-spared-jail-in-leak.html.

37. Kevin Robillard, *Bush AG: I Didn't Subpoena on Leak*, POLITICO (May 15, 2013), https://www.politico.com/story/2013/05/alberto-gonzales-subpoena-leak-091405.

38. Callum Borchers, *Sessions Says He Can't "Make a Blank Commitment" Not to Jail Journalists*, WASH. POST (Oct. 18, 2017), https://www.washingtonpost.com/news/the-fix/wp/2017/10/18/sessions-says-he-cant-make-a-blanket-commitment-not-to-jail-journalists/.

39. DAVID E. MCCRAW, TRUTH IN OUR TIMES: INSIDE THE FIGHT FOR PRESS FREEDOM IN THE AGE OF ALTERNATIVE FACTS 183 (New York: All Points, 2019).

40. *Id.* at 195.

41. Sari Horwitz, *Julian Assange Unlikely to Face U.S. Charges over Publishing Classified Documents*, WASH. POST (Nov. 25, 2013), https://www.washingtonpost.com/world/national-security/julian-assange-unlikely-to-face-us-charges-over-publishing-classified-documents/2013/11/25/dd27decc-55f1-11e3-8304-caf30787c0a9_story.html.

42. Superseding Indictment at 2, United States v. Assange, Crim. No. 1:18-cr-111 (CMH) (E.D. Va. May 23, 2019).

43. Jack Goldsmith, *The U.S. Media Is in the Crosshairs of the New Assange Indictment*, LAWFARE (May 24, 2019), https://www.lawfareblog.com/us-media-crosshairs-new-assange-indictment. This 2019 post viewed the Assange indictment as more of a threat to press freedoms than the current essay, which reflects my more considered views.

44. John C. Demers, Assistant Att'y Gen. for Nat'l Sec., Remarks from the Briefing Announcing the Superseding Indictment of Julian Assange (May 23, 2019), https://www.justice.gov/opa/press-release/file/1165636/download.

Chapter 13

* Portions of this essay draw on ALLISON STANGER, WHISTLEBLOWERS: HONESTY IN AMERICA FROM WASHINGTON TO TRUMP (New Haven, CT: Yale University Press, 2019).

1. Allison Stanger, *Whistle-Blowers Are the Last Defense against Global Corruption*, ATLANTIC (Oct. 22, 2019), https://www.theatlantic.com/ideas/archive/2019/10/europes-whistle-blowers-take-global-corruption/600139/.

2. John G. Coyle, *The Suspension of Esek Hopkins, Commander of the Revolutionary Navy*, 21 J. AM. IRISH HIST. SOC'Y, 1922, at 193, 225.

3. *Id.* at 226–32; *see also* 7 JOURNALS OF THE CONT'L CONG. 1774–1789, at 204 Worthington C. Ford et al. eds. (1907).

4. THE CORRESPONDENCE OF ESEK HOPKINS: COMMANDER-IN-CHIEF OF THE UNITED STATES NAVY 24 Alverda S. Beck ed. (1933).

5. 10 JOURNALS OF THE CONT'L CONG. 1774–1789, at 13 Worthington C. Ford et al. eds. (1907).

6. 11 JOURNALS OF THE CONT'L CONG. 1774–1789, at 732 Worthington C. Ford et al. eds. (1907).

7. 14 JOURNALS OF THE CONT'L CONG. 1774–1789, at 627 Worthington C. Ford et al. eds. (1907).

8. MARK WORTH, WHISTLEBLOWING IN EUROPE: LEGAL PROTECTIONS FOR WHISTLEBLOWERS IN THE EU 20–22 (2013), https://www.transparency.org/whatwedo/publication/whistleblowing_in_europe_legal_protections_for_whistleblowers_in_the_eu.

9. Margaret Rouse, Mary K. Pratt, & Ben Cole, *Definition: Whistleblower Protection Act*, SEARCHCOMPLIANCE, http://searchcompliance.techtarget.com/definition/Whistleblower-Protection-Act (last updated July 2018).

10. *Questions and Answers about Whistleblower Appeals*, U.S. MERIT SYS. PROT. BD., http://mspb.gov/appeals/whistleblower.htm.

11. For further distinctions between leakers, dissenters, civil disobedience, and whistleblowing, *see* Allison Stanger, *Whistleblowing as Civil Disobedience: Leaks in the Era of Trump and the Deep State*, HANNAH ARENDT CTR. FOR POL. & HUMAN. (Dec. 2019), https://hac.bard.

edu/amor-mundi/whistleblowing-as-civil-disobedience-leaks-in-the-era-of-trump-and-the-deep-state-2019-12-04.

12. *See* Whistleblower Protection Enhancement Act of 2012, S. 743, 112th Cong. § 105 (2012); *Whistleblower Protection Enhancement Act (WPEA)*, Gov't Accountability Project, https://www.congress.gov/bill/112th-congress/senate-bill/743/text .

13. Author interview with Louis Clark, Exec. Dir. and CEO, Gov't Accountability Project, and Bea Edwards, Exec. Dir., Gov't Accountability Project, in Washington, DC (Dec. 12, 2013); author interview with Tom Devine, Legal Dir., Gov't Accountability Project, in Washington, DC (Nov. 20, 2015); author interview with Dan Meyer, Exec. Dir. for Intelligence Cmty. Whistleblowing & Source Prot., Office of the Inspector Gen. of the Intelligence Cmty., in Herndon, VA (Nov. 20, 2015).

14. R. Scott Oswald, *A Closer Look into Presidential Policy Directive 19*, Law360 (Aug. 12, 2013), http://www.law360.com/articles/460838/a-closer-look-at-presidential-policy-directive-19; Joe Davidson, *Obama's "Misleading" Comment on Whistleblower Protections*, Wash. Post (Aug. 12, 2013), http://www.washingtonpost.com/politics/federal_government/obamas-misleading-comment-on-whistleblower-protections/2013/08/12/eb567e3c-037f-11e3-9259-e2aafe5a5f84_story.html; Charles S. Clark, *Intel Contractors' Whistleblower Rights Are a Work in Progress*, Gov't Exec. (Aug. 20, 2013), http://www.govexec.com/oversight/2013/08/intel-contractors-whistleblower-rights-are-work-progress/69026/.

15. Rodney M. Perry, Cong. Res. Serv., Intelligence Whistleblower Protections: In Brief (Oct. 2014).

16. Clark, *supra* note 14 (noting that President Obama's executive order provided the justification for Meyer's position in the Office of the Director of National Intelligence).

17. That language was added as part of the Intelligence Authorization Act and is part of the current U.S. Code. *See* Intelligence Authorization Act for Fiscal Year 2014, Pub. L. No. 113-126 128 Stat. 1390 (2014); 50 U.S.C. § 3033 (2018). The statutory language was preceded by Intelligence Community Directive 120 and Intelligence Community Directive 119. *See Intelligence Community Directive 120: Intelligence Community Whistleblower Protection*, Off. of the Dir. of Nat'l Intelligence (Mar. 20, 2014), https://www.dni.gov/files/documents/ICD/ICD%20120.pdf; *see Intelligence Community Directive 119: Media Contacts*, Off. of the Dir. of Nat'l Intelligence (Oct. 31, 2017), https://www.dni.gov/files/documents/ICD/ICD-119.pdf.

18. Author interview with Rajesh De, Former Gen. Counsel, Nat'l Sec. Agency, in Washington, DC (June 25, 2015).

19. *Remarks by the President in a Press Conference*, White House, Off. of the Press Sec'y (Aug. 9, 2013), http://www.whitehouse.gov/the-press-office/2013/08/09/remarks-president-press-conference.

20. Author interview with Stephen M. Kohn, whistleblower attorney, Kohn, Kohn & Colapinto, in Washington, DC (Feb. 13, 2015).

21. Benjamin Wittes, *Snowden Testimony before the European Parliament*, Lawfare (Mar. 7, 2014), https://www.lawfareblog.com/snowden-testimony-european-parliament.

22. David. E. Sanger, *N.S.A. Releases Email That It Says Undercuts Snowden's Whistle-Blower Claim*, N.Y. Times (May 29, 2014), http://www.nytimes.com/2014/05/30/us/nsa-releases-edward-j-snowden-email-and-undercuts-whistle-blower-claim.html?_r=0.

23. Author interview with Dan Meyer, Exec. Dir. for Intelligence Cmty. Whistleblowing & Source Prot., Office of the Inspector Gen. of the Intelligence Cmty., in Reston, VA (Mar. 25, 2015); *see also* Dan Meyer & David Berenbaum, *The Wasp's Nest: Intelligence Community Whistleblowing & Source Protection*, 8 J. Nat'l Sec. L. & Pol'y, no. 1, 2015, at 33, 49 n.57.

24. Darren Samuelsohn, *NSA Watchdog Talks Snowden*, Politico (Feb. 25, 2014), https://www.politico.com/story/2014/02/nsa-inspector-general-edward-snowden-103949.

25. Charles S. Clark, *Why the NSA Inspector General Lost His Job (and Wants It Back)*, Gov't Exec. (Dec. 16, 2016), http://www.govexec.com/defense/2016/12/why-nsa-inspector-general-lost-his-job-and-wants-it-back/133992/.

26. Andrea Peterson, *Key Intel Whistleblower Official Fired as Spy Agencies Face Oversight Crisis*, Project on Gov't Oversight (Mar. 21, 2018), https://www.pogo.org/analysis/2018/03/key-intel-whistleblower-official-fired-as-spy-agencies-face-oversight-crisis/; *see also* personal communication from Dan Meyer, Exec. Dir. for Intelligence Cmty. Whistleblowing &

Source Prot., Office of the Inspector Gen. of the Intelligence Cmty. (Oct. 4, 2018) (on file with author).

27. *NSA Inspector General Report on Email and Internet Data Collection under Stellar Wind*, GUARDIAN (June 27, 2013), https://www.theguardian.com/nsa-inspector-general-report-document-data-collection.

28. United States v. Edward Snowden, No. 1:19-cv-1197 (E.D. Va. Dec. 17, 2019), https://ia803106.us.archive.org/28/items/snowdenbookruling/snowden%20book%20ruling.pdf.

29. EDWARD SNOWDEN, PERMANENT RECORD 259 (New York: Metropolitan, 2019).

30. *Id.* at 221–22.

31. *Id.* at 221–22, 256–57.

32. *Id.* at 259.

33. *See id.* at 261–73.

34. Jennifer Valentino-DeVries & Siobhan Gorman, *What You Need to Know on New Details of NSA Spying*, WALL ST. J., (Aug. 20, 2013), http://online.wsj.com/news/articles/SB10001424127887324108204579025222244858490.

35. *See* Timothy Edgar, *Matinee Idols: Ryan Lizza's Flawed Account of Surveillance Law*, LAWFARE (Dec. 13, 2013), http://www.lawfareblog.com/2013/12/matinee-idols-ryan-lizzas-flawed-account-of-surveillance-law/; *see also* Robyn Greene, *Unintentional Noncompliance and the Need for Section 702 Reform*, LAWFARE (Oct. 5, 2017), https://www.lawfareblog.com/unintentional-noncompliance-and-need-section-702-reform.

36. Robyn Greene, *A History of FISA Section 702 Compliance Violations*, NEW AM. (Sept. 28, 2017) https://www.newamerica.org/oti/blog/history-fisa-section-702-compliance-violations/#all-702-compliance-violations.

37. Barton Gellman, Julie Tate, & Ashkan Soltani, *In NSA-Intercepted Data, Those Not Targeted Far Outnumber the Foreigners Who Are*, WASH. POST (July 5, 2014), https://www.washingtonpost.com/world/national-security/in-nsa-intercepted-data-those-not-targeted-far-outnumber-the-foreigners-who-are/2014/07/05/8139adf8-045a-11e4-8572-4b1b969b6322_story.html; *see also NSA Slides Explain the PRISM Data-Collection Program*, WASH. POST (July 10, 2013), http://www.washingtonpost.com/wp-srv/special/politics/prism-collection-documents/ (describing FISA 702 operations).

38. SNOWDEN, *supra* note 29, at 328.

39. Barton Gellman, *U.S. Surveillance Architecture Includes Collection of Revealing Internet, Phone Metadata*, WASH. POST (June 15, 2013), https://www.washingtonpost.com/investigations/us-surveillance-architecture-includes-collection-of-revealing-internet-phone-metadata/2013/06/15/e9bf004a-d511-11e2-b05f-3ea3f0e7bb5a_story.html?utm_term=.aeccb6b401cc.

40. Charles Savage, *Declassified Report Shows Doubts about Value of N.S.A.'s Warrantless Spying*, N.Y. TIMES (Apr. 24, 2015), https://www.nytimes.com/2015/04/25/us/politics/value-of-nsa-warrantless-spying-is-doubted-in-declassified-reports.html?_r=0.

41. Ryan Lizza, *Why Sally Yates Stood Up to Trump*, NEW YORKER (May 29, 2017), https://www.newyorker.com/magazine/2017/05/29/why-sally-yates-stood-up-to-trump.

42. Hannah Arendt, *Hannah Arendt: From an Interview*, N.Y. REV. OF BOOKS (Oct. 26, 1978), http://www.nybooks.com/articles/1978/10/26/hannah-arendt-from-an-interview/.

43. *Whistleblower Disclosure: Hearing before the H. Perm. Sel. Comm. on Intel.*, 116th Cong. (2019) (transcript), https://docs.house.gov/meetings/IG/IG00/20190926/110027/HHRG-116-IG00-Transcript-20190926.pdf.

44. Press Release, Off. of the Inspector Gen. of the Intelligence Cmty., Statement on Processing of Whistleblower Complaints (Sept. 30, 2019), https://www.dni.gov/files/ICIG/Documents/News/ICIG%20News/2019/September%2030%20-%20Statement%20on%20Processing%20of%20Whistleblower%20Complaints/ICIG%20Statement%20on%20Processing%20of%20Whistleblower%20Complaints.pdf.

45. Andrew P. Bakaj & Mark S. Zaid, Editorial, *We Represent the Whistleblower. Their Identity Is No Longer Relevant*, WASH. POST (Oct. 25, 2019), https://www.washingtonpost.com/outlook/we-represent-the-whistleblower-their-identity-is-no-longer-relevant/2019/10/25/d2ff25a2-f6a1-11e9-8cf0-4cc99f74d127_story.html.

46. I am indebted for this phrase to John Devitt, Head of Transparency International-Ireland, who used it at the first Whistleblowing International Network Conference, Glasgow, Sept. 10, 2019.

47. Michael J. Glennon, National Security and Double Government 118 (New York: Oxford University Press, 2015).

Chapter 14

1. Cass Sunstein, *Government Control of Information*, 74 Cal. L. Rev. 889, 890 (1986).

2. Louis Henkin, *The Right to Know and the Duty to Withhold: The Case of the Pentagon Papers*, 120 U. Pa. L. Rev. 271 (1971).

3. David McGraw & Stephen Gikow, *The End to an Unspoken Bargain? National Security and Leaks in a Post–Pentagon Papers World*, 48 Harv. C.R.–C.L. L. Rev. 473, 494 (2013).

4. *Id.* at 493–94.

5. *See, e.g.*, Brian Barrett, *The Latest Julian Assange Indictment Is an Assault on Press Freedom*, Wired (May 5, 2019), https://www.wired.com/story/julian-assange-espionage-act-threaten-press-freedom/ (quoting John Demers, head of the DOJ's National Security Division).

6. Michael M. Grynbaum & Marc Tracy, *"Frightening": Charges against Julian Assange Alarm Press Advocates*, N.Y. Times (May 23, 2019), https://www.nytimes.com/2019/05/23/business/media/assange-first-amendment-wikileaks.html(quoting Hersch).

7. Henkin, *supra* note 2, at 278.

8. Potter Stewart, *Or of the Press*, 26 Hastings L.J. 631, 636 (1975).

9. *See* Ctr. for Nat'l Sec. Studies v. Dep't of Justice, 331 F.3d 918, 934 (D.C. Cir. 2003) ("[D]isclosure of government information generally is left to the 'political forces' that govern a democratic republic."), *cert. denied*, 540 U.S. 1104 (2004).

10. David Anderson, *Freedom of the Press*, 80 Tex. L. Rev. 429, 528 (2002).

11. RonNell Andersen Jones & Sonja R. West, *The Fragility of the Free American Press*, 112 Northwestern L. Rev. 567 (2017) (sounding the alarm on the Trump administration's attacks on the customary norms of press access).

12. Steven Helle, *The News-Gathering/Publication Dichotomy and Government Expression*, 1982 Duke L.J. 1, 3 (1982) ("By according news-gathering less protection the Court has given implicit sanction to the presumption that it is the right of the government to deny information to its citizens.").

13. New York Times Co. v. Sullivan, 376 U.S. 254, 270 (1964).

14. *Id.* (internal quotations omitted).

15. *See, e.g.*, Hustler Magazine v. Falwell, 485 U.S. 46, 50 (1988) ("At the heart of the First Amendment is the recognition of the fundamental importance of the free flow of ideas and opinions on matters of public interest and concern."); Red Lion Broadcasting Co. v. F.C.C., 395 U.S. 367, 392 (1969) (citing the importance of an "informed public"); Thornhill v. Alabama, 310 U.S. 88, 103 (1940) (striking down law banning picketing because it "infring[es] upon the right of employees effectively to inform the public of the facts of a labor dispute").

16. *See, e.g.*, Near v. Minnesota, 283 U.S. 697, 714–15 (1931) (freedom from prior restraints "cannot be deemed to exhaust the conception of liberty guaranteed by state and federal constitutions").

17. *See, e.g.*, Va. State Bd. of Pharmacy v. Va. Citizens Consumer Council, Inc., 425 U.S. 748, 756 (1976) (noting that "freedom of speech presupposed a willing speaker," but when there is a willing speaker, "the protection afforded is to the communication, to the source and its recipients both"); Kleindienst v. Mandel, 408 U.S. 753, 762 (1972) ("It is now well established that the Constitution protects the right to receive information and ideas."); Stanley v. Georgia, 394 U.S. 557, 567–68 (1969) (recognizing the right to receive speech in striking down law banning private possession of obscenity).

18. Note, *The First Amendment Right to Gather State-Held Information*, 89 Yale L.J. 923, 924 (1980).

19. *See* Barry McDonald, *The First Amendment and Free Flow of Information: Towards a Realistic Right to Gather Information in the Information Age*, 65 Ohio St. L.J. 249, 258–61 (2004).

20. Citizens United v. FEC, 558 U.S. 310, 336 (2010).

21. *See, e.g.,* ACLU of Ill. v. Alvarez, 679 F.3d 583, 595 (7th Cir. 2012) ("The act of making an audio or audiovisual recording is necessarily included within the First Amendment's guarantee of speech and press rights as a corollary of the right to disseminate the resulting recording."); Glik v. Cunniffe, 655 F.3d 78, 82 (1st Cir. 2011) (the First Amendment "encompasses a range of conduct related to the gathering and dissemination of information"); Clay Calvert, *The Right to Record Images of Police in Public Places: Should Intent, Viewpoint, or Journalistic Status Determine First Amendment Protection?* 64 UCLA L. Rev. Discourse 230, 236 (2016).

22. Stewart, *supra* note 8, at 633–34.

23. *See, e.g.,* Minneapolis Star & Tribune Co. v. Minn. Comm'r of Revenue, 460 U.S. 575, 585 (1983) (alteration in original) (citation omitted) (quoting Grosjean v. Am. Press Co., 297 U.S. 233, 250 (1936) ("'[a]n untrammeled press [is] a vital source of public information,' . . . and an informed public is the essence of working democracy").

24. David Anderson, *Freedom of the Press in Wartime,* 77 U. Colo. L. Rev. 49, 69–70 (2006) (discussing the Court's jurisprudence).

25. C. Edwin Baker, *The Independent Significance of the Press Clause under Existing Law,* 35 Hofstra L. Rev. 955, 956 (2007).

26. *See* Lee C. Bollinger, Uninhabited, Robust, and Wide-Open: A Free Press for a New Century 8 (New York: Oxford University Press, 2010).

27. First Nat'l Bank of Boston v. Bellotti, 435 U.S. 765, 782 (1978).

28. Branzburg v. Hayes, 408 U.S. 665, 703–4 (1972).

29. *Id.* at 703.

30. 381 U.S. 1, 17 (1965).

31. *Id.* at 16–17.

32. 408 U.S. 665, 707 (1972).

33. *Id..*

34. *Id.* at 682.

35. 463 U.S. 547, 565 (1978).

36. 501 U.S. 663, 669 (1991).

37. Saxbe v. Washington Post Co., 417 U.S. 843, 850 (1974); Pell v. Procunier, 417 U.S. 817, 833–35 (1974).

38. Houchins v. KQED, 438 U.S. 1, 8 (1978) (plurality op.).

39. *Id.*

40. *Id.* at 9 (plurality op.) ("This Court has never intimated a First Amendment guarantee of a right of access to all sources of information within government control."); *see also id.* at 16 (Stewart, J., concurring) ("The First and Fourteenth Amendments do not guarantee the public a right of access to information generated or controlled by government.").

41. *Id.* at 12 (plurality op.).

42. *Id.* at 16 (Stewart, J., concurring).

43. *Id.* at 27–28 (Stevens, J., dissenting).

44. Richmond Newspapers, Inc. v. Virginia, 448 U.S. 555 (1980).

45. Globe Newspaper Co. v. Superior Court, 457 U.S. 596 (1982); Press-Enterprise Co. v. Superior Ct., 464 U.S. 501 (1984); Press-Enterprise Co. v. Superior Court, 478 U.S. 1 (1986).

46. *Richmond Newspapers, Inc.,* 448 U.S. at 575 (Burger, C.J., plurality).

47. *Id.* at 576 (Burger, C.J., plurality).

48. *Id.* at 587 (Brennan, J., concurring).

49. *Id.* at 582 (Stevens, J., concurring).

50. *See* McBurney v. Young, 569 U.S. 221, 231 (2013) ("This Court has repeatedly made clear there is no constitutional right to obtain all the information provided by FOIA laws."); Sorrell v. IMS Health Inc., 564 U.S. 552 (2011) (Breyer, J., dissenting) ("[T]his Court has *never* found that the *First Amendment* prohibits the government from restricting the use of information gathered pursuant to a regulatory mandate."); L.A. Police Dep't v. United Reporting Publ'g Corp., 528 U.S. 32, 40 (1999) (citing *Houchins* to support its statement that the government could decide "not to give out [police department] arrestee information at all").

51. McBurney v. Young, 569 U.S. 221, 233 (2013) (internal citations omitted).

52. *See, e.g.,* Near v. Minnesota, 283 U.S. 697, 714–15 (1931) (freedom from prior restraints "cannot be deemed to exhaust the conception of liberty guaranteed by state and federal constitutions").

53. Lillian R. BeVier, *Like Mackerel in the Moonlight: Some Reflections on* Richmond Newspapers, 10 Hofstra L. Rev. 311, 327 (1982) (questioning relevance of historical inquiry for determining whether right of access attaches).

54. *Richmond Newspapers, Inc.,* 448 U.S. at 589 (Brennan, J., concurring).

55. *See* Ashutosh Bhagwat, *Producing Speech,* 56 Wm. & Mary L. Rev. 1029, 1078–79 (2015).

56. *See, e.g.,* David Ardia, *Court Transparency and the First Amendment,* 38 Cardozo L. Rev. 835, 883 (2017); Thomas I. Emerson, *Legal Foundations of the Right to Know,* 1976 Wash. U. L. Q. 1, 29 (1976). Vincent Blasi's closely related "checking value" of the First Amendment likewise provides strong support for a right of access but for our purposes is easily subsumed under the broader self-governance umbrella. *See* Vincent Blasi, *The Checking Value in First Amendment,* 2 Am. B. Found. Res. J. 521, 527 (1977) (discussing "the value that free speech, a free press, and free assembly can serve in checking the abuse of power by public officials").

57. The self-governance theory of the First Amendment is most closely linked with Alexander Meiklejohn. Alexander Meiklejohn, Free Speech and Its Relation to Self-Government (New York: Harper Brothers,1948). *See also* Robert C. Post, Democracy, Expertise, and Academic Freedom: A First Amendment Jurisprudence for the Modern State 61 (New Haven, CT: Yale University Press, 2012) ("The value of democratic competence is undermined whenever the state acts to interrupt the communication of disciplinary knowledge that might inform the creation of public opinion.").

58. For this view, see Antonin Scalia, *The Freedom of Information Act Has No Clothes,* Regulation, Mar./Apr. 1982, at 19 (arguing that we should give up the "obsession" that "the first line of defense against an arbitrary executive is the public and its surrogate, the press," rather than "the institutionalized checks and balances within our system of representative democracy").

59. *See* Mary-Rose Papandrea, *Leaker Traitor Whistleblower Spy: National Security Leaks and the First Amendment,* 94 B.U. L. Rev. 449, 467–68 (2014).

60. Jen Kirby, *Trump's Purge of Inspectors General, Explained,* Vox (May 20, 2020), https://www.vox.com/2020/5/28/21265799/inspectors-general-trump-linick-atkinson.

61. For example, when evaluating a challenge to the government's decision to exclude a foreign citizen invited to speak in the United States, the Court rejected arguments that the First Amendment's right to receive speech could trump the executive branch's plenary power over immigration. The Court declared that such an argument "would prove too much," because almost every time someone is excluded from the United States, "there are probably those who would wish to meet and speak with him." Kleindienst v. Mandel, 408 U.S. 753, 768 (1972).

62. Anderson, *supra* note 24, at 85.

63. Branzburg v. Hayes, 408 U.S. 665, 703–4 (1972) (citing this definitional problem as a reason for rejecting a constitutional reporter's privilege).

64. *See* Mary-Rose Papandrea, *Citizen Journalism and the Reporter's Privilege,* 91 Minn. L. Rev. 515, 564–66 (2007) (summarizing approaches in state shield statutes).

65. *Id.* at 568–72 (summarizing "intent to disseminate" approach).

66. *E.g., Afghanistan War Leak Papers Will Take "Weeks to Assess,"* BBC News (July 27, 2010), http://www.bbc.co.uk/news/world-us-canada-10770682.

67. Floyd Abrams, *Justice Stewart and the Autonomous Press,* 7 Hofstra L. Rev. 563, 591 (1979).

68. Bollinger, *supra* note 26, at 110.

69. *See* Papandrea, *supra* note 64, at 525–34 (discussing contributions of nontraditional journalism to public discourse).

70. Emerson, *supra* note 56, at 17 (noting FOIA is a "good start" for determining how a constitutional right of access might work).

71. NLRB v. Robbins Tire & Rubber Co., 437 U.S. 214, 242 (1978).

72. Jacqueline Klosek, The Right to Know: Your Guide to Using and Defending Freedom of Information Law in the United States 43–116 (Santa Barbara, CA: Praeger, 2009) (listing successful FOIA requests).

73. Kissinger v. Reporters Comm. for Freedom of the Press, 445 U.S. 136, 156 (1980) (internal citations omitted).

74. 5 U.S.C. § 552(a)(3)(A). Executive records are subject to the Presidential Records Act.
75. The full list of exceptions is set out at 5 U.S.C. § 552(b). These exceptions include an exception for records that are "specifically exempted from disclosure by statute." *Id.* at § 552(b)(3).
76. Nat'l Archives & Records Admin. v. Favish, 541 U.S. 157 (2004) (denying FOIA request for death-scene photos of president's deputy counsel due to the family's interest in "personal privacy").
77. Paul Verkuil, *An Outcomes Analysis of Scope of Review Standards*, 44 Wm. & Mary L. Rev. 679, 719 (2002).
78. *Id.* at 712.
79. 5 U.S.C. § 552(b)(1) (excluding from disclosure matters "specifically authorized under criteria established by an Executive order to be kept secret in the interest of national defense or foreign policy and (B) are in fact properly classified pursuant to such Executive order"). Exemption 3 also permits agencies to withhold information protected from disclosure under other statutes, which include a number of other national security statutes. *Id.* at § 552(b)(3). The government also has successfully asserted Exemption 7, which permits withholding agency records for "law enforcement purposes" when disclosure would interfere with law enforcement proceedings, constitute an unwarranted invasion of personal privacy, or endanger the life of physical safety of an individual. *See, e.g.,* Ctr. for Nat. Sec. Studies v. U.S. Dep't of Justice, 331 F.3d 918 (D.C. Circ. 2003) (relying on 5 U.S.C. § 552(b)(7) to permit DOJ to withhold the names and other information about post-9/11 detainees).
80. Mary Cheh, *Judicial Supervision of Executive Secrecy: Rethinking Freedom of Expression for Government Employees and the Public Right of Access to Government Information*, 69 Cornell L. Rev. 690, 691 (1984).
81. F.B.I. v. Abramson, 456 U.S. 615, 631 (1982).
82. Exec. Order No. 13526, 75 Fed. Reg. 707, 707 § 1.1(a)(3)–(4), 709 § 1.4(c)–(d) (Dec. 29, 2009).
83. Susan Nevelow Mart & Tom Ginsburg, *[Dis-]Informing the People's Discretion: Judicial Deference under the National Security Exemption of the Freedom of Information Act*, 66 Admin. L. Rev. 725, 727–28 (2014).
84. *See, e.g.,* Ctr. for Nat. Sec. Studies, 331 U.S. at 926–28 (holding that government had met its burden of demonstrating that disclosure of post-9/11 detainees would interfere with the terrorism investigation; the Court explained that it is appropriate for the judiciary to defer to the executive branch whenever the government argues disclosure might harm national security).
85. Courts routinely allow the government to submit in camera a "Vaughn index" identifying and describing the disclosable documents to determine whether disclosure is appropriate.
86. David Pozen, *Freedom of Information beyond the Freedom of Information Act*, 165 U. Pa. L. Rev. 1097, 1118 (2017).
87. *See, e.g.,* CIA v. Sims, 471 U.S. 159, 178 (1985) (Disclosing "bits and pieces" of information "may aid in piercing together bits of other information even when the individual piece is not of obvious importance in itself.").
88. The term derives from the *Hughes Glomar Explorer*, a vessel purportedly owned and operated by the CIA, which the government refused to acknowledge. *See* Phillipi v. CIA, 546 F.2d 1009, 1010–12 (D.C. Cir. 1976).
89. Ctr. for Nat. Sec. Studies, 331 U.S. at 930–31 (rejecting a FOIA request for a complete list of post-9/11 detainees even though the government had already released a partial list).
90. *See, e.g.,* Trump v. Hawaii, 138 S. Ct. 2392, 2409 (2018); Holder v. Humanitarian Law Project, 561 U.S. 1, 34–35 (2010); U.S. v. Curtiss-Wright Export Corp., 299 U.S. 304, 320 (1936).
91. U.S. Dep't of Justice v. Reporters Comm. for Freedom of the Press, 489 U.S. 749, 771–72 (1989) (internal citation omitted).
92. David Pozen, *supra* note 86, at 1103.
93. Margaret B. Kwoka, *FOIA, Inc.*, 65 Duke L.J. 1361, 1361 (2016).
94. Pozen, *supra* note 86, at 1103–4, 1127–28.
95. *Id.* at 1104; *see also* Scalia, *supra* note 58, at 16 (observing that "[FOIA] and its amendments were promoted as a means of finding out about the operations of government; they have been used largely as a means of obtaining data in the government's hands about private institutions").
96. Exec. Order No. 12958, 60 Fed. Reg. 19825 (Apr. 20, 1995).

97. Members include representatives from the Departments of State, Defense, and Justice; the National Security Council; the Office of the Director of National Intelligence; and the National Archives and Records Administration. The director of the Information Security Oversight Office serves as executive secretary.

98. Elizabeth Goitein, *The New Era of Secret Law*, Brennan Ctr. for Justice (2016), https:// www.brennancenter.org/sites/default/files/2019-08/Report_The_New_Era_of_Secret_ Law_0.pdf, at 65.

99. *Id.* at 68.

100. Justice Scalia argued that agencies overclassify documents to take advantage of Exemption 1 of FOIA. *See* Scalia, *supra* note 58, at 15.

101. *See* Laurence Tai, *Fast Fixes for FOIA*, 52 Harv. J. Leg. 455, 460–65 (2015) (noting difficulties of automatic disclosure requirements).

102. *See* Scalia, *supra* note 58, at 18.

Chapter 15

* This essay draws heavily on Cass R. Sunstein, *Output Transparency vs. Input Transparency*, in Troubling Transparency, David Pozen & Michael Schudson eds. (New York: Columbia University Press, 2018). At the same time, there have been substantial changes, including different emphases and somewhat different conclusions.

1. Samantha Power, A Problem from Hell: America and the Age of Genocide (New York: Basic, 2002).

2. *See* United States v. Nixon, 418 U.S. 683 (1974).

3. 44 U.S.C. §§ 2201–2207.

Chapter 16

1. New York Times Co. v. United States, 403 U.S. 713 (1971).

2. *See* Branzburg v. Hayes, 408 U.S. 665 (1972); In re Grand Jury Subpoena, Judith Miller, 438 F. 3d 1141 (D.C. Cir. 2006).

3. *See* Bill Keller, *The Boy Who Kicked the Hornet's Nest*, in Open Secrets: WikiLeaks, War and American Diplomacy 12 Alexander Star ed. (New York: New York Times, 2011) (discussing how *New York Times* editors met with government officials prior to publication of sensitive material and withheld some material because of government concerns); David McCraw & Stephen Gikow, *The End of the Unspoken Bargain? National Security and Leaks in a Post–Pentagon Papers World*, 48 Harv. C. R.–C. L. L. Rev. 473, 483 (2013) (discussing how newspapers "will listen to government objections" before publication).

4. *See* Dan Berry, *News Analysis: In a Swirl of "Untruths" and "Falsehoods," Calling a Lie a Lie*, N.Y. Times, Jan. 25, 2017 (discussing decision by the *New York Times* to use the word *lie* in a headline describing a Trump statement); Jim Rutenberg, *Mediator: Trump Is Testing the Norms of Objectivity in Journalism*, N.Y. Times, Aug 7, 2016 (discussing challenges to and changes in journalistic standards in response to President Trump).

5. United States v. Progressive, Inc., 467 F. Supp. 990 (W.D. Wis. 1979).

6. *See, e.g.*, Branzburg v. Hayes, 408 U.S. 665, 684 (1972) ("the First Amendment does not guarantee the press a constitutional right of special access to information not available to the public generally").

7. As a practical matter, the settlement means that the government rarely tries to stop publication. As a legal matter, though, it remains theoretically possible for the government to threaten post-publication prosecution or to claim that a compelling state interest supports a prior restraint.

8. I do not mean to suggest that the rules that come out of this process should be vague or ambiguous. Both the press and government officials need to be able to know in advance the probable consequences of their actions. Many of the proposals I outline below are designed to make the process more predictable and transparent. My point is only that the people formulating the rules should avoid the rigidity and hyperbolic rhetoric that often accompany constitutionally based analysis.

9. Of course, the government would not have to punish the media if the leak did not occur in the first place. One might defend the current regime on the ground that harsh treatment of leakers minimizes government interference with the press by stopping leaking at its source. The problem, though, is that just as the press sometimes has good reasons for publishing secret information, so, too, leakers sometimes have good reason for leaking it. True, leakers are public employees, and they are given access to the information for only limited purposes. That means that leaking should sometimes be punished. But conversely, the very fact that media figures do not work for the government makes them less subject to a democratic check. Moreover, the assumption that they, unlike government bureaucrats, have the "right" to use the information they receive is parasitic on the very legal regime that is under debate. If the law prohibited the media from publishing the information, then it would no longer have a "right" to do so. Once one gets over free press romanticism, there is no reason in principle why one group of people seeking increased transparency should be assumed to be acting in the public interest, while the other group also seeking increased transparency should be assumed to be acting irresponsibly.

10. Unlike some other free speech problems, publication of classified information is susceptible to prior review, because a court can examine the material in question before it is made public. In cases involving matters such as whether crowd reaction to a speaker poses a clear and present danger, prior review is more likely to be impractical.

11. 18 U.S.C. § 793(d).

12. Int'l Counsel Bureau v. U.S. Dep't of Def., 723 F. Supp.2d 54, 62 (D.D.C. 2010) (to justify withholding information sought under FOIA, the agency must show "both that the information was classified pursuant to proper procedures, and that the withheld information meets the standard for classification"); United States v. Reynolds, 345 U.S. 1, 9, 11 (1953) (holding that "[t]he court itself must determine whether the circumstances are appropriate for the claim of [state secrets] privilege" and that "[w]here there is a strong showing of necessity, the claim of privilege should not be lightly accepted, but even the most compelling necessity cannot overcome the claim of privilege if the court is ultimately satisfied that military secrets are at stake").

13. Pub. L. No. 96-456, 94 Stat. 2025 (1980).

14. See Charles M. Bell, Surveillance Technology and Graymail in Domestic Criminal Prosecution, 16 GEO. J. L. & PUB. POL'Y 537, 544 (2018) (noting that "even CIPA's critics concede that it has been effective at preventing graymail though the full extent of its success is unclear").

15. See The Dissent Channel, https://www.afsa.org/dissent-channel.

16. Pub. L. No. 95-454, 92 Stat. 1111 (1978).

17. Intelligence Community Whistleblower Protection Act of 1998, 112 Stat. 2396 (1998).

Report of the Commission

1. See Alexander and Jaffer, chapter 2 herein; Haines, chapter 1 herein; Goldsmith, chapter 12 herein; PUB. INTEREST DECLASSIFICATION BD., TRANSFORMING THE SECURITY CLASSIFICATION SYSTEM: REPORT TO THE PRESIDENT 3 (Nov. 2012) ("Agencies are currently creating petabytes of classified information annually. . . ."); Seth F. Kreimer, The Freedom of Information Act and the Ecology of Transparency, 10 U. PA. J. CONST. L. 1011, 1043 (2008) ("The digital environment . . . serves as a force multiplier for leakers. . . ."); Margaret B. Kwoka, Leaking and Legitimacy, 48 U.C. DAVIS L. REV. 1387, 1402 (2015) ("Technology has changed the access to information lower-level government officials and contractors have, thereby enabling them to deluge leak.").

2. See Alexander and Jaffer, chapter 2 herein; Strauss, chapter 11 herein; Goldsmith, chapter 12 herein.

3. See Haines, chapter 1 herein; Kwoka, supra note 1, at 1402 ("[Technology] has . . . vastly increased the ease of distributing leaked information."); Jane B. Singer, Contested Autonomy: Professional and Popular Claims on Journalistic Norms, 8 JOURNALISM STUD. 79 (2007) ("A central claim of any profession, including journalism, is autonomy over articulation and enactment of its own norms, but the Internet has fostered a news environment in which definitions of professional concepts are open to reinterpretation. . . . "); Stephen J. A. Ward, Digital Media Ethics, UNIV. OF

Wis.-Madison Ctr. for Journalism Ethics (2020) ("The 'democratization' of media—technology that allows citizens to engage in journalism and publication of many kinds—blurs the identity of journalists and the idea of what constitutes journalism.").

4. *See* Deborah Charles & Ben Berkowitz, *NSA Leak Prompts Questions over U.S. Reliance on Contractors,* Reuters (June 10, 2013) ("The government workforce has pretty much stayed the same over the last 30 to 40 years but we've supplemented that with a contractor workforce that has grown dramatically." (quoting Scott Amey, General Counsel of the Project on Government Oversight)); Dan Taylor, *Bad Vetting: The NSA Keeps Leaking,* Outline (June 11, 2017) ("Critics argue that as long as the government depends so heavily on private industry for keeping an eye on employees with top secret clearances, there will be more Snowdens, Mannings, and Winners.").

5. *See* Morell, chapter 3 herein.

6. *See, e.g.,* Trevor Timm, *Obama Admits That "Top Secret" Is Not Always So Secret,* Colum. Journalism Rev. (Apr. 12, 2016); Ellen Nakashima, *Ex-Federal Official Calls U.S. Classification System "Dysfunctional,"* Wash. Post (July 21, 2012) (William Leonard, the Director of the Information Security Oversight Office under President Bush, asserted that the classification system "lacks the ability to differentiate between trivial information and that which can truly damage our nation's well-being."); Donald H. Rumsfeld, *War of the Words,* Wall St. J. (July 18, 2005) ("I have long believed that too much material is classified across the federal government as a general rule. . . . "); Daniel Patrick Moynihan, Secrecy (New Haven, CT: Yale University Press, 1999); Report of the Commission on Protecting and Reducing Government Secrecy, S. Doc. 105-2 (1997); Erwin N. Griswold, *Secrets Not Worth Keeping,* Wash. Post (Feb. 15, 1989) ("It quickly becomes apparent to any person who has considerable experience with classified material that there is massive over-classification and that the principal concern of the classifiers is not with national security, but rather with governmental embarrassment of one sort or another."); *see also* Clarke, chapter 5 herein (noting "the perception among national security professionals that routine designations . . . no longer provid[e] intended security levels"); Jaffer, chapter 8 herein ("[T]he government routinely classifies information whose disclosure could *not* reasonably be expected to cause damage to the national security, as many government studies have found").

7. Exec. Order No. 13526, 3 C.F.R. 13526 (2009); *see also* Exec. Order No. 12233 (1981).

8. Exec. Order No. 13526, pmbl.

9. *Id.* § 1.1(a)(4).

10. *Id.* § 1.2(a)(1)–(3). Further, the damage must pertain to one of the following categories: "(a) military plans, weapons systems, or operations; (b) foreign government information; (c) intelligence activities (including covert action), intelligence sources or methods, or cryptology; (d) foreign relations or foreign activities of the United States, including confidential sources; (e) scientific, technological, or economic matters relating to the national security; (f) United States Government programs for safeguarding nuclear materials or facilities; (g) vulnerabilities or capabilities of systems, installations, infrastructures, projects, plans, or protection services relating to the national security; or (h) the development, production, or use of weapons of mass destruction." *Id.* § 1.4.

11. *Id.* § 1.1(b).

12. *Id.* § 1.7(a)(1).

13. *Id.* § 1.7(a)(2).

14. Elizabeth Goitein & David M. Shapiro, *Reducing Overclassification through Accountability,* Brennan Ctr. for Justice 2 (2011), https://www.brennancenter.org/sites/default/files/2019-08/Report_Reducing_Overclassification.pdf.

15. *Id.; see* Haines, chapter 1 herein.

16. Goitein & Shapiro, *supra* note 14, at 2.

17. Exec. Order No. 13526, § 1.2(a)(1)–(3) (emphasis added); *see* 32 C.F.R. § 2001.10 ("There is no requirement, at the time of the decision, for the original classification authority to prepare a written description of such damage. However, the original classification authority must be able to support the decision in writing, including identifying or describing the damage, should the classification decision become the subject of a challenge or access demand pursuant to the [Executive] Order or law."); *see also* Goitein & Shapiro, *supra* note 14, at 34–40.

18. *See* Goitein & Shapiro, *supra* note 14, at 40–46.

19. Exec. Order No. 13526, § 1.7(a)(1); *see id.* § 5.5(b)(2) (authorizing sanctions where an individual "classif[ies] ... information in violation of [Exec. Order No. 13526]"); *see also* Alexander & Jaffer, chapter 2 herein (recommending "penalties for inappropriate classification").

20. Exec. Order No. 13526, § 1.5(a).

21. *Id.* § 1.5(b). "In practice," however, "'automatic' declassification is a misnomer." Transforming the Security Classification System, *supra* note 1, at 17. Prior to declassification, the records must be "reviewed on a page-by-page basis" to ensure that they do not contain information on atomic weapons or nuclear material. 50 U.S.C. § 2672(b).

22. Exec. Order No. 13526, § 3.1(d).

23. *Id.* For a discussion of the types of disclosures that may or may not serve the public interest, see Haines, chapter 1 herein (describing an instance in which declassification of "properly classified" information was "fundamental to a functioning democracy"); Sunstein, chapter 15 herein (arguing that, at least in general, "what most matters is what government actually does, not who said what to whom"). *See also* Monaco, chapter 4 herein ("Rather than wait for a leak to expose a controversial program and incur the potential damage to national security ..., a more meaningful and effective answer may come from trying to carefully maximize debate and transparency before, during, and after [such] programs ... are implemented.").

24. Transforming the Security Classification System, *supra* note 1, at 20–27. The Public Interest Declassification Board is an advisory committee established by Congress. *See* 50 U.S.C. § 3355a(a)(1). The Board is charged with advising the president on declassification procedures and is composed of nine individuals "appointed from among citizens of the United States" with expertise in history, national security, foreign policy, or other fields. *Id.* § 3355a(b), (c)(1).

25. Exec. Order No. 13526, § 3.1(d); *see* Strauss, chapter 11 herein ("[W]hile unauthorized disclosures of sensitive national security information can be very damaging to the national interest, we sometimes want there to be such disclosures[,] [which may] reveal errors or wrongdoing by the government or ... otherwise make important contributions to public debate....").

26. *See* Alexander & Jaffer, chapter 2 herein.

27. Exec. Order No. 13526, § 1.8(b).

28. *Id.* § 1.8(b)(2)–(3).

29. *Id.* § 1.8(b)(1).

30. *See* Goitein & Shapiro, *supra* note 14, at 48–49.

31. Exec. Order No. 13526, § 3.1(d).

32. *Cf.* Info. Sec. Oversight Office, 2017 Report to the President 28 (May 31, 2018) ("The ISCAP should recommend expanding its membership to include a member of the public[,] [which] would enhance sustained credibility in ISCAP decision-making activities.").

33. *See* Jaffer, chapter 8 herein; Monaco, chapter 4 herein.

34. *See, e.g.,* Monaco, chapter 4 herein ("[A] whistleblower who seeks to expose a policy she disagrees with is unlikely to be satisfied with the whistleblower process."); Stanger, chapter 13 herein ("Congress must address the legal ambiguities that have made utilizing the [IC Inspector General] system a risky proposition for whistleblowers.").

35. *See* Harold Edgar & Benno C. Schmidt Jr., *The Espionage Statutes and Publication of Defense Information*, 73 Colum. L. Rev. 929 (1973); PEN America, Secret Sources: Whistleblowers, National Security, and Free Expression 19–20 (2015), https://pen.org/sites/default/files/Secret%20Sources%20report.pdf.

36. *See, e.g.,* United States v. Morison, 844 F.2d 1057 (4th Cir.), *cert. denied*, 488 U.S. 908 (1988).

37. 18 U.S.C. § 793(a)–(f).

38. *See, e.g.,* 21 U.S.C. § 841 (imposing a graduated system of penalties for drug offenses in which the severity of the penalty increases as the drug quantity rises).

39. *See generally* Seidman, chapter 16 herein.

40. *See* Strauss, chapter 11 herein ("Intent has to play some role. Espionage on behalf of a hostile power is different from, for example, an authorized but well-intentioned disclosure of information about arguable government misconduct...."); *cf.* Adler & Brown, chapter 7 herein (describing a proposed amendment to the Espionage Act that would limit inchoate offenses

under the Espionage Act to situations where the individual acted with specific intent to cause harm to the United States).

41. *See* Seidman, chapter 16 herein; Strauss, chapter 11 herein (proposing a misclassification defense that would require defendants to show that they had "pursued remedies within the executive branch or . . . that those remedies were inadequate"); *see also* SECRET SOURCES, *supra* note 35, at 12.

42. *See* Seidman, chapter 16 herein.

43. *See* Sanger, chapter 10 herein (noting that the Trump administration's "indictment of Julian Assange" suggests that the government may be "edging" in the direction of prosecuting the press).

44. *See id.* (expressing concern that the potential for criminal prosecution may cause journalists from under-resourced news organizations to withhold stories).

45. *See* Adler & Brown, chapter 7 herein.

46. 18 U.S.C. § 793(e).

47. *See* Sanger, chapter 10 herein (arguing that the Espionage Act "plainly put journalists in its sights").

48. *See* Bartnicki v. Vopper, 532 U.S. 514, 529–30 (2001); Smith v. Daily Mail Pub. Co., 443 U.S. 97, 104 (1979).

49. *See* Alexander & Jaffer, chapter 2 herein.

50. 395 U.S. 444, 447 (1969).

51. *See* Potter Stewart, *Or of the Press*, 26 HASTINGS L.J. 631 (1975).

52. Branzburg v. Hayes, 408 U.S. 632, 704 (1972).

53. 28 C.F.R. § 50.10.

54. REPORTERS COMM. FOR FREEDOM OF THE PRESS, *Introduction to the Reporter's Privilege Compendium*, https://www.rcfp.org/introduction-to-the-reporters-privilege-compendium/ ("[Forty-eight] states and the District of Columbia have shield laws or court-recognized reporters privileges. . . . [Forty] states and the District of Columbia have enacted statutes— shield laws—that give journalists some form of privilege against compelled production of confidential or unpublished information.").

55. *See id.* ("[Shield laws] vary in detail and scope from state to state, but generally give greater protection to journalists than the state or federal constitution, according to many courts."); STUDENT PRESS LAW CTR., *State-by-State Guide to the Reporters Privilege for Student Media* (Sept. 15, 2010), https://splc.org/2010/09/state-by-state-guide-to-the-reporters-privilege-for-student-media-alabama-illinois/.

56. N.J. Stat. Ann. § 2A:84-21; *see id.* § 2A:84A-21a (defining "news media" as "newspapers, magazines, press associations, news agencies, wire services, radio, television or other similar printed, photographic, mechanical or electronic means of disseminating news to the general public").

57. *See* S. 987 (113th Cong.); *id.* § 11(1)(A) (defining the term "covered journalist"); S. Rep. No. 113-118 (113th Cong., 1st Sess. 2013).

58. *See* Journalistic Sources Protection Act, S.C. 2017, c. 22 (Can.); Contempt of Court Act 1981, § 10, c. 49 (Eng.) (Sources of Information).

59. *See* Strauss, chapter 11 herein.

60. *See* S. 987 (113th Cong.), § 11(1)(A)(iii)(II) (excluding various entities from definition of "covered journalist" in proposed federal shield law); 28 C.F.R. § 50.10(b)(1)(ii) (similar).

Closing Statement

1. New York Times Co. v. United States, 403 U.S. 713, 732 (1971).

2. 347 U.S. 483 (1954).

3. 376 U.S. 254 (1964).

4. *New York Times Co.*, 403 U.S. at 713.

5. *See, e.g., id.* at 732.

6. *See* Bartnicki v. Vopper, 532 U.S. 514 (2001). *Cf. Near v. Minnesota, 283 U.S. 697 (1931); Schenck v. United States, 249 U.S. 47 (1919).

7. *See* Cohen v. Cowles Media, 501 U.S. 663, 669 (1991) ("Generally applicable laws do not offend the First Amendment simply because their enforcement against the press has incidental effects."); Houchins v. KQED, 438 U.S. 1, 15–16 (1978) ("Under our holdings in *Pell v. Procunier* and *Saxbe v. Washington Post Co.*, until the political branches decree otherwise, as they are free to do, the media have no special right of access . . . than that accorded the public generally.").
8. *See* Mills v. Alabama, 384 U.S. 214, 218–19 (1966) (highlighting the "important role [of the press] in the discussion of public affairs" and the special place of freedom of the press in the development of the US Constitution).
9. *See* United States v. Morison, 844 F.2d 1057 (4th Cir. 1988); *The Chelsea Manning Case: A Timeline*, AM. CIVIL LIBERTIES UNION (May 9, 2017), https://www.aclu.org/blog/free-speech/employee-speech-and-whistleblowers/chelsea-manning-case-timeline.
10. *See Houchins*, 438 U.S. at 9 ("This Court has never intimated a First Amendment guarantee of a right of access to all sources of information within government control.").
11. *See* Schneider v. Kissinger, 412 F.2d 190, 194 (D.C. Cir. 2005) ("Absent precedent, there could still be no doubt that decision-making in the fields of foreign policy and national security is textually committed to the political branches of government."); Sosa v. Alvarez-Machain, 542 U.S. 692, 733 (2004); Gilligan v. Morgan, 413 U.S. 1, 10; Goldwater v. Carter, 444 U.S. 996, 1004 (1979).

INDEX

For the benefit of digital users, indexed terms that span two pages (e.g., 52–53) may, on occasion, appear on only one of those pages.

Inglis, Chris, 221
Inhofe, Jim, 51–52
Insider Threat software program, 94–95
Intel (computer processing company), 18
Intelligence Authorization Act of Fiscal Year
    2014, 220
Intelligence Community (IC). *See also* "Black
    Budget" (Intelligence Community); *specific*
    agencies
  background investigations for employees of, 98
  congressional oversight of, 79–80
  inspector general of, 144, 219, 220, 227,
    228–29, 278
  intelligence sharing within agencies of, 96
  leaks from former members of, 60, 61
  leaks' impact on, 65–68
  monitoring security clearances for staff and
    contractors at, 93–97
  motivations for leaking among members of,
    60–65, 72
  nonpartisanship and, 79
  polygraphy and, 98
  President's Daily Brief and, 58
  whistleblower process in, 46, 87–88, 144–45,
    216, 219–22, 229
Intelligence Community Whistleblower
    Protection Act of 1998, 220, 228–29
Inter-Agency Group on Unauthorized Disclosure
    of Classified Information (Willard
    Report), 126
Interagency Security Classification Appeals Panel
    (ISCAP), 242–43, 277–78
The Intercept, 41–42, 119, 147–48, 149
International Atomic Energy Agency, 110, 184
the internet
  democratization of access to information and,
    19–20, 197, 273–74
  disclosure of classified information amplified by,
    19–20, 34, 273–74
  encryption of traffic on, 225
  prior restraint opportunities reduced by, 34
  surveillance facilitated through design
    of, 224–25
Iran
  American Israel Public Affairs Committee leak
    case and, 133
  cyberwarfare attacks by United States against,
    170–71, 173, 183–84
  intelligence services in, 66
  missile program in, 173
  nuclear program in, 133, 163–64, 173, 183
  US partisan politics and, 52
Iraq
  Abu Ghraib prison abuse scandal (2004) and,
    140–41, 145–46
  intelligence failures prior to US invasion (2003)
    of, 166

Manning leaks (2010) about war in, 65, 67–68,
    106–7, 140–41
  US military abuses in, 61
ISIS, 66, 89
Israel, 12, 133, 170–71, 183, 184
I.T.T. Affair, 137

Jackson, Robert, 48
Jefferson, Thomas, 139
Johnston, Stanley, 132
Joint Worldwide Intelligence Communications
    System (JWICS), 55
Jordan, Jim, 160

Karzai, Hamid, 119
Kean, Thomas, 143
Keller, Bill, 202
Kennan, George, 15–16
Kennedy, John F., 132, 165
Khanna, Ro. *See* Wyden-Khanna bill
Khashoggi, Jamal, 61
Kim, Stephen Jin-Woo, 133, 168
Kim Jong-un, 173
Kiriakou, John, 134
Kirk, Mark, 51–52
Kohn, Stephen, 220–21
KQED (news station in San Francisco),
    13–14, 232
Kris, David, 88
Kwoka, Margaret, 19

Lamberth, Royce, 7
Landmark Communications, Inc. v. Virginia, 8–9
Ledgett, Rick, 116, 117, 120–21
Leibowitz, Shamai, 133
Le Monde, 202–3
Leonard, William, 143
Levi, Edward, 128, 138
Levine, Lee, 159–60
Levine, Mike, 134, 135
Lewis, Anthony, 161–62
Libby, Scooter, 133, 203
Lichtblau, Eric, 202
Litt, Robert, 113–16, 121
Lynch, Loretta, 226

machine learning
  analysis of employee network behavior via, 94
  Big Data companies and, 96–97
  Cambridge Analytica and, 96
  casino industry and, 95
  civil liberties issues regarding, 97
  Insider Threat software program and, 94–95
  intellectual property protection and, 95
  metadata analysis and, 94
  polygraphy compared to, 98
  Zero Trust software systems and, 95–96